Global Information Technology Education

Issues and Trends

Mehdi Khosrowpour
and
Karen D. Loch

 *IDEA GROUP PUBLISHING*

Senior Editor: Mehdi Khosrowpour
Series Associate Editors: Shailendra Palvia
                            Prashant Palvia
                            Ronald Zigli
Series Consulting Editor: Maryam Alavi
Managing Editor: Jan Travers
Copy Editor: Karen Cullings
Printed at: Jednota Press

Published in the United States of America by
        Idea Group Publishing
        Olde Liberty Square
        4811 Jonestown Road, Suite 230
        Harrisburg, PA 17109
        800-345-4332

and in the United Kingdom by
        Idea Group Publishing
        3 Henrietta Street
        Covent Garden
        London WC2E 8LU

Library of Congress Card Catalog No. 91-076953

British Cataloguing in Publication Data
A Cataloguing in Publication record for this book is available from the British Library

ISBN 1-878289-14-4

IDEA GROUP PUBLISHING

SERIES In Global Information Technology Management

Senior Editor:
Mehdi Khosrowpour
Pennsylvania State University

Series Associate Editors:
Shailendra Palvia
Prashant Palvia
Ronald Zigli

Series Consulting Editor:
Maryam Alavi

First release of this series
The Global Issues of Information Technology Management

Second release of this series
Global Information Technology Education: Issues and Trends

For more information, or to submit a proposal for a book in this series, contact:

Mehdi Khosrowpour, Senior Editor
Idea Group Publishing
Olde Liberty Square
4811 Jonestown Road, Suite 230
Harrisburg, PA 17109
1-800-345-4332

Table of Contents

PREFACE

The world today is undergoing sweeping change. The political affiliation of many countries has changed and their geographic boundaries quickly followed suit. The means by which we communicate has changed just as dramatically. The airline and financial services industry are classic examples of industries who conduct business 24-hours-a-day around the world via complex, international networks. The reality is that geographic distances, time zones and national boundaries are no longer barriers to global commerce. Information Technology (IT) has been a catalyst driving this global marketplace as well as offering a solution base from which to draw. Clearly change abounds and diversity is the norm.

As the globalization trend continues, companies have a growing need for employees who understand information technology in an international context. Business schools bear a major responsibility in educating and shaping future managers with a global vision. This book makes a unique contribution by providing insight into how countries around the globe currently define their MIS curriculum and how they are responding to the challenge of internationalization. Global IT programs, from both developed and developing countries, are presented. Several chapters identify and discuss key issues, problems, and opportunities related to the internationalization of curricula programs. For the first time IS faculty and researchers have access to course content, specific syllabi, and other materials to develop a program or individual courses in global IT, or to incorporate global IT topics within the existing curriculum.

This book contains sixteen chapters, organized into six sections. The first section introduces the issues related to delivering an internationally-oriented IT/IS curriculum. The second section contains two papers that discuss the significance of globalization to IT curricula. Chapter 2 provides an in-depth discussion of the drivers of globalization. It challenges educational institutions to develop relationships with the business community and public service and policy organizations in order to effectively incorporate the real world into course work. The following chapter addresses the question of how to internationalize an IT program. Section III, consisting of five chapters, offers a detailed examination of IT programs, the processes, and related issues to internationalizing the curriculum in different developed countries in the world. Similarly, Section IV has three chapters that present several developing countries' experiences. Section V consists of four chapters concerning useful strategies for teaching globalization. The strategies vary from outlining rationale for placement of topics in different IS/IT courses to the use of different media to deliver a global IT course. Finally, the last section discusses issues related to designing doctoral programs with an international component.

The book has significant value as a reference tool for several groups, e.g. practitioners, educators, researchers, and administrators of curricula programs. Many firms are doing business in other parts of the world. IS professionals will benefit from knowing MIS programs in other countries. This may affect their own hiring and organizational practices in other countries. In addition, it is likely they will be more sensitive to the need for global IT education in their own training programs.

Educators and administrators benefit from the extensive discussion of issues related to internationalizing IT programs in different countries. It quickly becomes apparent that methods used in one country do not apply to others. Different countries have different needs dictated by their stage of global information technology. As we seek to define curricula programs that address the global challenge, we must be cognizant of these differences. This book provides insight into questions such as:

- How might we define programs which address the different goals of MIS education in different countries?
- What should be the composition of MIS majors in different countries?
- What should the blend of technical and managerial content be in the curriculum?

Questions of administrative obstacles and faculty challenges are addressed as well.

Researchers will benefit from the extensive discussion on global IT issues as well as several IT educational models identified in the book. Current studies will gain from the knowledge provided. Future research studies may be designed drawing from the issues and models presented.

This book represents a joint effort on behalf of numerous people, and the editors would like to acknowledge their gratitude to several individuals. First of all, our deepest appreciation goes to the chapter authors. They worked hard to respond to the comments of reviewers and editors in a compressed time frame. We appreciate your efforts. We thank as well, the consulting and associate editors for their reviews of the submitted manuscripts. Considerable thanks is also extended to Idea Group Publishing, our publisher. Jan Travers, of Idea Group Publishing, provided constant support as she strived to keep the project on time. There are also others who have made their own special contributions. In particular, we would like to thank Karen Cullings, Pam O'Showy, and Carol Kalbaugh, also of Idea Group for their attention to the little details that took place behind the scenes.

Finally, we solicit and welcome the comments of you, the reader, as future editions and works can benefit from the valuable feedback. We believe that this is a new area in education that will continue to evolve as the global arena changes. It is our intent that our curricula programs reflect the dynamism of the world in which our graduating students must operate.

Karen Loch
Mehdi Khosrowpour

October, 1992

Section I

Introduction

Information Technology Education in Global Settings

1

Karen Loch
Georgia State University

Mehdi Khosrowpour
Pennsylvania State University

There are several forces that are prompting business schools and more specifically, IS departments, to assess their current programs in light of the globalization movement. Governing bodies such as the AACSB have placed increased emphasis on including international issues in each of the functional areas of business. This chapter first provides a macro-level view of international educational programs and their current inclusion of global issues. Several existing programs illustrate some basic elements critical to effectively internationalizing the curriculum. The chapter then focuses on the development of international information technology (IIT) curriculum. A review of past IS/IT curriculum development is covered. Common issues for IIT curricula developers worldwide are presented. A discussion on the shortcomings of existing curricula programs and obstacles to internationalization follows.

A review of the professional and popular literature makes it very clear that globalization is a topic of considerable interest and concern for industry and academia. Europe 1992, the opening of Eastern Europe and sweeping reformation in the former Soviet

Union are exerting a significant impact on the formation of the emerging global economy.

Information technology (IT) plays a major role in this globalization process. A heavy reliance on information technologies for coordination across geographic, cultural and organizational barriers is quickly becoming the norm. At an organizational level, IT assists firms operating in world-wide markets by helping them to identify market niches and to achieve far more control over resources scattered around the globe. IT has been an effective tool in turning formerly declining organizations in today's competitive world market into successful operations (Rockert and Scott Morton, 1984). One study concludes that a growing number of multinational corporations are utilizing the resources of information technology as the primary tool in the management and monitoring of their global businesses and business environments (Selig, 1984).

Leadership is profoundly affected by information technology as well. Bennett (1989) predicts that by the year 2000 it will be hard to find a chief executive who does not routinely receive information electronically from local, national, and international sources. Furthermore, top executives themselves predict that by the turn of the century, companies' choices of leaders will be affected by increased international competition, globalization of companies, advancements in technology, and the speed of overall change. Industry's future leaders will need multi-environment, multi-country, multi-functional, and possibly multi-company and multi-industry experience.

Similarly the requisite skill set for the IT executive reflects this new way of conducting business. IT executives are in the midst of transition from being technical custodians of the technology to being business strategists (Brancheau & Wetherbe, 1987). Traditional organizational structures, functions, job duties, and responsibilities have been either affected by IT or will be affected in the near future. This change requires IT managers to break out of their technical cocoons and behave and communicate in management teams. The IT manager must be conversant with profit and loss, return on investment, cost and benefits, forecasting, motivational theories, strategies, globalization, and other innumerable managerial issues; they must be able to speak the vernacular of managers (Bryce, 1983).

In summary, the existing literature on information technology and management clearly indicates that future general managers must possess an in-depth understanding of the coupling between business and information technology. Likewise, future managers of this technology should be strong planners with strong managerial talents and a good understanding of the potential and role of IT in support of globalization strategies. The resulting implications for education in general, and business education and IT education in particular, are profound.

This chapter provides an overview of the history of international business education programs and the common challenges of internationalization of curricula programs, irrespective of discipline. Several general models serve to demonstrate ways of creating viable curricula programs that respond to this new way of doing business. While not discipline specific, the concepts apply equally well to our IS/IT students and faculty . Next, we will discuss an evolutionary perspective of IT curriculum development and current status. We explore common issues for all developers of international information technology (IIT). Finally, we highlight challenges to the successful development of IIT curricula.

EDUCATION REFORM

Assessment of the United States' International Education Programs

The challenge of curriculum development is to define a coherent framework of course content that allows flexibility for a body of knowledge that is constantly evolving. Incorporating an international business perspective into the business school curriculum is a topic generating much interest and debate among our business school leaders. Accrediting bodies, such as the AACSB, and industry demands for students with a broader and more substantive understanding of international business issues are the primary forces behind this phenomena.

Some industry leaders believe strongly that the failure of education to respond will directly affect the competitiveness of the American work force in the world. John Patten, publisher of *Business Week*, states "American business will compete successfully throughout the world only as long as American education produces a work force that can prevail in a global economy driven by knowledge and skill. . . . Nothing less than our national fate is at stake" (Patten, 1990).

Several recent studies have called for American institutions to improve the level of international business education in order to improve the performance of American executives with international business responsibilities (The Excellence Report, 1982; Critical Needs, 1983; Global Competition, 1985). An in-depth report on education into the 21st century (Porter and McKibbin, 1988) found strong agreement among deans and faculty on the need for increased emphasis on international business / management issues. The topic ranked in the top four for both groups. Harold Leavitt of Stanford University and Noel Tichy of the University of Michigan both make specific recommendations as to what should be the end products of our programs:

> We need to provide our students with a global perspective, and a knowledge of foreign languages and cultures. We must also make them problem solvers, change managers, innovators, intra/entrepreneurs, versatile communicators, and technologically literate" (Kanter and Kesner, 1992: 467).[1]

A survey reported in *Management Practice Quarterly* clearly substantiates these points by indicating that to succeed in the business world, future MBA's will need to be multi-cultural in their sensibilities and highly flexible in their approaches to management.[2] Lest we think that American executives are overly harsh of our current status, or alone in this assessment, another study (Loch, 1991) reported a CEO of a leading European multinational firm echoing the same refrain:

> We need a different breed of managers for the future than the standard USA MBA - it was good for the 70s but not for today. They [the students] must rub shoulders with [their] peers in other countries and understand cultural differences. (Bernard Castaing, Président-Directeur Général - Procter & Gamble France)

There seems to be overwhelming consensus reflecting a perspective that (1) the United States must be prepared to compete in the fast-changing international arena and (2) education with an international component is a necessary part of the solution.

Internationalization of Curriculum

Despite acknowledgement of the need to address this issue, United States business schools are making slow progress (Porter and McKibbin, 1988). It is important to note that the notion of incorporating an international perspective into the business school program is NOT new. In fact, in the spring of 1974 the AACSB changed its accreditation standards to include a worldwide dimension in the curriculum. This standard is interpreted to say that "every student should be exposed to the international dimension through one or more elements of the curriculum" (Porter and McKibbin, 1988:59, 62: AACSB Curriculum Standards).

Funded by the General Electric Company, the AACSB launched a series of seminars/workshops in support of the new standard to further the internationalization of business school curriculum. They conducted 30 workshops in various parts of the country between 1977 and 1986. The workshops were of three types: (1) to assist the participants in adding an international dimension to the core courses in the curriculum at both undergraduate and MBA levels; (2) to aid faculty members in the design and teaching of an international course in their respective disciplines; and (3) to examine strategies that business schools can follow to internationalize the curriculum and the faculty. This third workshop type targeted deans, associate deans and departmental chairpersons.

These workshops might be viewed as successful in that 80% of the survey respondents (15% of the workshop participants) indicated that they shared what they learned with colleagues, creating a significant multiplier effect. Nevertheless, the percentage of faculty involved in these workshops represented less than 5% of total AACSB business school faculty. Ten years after the change in the accreditation standard, as much as 20% of the AACSB member schools[3] reported they had done nothing at one of the levels; 11% had done nothing at either the undergraduate or MBA level. Although the majority of the schools indicated that they had made a decision to incorporate an international dimension in some or all of their core courses, only about 10% had implemented the decision at the time of the survey.

Internationalization of Faculty

The ability to deliver an internationalized curriculum is also a concern. The small percentage of faculty who participated in the AACSB workshops is indicative of the small number of faculty who have ever studied international business or who are familiar with the international aspects of their respective disciplines. There is a tendency for administrations to focus on the curriculum and to neglect addressing the low level of internationalization of faculty and future faculty, and the peculiar problems and challenges associated with this fact. The recent surge of new international journals and established journals publishing articles with an international flavor reflects the academic community's heightened international interest and places pressure on faculty to "come up to speed." Unfortunately, faculty's lack of understanding of international issues (Deans and Goslar, 1990; Nehrt, 1987; Thanopoulos and Vernon, 1987) limits their ability to conduct international research and to introduce international issues into their courses. How bad is it? Approximately 15% of AACSB schools have formal faculty exchange programs. Less than 10% of these schools reported any faculty members studying or teaching at their foreign affiliates. During this same time frame, the reported annual average number of faculty who went abroad to teach or to do research under the aegis of their faculty foreign exchange programs was less than 1%. While 64 schools reported a total of 182 exchange agreements, 11 schools accounted for almost 50% of those agreements.

Internationalization of Future Faculty

Doctoral students represent the pool of future faculty members. It is thus relevant to assess to what extent they are being prepared to add an international dimension to the courses they will teach in their careers. Nehrt (1987) conducted two studies of doctoral programs to determine what percent of the PhD/DBA graduates had, at some point in their formal studies (masters and doctoral), at least one international business course. In 1976, 25% reported they had studied such a course.[4] The 1984 study surveyed the 53 largest doctoral programs. Ninety-one percent of the schools responded, representing 82% of all the doctoral graduates in the country. The study found that only 17% of the doctoral students who would graduate in the subsequent three years had taken one or more international courses. If the sample is adjusted so that it is equivalent to the 1976 study, only 15% of the doctoral students' studies included an international course. The prospect for future faculty trained in international issues looks grim.

MBA programs provide an additional level of concern. United States MBA programs churn out graduates in droves; 70,000 MBA degrees were awarded in 1990. This represents a 30% increase since 1980; a 15 fold increase since 1960 (Bryne, 1990). It is estimated that approximately 200,000 students are now studying for their MBA, without a significant international content. The current status of the internationalization of United States business school curricula, faculty, and students is seriously lagging, as these statistics indicate. Table 1 provides a summary of the statistics.

The picture appears bleak, yet there are several existing models that demonstrate ways of creating viable, truly international curricula programs. It is worthwhile to examine them for key elements critical to effectively internationalizing the curriculum. We can then apply these basics to the topic of development of international IT curricula.

Models for International Business Programs

Some prominent schools such as INSEAD (European Institute of Business Administration in Fontainbleau, France) and IMD (International Institute of Management Development in Lausanne, Switzerland), Ashridge Management College (Britain), and London Business School have extensive links with business. IMD, LBS, and Ashridge were set up with significant financial support from industry to provide a broad spectrum management program. IMD reports 90% of its annual revenues now come from international firms. Their curriculum is estimated to use almost twice as much international teaching material (Haynes, 1991). Their faculty represent the spectrum of nationalities. All of these schools are leaders in delivering continuing executive education.

An unique senior managers program was instituted in November, 1990 by Nokia Consumer Electronics, a Geneva-based subsidiary of Nokia, a Finnish telecommunications and electronics group. Its program lasts thirty-one months with a stated objective of grooming potential senior managers. The class composition is about half Nokia employees, the rest from outside the company. It offers a mix of education and experience. It beings with a four month introductory course followed by

Survey Items	Key Figures	Key Ratios
Number of AACSB Business Schools	564	
Number of faculty in AACSB Business Schools	24,000	
Number of AACSB Workshop Participants (1977-1986)[5]	1,071	4.4%[6]
Number of AACSB Business Schools with faculty foreign exchange programs[7]	64	15.4%[8]
Annual average number of professors who participate under the aegis of faculty foreign exchange programs	125	.5%[9]
Percentage of doctoral students with an international dimension in their program - 1976[10]		25.0%
Number of doctoral students graduating in years 1985-1987 with an international dimension in their program of study - 1984[11]	1,690	17.0%
Percentage of doctoral students graduating in years 1985-1987 with an international dimension in their program of study - 1984 = = = > sample equivalent to 1976 study		15.0%

Table 1: Summary Statistics of AACSB Business Schools and Internationalization Efforts (Source: Nehrt, 1986)

twelve months of on-the-job training overseas then three months at business school and then another year in a different overseas posting. Total on-the-job overseas training equals two years (Haynes, 1991). It is significant to note that two years, or 77% of the program is hands-on experiences; only seven months represents classroom studies.

There are some leading American examples as well. One of particular note is Arthur D. Little Management Education Institute in Cambridge, Massachusetts. A little less than thirty years old, this school represents probably the most internationalized business program in the country. The program is an intensive eleven month course. The faculty are made up primarily of international consultants who also play the role of mentor to the students. Its teaching methodology is case studies; multicultural teams are formed to work on the projects.

An extensive survey conducted by the Harbridge House Consulting Group based in London documents a growth in what it calls Consortium MBA programs (Baston, 1989). The consortium model's objective is to address the concern of managers that business schools are out of touch with business in general, and specifically global business practices. The consortium model is based on the creation of alliances among business schools, corporations, public-sector and not-for-profits for the purpose of designing and administering flexible and modular programs. University of Warwick Business School began a consortium with twenty-three participants. Manchester Business School began a masters in business management program that involves a partnership between the school and a number of major multinational corporations.

The Community of European Management Schools (CEMS) is a European consortium model that explicitly addresses the issue of internationalization of a curriculum program and all its stakeholders: university administration, faculty, students, and corporate, and the establishment of international research agendas. It combines academic institutions and companies working together to define the curriculum, pursues international research initiatives among the faculty, and extends their students' views beyond the traditional national boundaries of the institution.

A variation of the consortium model is a joint-venture model. It is another way of widening the schools' international perspective. An example is Britain's Cranfield School of Management alliance with France's Groupe ESC Lyon Business School and the establishment of the Sofia School of Management in Bulgaria. This arrangement provides international opportunities for both students and faculty. The corporate link, however, is missing.

These models exemplify different approaches to internationalizing business programs. Many of the programs illustrated efforts outside the United States. The majority comprised a single university with multiple corporate linkages or multiple academic linkages with no corporate involvement. All of the programs focused on masters or continuing executive level education with the exception of the CEMS model. CEMS's objective is to mold young, junior managers to be internationally competent. CEMS is distinctive from the other models also because it involves both multiple academic institutions and multiple corporations, representing multiple countries with diverse cultures.

Drawing from these models, we can identify six basic elements that are key to effectively internationalizing the curriculum. They are (1) a tight coupling with business to bring relevancy to the classroom, (2) an affiliation with other academic institutions, (3) internationally experienced faculty, (4) incorporation of international teaching materials to effectively illustrate international concepts, (5) inclusion of a hands-on learning work experience in another culture, and (6) language studies to maximize the benefit of the international experience.

We will focus now on the internationalization of IT curricula process. We begin with an overview of curriculum evolution. We then discuss the shortcomings of current curricula programs in view of the basic elements. A discussion of key obstacles to the internationalization process follows. Noting that this is primarily an American perspective, we provide discussion for IIT developers world-wide. Finally, we return to the basics and suggest different actionable strategies that may be used to begin the internationalization process locally.

INFORMATION SYSTEMS CURRICULUM EVOLUTION

Curriculum development for the information systems began in the early 1970s. Two professional associations ACM and DPMA, played majors roles in making curriculum recommendations. During the last twenty years, undergraduate and graduate IS curriculum recommendations have been made by both associations (ACM, 1979, 1986, 1991; DPMA, 1990). Pioneer IS programs were first introduced in the 1960s. A DPMA survey conducted in August 1989 provides some perspective on existing IS programs in the United States and Canada. In the last decade we have witnessed a convergence of the computer and telecommunications industries. In this short span of time, many organizations and even whole industries, such as financial services, have become reliant on information systems as the lifeblood to their businesses. It comes as little surprise, then, that of existing IS programs today, fifty percent have only been in existence since 1981 (DPMA, 1990). During this time period, the focus and content of the IS programs have changed dramatically in an attempt to keep pace with advances in technology. Yet contrary to the globalization trends in industry and information technology's key role, neither the ACM nor the DPMA explicitly included an international MIS course in its latest recommended curriculum. Moreover, they did not include an international MIS course among the electives.

We acknowledge that the way of doing business has changed, and the role of information technology in this change is monumental. Despite strong solicitation from outside observers (Porter and McKibbin, 1988) for curriculum reform, curriculum seems to be the last item on the agenda as we begin to internationalize the discipline.

Recently, some major MIS conferences have focused on global themes in acknowledgement of the trend. For example, the 1991 theme of the 2nd International Conference of the Information Resources Management Association was *Global Information Technology Management.* As of 1992, one of the official journals of the association is The *Journal of Global Information Management.* Similarly, the Eleventh Annual International Conference on Information Systems held in December 1990 in Copenhagen, Denmark had as its theme: *The Role of Information Systems in the Globalization of Business.* This meeting was its first "international" conference held at a non-US site. In an effort to promote non-US participation in the association, the Decision Sciences Institute (DSI), founded in 1969, held its first international meeting in June 1991 in Brussels, Belgium. Most recently, the Association for Computing Machinery (ACM) opened an ACM office in Europe in an effort to enhance its role as an international organization. In October 1990 the then president of the association, John White, challenged the organization to live up to its charter which implies an international scope for the Association (White, 1990). The ACM European Service Center in Brussels begins operations on October 1, 1992 (Bell, 1992).

We are also witnessing the introduction of several international IT journals to serve as outlets for scholarly research. To name a few: The *Journal of Global Information Management, International Information Systems, International Journal of Information Management,* and *Journal of Information Systems.* The latter two are published out of the United Kingdom. Both professional associations and publications are natural channels for faculty to expand their horizons and step out of their ethnocentric perspective. While these initiatives are laudable, they fail to adequately address the specific challenge of internationalizing the curriculum.

SHORTCOMINGS OF INFORMATION TECHNOLOGY EDUCATION IN THE INTERNATIONALIZATION PROCESS

The six basic elements identified earlier provide a framework by which to assess our progress in internationalizing IT curricula. The following sections provide an in-depth discussion of these shortcomings.

Lack of a Tight Coupling with Business

Similar to the international business education, field observers criticize our current programs for lacking relevancy and real-world ties. Companies are increasingly disenchanted with business school products. This criticism must be taken to heart as we begin to incorporate the international dimension. Henry Mintzberg of McGill University, a well-known, respected academic is not surprised by corporate reaction and predicts a loss of customers:

"If those people in business and government who support today's business schools really knew what was going on inside many of them - took the trouble, for example, to interview professors at random — they would be demanding revolutionary changes in faculty and curriculum instead of passively writing checks."

Active involvement of international corporations was a major component of almost all of the models examined.   The consortium model seems to offer particular promise as a means to exploit the strengths and diversities of the parties involved. Rehder, Porter, and Muller (1991) found that not only do such arrangements offer opportunities for participants [faculty, students] and business schools to utilize human and organizational resources of consortium members, they also provide other synergistic linking opportunities that might not otherwise be so apparent. Certainly a close relationship with industry provides several readily identifiable benefits. One, it opens the communications channels for guidance and feedback on course development and content. Two, it provides access to companies for case writing and applied research. Both of these benefits address the challenge of finding international teaching materials. Three, it may offer hands-on work experience for both faculty and students. It is time for businesses and business schools to work cooperatively.   Together they need to define what forms the requisite set of skills for an internationally capable manager and how to best deliver the product.

Lack of Cooperation Among Institutions

We are not adopting the paradigm of the 90s and beyond. Individualism abounds in the world of academe at all levels. While under the guise of collegiality and in the name of education, there is a spirit of cooperation among universities. However, the relationships are adversarial and highly competitive, modeling the win-lose relationship we teach so well to our students as they enter the corporate world.   This paradigm is very much contrary to the necessary mode of operation for our students as they operate in the global environment. The result is that we lack vision and understanding of how a 'live' organization operates in the real world, and more often than not, in a global context. Particularly in the domain of information technology, it is essential that we adopt a cross-functional approach to curriculum content and delivery. This will require significant attitudinal shifts by administration and faculty. Professor Noel Tichy of the

University of Michigan chastises the academic community. He contends that we are making only incremental changes, while what business needs is quantum changes (Mian, 1989). Robert O. Anderson, founder and former CEO of the Atlantic Richfield Corporation, describes our current individualistic approach as "teaching business in school is like teaching swimming without water" (Harris, 1989). There are advantages of learning the basic elements of the strokes outside the water, but the real test is whether the students put the two together. They must get into the water. For such changes to take place in academe, there must be a fundamental philosophical shift in our thinking, attitudes and approaches to delivering IT education.

Lack of Faculty with International Experience

Most faculty are not familiar with the international dimension of information systems. Hence they are unlikely to feel confident in introducing these dimensions into the courses they teach. Similarly, most faculty lack real experience in the international arena and therefore unable to appreciate the complexities of the global environment. Peter Drucker pithily stated

Management is a practice, not a science. Schools are staffed with young, rigid academicians who have no exposure to practice. They need to get their hands dirty (*Forbes,* August 19, 1991).

Likewise faculty are challenged to bring relevancy to their research programs which theoretically affect curricula. Rehder et. al. (1991) describe us as "frozen in time, with anachronistic theory and programs." Academicians typically claim that the research agenda is critical to staying abreast of or ahead of business trends and developments. Interestingly, there is currently very limited international research (Deans, Karwan, Goslar, Ricks, and Toyne, 1991; Deans and Kane, 1992; Deans and Goslar, 1990). Curriculum modifications, in theory, reflect the research findings and expose students to the cutting edge. In reality, there is a considerable time lag between research discoveries and curriculum changes. This theory also presupposes that we are researching the right things. Kaplan (1991) asserts that it requires a decade, or longer, to incorporate relevant material into the curriculum. This is not so far off the mark. The

AACSB identified the need to internationalize curricula almost seventeen years ago, yet there is only beginning evidence that adjustments have been made in research programs let alone in curricula.

Lack of Incorporation of International Teaching Materials

The cited exemplary models all make extensive use of international teaching materials, primarily cases, and many of the professors have extensive international experience.

Development and availability of international teaching materials, and faculty expertise affect the level of incorporation of materials. There are very few resources currently available that address the international dimension of IS. From a scholarly perspective, international research is limited. Teaching materials are also very limited. Only a handful of books are available on IIT, three of which were published within the last year: Deans et. al., 1992, Kefalas, 1990, Palvia, et. al., 1992, and Roche, 1992. As mentioned earlier, there is a growing number of scholarly publications which focus on international issues and there is some indication that other journals are expanding their topics to include international (Ives and Jarvenpaa, 1991).

The lack of ready availability of international teaching materials requires considerable effort towards development by those who are teaching international aspects of IT. IMD faculty, which are known for their extensive use of international cases, have the never-ending task of case development. They are able to build on IMD's extensive corporate network which provides opportunities for case development. Arthur D. Little's Institute builds on its faculty's extensive international expertise for development and in-class reference. However for the majority of schools, neither of these resources are readily available. This means that the first two initiatives, linkage with the business community and building relationships with non-domestic academic institutions, are key to development and availability of such materials.

Finally, the level of international expertise and interest of the respective faculty member plays a role. Most faculty are not trained in the international aspects of their fields. It is human nature to spend the most time on those topics with which we are most familiar; unfamiliar topics receive little attention. Furthermore, it is a false assumption that every faculty member has an international interest, and is so inclined, to include international material in the course content.

Lack of Inclusion of Hands-on Work Experience

McFarlan (1992) of Harvard University describes the challenges for the multi-national CIO. He states that internationally capable CIOs need both intellectual and visceral sensitivity to the international complexities of information technology management. He reports a recent interview of a CIO of a large chemical company who noted a key requirement for his successor is that he have had substantial international experience, including a period of overseas residency. The models described earlier all included some form of hands-on experience. Our students are frequently described as products of ivory towers with little practical understanding and real-world appreciation (Drucker, 1991; Bryne, 1990). The bottom line is that book learning is viewed as necessary but not sufficient. Students must experience working with their peers in other cultures, and acquire some visceral understanding of what it takes to conduct business in another culture and language.

Lack of Multi-language Proficiency

There is the additional issue of foreign language training in which most American students are woefully lacking. Many business schools do not require language courses as part of the core program. Graduate programs have increasingly dropped the foreign language requirement as a necessary tool to conduct research. The question of language requirement, and internships as well, really touches a much more significant issue: length of program. We in academe are always concerned with the length of programs and whether the students will make a commitment to a longer program. A truly internationalized program which requires language proficiency, study abroad and internships will take more time. A frequent explanation for not including language courses is that it extends the program beyond the conventional four-year or two-year norm. It is unfortunate that we take such a short-term view of developing students for a life-long career. In turn, the students adopt a short term view of things. The short term view pervades in management. And so the cycle continues. It would seem that other countries are much ahead of the United States in addressing this issue.

OBSTACLES TO THE SUCCESSFUL DEVELOPMENT OF IIT CURRICULA IN THE UNITED STATES

Certainly the internationalization of IT curricula is in its infancy. There are several obstacles that exist as we strive to move forward.

Lack of Leadership

Lack of leadership in the profession prevails. Within the ranks, there is little consensus as to what the international IT dimension should include and how it should be incorporated into an existing program. While the professional societies are increasing their public visibility concerning international issues, they are failing to provide leadership to address the curriculum questions head-on. Rather it is more individual efforts by a handful of schools and colleagues that are spearheading the effort to incorporate a global dimension in their respective IS/IT programs.

Lack of Recognized Discipline

Two, MIS is still not a recognized discipline such as finance, accounting, or marketing. Rather it is viewed as a subset of other disciplines such as accounting, operations, or management. This perspective is perpetuated by the fact that in many schools, MIS / IS are part of other departments. In many non-US institutions it is not even part of the Business School but rather part of the Engineering School. Additionally, there is a lack of understanding by other disciplines of the need for international IT curriculum. This makes it difficult for the discipline to introduce new courses such as international MIS into an already full program. Arguably, if something comes into the program, something else must go out.

Lack of Conducive Environment

Part of the slow reaction may be explained by how academe operates. Faculty tend to be functional specialists for which they are recruited, promoted, and rewarded yet international research and instruction require multi-disciplinary skills. We propagate this limited formation through our doctoral students.

An additional factor is related to the reward system in academe. Curriculum research and development are often viewed as being less scholarly and not real research. Recognition in our field is heavily based on the number and placement of publications. The goal is to publish in the tier one, or premier journals of the discipline. For the most part, the respected journals do not view international issues as a premier research topic. This is reflected by (1) the small number of premier journals - those journals that count the most in tenure decisions - that present an international perspective and (2) the number of international articles in the premier journals. In turn, the journals that publish curricula related issues are not considered part of the premier list.

The circuitous relationship between editors, referees, and the contents of the journal further ensure the limited publication options for international research. The lack of recognition and the limited publication opportunities for international research discourage junior faculty from pursuing international research agendas. From a tenure and promotion perspective. it is more circumspect to develop a research agenda that is of interest to the key journals so as to successfully publish and in turn, be awarded tenure. Changes in the journals and the editorial review process must be effectuated to reflect today's global business environment.

These facts present a great disincentive for non-tenured faculty to pursue any initiatives in the area of curriculum development. It is time for administration to re-evaluate seriously the reward and tenure and promotion processes, and to reward well-received international research and curriculum innovation.

COMMON ISSUES FOR IIT DEVELOPERS WORLD-WIDE

The effects of the globalization trend is not unique to the United States but being felt world-wide. Regardless of the country of origin, mangers and IT managers in multi-national firms need to understand the factors which influence the global IT environment. Likewise, academic institutions world-wide are re-evaluating their current IS/IT programs as they strive to respond to industry.

The shortcomings highlighted apply equally well to programs world-wide. The representative models examined earlier included many non-American programs. It provides strong evidence that the six critical elements are applicable to all IIT developers, irrespective of geographic location. As an example, the CEMS program currently involves 12 European countries and more than double the number of multinational firms. It also recently included IT as a part of its required core. The most basic argument for IT inclusion in the core is that it touches all the functional areas of business.

All of the programs have highly internationalized faculty. Many of the faculty are also international consultants with extensive real-world experience. Incorporation of materials was specifically addressed by most of the programs through exploitation of their industry and academic networks, and considerable effort towards developing their own materials. Finally, internships, hands-on work experience, and extensive language requirements were requisite for the programs.

The first two obstacles are likely common issues for IIT developers in other countries. The lack of leadership and definition of the field is not country specific. The third obstacle, the prevailing academic environment is more likely country specific. Reward systems vary even from institution to institution. In many countries, there is a very close relationship between academia and government. Most probably, each country's IS professionals can identify their unique obstacles to effectively internationalizing their IT programs.

Variations on common issues also need to be addressed. We know that we do not all perceive MIS issues through the same set of lenses. Palvia, Palvia, and Zigli (1992b) found that key MIS issues correlate with a country's computer industry and technological development. Classifying countries as either developed, developing, and less developed, they found that perception of MIS issues, and therefore what IS executives and corporate general managers view as important, was closely associated with the technology environment of the country. They proposed a three- stage life-cycle model for IT and IS development in nations.

Stage one emphasizes infrastructure which remains largely in the domain of governments and/or large powerful organizations. Stage two includes primarily operational problems which are in the decision realm of lower and middle management. Finally, stage three reflects the maturation process where the IS and IT can be used in a strategic manner to enhance competitive and organizational posture of the firm.

Development of an IIT curricula necessarily reflects the respective country's national IT environment. The country's multinational organizations and responsible managers must however understand the issues and opportunities of using information technology on a multi-country, world-wide basis. The other countries in which they operate are very likely at different stages in the life-cycle model. This means that the curriculum must provide a true international perspective rather than limited to the domestic issues of the country. Furthermore, all countries are at some point in the life-cycle model. While one country may have passed through an earlier stage, the issues of the previous stage do not cease to exist but rather become of secondary concern. The concerns for MIS executives and general managers simply carry different degrees of import depending on the national IT environment.

Drawing from the literature (Palvia et. al., 1992; Roche, 1992), we propose five common themes to include in IIT curricula programs: (1) technical issues (e.g. hardware, software, data and telecommunications, data and standards, role of protocols, security), (2) people issues (e.g. culture, education, religion, language), (3) political / legal issues (e.g. government regulation, labor unions, transborder data flows, legislation), (4) economic issues (e.g. export/import restrictions, currency, national infrastructure), and (5) managerial and strategic issues (e.g. training, end-user computing, use of IT for competitive advantage, organizational structure, interorganizational systems). One possible approach is for the curriculum to address the five themes, and overlay the national IT environment on these five themes. Inclusion of international teaching materials and other classroom resources could then be used to illustrate how the IT environment influences the degree of importance of the respective issues within the theme framework.

ACTIONABLE STRATEGIES

There are several actionable strategies that we can begin to do as we move to internationalize the IT curricula. We can categorize these strategies by the six elements previously outlined.

Tight Coupling with Business

Considerable evidence has been provided as to the benefits of a strong relationship with industry. The relationship may be at different levels. Possible level of interaction may include special speakers in classroom or other forums, workshops for faculty on international IT issues, executive roundtables or other industry representation on committees, or internships and practicum options for both faculty and students. A regular dialogue is necessary and should be a primary objective.

Affiliation with Non-domestic Academic Institutions

Formalized affiliation with schools in other countries opens a host of opportunities to be exploited. Possible strategies include exchange of faculty to provide international experience. Student exchanges are another option. A less formal relationship may include exchange of teaching materials, joint development of teaching materials, and joint research projects.

Internationalization of Faculty

Both of the above items include strategies that will contribute to the internationalization of faculty. Another strategy is to bring visiting faculty from other schools; a sort of internationalizing on-site. Grants for international travel permit faculty to attend programs to develop their international skills. Workshops conducted by key business personnel on selected topics provides an applied perspective to a specific topic of interest. Internships with an international emphasis is a tangible way for faculty to get on-the-job experience that they lack. Optimally, they take place overseas. In either case, the project should be international in scope and the duration of sufficient length to be able to do something of value.

Incorporation of International Teaching Materials

Once the first three elements are addressed, this element follows naturally. The more basic concern is the development and availability of the teaching materials. The future looks promising in this regard. One consideration is to exploit more fully inter-faculty relationships in order to develop materials. The CEMS model specifically created inter-faculty teams in each discipline in order to develop internationally oriented cases in cooperation with the corporate members. The corporate members provided the sites for the case studies. The multi-country perspective of the team members brings much richness to the process. An additional factor to explore is the need for an interdisciplinary focus which should be present in international materials.

Hands-on Experience and Language Studies

These two elements were really requirements for the participants in the programs examined. The MIT Commission on Industrial Productivity (Dertouzos, Lester, and Solow, 1989) recommended that students be given increased opportunities for substantive interaction with people and cultures of other countries for considerable duration. International study abroad programs provide some hands-on exposure and most often involve language studies. Generally, they are viewed as an invaluable experience which should be linked to an internship program. Internships and practicums are other strategies. The emphasis should be on international projects and tasks. The usual distinction made between internships and practicums is that internships are overseas, practicums are local. Both provide hands-on experience. Corporate interviews suggest that it is not adequate for the students to simply study in another culture; they must also experience the business environment. Working and living in a different culture and language are very different from being a tourist. This argues strongly for a combined study abroad / student internship program. Duration is also of concern. CEMS requires a minimum of one term per component. Graduates of the program stated unanimously that while they found the experience invaluable, a longer period of six months would be even more worthwhile.

Financial considerations are significant. Study abroad and internships require considerably more commitment of resources by both the student, and the academic institution for locating, administration and logistics. Business relationships might be one source of establishing scholarship programs to specifically support this initiative.

CONCLUSION

All of the actionable strategies require that as a business school, and a department, the overall objective must be defined. The objective will direct which strategies are most appropriate. Likewise, allocation of appropriate resources by administration in order to implement the strategies is also important. Strong business commitment is needed to jar loose the staid administrative bureaucracy of business schools. While administration says that it supports the internationalization of the program, it has heretofore been unwilling to commit the dollars necessary to internationalize the faculty and revamp the curricula. Active involvement of the business community will go far in breaking down this barrier. Active involvement of the business community will help us to deliver a more valuable product. Finally, a long term commitment to the process is required. Change of this magnitude will not occur overnight.

Porter and McKibbin (1988) suggest that the key question we must ask ourselves ". . . is whether the current curriculum is as appropriate for the future—the 1990s and beyond—as it ought to be" (1988:79). Globalization of industries has occurred across the board: textiles, machinery, food, finance, petroleum products, metals, entertainment, and so on. This in turn requires a massive, dynamic, sophisticated information technology infrastructure with the capability to support the organization at all levels spanning time and geographic boundaries. It is our job as IS faculty to prepare the future information system specialists for this challenge. We are headed in the right direction, but will we be able to deliver, and how soon?

ENDNOTES
[1]Harold Leavitt and Noel Tichy as cited in the Johnson, Smith, & Knisely, Inc. study Management Practice Quarterly (Spring 1989) p. 3.

[2]See also Management Practice Quarterly (Summer/Fall 1989) p. 96; Johnson, Smith & Knisely, Inc. study Executive Search/Europe 1992, New York: Johnson, Smith & Knisely, 1989; Babson College Excel Committee on Management Education in the 21st Century, "Management Education in the 21st Century," Wellesley, MA: Babson College, 1990.

[3]Findings from a second survey of all 564 AACSB member schools conducted by Nehrt in 1984. Reported response rate was 99%.

[4]The 1976 study surveyed the 25 largest doctoral programs in the country. As of 1986, 100 business schools in the United States offer doctorates in business. The 53 largest programs produce 92% of all doctoral graduates.

[5]Statistics taken from a 1985 survey conducted by the AACSB of all participants of AACSB workshops/seminars to determine the effects of their efforts. All the participants (1071) received a survey; 162 responded for a 15% response rate.

[6]Ratio of number of faculty who participated in the AACSB seminars / total number of estimated faculty in Business Schools.

[7]AACSB conducted a survey in 1983 to determine the number of schools with faculty and student exchanges. Out of 414 responding institutions (a 68% response rate), 82 or 19.8% reported that their school had formal ties with foreign business schools. The schools also indicated a variety of other types of exchange relationships. Nehrt resurveyed the 82 schools in 1984 to assess how many of the schools' faculty actually participate in these exchange programs. Eighty-one schools responded. Only 64 schools remained with valid exchange programs, reporting a total of 182 exchange programs, of which 96 involved 'formal' agreements.

[8]64 of 414 institutions with valid exchange programs in 1984.

[8]Average annual number of participating faculty / estimated number of faculty in AACSB member schools -1984.

[10]Survey of the 25 largest doctoral programs in 1976.

[11]Survey of 53 largest doctoral programs, representing 92% of all doctoral graduates. As of 1986, there are 100 U.S. business schools which offer doctorates in business. Only 287 students reported having had one or more international courses.

REFERENCES

ACM. (1979). Recommendation for the undergraduate program in computer science. *Communications of the ACM, 22*(3), 147-166.

ACM. (1986). Recommendations for the undergraduate program in computer science. Curriculum Committee on Computer Science Curriculum 68. *Communications of the ACM, 11*(3), 151-197.

ACM. (1991). *Computer Curricula.* ACM, New York.

Baston, R. W. (1989). *The Company-Based MBA.* London: Harbridge House Consulting Group, Ltd.

Bell, Gwen. (1992). President's letter: ACM in Europe. *Communications of the ACM, 35*(9), 17-18.

Bennett, Amanda. (February 27, 1989). The Chief Executives in the Year 2000 Will Be Experienced Abroad. *Wall Street Journal,* 1.

Brancheau, J. C. & Wetherbe, J. C. (1987). Key issues in information systems management. *MIS Quarterly, 11*(1), 23-45.

Bryce, T. (1983). Information systems - a field in transition. *Journal of Systems Management, 33*(8), 6-13.

Bryne, J. A. (Associate Editor). (1990). *Business Week's Guide to the Best Business Schools.* New York: McGraw-Hill Book Company.

Critical Needs in International Education: Recommendations for Action. Washington: National Advisory Board on International Education Programs, December, 1983.

Deans, P. C., & Goslar, M. D. (1990). *Incorporating an International Dimension into IS Curriculum: A Conceptual Model with Emphasis on the Foreign Component.* Presented at the International Academy for Information Management, Chicago, IL.

Deans, P., and Kane, M. (1992). International Dimensions of Information Systems and Technology. Boston, MA:: PWS-Kent Publishing Company.

Deans, P., Karwan, K., Goslar, M., Ricks, D., and Toyne, B. (1991). Identification of key international information system issues in U.S. based multinational corporations. *Journal of Management Information Systems, 7*(4):1-24.

Dertouzos, M. L., Lester, R. K., & Solow, R. M. (1989). *Made in America: Regaining the Productive Edge.* Cambridge, Mass.: MIT Press.

DPMA. (1990). *Information Systems: The DPMA Model for a Four Year Undergraduate Degree-Draft.* Data Processing Management Association, Park Ridge, IL.

Drucker, P. (August 19, 1991). *Forbes.*

Global Competition: The New Reality. (January 1985). Report of the President's Commission on Industrial Competitiveness, Vol. 1, Washington: Government Printing Office.

Haynes, P. (March 2, 1991). Passport to prosperity. *The Economist, 3*(13).

Ives, B. and Jarvenpaa, S.L. (1991). Applications of Global Information Technology: Key Issues for Management. *MIS Quarterly, 15*(1): 33-49.

Kanter, Jerry and Kesner, Richard. (1992). The CIO/GIO as catalyst and facilitator: Building the information utility to meet global challenges. In Palvia et. al. (Eds.), *The Global issues of information technology management.* (pp. 465-483). Harrisburg, PA: Idea Group Publishing Series in Global Information Technology Management Series.

Kaplan, R. S. (April 1991). The Topic of Quality in Business School Education and Research. *Selections,* 13-21.

Kefalas, A.G. *Global Business Strategy: A Systems Approach.* Cincinnati, OH: South-Western Publishing Company, 1990.

Loch, Karen D. (1991). Education and Global Business. Report funded by Society for International Business Fellows.

McFarlan, F.W. (December, 1986). Editor's Comments. *MIS Quarterly, 10*(4).

Mian, J. (July 17, 1989). B-Schools Get a Global Vision. *Fortune,* 80.

Nehrt, L. C. (1987). The Internationalization of the Curriculum. *Journal of International Business Studies, 18*(1), 83-90.

Palvia, S., Palvia, P., & Zigli, R. M. (1992a). *The Global Issues of Information Technology Management.* Harrisburg, PA: Idea Group Publishing Series in Global Information Technology Management Series.

Palvia, S., Palvia, P., & Zigli, R. M. (1992b). Global information technology environment: Key MIS issues in advanced and less-developed nations. In Palvia et. al. (Eds.), *The Global issues of information technology management.* (pp. 2-34). Harrisburg, PA: Idea Group Publishing Series in Global Information Technology Management Series.

Patten. (December 17, 1990). The Technology Revolution comes to Education. *Business Week* Special Section.

Porter, L. W. & McKibbin, L. E. (1988). *Management Education and Development: Drift or Thrust into the 21st Century?* NY: McGraw-Hill Book Company.

Rehder, R., Porter, J. L., & Muller, H. J. (May 1991). Challenging the Management Education Monster: The Learning Alliance MBA. *Selections,* 13-25.

Roche, E.M. (1992). *Managing Information Technology in Multinational Corporations.* New York, NY: Macmillan Publishing Company.

Rockart, J.F. & Scott Morton, M.S. (1984). Implications of change in information technology for corporate strategy. *Interfaces, 14*(1), 84-95.

Selig, Gad J. (1983). *Strategic Planning for Information Resource Management: A Multinational Perspective.* Ann Arbor, Michigan: UMI Research Press.

Thanopoulos, J. & Vernon, I. R. (1987) International Business Education in the AACSB Schools. *Journal of International Business Studies, 18*(1), 91-98.

The Excellence Report: Using It To Improve Your Schools. (1983). Arlington, VA: American Association of School Administrators, 3-12. (Contains the report to the President. 1982. A nation at risk: The imperative for educational reform).

White, J. R. (1990). Enhancing ACM's Role as an International Organization. *Communications of the ACM, 33*(10), 11-12

Section II

Significance of Globalization

Drivers of Globalization
2 The Intertwining of Business and Information Technology

James A. Senn
Georgia State University

Foundations which have served as the base for business practices of many years are in rapid transition, including the drive toward globalization. Information technology is both a driver of globalization and an area where organization response is also required to ensure that emerging issues are addressed in an effective manner.

This chapter examines the intertwining of business and information technology in international business. The forces driving globalization are examined as a structural change in business. Related responses needed from managers of information technology are also explored. Key challenges for educators are examined with an eye toward the evolution needed in curricula and delivery systems.

The world of business is undergoing shifts that are unprecedented in the twentieth century. In many respects, the very foundations on which organizations build their strategies, products, and services, are in transition. Globalization is at the same time both a driver of the transition and a result.

Information technology (I/T) is also undergoing tremendous changes due to shifts in economic and performance levels, and in the role it plays in organizations. I/T plays a pivotal role in the capability of firms to be successful in a global business community. It is therefore a resource that must be managed in new ways to accommodate the very changes it is helping to bring about. In this sense, business and information technology are intertwined.

Managers and executives are finding they have little choice but to be responsive to business and I/T changes, often in ways they have not anticipated. Educators in business and information technology must also change their perspectives. Yet little attention has been paid to either the nature of the response needed or to the manner in which it will come about.

To date, a scant literature on the globalization of information technology has emerged. This appears to be attributable to a variety of causes:

• International aspects of I/T have not been a significant research area for I/S researchers
• Practitioners focus more on meeting the challenges they are facing than on creating frameworks, models, and theories that can be transfered into research or education settings
• Internationationally oriented business training programs, and the materials used in them, are company specific and not readily applied to research and education settings
• There has not been widespread interest in global information technology by the press

Changes are starting to occur in all of these areas. Practitioners are recognizing the value as well as the national and corporate significance of assisting academic organizations in "internationalizing" core and elective courses.

Only in the last decade has the link between information technology and global business become a matter of recurring, deliberate consideration at the senior management levels of the organization. Practioners and scholars alike are seeking to formulate frameworks and models that can serve as a guide to research and application.

The first section of this chapter examines the intertwining of two platforms—business and information technology— which are each evolving separately. The next two sections examine different aspects of each platform. One addresses the drivers behind globalization of business. The other explores the challenging decisions information systems professionals must formulate to adjust the information technology platform to the forces of globalization. The last section presents a challenge to educators who must recognize the force of globalization and reshape curricula and delivery systems accordingly.

DOMINANT PLATFORMS

A platform is a foundation from which to begin building virtually any structure, whether physical or conceptual. The features of the resulting structure are influenced—often determined—by the characteristics of the platform. A design of a building, for example, accommodates the characteristics of the land (the platform) on which it is constructed. Every attempt is made to leverage the platform characteristics to achieve the desirable objectives (aesthetics, functionality, efficiency of use, etc.). Likewise, limitations resulting from the platform are also recognized and taken into consideration when creating the structure (e.g., because of a high water table, buildings in some geographic areas do not have basements).

Physical platforms are typically treated as if they are fixed in nature. Changes take place very slowly, in an evolutionary fashion. Only in rare instances do abrupt shifts occur (e.g., when an earthquake causes entire land masses to shift or when science creates a breakthrough in research that unlocks another mystery). Conceptual platforms are only slightly more likely to shift (e.g., recognition that the world is not flat, that the earth rotates around the sun—or that a mainframe is just another node on a network).

Organizations that are commercial enterprises are subject to the influences of two dominant platforms: business and information technology. Each one is comprised of individual components (planks) that collectively determine strength while creating opportunity or limitations. The interconnection, directly or indirectly, between these two platforms creates opportunity, value, and impact. The next section discusses the master platform driving business.

THE BUSINESS PLATFORM

Among the planks making up the master business platform (Exhibit 1) are the state of the economy (e.g., interest rates

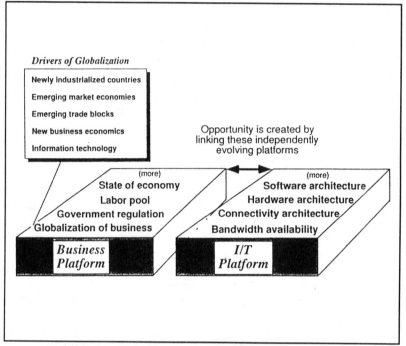

**Exhibit 1: Globalization and The Master Platforms
of Business and I/T**

and money supply), the labor pool (size of workforce and educa-
tion/training level), government regulations (e.g., antitrust and
interstate commerce laws), and globalization of business.

When applied to business, globalization refers to the
tendency of organizations to view their opportunities and their
influences as extending well beyond national or country boundaries. Global firms view themselves as competing in many regions
of the world, crossing time zones and cultures in the process.

The tendency toward globalization is evident by the
increasingly familiar practices of such companies as Honda
Motors, The Coca-Cola Company, Nestlé, Inc., and Asea-Brown
Boveri (Reich, 1991). Each views the greatest base of potential
consumers as being outside of its home country. They believe
they compete in a world market.

Globalization in business is an outgrowth of at least five
driving forces. Each is a causal factor in its own right. Together
the five forces described in this section form the basis of a

convincing argument that globalization of business is a permanent, structural change in trade and commerce. The five forces are: aggressive newly industrialized countries; emerging market economies; emerging trading blocks; new business economics; and information technology.

The Newly Industrialized Countries

Four newly industrialized countries (NICs)—the Republic of South Korea, Taiwan, Hong Kong, and Singapore—are visible in the world market. Not considered an economic threat by the industrialized world for many years, they have emerged as formidable competitors. NICs show substantial economic growth year after year (see Exhibit 2). (Mexico is also industrializing and may be considered an NIC in some economic analyses.) It is anticipated that a sustainable growth rate for the first half of the nineties will range between 5 and 7 percent per year, even when the impact of world recession is considered.

At first the NICs focused on the high volume production of commodity products such as consumer electronics. In fact, the countries played a central role in changing them from

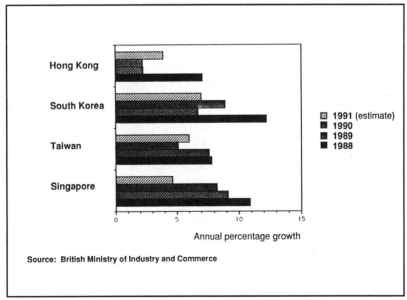

**Exhibit 2: Economic Growth of Newly
Industrialized Countries (NICs)**

expensive specialty items into commodity products. NIC manufacturers also perfected processes for achieving consistently
high quality products and cost effective manufacturing and
distribution systems, all while demonstrating a high degree of
patience in the creation of export destinations.

In each NIC, exports are growing rapidly. Singapore is a
typical example. It doubled its manufacturing exports to the
United States between 1980 and 1988, and the level is currently
near 45 percent of the island state's total manufacturing output
for export. Increasingly the NICs can be expected to move to
greater export levels, often relying on the manufacturing and
distribution of higher price, value-added products. The Japanese auto manufacturers have followed precisely this strategy.

Emerging Market Economies of Europe

While the change in government style and economic
philosophy in the countries of Eastern Europe was not predicted
by experts in trade or foreign affairs, there is widespread agreement on the potential impact of the shift to a market economy.
Countries such as Poland, Czechoslovakia, Hungary, and the
former East Germany have a highly skilled and determined work
force—a basis for entering world markets (Exhibit 3), even
though they lack a modern industrial facility and a suitable
information technology infrastructure.

Yet with the countries now open to the West, and under
effective leadership, these apparent disadvantages can be turned

COUNTRY	POPULATION	GNP	EXPORTS	IMPORTS
Albania	3.2 million	$2.8 billion	$345 million	$335 million
Bulgaria	9.0 million	$25 billion	$13.7 billion	$14 billion
Czecho-slovakia	15.6 million	$142.5 billion	$18.0 billion	$18.1 billion
Hungary	10.6 million	$83.8 billion	$9.9 billion	$9.3 billion
Poland	38.4 million	$259 billion	$10.5 billion	$12.6 billion
Romania	23.2 million	$137 billion	$12.7 billion	$10.6 billion
Yugoslavia	23.7 million	$145 billion	$11.4 billion	$12.7 billion

Exhibit 3: Profile of East European Countries

into opportunities, all of which may have a sizeable impact on global competition.

Since the countries need not evolve from an existing, operational infrastructure, they can leapfrog competitor nations by acquiring, installing, and building on the most modern technologies and advanced manufacturing processes developed elsewhere in the world. The advantage will not only be one of having modern technology, but also of avoiding the need to adapt an existing infrastructure to new requirements. Telecommunications systems, for example, will likely be installed quickly, often funded by US carriers and European post, telephone, and telegraph units (PTTs). Since they will most likely rely heavily on cellular and fiber optic methods, developers are not distracted by the need to replace an installed base of copper cables (even if an extensive one existed).

Likewise, newly constructed factories will use modern designs, advanced machine tools and production lines, and quality-driven methods. Some initiatives, like the creation of transportation and financial service systems, may be provided by Western companies through a combination of direct aid and operating alliances.

Most important for the long term, these countries will have both internal and world markets available to them. Already, the Western World is seeing East European leaders, such as Leke Walsena of Poland, seeking trading agreements rather than financial aid.

All of the above are indicators that Eastern Europe will play a role in the greater globalization of business. Even though it appears as if time stood still in Eastern Europe for nearly 50 years, the walls are down and momentum will be regained quickly. Efforts to fulfill a vision of global markets is gaining momentum. Opportunity for the East means competition for the West—on a worldwide basis.

Emergence of Trading Blocks

Additional trading power blocks are emerging from the intertwining of political and economic forces, resulting in a shattering of commonly accepted wisdom about local trade. Three dominant blocks (Exhibit 4), sometimes referred to as the Triad (Ohmae, 1985), include 600 million persons—one-half of the most developed portion of the world and 12 percent of the total population. Japan and the United States account for 30 percent of the free world trade. The percentage grows to 45 percent if the dominant EC countries of France, Germany, Italy, and the United Kingdom are included.

One block is the 12-country European Community (EC). The EC's efforts to establish a truly common market, with the trade barriers down, are aimed at its published target date of December 31, 1992. The Single European Act, which triggered the calculated movement toward the 1992 open market goal, identified the various pieces of legislation needed to create a truly open market. Many of the 279 laws will be passed by the deadline. However, it should not be assumed that complete fulfillment of the EC objective is a fait accompli. Serious obstacles still remain, including the challenge of creating a single European currency and the related monetary union, reaching agreement on key agriculture policies and programs, and harmo-

Trading Block	Member Countries	No. of Consumers
Association of southeast Asian Nations (ASEAN)	Brunei, Indonesia, Malaysia, The Philippines, Singapore, Thailand	332 million
European Community (EC) Formerly European Economic Community (ECC)	Belgium, Denmark France, Germany, Greece, Ireland, Italy, Luxembourg, The Netherlands, Portugal, Spain, United Kingdom	325 million
European Economic Area (EEA)	Emerging trading agreement and regional political/economic block consisting of countries of EC and EFTA	378 million
European Free Trade Association	Iceland, Liechtenstein, Norway, Sweden, Switzerland	33 million
South Asian Association for Regional Cooperation (SAARC)	Bangladesh, Bhutan, India, Maldives, Nepal, Pakistan, Sri Lanka	268.4 million
United States-Canada North American Free Trade Zone	United States, Canada (discussions in progress with Mexico)	US & Canada: 278 mil US, Canada, & Mexico: 366 mil

Newly Industrialized Countries:

Hong Kong	5.8 million consumers
Singapore	2.7
South Korea	42.1
Taiwan	20.2
Mexico	88.6

Exhibit 4: Representative Global Trading and Power Blocks

nizing tax policies. Nonetheless, the sentiment toward creating an economic and political organization of 325 million consumers is a sign that Europe will be a regional power block and that it will change the nature of global competition.

Similar philosophies are emerging in the United States with the creation of the US/Canada trade agreement and a proposed trade treaty with Mexico. Such a move would establish a North American block of 366 millon consumers, ranging from the Yukon to the Yucatán.

Japan, the third component of the Triad, is a large market of 123 million consumers. Most visible is the success of the giant Japanese exporting firms in industries such as automobiles and consumer electronics.

Although the Japan, US/Canada, and EC regions receive a great deal of attention, other trading blocks have also emerged, as shown in Exhibit 4. Still others are being formed. Each is designed to enhance member economic welfare by encouraging trading within the member countries, while seeking to facilitate greater global business opportunities. As they gather strength and visibility, they too will influence globalization of business, perhaps in unexpected ways.

New Business Economics

Globalization itself is bringing about a change in fundamental business economics, for it means that isolationism will not be feasible. Even those firms choosing not to seek out international markets are being affected by the competitive onslaught of foreign companies seeking to enter their markets. For commerce, this means "there is no longer any place to hide."

On another economic level, countries and corporations are finding that it is increasingly difficult to compete on the basis of low wages. Any advantages gained from a low labor cost strategy are likely to be short lived. Japan, once a low cost producing nation, now finds itself competing against the very same tactics it used only a few years ago—utilized by the NICs. They in turn are being pressed competitively by other emerging nations, such as Indonesia and Malaysia. In the long run, companies cannot escape rising wages.

Still another change in business economics is the growing magnitude of product costs. Large bases of fixed costs are part of the new economic reality (e.g., to develop a new drug currently requires an average up-front investment of $235 million). With high fixed cost bases, and shorter time periods in which to recover the costs, firms have little choice but to spread the costs across more distant and expansive markets—global markets. It is evident that, like globalization itself, this too is an emerging structural change in business: Firms must seek global markets to recover huge research and development costs.

Information Technology

A growing number of executives realize that information technology has become a formidable driver of globalization: It facilitates interaction between organizations and delivery of information, both essential for competitive success and market dominance. The I/T influence extends well beyond yesterday's lifestream systems of business (order entry, accounting processes, and inventory management), even when augmented by more modern just-in-time manufacturing and quick-response strategies. It has strategic impact (Porter, 1990).

Data communication capabilities often make a critical difference in global business support. Connectivity offers a means for overcoming the two main business barriers of distance and time. Geographic distance affects corporate strategy when it prohibits a firm from delivering products or services, monitoring activities of competitors, or maintaining the flow of information between employees or business partners. An organization's communications capabilities take on strategic value when they allow the firm to overcome these barriers and provide a business benefit.

When applied to international business activities, the connectivity provided through I/T will enable firms to establish an electronic presence in a region where a physical presence may be undesirable due to economic or physical constraints. Likewise, direct connection and a routine, obstacle-free flow of information between businesses may improve service and control to new performance levels. Some locations do not have the desired level of connectivity. That's one of the challenges of doing business globally.

Compressing the business process is often essential in global business. This means that the delay in transmission of information between locations must be eliminated. Networks provide that essential capability.

THE I/T PLATFORM

Even though the master platform and global conditions of business are changing rapidly, the I/T world appears to be moving even more quickly. Product lines frequently have only a 12 to 18 month life before replacement. Software generations are enhanced yearly. Regulatory policies undergo dramatic shifts. Yet the most fundamental platform shifts are in the major components of the I/T platform: computers and communication systems.

The primary planks of the I/T platform include hardware and software architectures (sometimes referred to as vendor master architectures), connectivity architecture, and bandwidth alternatives. I/T professionals must not only monitor the platform changes, but continually adjust their architectures to support global competitive needs. This section addresses seven such challenges which are grouped for convenience into the two categories of policy and technology, and global architecture issues.

Creating The Right I/T Architecture

The architecture of I/T is a direct outgrowth of the options provided through the capabilities built into the I/T platform. As shown in Exhibit 5, it is an adaption of the platform to the needs of the organization's products, services, and processes.

The I/T architecture, while varying from organization to organization, is generally described accordingly to include the following well-known categories of components:

- Data architecture
- Communications architecture
- Computing architecture
- Applications architecture

There is more than one way to formulate the architectures to leverage the features of the platform and the alternatives each provides. Any architecture should be developed with an objective of leveraging the capabilities offered by information technology, while also fitting the needs of the business.

It is in the creation of the organization's I/T architecture that decisions about solutions like open systems, client-server architecture, distributed processing, systems integration, systems engineering, and object orientation must be made. Resisting the tendency to favor one over all others is essential, since proponents of specific solutions often view the other solution options as competitors. More likely, they all play a role in the global future.

Synchronization of Policy and Technology

To what extent are technology questions and policy questions jointly addressed and synchronized? In the context of current I/T management issues, such as outsourcing, downsizing (rightsizing), use of packaged rather than custom software, and reliance on systems integrators (none of these are unique to globalization), one must balance the other. Key concerns are the mix of architectures that will be supported and the responsibility for making such decisions.

What Mix To Support. In creating a global architecture, a headquarters mindset may doom global systems to failure. Abdication to country managers may do the same. The intertwining of management processes and technology issues means I/T directors are faced with the challenge of determining whether they will support:

- Varied computer architectures
- Local standards for each country
- Identical application portfolios
- Identical software packages
- Single/multiple/multiple but identical networks
- Identical procedures for development and operations

Even though there are technical issues underlying each decision, cultural, nationalistic, logistics, monetary, and legal issues are likely to surface early in any analysis.

Who Determines the I/T strategy. Addressing these fundamental matters triggers a related discussion of which global I/T strategy the firm will endorse. There appear to be four dominant strategies:

1. Independent global I/T operations:

I/T responsibility rests with country units
2. Headquarters driven global I/T strategy:
   National solutions are modified to fit country operations
3. Shared Synergy:
   Cooperative development occurs with some identical
   solutions and others that are developed locally or regionally [1]
4. Integrated global I/T:
   A compelling business need drives management to agree on
   the need for integrated systems and databases for key
   business processes; Move toward consistent worldwide
   architecture.

Unfortunately, there is little evidence to suggest that most firms wishing to compete globally, i.e., to be global, have adequately addressed I/T strategies in relation to their business aspirations (Ives and Jarvenpaa, 1991).

Global Architecture Issues

This section discusses four issues specific to the support of global business. Although each is significant by itself, collectively they form the basis for functionality and effectiveness.

Common Systems Determining whether information systems should be common globally or tailor-made to fit market regions will provoke vigorous discussion between corporate and country units. The growing importance of accommodating local taste while achieving the levels of effectiveness firms need to be competitive across many borders also raises a question of uniformity across information systems: Should applications be tailor-made to fit local needs or common across markets, thus having a universal design?

More multinational firms are emphasizing use of common systems.   Corporate information systems professionals define data standards, processing characteristics, and application interfaces. Local development teams carry out the implementation, giving them ownership and involvement. At the same time, they pass back experience that may influence common system features as the applications evolve.

Ability to Interconnect Global organizations are obliged to span a wide variety of organization boundaries in order to link with customers, suppliers, service providers (e.g., shippers), and government agencies. Both cross-country and cross-application connectivity are fundamental requirements. Not all architectures provide the degree of interconnection needed to drive global business processes. It is for this reason that I/T gatekeepers in the largest trading blocks, including the European Community and the U.S./Canada/Mexico block, have paid a great deal of attention to the development of an interconnect capability in telecommunications. While such a capability is taken for granted in North America, the opposite is true in Europe. EC governmental units have assigned to high level authorities the responsibility for developing cross-country (i.e., within the EC) standards to which all countries must adhere (European Community, 1989), at least at the information services (rather than voice) level—the portion of the data communications spectrum most important to business.

In Japan, government officials are studying carefully a proposal to break up Nippon Telephone and Telegraph in a fashion similar to the United States' break-up of AT&T in the 1980s. New services, greater connectivity, and more efficiency are the targets. Tremendous economic and trading significance is attached to the result. The driving force, however, is the ability to interconnect in support of global business.

Reach Across Markets The ability of an organization to reach across country markets is an essential competitive characteristic, since local accommodation will be mandatory for most businesses. Growing evidence (Reich, 1991; Senn, 1991) suggests that global business will now mean customers and business practices will also be global. Even though this is happening, individual customs and cultures still prevail and firms are learning that they must accommodate them to be successful. Although the strategies vary, I/T is frequently the facilitator.

Monitoring sales in geographically dispersed stores through interorganization systems (Cash and Konsynski, 1985) is one vehicle for accommodating the unique needs of specific markets and regions. This in turn leads to markets that are electronic in nature (McNurlin, 1987) where information is exchanged via vast global networks. The sharing of manufacturing and shipping schedules, facilitated by EDI, is another vehicle (Malone, et al., 1987). Still other organizations are turning operations responsibility for inventory management and order fulfillment over to third party agents. An alternative to "just-in-time" methods, this strategy requires timely and accurate coor-

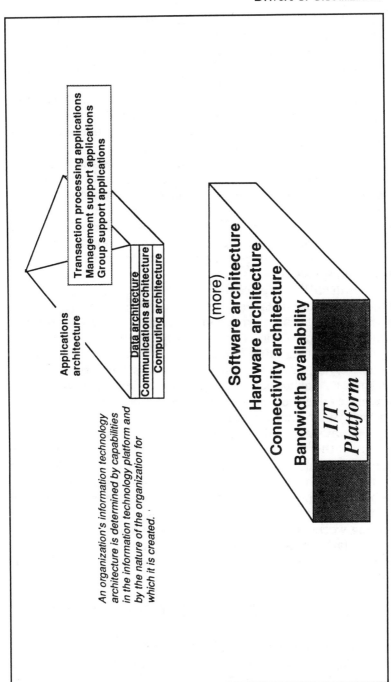

Exhibit 5: Information Technology Architecture

dination between all parties, even if the manufacturer is a geographically distant NIC manufacturer.

Location Base Determining the most desirable location of application and processing centers takes on greater significance in international business. The choice of hardware and software platform on which to build global applications will raise many challenges, as it does in any large system. The need to meet local market requirements may result in a tendency toward distributed functionality and localized data.

Price/performance trends in computing and data communication make the distribution of information technology economically attractive and the continued evolution of high-power workstations, attractive mid-range systems, and effective networking techniques increases local performance levels. On the other hand, the need to be responsive at corporate levels will, in some instances, suggest large processor platforms and a centralized system.

Suitability of Architecture The need for a coherent I/T architecture is often realized as soon as an enterprise undertakes globalization of its information systems.   Firms assembling cross-border applications, particularly in European countries, are finding that national operations were built from individual designs relying on local technology—the state computer firm. This may be particularly troublesome if decisions were made years ago to use the technology of a major computer or communications vendor in the country of interest.

Many firms will find that they do not have an architecture, but rather a series of incompatible facilities, and worse yet, incompatible application systems. The accrual of long-run advantages will occur only when firms establish a platform which can be used repeatedly as new applications are created or new features are added to existing systems. Identifying the criteria for selecting workstations, local area networks, value-added carriers, and database systems is the starting point for a foundation, not the end-point. The latter requires a full evaluation of information delivery requirements.

IMPLICATIONS FOR EDUCATION

Information systems education in North America has the opportunity, and indeed the necessity, to begin a process of incorporating global thinking and international issues into the programs and activities that comprise the curriculum. Adding an internationally oriented course is as insufficient as adding a lecture on global business in each course. Rather, the many issues surrounding globalization need to be integrated into the sequence of instruction and learning experiences just as they are now woven into the fabric of business.

The challenge to educators is to continue to develop the knowledge which forms the basis of the field, to improve the manner in which it is transmitted, and to broaden the base at the same time. Globalization is an essential part of that base.

There is no single approach to doing this. However, at least the following set of concerns must be addressed, regardless of approach:

• Create awareness

A huge number of people feel they are untouched by globalization. They do not recognize it as a fundamental change in the platform of business, but rather a factor that affects only selective industrial sectors. Creating awareness is thus the starting point, and must involve faculty, administrators, students, and program supporters from the business and governmental communities.

• Educate the educators

The majority of faculty members responsible for information systems education have not developed systems, applications, or development plans for international businesses. Only a portion have even traveled extensively outside of their own geographic or cultural sphere. Yet it is these same academic leaders who have the responsibility for meeting these challenges. New programs, methods, and instruments of education must emerge to overcome this critical challenge.

• Introduce globalization into the curriculum

Incorporate international, multinational, and global issues into virtually every aspect of the information systems curriculum. The information systems core course(s), whether for I/S majors or for "user-managers" is the starting point. The four areas which comprise the typical introductory course need to be

rethought in this manner:
— The impact of information technology on organizations
— Fundamentals of information technology use
— Developing and acquiring information systems
— Management of information technology

The courses for I/S majors, spanning development methods, data resources, policy and administration, data communication, and beyond likewise merit additional consideration in this regard.

• Recognize the shifting platforms

Business and information technology cannot be separated. The analogy of platforms features the independent evolution of each. Yet it demonstrates the importance of creating links and levers between them, for unless that occurs, I/T will be largely irrelevant.

• Emphasize diversity

Diversity of culture, individuals, and organization environment is the real norm. Yet academic (and other) programs implicitly emphasize "sameness," "normal circumstances" or the "usual conditions." I/T plays a role in creating and in accommodating the great resource of diversity.

Exhibit 6 shows the interrelation between three entities that can collectively address these concerns. A great deal of the information needed to drive international issues into course work will of necessity be anectotal and case based. Business and corporate organizations are the most appropriate source of information on the challenges, alternatives, strategies, and decision processes associated with international business. Many are willing to share their insight and experience with informed educators wishing to integrate such information into their I/S programs.

Often overlooked, but an extremely important resource, are the public service and policy groups who specialize in international commerce. Chambers of Commerce, regional trade and export offices, and economic bureaus routinely capture and maintain a wealth of data on global opportunities and threats from foreign competitors. Most focus on trends affecting both large and small businesses.

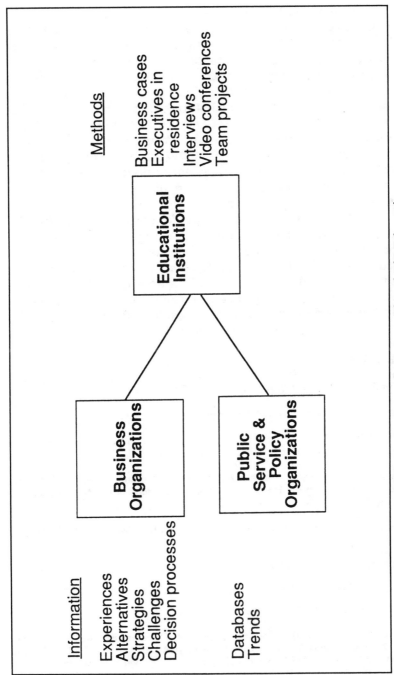

Exhibit 6: Partners for International I/T Education

Educational institutions, the third component, have the opportunity, indeed the responsibility to develop relationships with the other component. Doing so can lead to a wealth of resources, including business cases, executives in residence, and education projects. Executives and managers, trade representatives, and consultants are often very willing to help develop cases and other instructional material, visit with student project teams, and put faculty in touch with staff members. When personal appearances on campus are not feasible, they often offer to participate in conference calls with students, particpate in video conferences, and arrange for interviews in their offices. Similar experiences are likely with officals of public service agencies and foreign trade delegations.

The diversity of ideas and opportunities is virtually unlimited, providing educators are willing to focus on international business as an integral, rather than add-on element of I/T education. The chapters in this book will add to the diversity as they provide differing strategies for accomplishing the objectives outlined in the preceding discussion. Each strategy merits careful consideration, for it is altogether too easy—even in a learning environment—to think local.

REFERENCES

Cash, James I. and Benn R. Konsynski, (1985) "IS Redraws Competitive Boundaries," *Harvard Business Review.* 63,2 March-April, pp. 134-142.

European Community, (1989) *The Green Paper.* Brussels.

Ives, Blake and Sirkka L. Jarvenpaa, (1991) "Applications of Global Information Technology: Key Issues for Management," *MIS Quarterly,* 15, 1, pp. 33-49.

Malone, Thomas W., J. Yates, and Robert I., Benjamin, (1987) "Electronic Markets and Electronic Hierarchies," *Communications of the ACM.* June, pp. 484-497.

McNurlin, Barbara, (1987) "The Rise of 'Cooperative' Systems," *EDP Analyzer* 25,6 June.

Ohmae, Kenichi, (1985) *Triad Power.* Free Press.

Porter, Michael E., (1990) *The Competitive Advantage of Nations.* Free Press.

Reich, Robert B., (1991) *The Work of Nations.* Knopf.

Senn, James A., (1991) "Assessing The Impact of Western Europe Unification in 1992: Implications for Corporate I/T Strategies," in Palvia, S., Palvia, P., and Zigli, R.M., *The Global Issues of Information Technology Management.* Harrisburg, PA: Idea Group Publishing.

3 Alternative Curriculum Approaches for Global IT Education

P. Candace Deans
Wake Forest University

Martin D. Goslar
New Mexico State University

Business today must be concerned with foreign as well as the domestic (U.S.) marketplaces in order to compete successfully. Business school curriculum can no longer narrowly focus on the business environment of the past. It is necessary that educational institutions anticipate the demands of a rapidly changing world and better prepare students to meet the challenges of the 21st century.

There is a clear need to address the international issues specific to the information technology (IT) curriculum if we are to provide a relevant and dynamic education for our students. Globalization of the marketplace and the impact of information technology on the firm are certainly two major forces transforming business today. In an international context, information technology can be viewed not only as a catalyst that is driving the global marketplace but also as a solution base from which to address international managerial challenges.

Until recently, very little research has been directed toward international issues specific to information systems and technology. Likewise, there has been very little evidence of efforts to incorporate international issues into specific courses. Only now are we at a point where research and information that provides

*relevant curriculum resources and materials specific to informa-
tion technology is becoming available.*

*As academicians, we are in the beginning phase of ad-
dressing the issue of how to best internationalize the information
technology curriculum. A better defined international component
will evolve over time as more attention is devoted to these issues
by leading academicians in the field.*

*In this chapter, we will discuss the present state-of-the-
art, current trends and future directions for internationalizing the
IT curriculum. A discussion of alternative curriculum models for
international business education in general and resulting implications for IT curriculum development is presented. This discussion
will provide a foundation from which to evaluate the best alternatives for incorporating an international component into the existing IT curriculum.*

*Progress toward internationalizing the IT curriculum is not
at a point that we can provide tested international IT curriculum
examples since to our knowledge none currently exists. We will
provide possible alternatives and recommendations to consider.
This will provide a starting point from which to proceed as we as
academicians address these issues and possible future directions.*

As we move toward the next century, information technology will play an increasingly significant role in a rapidly
evolving interdependent international economy. Business schools
must respond to increasingly demanding industry environments replete with international information laden challenges.
A global marketplace requires that students be educated with a
broader base of knowledge. Although extensive curriculum
material has been developed that addresses the international
dimensions of marketing, accounting, finance, and management, very few resources are currently available that address the
international dimensions of information systems (IS). "Internationalization" of the information technology (IT) curriculum is
presently receiving increased attention by those in the field.
There is clearly an increasing demand for supplemental material
that addresses relevant international information systems and
technology issues.

In this chapter, a model is presented that describes
foreign influences that may directly or indirectly influence IT
curriculum trends. These foreign influences contribute to an

overall understanding of the international issues that comprise the international IT curriculum component. Based on current research and information, an outline is developed that identifies the key topics and dimensions that should be included in the international component of the IT curriculum. This outline may be used as the basis for a separate course in international information systems. Alternatively, these topics may be infused into the existing IT curriculum to enhance the international dimensions of the courses. The development of this outline is the result of empirical work designed to identify key international information systems issues and trends toward internationalizing the information technology curriculum (Deans et. al., 1991). The topics covered represent the current state-of-the-art knowledge on the topic. In many areas, very little international research has been done and limited information is available. Much research is currently in progress, however, and the quest for knowledge in this area is evolving.

The specific objectives of this chapter are basically three-fold: 1) to discuss the current state-of-the-art in terms of curriculum development and approaches for internationalizing IT education, 2) to describe alternative curriculum models for internationalizing business education and the resulting implications for the IT curriculum and 3) to provide a discussion of the pros and cons of each alternative in the context of overall business school objectives. Finally, we will provide some recommendations for internationalizing the IT curriculum.

In our discussions, we will generally use the term information technology (IT) as a broader description for the traditional MIS or IS curriculum. In much of the literature IT and IS are used interchangeably. We will, therefore, not make a formal distinction between these terms.

BACKGROUND

The information technology (IT) curriculum is currently void of a well-defined international component.   There is presently very little consensus as to what the international dimension of the information systems field should include or how it might best be incorporated into the existing curriculum. Literature relevant to international dimensions of the IT curriculum is scarce. Very little information is available that would provide a better understanding of IT curriculum trends in foreign schools of business or their effects on IT curriculum in U.S. business schools.   Previous domestic (U.S.) IT curriculum studies focus on either the undergraduate IS course (McLeod, 1985) or graduate IS course (Gupta and Seeborg, 1989). Results of these studies indicate that IT courses and programs in U.S. business schools strongly emphasize the U.S. business perspective and provide little, if any, international content. In a like manner, very little academic research has addressed the issue of internationalizing   the IT curriculum in U.S. schools of business.   Studies have been   reported in the international business literature (Thanopoulous and Vernon, 1987; Nurht, 1987) that focus on internationalization of the business school curriculum from the perspective of both U.S. and non- U.S. business schools. These studies are, however, broad in focus and do not concentrate on specific curriculum content for each of the functional areas of business. An extensive literature search reveals very little empirical data to describe IT programs worldwide. A few fragmented studies have been reported that may provide some related insights. Trujillo (1989) describes academic computing approaches in Columbia, South America. Van Weert (1987/88) describes educational IT usage in The Netherlands.   Computer science programs in China have been studied by Cheng (1987) and by Wilson, Adams, Baouendi, Marion and Yaverbaum (1988).   Keefe (1990) provides some insights into Soviet computer skills. These studies provide limited insights into IT curriculum trends and future directions on a broad scale. Worldwide trends are not available and general implications and influences on U.S. IT programs are not apparent.

Influences Toward Internationalization of IT Education

There are clearly many trends today that indicate a shift toward   enhanced awareness of international issues in the IT curriculum. A rapidly changing international business environment has contributed to enlightened awareness of the opportunities and challenges of the worldwide marketplace. Moreover, there has been a continued increase in the number of foreign and U.S. multinational corporations during the last decade. At the same time, the competitive position of the United States in the global marketplace has declined. Because of these trends, demands for students to have some international background have become more pronounced, both by businesses that hire graduates of our business programs as well as by academic governing bodies such as the American Assembly of Collegiate Schools of Business (A.A.C.S.B.). The A.A.C.S.B. has placed increased emphasis on incorporation of international aspects into the functional areas of business. Although schools have made progress in this regard, the conclusions of a study by Porter and McKibbon (1988) reveal that a majority of business schools still have a long way to go in terms of truly integrating international business throughout the overall curriculum.

The impacts of IT curriculum trends worldwide and their influence on IT programs in the United States is currently not clear. Several trends indicate a flow of influence on curriculum content from U.S. IT programs to foreign IT programs and vice versa. Interviews with several academicians in European business schools indicate that IT courses traditionally housed within computer science departments are increasingly being housed in schools of commerce or management departments. Rifkin (1989) calls attention to data indicating a high percentage of foreign students enrolled in graduate level IT programs in U.S. universities. Furthermore, U.S. schools of business currently employ a high percentage of foreign faculty, a trend that appears to be continuing. The impacts of these trends and their influence on internationalization efforts for U.S. IT programs have not been studied.

As IT continues to play a prominent role in the global marketplace, these effects will eventually filter to the curriculum level. As corporations utilize IT applications to link with buyers, suppliers, and customers worldwide, the effects and consequences cannot be overlooked in the classroom. Information technology will provide the means for addressing managerial problems and international obstacles of operating outside the United States. As corporations are forced to develop a broader perspective and better understanding of worldwide telecommunications opportunities and obstacles, greater emphasis will be necessary in the IT curriculum in order to meet changing market demands.

Change is an inevitable part of doing business today. Curriculum revision will likewise be necessary to reflect the realities of the changing global business environment.

IT Curriculum Guidelines

Curriculum guidelines have been in existence for the information systems area since the early 70's. The first of these, and the most widely accepted recommendations, were developed by the Association of Computing Machinery (ACM), the Data Processing Management Association (DPMA) and the International Federation for Information Processing (IFIP). Both the ACM and DPMA gudielines were recently revised to reflect the dynamic changes resulting from rapid developments in information technology. A review of the newly revised guidelines from both of these organizations reveals no efforts to include international aspects in the IT curriculum or to recognize the significance of the international component. This is disappointing given the continuing trends toward globalization of the marketplace and the role of information technology in this newly evolving business environment.

At this point, formal guidelines or recommendations have not been established that provide IS educators with clear direction in the international curriculum development arena. Clearly, IT educators are in the beginning stages of developing a well-defined internationalized curriculum. At this point, only recommendations and possible alternatives can be presented as a starting point from which to build.

FOREIGN INFLUENCES ON IT CURRICULUM TRENDS

As we continue to move toward a more global economy, factors alluded to in the previous discussion will contribute to and influence our understanding of international IT curriculum issues. A model developed to describe many of these influences (Deans and Goslar, 1990) identifies several categories of variables that have varying effects on IT curriculum development. This model, presented in Figure 1, focuses specifically on the influences from the foreign environment. These categories of influences will be discussed in the following paragraphs.

The Contextual Factors

Contextual factors are those that most indirectly influence IT program characteristics in various parts of the world.

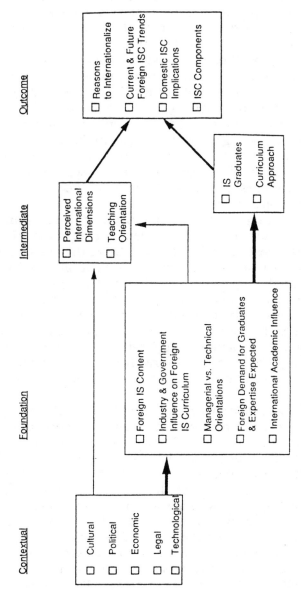

Figure 1: IS International Curriculum Research Model-Foreign Dimension

These contextual factors are those environmental constraints that represent the foundational base for the international business discipline: political, cultural, economic and legal (Farmer and Richmond, 1970). An additional category added by Skinner (1964) incorporates the technological dimension that has also been determined to be appropriate for addressing international IT issues (Deans and Ricks, 1991).

The *political* dimension may have tremendous underlying consequences for educational programs from a broad perspective.   Political orientations may be derived from governmental support and directions, industry interests motivated by goal-driven perspectives, academic units or other geographically unique competing interest groups. In the foreign environment, government takeover in some countries is commonplace and may result in immediate change in policies and directions. These changes can have substantial effects on educational institutions and their programs.

Cultural characteristics may play an important role in the direction curriculum development may take in particular institutions. These are influences and mores that a society maintains to establish its value systems and eventual "view" of the world. Appropriate applications of information technology may depend on these cultural characteristics and vary considerably depending on the country or geographical region of the world. In some countries, for example, automated teller machines may not be acceptable for banking applications because of cultural constraints.   These cultural directives may mandate substantial variations in IT directions and influence IT teaching orientations.

Economic concerns also underlie and indirectly influence the eventual direction and focus of IT curriculum from the foreign   perspective.   Clearly, less developed countries will address the issues from a different perspective than will the more industrialized nations of the world. Due to the resource-intensive requirements of the IT curriculum, economic support is necessary in providing state-of-the-art computer hardware, software and network firmware. Quality IT programs, both in the United States and outside the United States may depend on industry and/or government contributions and influence. Economic resources for IT programs many times go beyond those required by other academic areas. The degree of economic support provided by these outside publics may in turn reflect high influence on the emphasis and direction of IT programs. Economic variables will also affect the orientation of IT programs since curriculum orientation is highly correlated with instructional funding for hardware and software.

Legal influences cannot be overlooked as still another dimension of the environment that affects educational directions in a broad sense. Legal influences may include those associated with mandated educational structures, policies and procedures relevant to educational privileges, rights of citizens of the country or region, minimum training and educational levels of employed professionals of the system, and any other established legislation designed to regulate educational pedagogy and related technologies.

The *technological* component has particular relevance for IT curriculum development and trends. The technological infrastructure that is in place will most certainly filter down to the IT curriculum level. As the level of technological sophistication in a country increases, orientations and directions for the IT curriculum change as well. From a technological perspective, variations in different parts of the world may be substantial. The technological dimension is closely interrelated and influenced by the other contextual dimensions.

Foundation Factors

Several factors have been recognized that strongly influence eventual IT curriculum directions and trends. These variables are described as foundation factors that are strongly influenced by the contextual factors and in turn have the greatest effect on IT curriculum trends. From the foreign perspective, the content of the IT curriculum includes several components: IT topics included in the program offerings, the combinations of the specific courses offered, IT faculty credentials and experience, qualifications of the student populace and their prior training, experience, skills and educational levels, applied versus theoretical knowledge dissemination, traditional versus more state-of-the-art IT techniques and undergraduate versus graduate program content.

A second category of foundation variable includes industry and government influence. These entities exert political and economic influence on IT curriculum and they also strongly affect the IT specialty knowledge (through market demand) of those who graduate from these programs. Graduate demand is highly correlated with industry and government support. The IT specialty survives because of the interest by these sectors of the economy.

Intermediate Factors

There are also some identified intermediate factors that play a role in eventual IT curriculum directions and are dependent on the foundation factors of the previous discussion. These intermediate factors are differentiated according to their influence by other factors in the overall model. As depicted in Figure 1, the intermediate factors may be influenced to varying degrees by the contextual and foundation variables. Perceptions of "international" and what that encompasses will vary among institutions around the   world.   Not only do perceptions of business administration education vary, but perceptions of the IT area of study are also far from consistent across foreign business schools. In many foreign schools of business, the IT curriculum may be housed with computer science or engineering rather than in a business program. Only recently have these schools moved toward including information technology as a part of their commerce education and management programs.

Teaching orientation is more specific and refers to whether IT courses are taught from a domestic or global perspective. In the   United States, for example, IT courses have traditionally been taught strictly from the U.S. business perspective. This view of a domestic orientation does not necessarily hold in other countries. The European approach to business administration education, for example, has a more global orientation.

Two other intermediate factors depicted in the model, IS graduates and curriculum approach, are affected to a greater degree by the foundation factors. Graduates of IS programs are a clear reflection of the content of the program in which they participate.

The curriculum approach, whether managerial or technical, will be directly influenced by market demands for skills and industry/government motives. All these intermediate variables directly affect IT curriculum trends and changes.   The factors identified for each of the previously discussed components of the model provide the impetus for interactions that provide the criterion from which to develop an international IT curriculum. These response variables include: the reasons to internationalize, future trends for foreign IT curriculum, the implications for

U.S. IT programs and the specific content components for IT programs in both U.S. and non-U.S. schools of business.

This model recognizes foreign influences affecting IT curriculum trends as efforts are made to internationalize the curriculum. Presently, these influences may be minimal. Their influence is difficult to gauge. It should be recognized that the factors identified in this model are not unique to the foreign environment. Certainly, cultural, political, legal and economic factors in the United States will influence the content of IT programs. The degree of influence of each of these factors and the resulting implications for curriculum content may be substantially different in the United States context. Our focus here has been on those influences from outside the United States that may have some influence on existing IT programs.

CURRICULUM TRENDS:
THE BROAD PERSPECTIVE

Many factors complicate the issue of how best to incorporate an international dimension into the existing IT curriculum. Internationalizing IT education cannot be addressed as a stand-alone issue. Implications for internationalizing the IT curriculum will depend on characteristics of the existing IT program and the present emphasis on international business in the overall curriculum.

IT Curriculum Trends

Although the information technology curriculum has evolved through several stages, there are many models and approaches currently in existence. Business schools vary considerably in their approaches and progress toward developing a broad based information technology curriculum. Schools that provide a major in information technology may vary to a large degree in terms of curriculum focus and breadth of topic coverage. Some IT degree programs tend toward a strong technological emphasis including extensive programming skills. At the other extreme, the focus may be almost entirely managerial with little, if any, devotion to programming and hard core technical skills. Clearly, a consistent model that can be viewed as a standard for the field does not currently exist. The problems may be further compounded for smaller business schools that do not include information technology as a concentration or major in their degree programs. These schools may have more flexibility in IT curriculum decisions, but at the same time, this may lead to even greater variability in course content and overall emphasis. When an IT major is not offered, pressures to respond to rapidly changing technology and the dynamic demands of the business community may not get top priority attention. Availability of resources is likely one of the most important factors influencing the directions for IT curriculum development. Curriculum change is also highly influenced by the background and enthusiasm of the faculty that play the strongest roles in the decision making process.

An alternative approach taken by some institutions is to incorporate information technology throughout the functional areas of business with less emphasis on the traditional separate IT curriculum. This approach tends to be gaining some acceptance as advancements in IT continue to proliferate as an integral component of all the functional business areas. These issues add increased complexity to the development of alternative models that incorporate the international dimensions of information technology.

International Business Curriculum Trends

The international business curriculum in U.S. schools of business is, likewise, very diverse with many alternative approaches and curriculum models. As with IT education, change is taking place at an unprecedented pace and schools are struggling with the issue of how to best incorporate the interna-

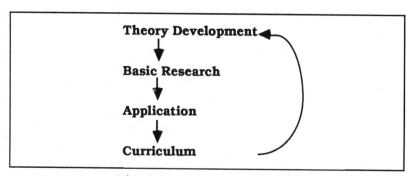

Figure 2: Research Levels

tional dimensions into the existing curriculum. Although some schools have developed specialized programs in international business, the general trend for most schools has been to include international dimensions into the traditional functional areas of business (Arpan, 1991). In many schools, a stand-alone International Business course has been added to the degree requirements. It cannot be overlooked, however, that a large percentage of schools have done very little in terms of internationalizing their overall curriculum (Porter and McKibbon, 1988). Many factors are now contributing to a more heightened interest in this dimension of business education. Rapid changes are currently taking place in the international business environment. The economic integration of Europe and the shift of Central and Eastern European countries to market-based economies are certainly significant events that will impact the U.S. business community. We can no longer ignore the significance of a truly global marketplace.

Information technology education and international business education have many aspects in common. Both areas are an integral component of each of the functional areas of business and there are many alternative methods by which to incorporate these into the overall business school curriculum. The challenges presented in this discussion present additional complexities as academicians face the task of internationalizing IT programs and courses.

Premises for IT Curriculum Development

Many of the issues presented previously contribute to the complexity of curriculum development for the international IT domain. The established IT curriculum varies more extensively among institutions than for most other functional areas. This makes the task of incorporating an international component even more difficult. Since very little work to date has been done to address the international dimensions of the IT curriculum, few resources are available for developing curriculum materials.

Curriculum development is based on the premise that research provides the foundation and input from which to build. As outlined in Figure 2, there are several research levels that must be addressed before the curriculum level can be adequately addressed. Theoretically based research is aimed primarily for the academician and provides the foundation from which to build. On the second level, basic research may incorporate both theory and an applied dimension that may include empirically based work aimed at both the academician and practitioner. A third level includes work that is mainly practitioner / application oriented and focuses on specific problems and implications for the practitioner. Once these dimensions have been addressed, it is then appropriate that this information be incorporated back into the curriculum. Only now is research and information becoming available to address the international IT curriculum issues.

ALTERNATIVE CURRICULUM MODELS FOR INTERNATIONAL BUSINESS EDUCATION

It is imperative that plans for internationalizing the IT curriculum fit with the overall business school plans for internationalization. Consistent implementation plans across the functional areas of business will lead to a more successful long-term program. There are several relevant factors that should be evaluated when assessing the resources available for internationalizing the business program. Only then can the most appropriate overall international curriculum model be determined.

It is necessary that the following issues be examined in the context of each institution's individual business program: 1) the composition of the student body, 2) the background of the faculty and 3) the specific goals and objectives of the institution (Arpan, 1991). In order to evaluate student composition, the following questions are pertinent and should be asked by each institution:

- Who are your students?
- What are their interests?
- Where do they go after leaving your institution?
- What companies hire them?
- How international are they to begin with?

Only after examining the background of the students can the degree of value added that should be provided be determined. A master's in international business, for example, may attract a type of student that would not normally apply to the university.

This may add to the cultural diversity on campus and provide positive benefits.

The school's focus and direction for internationalizing the curriculum should also include an assessment of the background of the faculty. The following questions are among those that should be asked:

- Do the faculty have an interest in international business?
- Are incentives in place for internationalizing the curriculum?
- What is the background and power of the administrators who will play the significant roles in the internationalization efforts?
- What institutional linkages currently exist?

Beyond the students and faculty, it is necessary to evaluate the objectives and goals of the business school. In this context, there are typically three broad objectives that are considered. These objectives correspond to the educational levels: awareness, understanding and competency (Arpan, 1991). On the *awareness* level, the objective is only to provide students with an *awareness* of a larger world beyond the boundaries of the United States. The objective of *understanding* requires a more in-depth knowledge of this world and provides answers to the why questions that go beyond superficial facts. The *competency* objective assumes the development of more specific skills and the ability to do something with the understanding that is acquired.

Various curriculum methods correspond to each of these three dimensions (Arpan, 1991). On the awareness level, an infusion approach would be most suited to the curriculum

---

I. Infusion into Existing courses
- Throughout the curriculum
- In introductory course

II. Freestanding International Information Systems/ Technology Course

III. Combination of Infusion and Freestanding Course

Tradeoffs: Meeting the Overall Goals of the Business School Curriculum

---

Figure 3: Alternative Curriculum Approaches

objectives. Infusion would involve adding some international content to every course or to some courses in each of the functional areas. This approach is usually the lowest cost and least complicated to implement. Infusion does not require the faculty to have a lot of knowledge and training in international business. This method also becomes the one that is easiest to implement for accreditation requirements.

On the understanding level, it is necessary that specialized international business courses be provided as a part of the curriculum offerings. Most likely, an array of international business courses are established (e.g., international marketing, international finance and international accounting). The understanding level requires a moderate level of cost and complexity. From a faculty perspective, it is necessary to have people with knowledge of the topic beyond the superficial level.

The competency level is hardest to implement successfully. This dimension represents one of high cost and complexity and should match a strong commitment on the part of administrators to provide the resources necessary to move to this level. From a competency perspective, it is no longer sufficient just to receive a degree in business. Interdisciplinary programs become an important part of the degree requirements. Supporting disciplines such as foreign language, political science and anthropology make important contributions to this overall program. Language requirements, cultural training and internships play an important role in meeting the objectives of the competency level.

Clearly, many factors go into this decision making process. It is, however, necessary to evaluate tradeoffs in the context of the overall business school curriculum. Decisions for internationalizing the IT curriculum should then be based on the foundation that has already been defined for the business school program and, specifically, for the internationalization plan.

IMPLICATIONS FOR IT CURRICULUM DEVELOPMENT

Based on the previous discussion and as summarized in Figure 3, two general approaches that may be taken for internationalizing the IT curriculum include the infusion method and the freestanding international IT course. The infusion approach incorporates relevant international topics throughout the traditional information technology courses. The international emphasis may be focused toward the introductory level course or may be dispersed throughout all courses. The freestanding approach, on the other hand, supports a separate international IT course. This course is more appropriately an upper level course that builds and expands on topic areas covered in the management oriented courses as well as the telecommunications course. The freestanding course would focus on the broader global view of information systems and technology and emphasize unique challenges of operating in an international environment as opposed to strictly domestic (U.S.) operations. It should be stressed that a third approach may involve a combination of these methods and may be the more appropriate approach, depending upon the school's objectives, resources and commitment to internationalization of its overall curriculum.

The Tradeoffs: Infusion Versus Freestanding Approach

There are clearly advantages and disadvantages with each approach that can only be evaluated in the context of each individual school's objectives and goals. There are, however, general pros and cons that are to a large degree standard across schools. An advantage of the infusion approach is that it exposes more students to the international dimension. Infusion through a required introductory level course exposes all students, not just those majoring in information systems. Infusion in the upper level courses exposes only majors. The infusion method also involves a larger number of faculty and this can lead to difficulties in terms of faculty qualifications and coordination across courses. For these reasons, a majority of schools currently utilize the infusion approach focusing on the introductory level course or an appropriate course in the curriculum.

The freestanding approach requires faculty well versed in the international dimension of the functional area being addressed. This approach would, however, limit the number of faculty that would need to be prepared to teach international topics. If the freestanding course is only offered as an elective, the number of students exposed to the international dimensions may be limited. Currently, finding well qualified and interested faculty may be difficult. Faculty with formal academic training in both information technology and international business are scarce. The costs of faculty development in this area may be substantial. As such, planned benefits should be considered and well documented. Faculty expertise and available resources are important considerations when evaluating the tradeoffs of these approaches.

Internationalization trends in general suggest infusion as the most common approach for a majority of schools (Arpan, 1991). At some point later, an additional freestanding course may be considered. Using this combination of approaches may be the more appropriate alternative for some schools. This approach may be the best direction for schools with undergraduate programs that must be coordinated with graduate programs at both the masters and Ph.D. levels. The freestanding course is likely to initially be incorporated through graduate programs that have a concentration in information systems.

Most schools should find one of these two methods or a combination of approaches to be quite effective for their intenationalization plans. If the overall objective of the business school is awareness, infusion would be the most viable alternative. If the goal is more in-depth understanding or competency, a required freestanding course or some combination of these approaches may be the better alternative. In any case, these decisions must be made in the context of the school's overall objectives and goals. The school's current emphasis on internationalizing the other functional areas may be a good indicator of the most appropriate approach for the IT curriculum. If the school has developed a pattern of implementing stand-alone international courses for the other functional areas, this may also be an appropriate approach for the IT curriculum. If no other international courses currently exist, it is very unlikely that a stand-alone international IT course would be approved or even appropriate.

RECOMMENDATIONS FOR EACH APPROACH

It is necessary that the international IT curriculum approach that fits best with the overall business school objectives and internationalization plans be determined initially. In this context, specific plans for implementation can then be

I. **Setting the Stage for Global IS: The International Business Environment**
 The Changing International Business Environment
 The Changing Role of the Information Systems Function
 The Significance of the International Dimension
 The Relevance of Linkages Between Information Systems and
  International Business
 The Role of Information Technology in the Evolving Global
  Marketplace
 Information Systems: The Global Communications Link
 International Management and IS

II. **International Business and Environmental Influences on the IS Function**
 International Business Background
  Definition of International Business
  The Multinational Corporation
  Evolution of the Multinational Enterprise
  Types of International Business Activity
 The International Management Environment
  The Economic Environment
  The Political Environment
  The Cultural Environment
  The Legal Environment

A Conceptual Model Linking the IS Function With Its International Environment

 Overview of International IS Issues
  Country-specific Issues
  Technological Issues
  Managerial Issues
 Perspective of the U.S.-Based MNC
 Perspective of Developed Countries
 Perspective of Less Developed Countries
 The International Perspective

III. **A Closer Look at International Issues and Influences Impacting the IS Function: Emphasis on Service Versus Manufacturing**
 Multinational Service versus Manufacturing
 International IS Issues for Service and Manufacturing MNCs
 General International Influences
 International Organizational Influences
 International Barriers to the Transfer and Management of IS
  Technology

IV. **The Technological Issues: Transnational Information Flows and Global Connectivity**
 The Nature of Transborder Data Flows (TBDF)
  TBDF: The Key Issues

Table 1: Global Information Systems Course Outline

TBDF Regulation by Host Country Governments
MNC Operations and TBDF

Global Connectivity
    International Telecommunications/ Networking
    International Standards
    Postal, Telephone and Telegraph Companies
        (PTTs)
    Price & Quality of Telecommunications Support
    Data and Systems Security
    Vendor Selection and Support
    Integrated Services Digital Networks
    Electronic Data Interchange (EDI)
    End-User Computing

Global Integration of Technology

**V. The Managerial Issues: Planning and Strategic Implications of
    Global Information Systems**
    Planning for Global Information Systems
        The Need for a Global IS Plan
        The Evolution of IS Planning
        Assessing the Status of International IS Planning
        Barriers to an International IS Plan
        Alternative Planning Approaches
    Strategic Implications of IT
        Strategic Information Systems (SIS)
        The Global Value Chain Approach to SIS
        Strategic Information Systems in Multinational
            Industries
        Strategic Information Systems in Global Industries
        Strategic Opportunity in Multidomestic and Global
            Industries

**VI. Tying It All Together: Current State of the Art, Future Directions
    and Emerging Trends**
    IS Issues Around the Globe
    Impact of Europe Unification in 1992
    Eastern Europe in the Information Age
    Growth of On-Line Databases
    Intellectual Property Protection
    Ethical Issues: The International Perspective

Table 1: Global Information Systems Course Outline (Contd.)

examined. In the following sections a discussion of specific recommendations that might be considered for each alternative is presented.

The Freestanding International IT Course

A comprehensive outline is presented in Table 1 that identifies the major topics and components that should be included as the basis for a stand-alone international IT course. This outline represents iterative development phases based on empirical work designed to identify the major international IS topics of importance both to IS practitioners as well as academicians (Deans et. al., 1991; Deans and Ricks, 1991). The organization of topics and integration of the overall course outline is based on extensive interviews with practitioners as well as feedback from academicians. A rationale for the outline model presented in Table 1 is provided in the following paragraphs.

It is imperative that an international IT course begin with an appreciation for global business activity and the role of information technology in this evolving global marketplace. Students cannot fully understand the concepts without an awareness of the setting and significance of changes taking place in the global business environment. Clearly, the IS manager will encounter a different set of challenges depending on the part of the world in which he operates.

From this broad awareness base, the student can more easily focus on the specific dimensions of the international environment that affect business operations. These include economic, cultural, political, and legal environments of each foreign nation. These dimensions correspond to the contextual factors identified for the curriculum model in Figure 1. Focus may then shift from this broad awareness to the specific and unique issues and concerns that confront the IS manager in each of these four dimensions. These issues may be discussed from various perspectives, including those of the U.S.-based MNC, those of MNCs in developed countries, and those of MNCs in less developed countries. An overall global perspective of international IT issues can then be addressed. The topics have moved from broad- based awareness to a more specific focus and finally back to a broader emphasis.

International IT issues can be further evaluated from the

perspective of the multinational service MNC and manufacturing MNC. In general, the nature of the business activity of service firms is different from that of manufacturing firms. From an information systems perspective, the firm's information requirements may differ and it has become necessary to look at these differences. Many international variables (e.g., number of foreign subsidiaries, level of international involvement, number of countries of operation, and location of foreign subsidiaries) may influence the significance of international IS issues and these can be discussed in the context of differences between service and manufacturing MNCs. International organizational variables (e.g., international organization structure, and international data processing operations) may also play a part in these influences.

The focus of the course might then shift to a more detailed discussion of specific issues. These issues tend to fall into two broad categories that focus on technological and managerial dimensions. Two general areas drawing particular attention from the technological domain include issues relevant to the transfer of data and information across national borders and issues specific to the firm's international telecommunications function. From the managerial perspective, two broad areas of focus include issues specific to planning for international information systems and the strategic implications of information technology.

The final focus of the course should tie the various perspectives into a comprehensive whole. This may be accomplished by summarizing the current state of the art and then identifying future directions and emerging trends. The outline presented here represents one means by which to internationalize the information technology curriculum content. It allows for flexibility in terms of supplementary readings and student involvement. Research papers, projects and student activities can be incorporated to best meet the needs of the course requirements. Detailed curriculum material closely following this outline can be found in a supplementary text (Deans and Kane, 1992).

The Infusion Approach

Alternatively, specific components from the outline in Table 1 may be infused into the curriculum through appropriate courses. This approach will require coordination among the IS faculty and a more formal internationalization plan. Again, there are many factors that will affect the direction most appropriate for a given IT program. The number and variety of courses offered, whether a major or concentration in IT is available, and the existence of both undergraduate and graduate IT programs and the specific requirements and relationships between these programs become important factors. Emphasis will focus on breadth as opposed to depth of coverage.

When a variety of courses are offered as part of the IT program, the infusion approach may be implemented throughout a wider spectrum of the curriculum. For example, a separate course in telecommunications may incorporate Section V from the outline in Table 1 addressing "global telecommunications issues." An in-depth discussion of international telecommunications standards, Postal, Telephone and Telegraph companies, and vendor selection and support may be integrated into the course material. Likewise, a separate course in strategic information systems may focus on the managerial topics identified in Section VI of Table 1. A discussion of strategic information systems in multidomestic versus global industries would provide a more in-depth coverage of the international dimension.

Incorporating specific international topics throughout the traditional introductory information systems course both at the undergraduate and graduate levels is a viable alternative that will mazimize the number of students exposed to these topics. An introductory course typically provides some coverage of telecommunications issues as well as managerial topics specific to IS planning and strategic implications of information technology. The telecommunications chapter may be supplemented with some discussion of transborder data flow (TBDF) regulations and a general overview of issues relevant to international telecommunications and connectivity. A discussion of global IS planning and specific barriers to the implementation of an international IS plan may be incorporated into the IS planning chapter. This approach will provide students with a broader awareness of issues that must be considered on an international scale.

When the international topics are dispersed throughout a wider range of courses better coordination among faculty will be required in order to avoid duplication of topics. Faculty expertise and interest will also play a part in the eventual success of each alternative.

The Combination Approach

A combination of the free standing international IT course and infusion of international IT topics throughout the curriculum may be a more appropriate alternative, especially for larger IT programs that must address both undergraduate and graduate level interests. The stand-alone course may be offered as an elective, while at the same time providing for integration of international IT topics throughout additional courses. This alternative may be more complex, but at the same time may more closely match the objectives, resources and internationalization plans of the business program.

FUTURE TRENDS FOR INTERNATIONAL IT CURRICULUM DEVELOPMENT

There is presently a heightened interest in international IT issues both from a research as well as curriculum development perspective. Research results specific to the international IT domain have only recently appeared in the literature. Much work is currently in progress and relevant studies are expected to increase in the literature. In support of these trends, a new journal with a specific focus on international information systems has recently been established. Professional IS organizations are also becoming more international in focus and in their membership status. Greater interaction among colleagues from foreign business schools will lead to collaborative research studies and access to information that is difficult to obtain. As additional information becomes available through international research efforts, more emphasis will be directed to the IT curriculum level. This process will take time, since international research is frequently more difficult and data collection becomes a more complex task than in the strictly domestic (U.S.) context.

Trends for internationalizing IT education will likely follow similar directions as have preceeded for the other functional areas of business. Considerable literature and curriculum material have evolved in the areas of international marketing, international finance and international accounting. Many business programs now offer separate courses in these areas. Curriculum material in the information technology area will, likewise, eventually evolve to a point that separate coursework may become commonplace. Rapid changes in information technology as well as in the international business environment will demand continual revision and curriculum change. Currently, very few schools offer a separate course for international information systems and technology. Those that do are primarily at the graduate level and tend to have a large information systems faculty and degree program. Current business trends certainly indicate that international IT issues will continue to receive increased attention by those in the field. This emphasis will filter to the curriculum level as academicians strive to continue to provide a relevant curriculum for students.

CONCLUSIONS

In this chapter we have discussed current trends and practices for incorporating an international dimension into the IT curriculum. IS academicians are only now in the beginning phases of developing this international component. There are clearly many worldwide trends and influences currently playing a part in this process and providing the impetus for continued efforts.

As decision makers for IT programs consider the alternatives and resource commitments for internationalizing the curriculum, it is necessary that the overall objectives and goals of the business school curriculum be evaluated in order that international plans for the IT component be consistent and fit with the mission and objectives already in place. In matching these goals, several alternative curriculum approaches might be considered. Infusion meets the requirements of the awareness level and exposes the largest number of students to international topics. At the other extreme, a freestanding course may be more appropriate for a subset of students when the goals require more in-depth understanding or competency. The approach most likely to fit the objectives of most schools will be a combination of these. Combining methods provides the greatest flexibility for programs that will inevitably need to respond to change.

As we develop curriculum that will prepare managers for the 21st century, globalization of the marketplace cannot be ignored. It is imperative that our curriculum reflect the realities of the world in which our students will work.

REFERENCES

Arpan, J. (1991). Presentation at the Southeast Academy of International Business meeting, Columbia, South Carolina.

Cheng, C. (1987). The computer science program of a college in China. *Technological Horizons in Education, 14,* 64-66.

Deans, P.C. & Goslar, Martin D. (1990). Incorporating an international dimension in IS curriculum: A conceptual model with emphasis on the foreign component. *Proceedings of the International Academy for Information Management,* Chicago, Illinois.

Deans,P.C. & Kane,M.J.(1992). *International dimensions of information systems and technology.* Boston: PWS-Kent Publishing Company.

Deans,P.C.;Karwan,K.R.; Goslar, M.D.; Ricks, D.A.; & Toyne, B. (1991). Identification of key international information systems issues in U.S- based multinational corporations, *Journal of Management Information Systems, 7*(4), 27-50.

Deans, P.C. & Ricks, D.A. (1991). MIS research: A model for incorporating the international dimension, *Journal of High Technology Management Research,* 2(1), 57-81.

Farmer, R.N. & Richman, B.M. (1970). *Comparative management and economic progress.* Indiana: Cedarwood Publishing Company.

Gupta, J.N.D. & Seeborg, I.S. (1989). The graduate MIS course in colleges of business. *Journal of Management Information Systems, 5*(4), 125-136.

Keefe, P. (1990). Comrades, we were born to code. *Computerworld,* 24, 95,99.

McLeod, R., Jr. (1985).   The undergraduate MIS course in A.A.C.S.B. schools. *Journal of Management Information Systems,* 2(2),   73-85.

Nehrt, L.C. (1987). The internationalization of the curriculum. *Journal   of International Business Studies, 18*(3), 83-90.

Porter, L.W. & McKibbin, L.E. (1988). *Management education and development: drift or thrust into the 21st century?* New York: McGraw-Hill.

Rifkin, G. (1989). MIS education assumes a foreign accent. *Computerworld, 23*(1), 66-67.

Skinner, W.C. (1984).   Management of international production.   *Harvard Business Review, 42*(5), 125-136.

Thanopoulos, J. & Vernon, I.R. (1987). International business education in the

A.A.C.S.B. schools. *Journal of International Business Studies, 18*(1), 83-90.

Trujillo, I. (1989). Academic Computing: The Los Andes strategy. *EDUCOM, 24,* 32-37.

Wilson, J.D.; Adams, E.S.; Baouendi, H.P.; Marion, W.A.; & Yaverbaum, G.J. (1988). Computer science education in the Peoples Republic of China in the late 1980's.*Communications of the ACM,31,*956-965.

Van Weert, T.J. (1987/88). Information technology in education: the situation in the Netherlands. *T.H.E. Journal, 15,* 77-80.

Section III

Global IT Education in Selected Developed Countries

Information Systems Education Issues:
The U.S. and European Perspectives

4

R. Ravichandran and Jatinder N.D. Gupta
Ball State University

The rapid changes in the IS industry coupled with the expansion of the information services sector of the economy make it critical that the IS education process stay current and in tune with the needs of the organizations. Many past studies, taking a descriptive approach, have dealt with current industry trends and available IS curricula. IS education should meet the demands of the employers. A demand side model of the IS education process is proposed. This model considers various factors affecting job performance of IS employees. IS curricula in US and Europe are discussed. A preliminary survey of IS employers identifies important subject areas and areas of deficiency. Collaboration between industry and university is examined. Implications of differences in IS management practices at various levels are explored. Suggestions to improve IS curricula are presented. Integration of curricula across the Atlantic is discussed along with a model international IS course component.

Information Systems (IS) are increasingly being used as competitive weapons by many organizations. The rapid changes in the IS industry, coupled with the expansion of the information services sector of the economy, make it critical that the IS education process in universities stay current and in tune with the needs of the organizations. Many past studies have looked at the IS education process from the viewpoints of the industry and university. However, most of them have taken a descriptive approach and have described current industry trends and current IS curricula. This chapter offers a supply side view rather than a demand side view. In order to make sure that the IS education meets the demands of the employers, a better understanding of the IS education process is needed. In this chapter a model of the IS education process is proposed. This model considers various variables affecting job performance of IS employees. University education and university-industry collaboration are considered in detail.

Information Systems are being utilized as a strategic weapon by many organizations around the world. However, the way in which IS are employed in organizations can differ across countries. For successful IS implementations, the nature of IS function in organizations needs to be better understood. By recognizing cross-cultural differences, lessons from successful IS implementations from one culture can be transferred to another culture. Such an understanding also promotes the effective integration of the world through information technologies.

This chapter will explore several issues: IS education process, IS curriculum, the demand and supply sides of the IS educational system, the nature of interaction between industry and educational institutions, the nature of differences in IS educational systems in the US and Europe, educational changes recommended for effective integration of IS curricula across the Atlantic, and improvements to the IS education process.

The discussion will be based on literature, preliminary results from a survey of IS employers and personal observations.

IS EDUCATION PROCESS

The process of IS education is a complex one. Understanding this process will help in building a quality IS program in universities. From the viewpoint of the IS employer, the most important outcome is job performance. For the employer, a student must be well prepared by the university to effectively perform in the workplace. However, adequate IS education alone is not sufficient to guarantee good performance on the job. Another important contributing factor to job performance is the level of training possessed by the IS graduate. Training for IS employees is critical given the fast pace of technological changes in the IS arena. Employers routinely spend a great deal of their time and effort in training IS graduates (Rifkin, 1988). The other major factors affecting job performance can be grouped under two categories: (a) organizational factors (such as organizational environment, reward systems, and culture) and (b) personal factors (such as worker intelligence and ability to learn new skills).

A simplified model of the IS education process is depicted in Figure 1. A high school graduate is viewed as the basic input to the IS education process. The student who enters the university can be seen as influenced by the high school educational process. The university prepares the student through IS education. Then the employer organization trains the student for the workplace. The various components of the model are discussed next.

High School: High schools provide their end-products as inputs to the universities. The level of training that they provide in verbal, quantitative, and reasoning skills affects the ability of the students to learn and apply advanced IS concepts later in the universities. Concerns have been raised about the

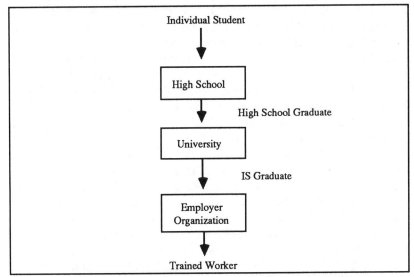

Figure 1: A Process Model of IS Education

quality of education provided by high schools. Increasingly many high schools provide significant computer learning experiences as part of their curriculum. They also train the students in programming languages such as BASIC. The students are learning to accept computers as normal components of their daily lives, thus avoiding the computer phobia manifested by older adults.

University: The IS education process is carried out by the universities. They make sure the requirements of the employers in the industry are met by the graduates. Though community colleges are not specifically included in the discussion, they are part of the academic institution whose outputs become the inputs for the four-year colleges and universities.

Employer Organization: Organizations here include corporations, not-for-profit institutions, educational institutions, and public institutions. They are the consumers of the products from the educational process, and for successful IS education their needs should be kept in mind.

A Model of IS Education Process

The model in Figure 1 espouses a process view of the IS education system, following a step-by-step sequential approach. However, there are interactions within the various components which are not captured by the model. The model can be expanded further as shown in Figure 2 to include various interactions to facilitate further discussion. This model deals with the various factors that affect the job performance variable and how the IS education process is related to them. The model specifically deals with college IS graduates. To focus on the IS education process and to keep the model manageable, several important factors are abstracted at a higher level, namely personal factors and employer organization.

Personal Factors: Personal factors come into play at three different places in the IS education process, namely the high school, university, and workplace. It is a high level abstraction designed to represent the individuals as they get themselves prepared for the workplace. This set of factors attempts to capture various factors such as level of knowledge possessed (e.g., verbal and mathematical skills), intelligence, motivational levels for learning and training, and family backgrounds. For instance, a major disruption in the family life might

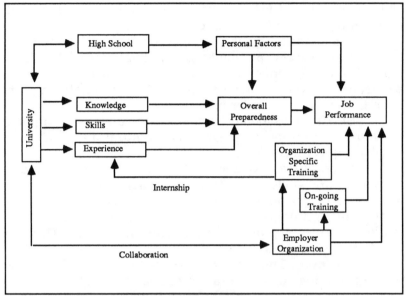

Figure 2:   A Model of IS Education Factors

affect job performance. Some of these factors may change over time. Since the focus of this chapter is on IS education, detailed accounts of personal factors are not included in the model. But it is important to recognize their influence on overall preparedness and job performance. A student inadequately prepared in the high school and who, as a result, does not possess the required knowledge assumed of a college freshman may not derive the full benefits from the university IS education and hence may not be as well prepared for the workplace as other IS graduates.

Employers provide both ongoing training and organization specific training to the new IS graduates to prepare them adequately for the organizational workplace. Apart from IS training, organizations provide the environment within which to work. Organization here is a higher level abstraction which tries to capture the effect of many organizational factors on job performance. Factors which fall under this category include such variables as reward systems, work environment, and authority and responsibility issues arising from different organizational control systems.

University: University IS education is seen as having three components: knowledge, skills, and experience. The effect of the university on these three variables contribute to the overall preparedness of the IS graduates.

Knowledge: This is the basic core IS curriculum. Basic concepts and various principles form the fundamental building blocks of the IS education.   Concepts such as data independence, life cycle development methodology, prototyping, and user satisfaction fall under here.

Skills: Skills include, among other things, programming in a fourth generation language, user communication skills and database query formulation.

Experience: Experience deals with the application of knowledge and skills to practical situations. Students learn by working on programming projects, systems analysis, design and implementation projects. Such experience integrates the curriculum in a meaningful way for students and prepares them for 'real-world' situations.

Training: The model considers two types of training, ongoing training and organization-specific training.

Organization-Specific Training: IS graduates need to be trained to have knowledge of the organization in which they will be working. Such training might include training in the specific operating systems which are used by the organization. The IS graduates also need to be familiar with the organizational structure, with the various departmental functions, and with the product lines and services performed by the organization. They need to know the current state of computing in the organization, and the organizational blueprint for future computing. On a more micro level, they need to be conversant with the needs of the individual computing clients with whom they will be working. Such training is essential before the IS education that the workers received at the universities can be fruitfully employed. While such training is required of all new workers, both IS and non-IS graduates, the need for organization specific training for IS graduates tend to be higher than that for non-IS graduates. For instance, systems analysts need to intimately know the functions of the departmental unit with which they are working. Network analysts and specialists in enterprise-wide computing need to be aware of the global data needs and information resource availabilities in the organization across departmental boundaries.

Ongoing Training: Information systems field is fast changing. New breakthroughs in hardware technology necessitate new ways of thinking and application development methodologies hitherto considered impractical. Software applications also tend to change constantly (Raths, 1991). Also new software products keep emerging to meet specific organizational needs. As software products proliferate, the knowledge needed to maintain compatibility and interoperability across different platforms increases. As a result, several organizations spend large amounts of money for ongoing training of their employees. For instance, IBM spends about $78 million dollars a year for ongoing training of its employees (Rifkin, 1988). Notice that ongoing training is difficult to avoid. It has to be done either by the organization or by some outside agencies hired by the organization.

   Outcome Variables: Two outcome variables namely overall preparedness and job performance, are considered in the model.

   Overall Preparedness: How well are the IS graduates prepared for the workplace? While the focus of this chapter is on IS graduates who enter the workplace after four years of college, the job specification need not be restricted to traditional jobs such as programmer, systems analyst, and end-user specialist. It may include IS strategy positions for MBA/MS graduates and teaching and research positions for Ph.D. graduates. This variable measures how well the IS graduates are prepared to meet job demands.

   Job Performance: Job performance is a measure of how well the IS graduates perform on their jobs. It is a complex construct and several measures exist for it in the organizational behavior literature (Miner, 1980; Tosi et al., 1986). Many factors have been found to influence job performance. Only three specific factors are considered in this model, namely overall preparedness, organization-specific training, and ongoing training of the IS graduate. Other factors are abstracted in two high level boxes, namely personal factors and employer organization.

   Interactions: Although the model considers various interactions between different components, two interactions are of special interest: (a) internships and (b) collaboration.

   Internship: Internship in this context includes different types of experiential learning activities in which students participate. It includes traditional student internships in organizations during summers and project work done for various organizational units. There are several advantages resulting from such interactions (Ruiz and VanderMeer, 1989). The students enhance their learning experience (Taylor, 1988). As for organizations, they know a great deal more about prospective employees and, as a result, they can hire only those students who have proven their worth during their internships. This reduces their risks in hiring new employees. Also, interns frequently complete projects which, if accomplished through the hiring of consultants, would have cost the organizations quite a bit more (Lindmeyer, 1987). If the organization hires interns, then the need for organization-specific training after hiring is vastly reduced. However, the employers do have to pay a price for all these benefits, since they have to invest their efforts in training the students and some of them may not be hired.

   Collaboration: Collaborative efforts between the industry and the university can enhance the IS education process (Burn, 1989; Fielding, 1989). By interacting with universities, industry can convey its expectations for new graduates. Possible ways of collaboration include consulting projects, contract works, sabbatical leaves, visiting professorships, research grants, endowed professorships, equipment grants, and software grants. Communication methods include direct communication to professors by personnel directors, conference contacts and networking, training programs by universities, collaborative research ventures, and journal articles.

Functional Specification

   The interactions between the various components that are shown in the model in Figure 2 can be formulated as functional relationships. This will help in future studies exploring the IS education process model. The following functional relationships are proposed:

Preparedness = f (Knowledge, Skills, Training, Personal
                  Factors)   (1)

Job Performance = f (Preparedness, Training, Personal Factors,
                     Organizational Factors)   (2)

   Initially, these relationships can be studied. Similarly, other relationships can be specified and empirically investigated later.

IS CURRICULUM

The Information Systems curriculum in the U.S. is primarily structured along the guidelines provided by the Association for Computing Machinery (ACM, 1968; ACM, 1979) and more recently by both ACM and IEEE-CS (ACM, 1991; Mulder and Dalphin, 1984; Tucker et al., 1991) and the Data Processing Management Association (DPMA, 1990). ACM has proposed a revised set of courses in 1991. The set of revised courses is presented in Table 1. Integration of IS with other functional areas such as production and marketing has been pursued (Adams and Song, 1989). Other efforts have been made in this arena such as the curricula for a liberal computer science major (Gibbs and Tucker, 1986). Other agencies have also been involved in this process (CSAB, 1987).

Most of the curriculum recommendations made by both the ACM and the DPMA have been predominantly reactive in nature. The curriculum committee has been slow in reacting to the fast changes in the computer industry. For instance, the focus is still on data structures in the basic courses, e.g., IS02 Data and File Structures. While it can be argued that students need to know data and file structures, a complete course need not focus on that topic. It will be similar to having a course in assembly language programming. While knowledge of assembly languages is useful for all IS graduates, skill in assembly language programming needs to be possessed by specialized programmers. The majority of the programming can be accom-

Code	Course Title
IS01	Computer and Programming Concepts
IS02	Data and File Structures
IS03	Systems and Information Concepts in Organization
IS04	Database Management Systems
IS05	Fundamentals of Information Systems
IS06	Computer Communication Networks and Distributed Processing
IS07A	Decision, Executive, and Cooperative Work Support Systems
IS07B	Knowledge-Based and Expert Systems
IS08	Information Systems Development Tools and Techniques
IS09	Information Management
IS10	Information System Projects

Table 1: Preliminary ACM 1991 IS curriculum courses

Code	Course Title
CIS-01	Fundamental Concepts of Information and Computer Technology
CIS-02	IS Concepts
CIS-03	Computer Concepts
CIS-04	Application Development
CIS-05	Application Design and Implementation
CIS-06	Systems Development 1 (Single User Systems)
CIS-07	Systems Development 2 (Multi User Systems)
CIS-08	Systems Project
CIS-09	Management of IS

Electives

Code	Course Title
CE-01	IS Professionalism and Ethics
CE-02	Information Center Concepts and Management
CE-03	Audit and Security Management
CE-04	Telecommnications
CE-05	Distributed Processing
CE-06	Implementation of PC Network Systems
CE-07	Office Automation Systems
CE-08	Group Decision Support/Electronic Meeting/Executive Support Systems
CE-09	Decision Support/Expert/Neural Net Systems
CE-10	Software Engineering
CE-11	Alternative Analysis and Design methodologies
CE-12	Computer Graphics
CE-13	Systems Simulation
CE-14	Software and Hardware Architecture
CE-15	Advanced Database concepts
CE-16	Human-Computer Interaction

Table 2: Preliminary DPMA 1991 IS curriculum courses

plished in fourth generation and object-oriented languages. This becomes even more important given that enormous productivity increases are required to adequately meet the software needs of the industry. It is much more fruitful to introduce object-oriented programming constructs in the basic IS course.

As another example, consider the emphasis on hierarchical and network database management systems in the database management course. Relational, textual and object-oriented systems can be made the primary focus of the database course as opposed to the current focus on hierarchical, network and relational databases.

EVALUATION OF IS CURRICULUM

Any curriculum needs to be constantly monitored using outside evaluators (Tamir, 1985). Feedback from the practitioners is critical in making sure that the skills and knowledge required in the workplace for effective functioning of the graduates are provided to the students. Although universities are neither vocational training schools nor training centers for the employers, it is important that the basic principles and the knowledge imparted by the universities are grounded in reality and strengthened by practical project experiences.

Are employers of the IS graduates satisfied?   Some authors have argued that IS education needs a lot of improvement (Freedman, 1986; Rifkin, 1988; Yaffe, 1989). However, no systematic exploration of this issue has been made so far. A survey of skill requirements for IS professionals was performed more than a decade ago (Cheney and Lyons, 1980). A literature search for articles in ABI/INFORM and CompuCite databases during the period 1986-1991, using the key words IS and education and combinations thereof, revealed very few articles (Anonymous, 1990; Adams and Song, 1989; Cardinali, 1988; Gordon et al., 1986) in the IS education area.

IS Curriculum Needs

Knowledge in the area of information systems is fast-growing. Given the limited time and resources available at the disposal of both the faculty and the students, the focus in the IS curriculum should be on the most important topics and the most needed topics. Area or topic in this context denotes knowledge, skill and/or experience in the specified area or topic. What topics should be covered in the IS curriculum?

Various topics covered in the undergraduate core MIS class include systems analysis and design, database management systems, information systems by functional areas, computer hardware, and computer security (McLeod, 1985). A survey of the introductory MIS core course offered among the AACSB - accredited business schools indicated that a similar set of topics was covered in the graduate MIS course (Gupta and Seeborg, 1989).   However, these studies have looked what is being offered in various programs. For the graduate IS education, summaries of the leading IS programs in the US which participated in the IBM Management of Information Systems (MoIS) project are available (UCLA, 1990a; UCLA, 1990b). This is a supply side view. But IS education needs to be looked at from the demand side. What do the employers need? Are the IS graduates overprepared in certain areas and underprepared in others?

In answering the question as to which areas should be covered in the IS curriculum, two important factors should be kept in mind. One is the importance of the area. In each of the areas, different levels of mastery of the subject may be needed by the employers. Do the IS graduates possess appropriate levels of expertise in each of the areas? In one important area, the IS graduate may possess more expertise.   This is a case of overpreparedness of the IS graduate. In another important area, however, the level of mastery may fall short of the expected level of mastery. Time and effort that results in overpreparedness in certain topics can be reallocated to deficient topics. A proper assessment of IS curriculum ought to take care of important areas and appropriate levels of mastery in each of the area.

Higher levels of deficiencies demand higher levels of on-the-job training sponsored by the employers. Such measures can help in refocusing educational efforts from areas in which overpreparedness exists to deficient areas. Such a reallocation must be from the least important areas to the most important areas. It is unrealistic to expect IS graduates to be prepared at the maximum possible level in each important area. Also, other components in the model such as university-industry collaboration can be measured and empirically validated. To keep the discussion brief, further details will be omitted.

The model does not take into account differences in effort levels that may be required to reach the same level of expertise in each of the areas. For instance, consider an average level of expertise in the database area defined in terms of an ability to create, populate, and query a database. The efforts required to attain that level of expertise in the area of relational databases will be much less than those in the areas of hierarchical and network databases.

It is easy to extend the model to take into account levels of resources required for university education and employer training in each of the areas and formulate an overall educational effort optimization model which matches the resources to the most important areas. However, a simple model needs to be explored in depth before more complex formulations are pursued. Moreover, an awareness and focus of the various variables in the models and their interactions will facilitate the IS education process. Previous studies in training and skill development have found awareness to be a major contributory factor to the final improvements (Miner, 1980).

AN IS EDUCATION STUDY

In order to operationalize the above model, a study of the IS educational needs was undertaken. Preliminary results from the study will be discussed next.

Participating Organizations

The data reported come from the responses from 13 Fortune 500 companies during the summer of 1991. The respondents were the Chief Information Officers of these organizations. Background information for these companies is given in Table 3. It is difficult to generalize about most of the discussion and observations. They hold true for the thirteen participating organizations. Given the small sample size, median values are reported for all the variables in the study, unless otherwise specified. Mean values of the variables under study were very similar. Annual revenue for these companies for the current year was 1.308 billion U.S. dollars, with an expected revenue of 1.350 billion U.S. dollars in 1992-1993. The organizations are large employers with 4900 employees as the median value of the

Employment Information	Current	One year from now
Total number of employees in organization:	4900	6400
Number of IS/IT employees:		
Primarily working in IS department	144	219
Primarily working in functional areas (e.g., finance)	40	55
Number of new IS/IT employees hired each year:	8	5
Number of new IS/IT graduates hired each year:	3.5	2
Annual revenue (in millions of US Dollars) :	1308	1350

Table 3: Background Information for Responding Organizations (N=13). All figures are median values

number of employees. All organizations reported possible future expansion of the employee base, with the median value being 6400.

IS Employees

The number of IT employees were 184, with 144 of them working in the IS department and 40 of them working with end-users in various functional areas.   A small number of IS employees are supporting a large corporate workforce, which may be attributed to several factors: enhanced productivity of IS employees, increasing computer sophistication of general non-IS workforce (e.g., skills in using spreadsheets and word processors), and ability of large centralized systems to support a large service-oriented workforce (e.g., in banks). The distribution of IS employees in the MIS department and functional departments shows that a significant number of IS employees are being spread across functional areas to support end-users. The number of new IS employees for the current year is, however, low at 8 and for the forthcoming year is even lower at 5. Comments from the respondents indicated that many firms were holding off on their new hires given the recession and indicated that more employers would be hired in the coming years. Out of the new IS employees, new IS graduates represented even a lower number. One of the possible causes for this phenomenon is personnel turnover, in that employees may be hired from other organizations, rather than fresh from the universities.

Educational Background of IS employees

Educational background information of current IS employees of the participating organizations is summarized in Table 4. More than 50% of the IS employees possess undergraduate degrees, while a significant minority has had some university courses. Only a handful of employees had graduate IS education. Note that some employees have not taken any university courses. Such IS employees may be 'old-timers' and may have started as computer operators.

Minimum educational background required for new IS employees is summarized in Table 5. Most of the new employees are required to have undergraduate degrees, with the number of

Qualification	Percentage of Employees with Qualifications
No University Courses	12
Some University Course	21
Technical College Certification	8
Bachelor's Degree	50
Master's Degree	7
Doctorate	2

Table 4: Educational qualification of current IS employees for responding organization

Qualification	Percentage of Employees with Qualifications
No University Courses	5.5
Some University Courses	5.5
Technical College Certification	4.4
Bachelor's Degree in IS	10.5
Bachelor's Degree in other areas	35.4
Master's Degree in IS	2.8
Master's Degree in other areas	0
Doctorate in IS	0
Doctorate in other areas	0
Diploma in IS	0
Diploma in other areas	0

Table 5: Minimum Educational Requirements for new IS hires in responding organizations

IS graduates less than non-IS graduates. Some masters degrees were required, but no masters degrees in other areas were required as a minimum qualification. Doctorate degrees were not required as minimum educational requirement for any new IS employee. However, such terminal degrees may be required for research-oriented IS positions in companies such as Boeing, and for teaching positions in universities.

IMPORTANT IS AREAS

What are the important areas to be taught under the IS curriculum? For ascertaining the important topics, a multi-pronged approach was taken. First, the literature was surveyed to find out what the industry felt to be important (Cardinali, 1988; Cheney and Lyons, 1980). Second, areas from various recent curriculum proposals such as those shown in Table 2 (DPMA, 1990) and in Table 1 (Tucker et al., 1991) were taken into consideration. Third, a list of recent promising developments (such as object-oriented programming and graphical user interfaces) was compiled, based on the personal observations of the topics most frequently touched upon by various industry magazines and by conferences in the IS area. Fourth, views of the leading employers of IS graduates in the Midwest region as observed from personal contacts and conversations were taken into account. Fifth, results from surveys of top IS executives about critical IS related issues (such as 'Top Ten Issues in Information Systems' over the past several years) were considered (Eliot, 1991). Combining the results from all the approaches yielded 29 areas. Using personal judgment, these areas were subdivided into three groups on the basis of the breadth of the topic: broad areas, subject areas, and specific areas. The areas covered the three components of IS education as in Figure 2, namely, knowledge, skills and experience.

Broad areas included hardware knowledge, software knowledge, user issues, IS management issues, communication skills, and hands-on experience. Subject areas are structured around traditional IS course offerings and included systems analysis and design, databases, telecommunications, management of IS, decision support systems, expert systems, and programming. Within these broad and subject areas, sixteen specific areas were considered. They were Computer Aided Software Engineering (CASE), Object Oriented Programming (OOP), Graphical User Interfaces (GUI), Relational Databases, Local Area Networks (LAN), Computer Aided Design (CAD)/ Computer Aided Manufacturing (CAM), Logic Programming, Knowledge Engineering, Hardware and Software Selection, Operating Systems, Logical Data Models, Data Flow Diagrams, Application Generators, Information Centers, IS/IT Strategic Planning, and IS/IT as a Competitive Weapon. Respondents were given the opportunity to specify additional areas as they deemed fit.

A list of areas such as this cannot be comprehensive in covering every possible IS topic. Rather, it is aimed to be as useful as possible without becoming too long.

The respondents ranked these areas on their level of impor-

	Level of Importance in Job	Desired Expertise Level	Actual Expertise Level Possessed by
Graduates			
Broad Areas:			
Communication Skills	8	8	5
Software Knowledge	7	7	5
User Issues	6.5	7	3
Hardware Knowledge	5	5	4
IS Management Issues	5	5	3
Hands-on Experience	5	5	4
Subject Areas:			
Programming	8	8	6
Systems Analysis and Design	7	6.5	5
Databases	6	6.5	4
Telecommunications	5	5	3
Management of IS	3.5	3	2
Dec. Support Systems	3	3.5	3.5
Expert Systems	2	2	2
Specific Areas:			
Relational Databases	6	6	4.5
Local Area Networks	5.5	6	3
CASE	5	5.5	3
IS/IT as a Competitive Weapon	5	6	2
Logic Programming	5	5	4
Logical Data Models	5	5	3.5
Data Flow Diagrams	5	6	4
Application Generators	5	5	4
Graphical User Interfaces	4	5	4
Object-Oriented Programming	3	3.5	3
Knowledge Engineering	3	2	2
Hardware and Software Selection	3	3	2
Operating Systems	3	2	2
Information Center	2	2	2
IS/IT Strategic Planning	2	3	2
CAD/CAM	1	1	1

All values are on a scale of 1 to 9 (1 = very low, 9 = very high)

Table 6: IS Subject Areas

tance in job on a nine point Likert-type scale (1 = very low, 9 = very high). They also provided desired expertise level in each of the areas and actual expertise level possessed by graduates on nine point scales. These results are summarized in Table 6. Within each category of broad areas, subject areas, and specific areas, the topics are listed in the order of perceived importance.

Among the broad areas communication skills was considered the most important issue with a score of 8 (with the highest possible importance score being 9), closely followed by software knowledge and user issues. Hardware knowledge, IS management issues and hands-on experience were perceived to have the same importance. As for the desired expertise level, a high level of communication skills with a score of 8 was expected from the graduates. But the actual communication skill level was only 5. Communication skills are important in the interaction of the IS professionals with the users and in the process of specification of system requirements. In all the broad areas IS graduates did not possess the desired levels of skills. They fell short of the expected skill level most in communication skills and user issues. Actual expertise in software knowledge and IS management issues were also deficient. The difference between actual and expected levels of skills were not that high in the areas of hardware knowledge and hands-on experience.

In the subject areas, programming was considered the most important for good job performance followed by systems analysis and design, and databases. Business telecommunications was perceived as the fourth most important area. Management of IS, decision support systems and expert systems were not considered important by the participants. As for deficiency, IS graduates were most lacking in the database area, followed by programming and telecommunications. Deficiencies in systems analysis and design and management of IS subjects were perceived to be low. IS graduates were adequately prepared in the expert systems and decision support systems areas.

In specific areas, the relational databases area was considered the most important closely followed by Local Area Networks. Six topics, namely, CASE, IS/IT as a competitive weapon, logic programming, logical data models, data flow diagrams, and application generators tied for the third place. Graphical user interfaces, object-oriented programming, knowledge engineering, hardware and software selection, operating systems were considered to be of some importance. The specific

Variable	Score
Preparedness(1)	5.5
Additional Training(2)	6
Current Level of Collaboration(3)	3
Desired Level of Collaboration(3)	5
Benefits from Collaboration Efforts(4)	5

(1) 1 = very poor, 9 = excellent
(2) 1 = none, 9 = extremely high
(3) 1 = none, 9 = very high
(4) 1 = none, 9 = very significant

Table 7: Overall measures of IS education process

areas of Information Centers and CAD/CAM were not considered important. In terms of deficiencies, expertise in the area of 'IS/IT as a competitive weapon' was the most lacking, followed by LANs, CASE, relational databases, and logical data models. Deficiencies in other areas were perceived as negligible.

Two overall measures were also obtained in the study. One related to the overall level of preparedness of new IS graduates recruited by the participating organizations. The other variable measured the amount of additional training efforts required on behalf of the participating organization to bring new MIS graduates up to desired skill levels. The results for these two measures are presented in Table 7. On a nine point scale (1 = very poor, 9 = excellent), overall level of preparedness was rated 5.5. This score represents a slightly above average rating for the new IS graduates and emphasizes the need to improve IS curriculum. Additional training efforts was given a rating of 6 on a nine point scale (1= None, 9= extremely high). Thus, additional training efforts were moderate, which indicates the need for more university-industry collaboration endeavors, such as internship programs, to reduce training to minimal levels. Such efforts can reduce wastage of resources in retraining, additional training, and unused university training. With a larger sample size, it is possible to empirically build and test the model.

UNIVERSITY-INDUSTRY COLLABORATION

In recent years, many stakeholders in the education process have called for increased university-industry collaboration levels. There is no doubt that students, universities, and employers will benefit from such efforts. But it is not clear to what extent such collaboration programs are needed. What are the various collaboration programs available to IS educators and universities? What are the current levels of such collaboration programs? What are the desired programs? Which programs are perceived to be the most beneficial? Answers to such questions were sought as part of the study.

What are the possible collaboration programs in the IS education process? A list of seventeen such programs were generated using a multi-pronged approach. They were grouped into three categories, namely student interaction, communication methods, and professor interaction. The student interaction grouping included field trips/tours, internship programs, cooperative programs, guest/visitor lectures, student projects, equipment grants (for primarily teaching purposes), and software grants. In the communication methods group, such activities as direct communications to professors by personnel directors, training programs by the university, conference contacts/networking, collaborative research ventures, academic journal articles, and practitioner journal articles were included. The professor interaction group included five activities, namely consulting projects, sabbatical leaves, visiting professors, research grants, and endowed chairs. Respondents were given the opportunity to specify additional collaboration programs.

Responses as to the importance of these collaboration programs and number of such programs were sought from the participating organizations. Results of the survey based on initial data from the participating organizations is summarized in Table 8. Since no collaborative programs under the professor interaction category were present in any of the responding organizations, such programs have been omitted in Table 8.

Among the student interaction category, guest/visitor lectures and internship programs were most prevalent followed by field trip/tours. Other programs were not present. Internship programs were considered the most important, followed by guest/visitor lectures, cooperative programs, and field trips/

	Number of Programs in a Year	Importance (1)
Student Interaction:		
Field Trips/Tours	2	3
Internship Programs	1.5	7
Cooperative Programs	0	3
Guest/Visitor Lectures	3	3
Student Projects	0	1
Equipment Grants	0	1
Software Grants	0	1
Communication Methods:		
Direct Communication to Professors by Personnel Director	2	6.5
Training Programs by University	1	2
Conference Contacts/Networking	1	1.5
Collaborative Research Ventures	1	1
Academic Journal Articles	0	1
Practitioner Journal Articles	0	1

(1) 1 = very low, 9 = very high

Table 8: University Industry Collaboration

tours. Other collaboration programs were not currently under way and were perceived as having a very low level of importance.

Under communication methods employed to enhance the university-industry collaboration process, 'direct communication to professors by personnel directors' was considered the most important. Such direct communications were undertaken by all participating organizations. Training programs, conference contacts/networking, and collaborative research ventures were present. But academic journal articles and practitioner journal articles were not used as a medium of communication by any of the participating organizations. Except for the direct communication to professors by personnel directors, all other collaboration programs were considered to be of little importance. One reason for the limited number of collaboration programs may be the limited number of organizations participating in the study. Also some of the collaboration programs may be specialized in nature. Consider as an example software grants. A manufacturer might donate CAD/CAM software and hardware which is currently used by the manufacturer. By donating specialized software programs, employer organizations avoid the cost of in-house training of the future IS employees. Such organizations may be very specialized in nature and will be hopefully covered under the study with a larger sample size.

Overall measures for the university-industry collaboration process are presented in Table 7. On a nine point scale (1 = None, 9 = Very High), current level of collaboration is rated three and desired level of collaboration rated five. This shows that more collaboration is desired by the participating organizations. The overall benefits to the participating organization resulting from the current collaboration efforts is given a score of five on a nine point scale (1 = none, 9 = very significant). For a lower level of effort, the participating organizations seem to be gaining beneficial returns. This implies that for a little higher level of collaboration efforts, they may be able to get even higher levels of benefits from the collaboration programs.

GLOBAL INFORMATION TECHNOLOGY EDUCATION

One of the important developments in the IS field is the globalization of the information technology. Multinational corporations are on the rise, and many organizations are getting involved in imports, exports, and offshore plants. Increasingly, data entry and software development functions are being carried out of the country. As the world is becoming a global village, the students need to be aware of such developments and be prepared to handle cross-country transactions in products and services. For the IS graduates it becomes even more critical to be prepared for such global developments. Many multinational companies view IS related issues as among the most important issues that they have to deal with (Deans et al., 1991). Major markets in the world economy are spread across countries, with U.S., Japan, and the European Economic Community as dominant players.

Examining the IS education process in different countries is beneficial in several ways. First, by closely examining the IS education process across national boundaries, insights into national educational delivery systems can be obtained. Second, differences in important IS related issues can be perceived, which can be then integrated into the IS curriculum. Third, any advantageous features observed in one IS education system can be implanted into the other systems. Fourth, such examination enables the IS educators to play a larger role in enhancing increased global cooperation by focusing on information exchange standards and information services markets.

European Perspective

The key differences observed between the U.S. and Europe can be discussed in terms of the components in the IS education process model depicted in Figure 2. Most of the comparisons are based on personal observations of the IS education systems in the following countries: the U.S., Sweden, France, Holland, Belgium, Austria, Switzerland, Denmark, Italy, Finland, Poland, Czechoslovakia, and Hungary. A survey is currently being undertaken to test the applicability of these observations in European countries.

Trimester	Class Title	Hours
1.1	Orientation to Information Systems	1
1.2	Orientation to Information Systems	2
1.3	Pascal	3
2.1	Expert Systems	2
2.2	Organizing Information Flow Within Companies	2
2.2	System Components	2
2.3	Company and Information Analysis	3
3.1	Applied Information Technology	2.5
3.1	4th Generation Aids	2.5
3.2	Information Management	2.5
3.2	IS Electives	5
3.3	Information Planning	2.5
3.3	IS Electives	5
4.1	Practical or Theoretical Project in Information Systems	5
Electives:		
	4th Generation Language	2.5
	Impact of Automation on Management	2.5
	Information Management Engineering	2.5
	Information Systems	3
	Information Delivery and Capital Information Decision	2.5
	Applied Information Technology	2.5

Table 9: A typical European university IS curriculum

A typical European IS curriculum of a middle level university is shown in Table 9. Several observations can be made by comparing this European curriculum with those US curricula proposed by the ACM, as in Table 1, and by the DPMA, as in Table 2. In the third trimester of the first year of the European curriculum, a specific programming language is required namely, PASCAL. In the US, only one programming language course is required and the student is often exempted from this course by allowing credit for any prior programming experience in languages such as BASIC obtained in high school. Programming proficiency of the IS graduate is further diluted in many IS curricula in the US because programming is made part of a course in which wordprocessing and spreadsheet skills are given the central focus. This would fit well with the perceived importance and deficiency of the US IS graduates in the programming languages area by the US employers.

Expert systems are introduced early in the European IS curriculum, emphasizing its application orientation. This might motivate the student in a better way than a data and file structures course as recommended by the ACM and the DPMA. While the current IS curricula in the US do not necessarily have an expert systems course, at least the proposed ACM IS07B course deals with it, while the DPMA makes it part of a potential elective (CE08). It is critical that the IS student is exposed early on in the curriculum to useful and concrete applications of information technology. This may be better than the usual hurdle courses consisting of data and file structures, databases, systems analysis and design. Also, throughout the European IS curriculum, applications are emphasized to a greater extent, e.g., Applied Information Technology course in the first trimester of the third year. In the US business schools, significant IS concepts are introduced in the third and fourth years, as compared with the first year in the European IS curriculum. Traditionally, the first two years in the US undergraduate program are spent on getting into the business school, i.e., fulfilling the basic minimum requirements in all functional areas such as introductory marketing and introductory finance courses. It may be more useful for students to be exposed to different IS technologies throughout a four year period rather than the last two years. Moreover, more course work in IS courses is performed by the European IS majors than the US IS majors (as measured by credit hours).

Integration of IS Curriculum Across the Atlantic

Most of the multinational U.S. manufacturing firms with a quarter or more of their sales abroad have set up separate departments for IS. Education of senior personnel was cited as the number one concern by many multinational corporations based in US (Deans et al., 1991). It is critical that IS graduates be trained in global issues. IS curricula should be integrated across the Atlantic and Pacific Oceans. This calls for the understanding by the students of the differing cultural, social, and economic systems around the globe.

Traditionally, top US business schools such as MIT, Stanford and Harvard have focused on the US. Only recently have they started to incorporate global components into their curriculum. This applies equally well to the IS curriculum in business schools. Contrast such a nationalistic approach with the truly international approaches of top European schools as such as IMD and INSEAD. Lessons can be learned from the experiences of IMD and INSEAD by US schools to improve their IS curricula.

IS Management

Are there any differences between U.S. and European IS management issues? Why are such differences present? What are the implications of such differences to the IS educators in the US and in Europe? Three such differences are explored next: (a) user issues at the single user level, (b) the role of the IS department at the organizational level, and (c) the role of politico-economic forces at the industry level.

The first difference is that the most of the attention in IS education in Europe is focused on the technical side of IS rather than the soft side of the IS (such as end user satisfaction). This is reflected in the fact the most of the IS education in many European universities is housed in engineering departments and divisions of the universities. Even when the IS program is offered by the business schools, many of the courses are taught by engineering departments. Most of the IS programs are labeled as Information Technology (IT) programs. One way of looking at the phenomenon takes into consideration the evolution of computing in organizations and cultures. One might argue that the perceived importance of the human issues in IS increases as the cost of hardware and software drops in comparison to the human cost. As societies progress on the ladder of computing evolution, they will increasingly place higher emphasis on the soft IS issues. Consider the US in the 1960s, and third world countries such as India in the 1980s and early 1990s. Most of Europe is still lagging behind the US in the application of computing technology. For instance, the number of workers who do not have personal computers at their desktops as a percentage of the total workforce is still rather high in Europe.

Another interesting difference is that the IS function within the European organizations is not as centralized as in the US organizations. As end-user computing proliferates in an European organization, each department provides the local support needed for the IS computing. Support outside the organization such as university consulting projects is often sought. This is seen as natural by many participants in the end-user computing perspective in Europe. In the US, end-user computing is being brought back under the control of the MIS department under the guise of corporate-wide standards. For instance, consider the proliferation of Local Area Networks (LAN) and their centralized control in the name of standardization. Sophisticated LAN management software packages give the LAN administrator complete control of the network resources. End users can no longer acquire needed software on their own and install them on the network. Everything needs the approval of the central IS department. Since many such political control and power problems do not arise in European organizations, projects do not fail as they do in the US organizations due to political power maneuvers. As a result, there may not be much of a need for emphasis on power and control issues in the European IS curriculum.

Another observable difference in IS education concerns the impact of factors operating across the industries as a result of governmental regulations. One of the fastest growing sectors in the IS industry is the telecommunications sector. In order to achieve complete integration of organizational networks across local, national, and international boundaries, telematic technologies have to be standardized. Two standards critical in this area are Integrated Services Digital Network (ISDN) and Open Systems Interconnection (OSI) model. Students need to be aware of the various issues involved in the adoption of these standards.

First, different levels of regulation are present in the telecommunications area. For instance, in the U.S. the market is fairly open and the federal government does not own any of the telecommunications players such as AT & T, MCI and US Sprint. Many regulations in place are geared toward ensuring that AT & T does not dominate the telematics market. Many European governments, on the other hand, control the telecommunication companies. Even though some efforts have been made in the recent past toward deregulation, such efforts have not resulted in open markets. Subsidization of investments in telematics network is common. IS graduates should be aware of such differences across countries so that they can be contribute to the international competitiveness of their employers.

University - Industry Collaboration in Europe

Most of the industry support for student interaction programs in the U.S. is in the form of internship programs. Software and hardware grants come only from software and hardware vendors, not from employer organizations. In Europe doctoral and graduate students in the IS area are supported by industry sponsors. They regularly receive fellowships, which is a common practice for most of the universities, both top and medium-level institutions. For instance, travel outside the country by students is regularly supported by the sponsoring organizations.

In the US, most of the academic research tends to be supported by the university system itself. Most of the outside research funding either comes from federal programs such as the National Science Foundation (e.g., DRMS program supporting GDSS research) or large corporations such as IBM. However, the lion's share of the research funding goes to a handful of top research institutions. Consider that none of the thirteen responding organizations had any collaboration programs with professors such as research projects and visiting professorships. In contrast, most of the IS research in Europe is supported by industry sponsors. For instance, under cooperative work arrangements, corporate sponsors provide for the salary benefits of university researchers. This practice is fairly common for most of the universities.

One of the reasons for broader research support may be the applied nature of IS research in Europe. Research studies use more case-based and ethnomethodological approaches for studying issues related to IS. As a result, most of the research done in Europe is sponsored by a corporation. Case studies are conducted by university faculty for corporations. Also, there is a greater involvement in governmental or quasi-governmental projects. Most of the research projects tend to address pressing business problems at hand. In areas such as database systems and expert systems, descriptions of systems implementations and frameworks abound.

Research in US tends to be more academic, using more rigorous methods. Case studies, once the predominant method of MIS research, are still being carried out. Multi-organizational studies using survey methodologies and field studies using experimental and quasi-experimental designs are on the increase. In areas such as database management systems, mathematical modeling and simulation techniques are often used. These trends reflect a maturing of the IS field in the academic circles in the US. However, many of the applied projects that are performed for corporations are not published in US due to the proprietary nature of the results. Hopefully, the lessons learned from such projects are communicated to the future IS workers in the classrooms by professors who consult on these projects.

IMPROVEMENTS TO IS EDUCATION

IS Curriculum Improvements

Attention should be given to developing communication skills in the IS curriculum. Communication skills were perceived to be very important by employers. Both oral and written skills are important. Oral skills are a must in interacting with the IS users during systems analysis and design and implementation phases. IS students should be prepared well to interact with the users. They should be prepared to make oral presentations such as system walk-throughs and training sessions. Written skills are important in areas such as user documentation, on-line help, and project reports.

Many IS curriculums are moving away from program-ming, forcing the students to take such courses from computer science departments. But many IS employers see it as the most important area. Also, the expected level of expertise is not possessed by the IS graduates in the programming area. Efforts should be made to train IS graduates in programming languages and recent developments such as object-oriented programming and GUI programming. Most IS curriculums do not have a business telecommunications course. There is a need for such a course. The most discrepancy between expected and actual expertise levels exists in the database area. In terms of specific areas, students should be trained to use IS/IT as a competitive weapon. Attention should also be given to CASE, LANs, and relational databases.

Improved University - High School Interactions

The link between information systems and high school curriculums has been studied (Burn, 1989; Fielding, 1989; Kraemer et al., 1986). However, high schools have been found to be lacking in providing fundamental education in many critical areas including IS (Gries, 1991). If the outputs from the high school system are not good, then the university system will be wasting its resources on bringing the students up to required proficiency levels. Universities can be perceived as manufacturers. Just as manufacturers are demanding quality components from their subcontractors and suppliers, universities should demand high quality graduates from the high schools. Like many manufacturers who are getting involved in training of the suppliers to produce quality components, universities should focus some efforts in improving the high school education process. They should communicate their needs to schools and should help them in providing a quality education.

A Model International IS Curriculum Course Component

Organizations around the world are fast adopting computer and communications technologies. However, blind adoption of technology and management practices may result in adverse consequences. As nationalistic barriers are broken and the size of global economic trade in information services industry grows, exports and imports of technology and management practices must be carefully undertaken. The need for integrating international components into the IS curriculum is critical. IS professionals should be able to grasp the national differences that need to be taken into account in the global information trade. IS curriculum should explicitly recognize such differences. IS graduates should be prepared to deal with international IS issues related to both technology and management practices.

It is interesting to note that none of the CIOs in the preliminary study of IS employers noted the need for an international IS curriculum component. There may be several reasons for this low level of interest in international IS issues. First, the employers may not be directly engaged in international trade. They may not give IS employees direct international assignments, which can range from overseas transfers to international telemarketing. Second, the small number of firms included in the study may have led to omission of those IS employers who are engaged in international trade. Third, the employers may perceive speaking and writing skills in foreign languages to be more important for management of international activities than skills in international technical and managerial issues. In a study of multinational corporations, it has been found that education of IS professionals is one of the most important concerns of the corporations (Deans et al, 1991). Given this observed interest for coverage of international dimensions in IS curriculum, a study of a larger number of employers is likely to provide strong support for an explicit international IS curriculum component.

There are two possible approaches for dealing with international issues in the IS curriculum. First, there can be a course that deals with international IS issues per se. Second, international IS issues can be spread throughout the curriculum. The advantage of the first approach involving a single IS course is an in-depth treatment of IS issues made possible by it. For instance, a project exclusively focused on international IS issues can be undertaken by students. However, this approach suffers from a practical, but serious, disadvantage. The number of different subjects that IS curriculum has to deal with (along with material to be covered) keeps constantly increasing. Students cannot be required to take too many IS courses. This is especially true for undergraduate and graduate business programs. Accreditation bodies such as the American Assembly of Collegiate Schools of Business (AACSB) restrict the number of required IS major courses. The second approach, which spreads the international aspects throughout the curriculum, has its own merits and demerits. Such an approach permits constant attention to international IS issues as the student goes through the IS study program and does not impose an extra course load requirement on the student. However, the real effect of such an approach might be a cursory examination of international chapter material in one or two class meetings. This may not adequately expose the student to the the complexities of international IS issues. Also, it becomes difficult to monitor the breadth and depth of coverage of international issues in various courses taught by different instructors.

Irrespective of the approach taken toward handling international IS issues, certain issues should be dealt in the basic IS curriculum material. A brief discussion of potential issues follows. In the area of hardware, the nature of differences between operating environments should be clearly observed. For instance, there are differences in voltages and cycles, availability of mostly uninterrupted power supply and air conditioning, monitor emission standards and communication cable installation regulations. Different operating systems may be employed. However, the spread of personal computers has mitigated many of the problems arising from incompatible minicomputer hardware platforms. Developments in standards need also to be covered. For example, the existence of a universally accepted Group III fax transmission standard has made it possible to send and receive fax messages all over the world. The spread of electronic mail and the effects of high bandwidth available in satellite communications need to be explored.

In the area of software, there have been developments which portend well for the IS professionals. Programs such as Lotus 1-2-3 have become a staple of IS users in business applications around the world. However, language specific programming needs to be explored in the IS curriculum. In the area of management practices, differences arising from national attributes and culture need to be taken into account. For instance, in the US, the annual labor cost of a worker far exceeds the cost of hardware. The key issues pertain to training, user satisfaction, effective usage, etc. On the other hand, in many East European block countries and third world developing countries such as India, the cost of hardware and software still far outweighs the cost of labor. Given such a cost difference, IS management practices will focus on more efficient use of hardware and software. IS graduates must be aware of such differences and should be able to take them into account as they start dealing with more and more international issues in the workplace. Blind acceptance of technology and management practices from other countries would be deleterious to productivity enhancements arising from the application of computer and communication technologies in the workplace.

DISCUSSION AND CONCLUSION

This chapter proposed a model of the IS education process. The model considered various factors influencing job performance as the model's final outcome. A process-oriented view of IS education was taken. Such an approach is suitable for identifying deficient areas and arriving at prescriptive guidelines. As a first step to operationalizing the model, a study was undertaken to assess the perceptions of IS employers about their needs and their IS employees. Preliminary findings yield interesting insights. Tentative recommendations for IS educators were provided. Results from a larger set of organizations may follow a similar pattern or may yield different results. This can be seen as a first step in improving IS education. Such results are useful in several ways. First, such results can be used by universities to restructure and improve their IS curricula to meet changing needs. Second, the results are useful to accrediting agencies such as AACSB in their review of the IS curriculum. Third, the findings are very important to the organizations devoted to the development of the field, such as DPMA, SIM, and ACM. Training courses can be offered by such institutions to IS faculty members. Fourth, publishers can take the lead in developing textbooks in needed areas to meet the expected demand. Fifth, doctoral institutions can modify their doctoral programs to train their doctoral students to possess expertise in important areas.

The approach presented in this chapter is amenable for adoption by a set of schools in a specific region to assess the needs of its clients, namely leading employers of their graduates. Such an assessment, if followed up by appropriate changes in the IS curriculum, will result in better prepared IS graduates. The universities can use their strengths to offer needed training programs to employees of their client organizations.

The need for internationalization of the IS curriculum was emphasized. As a specific example, the European IS education system was contrasted with the US education system.

Drawing on personal observations of the educational system in multiple European countries, differences in IS education at individual user, organizational, and national levels were explored. IS curriculums and research tends to be more applied in Europe than in the US. This goes well with the higher levels of university-industry collaboration observed at European universities. The US educational institutions and employers can collaborate at higher levels, so that they will be better prepared to the meet the challenges arising from the the European unification in 1992. Also, the IS curricula across the Atlantic need to be integrated so that the IS students in both the US and Europe are aware of differences among the various economic and cultural zones. This will lead to effective utilization of the information systems and information technology toward the realization of an integrated global economy.

Many of the issues that have been discussed in this chapter need to be investigated by future researchers in this area. A large scale survey of IS employers in both the U.S. and Europe is currently being undertaken. Results from such a study will be useful in ensuring that IS education meets the demands of employers. It will also support integration of IS education across the Atlantic. It will be a first step toward effective management of global information technology education issues.

Appendix

This appendix contains course descriptions for undergraduate and graduate IS programs offered by the business school of a typical US university. Note that all the courses are required to be taken by the students. Also, proposed model curricula from ACM and DPMA (which are included in the Tables in the main body of the chapter) are reproduced again for ease of reference.

Course Descriptions
Undergraduate IS program

1. **Business Application Programming**. (3 credit hours)
   Basic COBOL and programing skills using illustrative examples, exercises, and topics that emphasize applications in commercial data processing.

2. **Information System Concepts and Techniques** (3 credit

hours)
Introduction to various concepts and techniques of information systems with application to solving managerial problems.
Topics covered include information flows, application of computer-based information systems, managerial decision making, and mutual influence of organizations and information
systems.

3. **Business Systems Analysis and Design** (3 credit hours)
Various systems analysis and design concepts and techniques, including the key steps in the systems-design and
development cycle. Emphasizes the consideration of practical
applications within the business environment.

4. **Database: Structures and Management** (3 credit hours)
Logical and physical organization of data. Data description,
command, and interrogation languages. Examines function
of databases in information systems.

5. **Information Systems Management** (3 credit hours)
Equipment selection, equipment acquisition, computer operations management, project management, computer personnel management, financial control, systems security and
control, and the relationship of the information systems
function to an organization.

6. **Business Data Communications** (3 credit hours)
Concepts and problem of transmitting, communicating, and
managing business data needs through the use of computer-
based telecommunication systems. Includes applications of
integrated and distributed systems to problems in various
functional areas of business.

7. **Problems in Information Systems** (3 credit hours)
An integration of various information systems principles,
theories, and techniques for implementing information systems in organizations, including strategic issues. Includes
lectures, tours, readings, cases, and the completion of a
major individual project.

Course Descriptions
Graduate IS program

1. **Management Information Systems** (3 credit hours)
   Concepts and techniques of managment information systems including information flows, information needs, and the design, development, and implementation of information systems in organizations. Case studies demonstrate the use of various concepts and techniques in solving practical problems.

2. **Systems Analysis and Design** (3 credit hours)
   Concepts and techiques for the analysis of information needs, specification of system requirements, system development life cycle, and the design, development, and implementation of computer-based information systems in organizations including structured and prototype approaches.

3. **Data-Base Management Systems** (3 credit hours)
   Data structures and the principles of data modeling applied to analysis and design, including an examination of such commercially available data-base models as inverted, hierarchical, CODASYL network, and relational data bases. Discusses issues in the implementation of each model.

4. **Decision Support Systems** (3 credit hours)
   Decision support systems as tools for improving managerial decision making. Strategies for designing decision support systems for various managerial functions. Case studies and commercially available software are used to solve practical problems.

5. **Information Resource Management** (3 credit hours)
   Concepts and techniques of information resource planning and management, including a discussion of the design, development, operation, and evaluation of information resource planning strategies in the context of corporate plans and objectives.

6. **Teleprocessing Networks for Business** (3 credit hours)
   Concepts and techniques of teleprocessing network technology for business applications, including digital network error

detection, network protocols, line controls, system planning considerations, and integrating information processing for business applications.

7. **Information Systems Research and Applications** (3 credit hours)
The application of information system concepts, data-base systems, and related techniques to practical situations selected from public or private sectors, including a discussion

Preliminary ACM 1991 IS curriculum courses

Code	Course Title
IS01	Computer and Programming Concepts
IS02	Data and File Structures
IS03	Systems and Information Concepts in Organization
IS04	Database Management Systems
IS05	Fundamentals of Information Systems
IS06	Computer Communication Networks and Distributed Processing
IS07A	Decision, Executive, and Cooperative Work Support Systems
IS07B	Knowledge-Based and Expert Systems
IS08	Information Systems Development Tools and Techniques
IS09	Information Management
IS10	Information System Projects

Preliminary DPMA 1991 IS curriculum courses

Code	Course Title
CIS-01	Fundamental Concepts of Information and Computer Technology
CIS-02	IS Concepts
CIS-03	Computer Concepts
CIS-04	Application Development
CIS-05	Application Design and Implementation
CIS-06	Systems Development 1 (Single User Systems)
CIS-07	Systems Development 2 (Multi User Systems)
CIS-08	Systems Project
CIS-09	Management of IS

Electives

Code	Course Title
CE-01	IS Professionalism and Ethics
CE-02	Information Center Concepts and Management
CE-03	Audit and Security Management
CE-04	Telecommnications
CE-05	Distributed Processing
CE-06	Implementation of PC Network Systems

CE-07   Office Automation Systems
CE-08   Group Decision Support/Electronic Meeting/Executive
        Support Systems
CE-09   Decision Support/Expert/Neural Net Systems
CE-10   Software Engineering
CE-11   Alternative Analysis and Design methodologies
CE-12   Computer Graphics
CE-13   Systems Simulation
CE-14   Software and Hardware Architecture
CE-15   Advanced Database concepts
CE-16   Human-Computer Interaction

---

of implementation strategies of   these concepts and techniques. Requires the completion of a major research project. Normally taken during student's last semester.

REFERENCES

ACM (1968). Recommendations for the undergraduate program in computer science Curriculum Commitee on Computer Science Curriculum 68. *Communications of the ACM, 11*(3):151-197.

ACM (1979). Recommendations for the undergraduate program in computer science. *Communications of the ACM, 22*(3):147-166.

ACM (1991). *Computing Curricula.* ACM, New York.

Adams, C. R. and Song, J. H. (1989).   Integrating decision technologies: Implication for a management curriculum. *MIS Quarterly, 13*:199-209.

Anonymous (1990). ISM interview...Hugh J. Watson on the status of and business's role in IS education. *Journal of Information System Management,* 7:87-91.

Burn, K. J. (1989). Restructuring school and curriculum for a global, technological society. *NASSP Bulletin, 73*:29-36.

Cardinali, R. (1988). Business school graduates-Do they meet the needs of MIS professionals? *Words, 16*:33-35.

Cheney, P. H. and Lyons, N. R. (1980). Information systems skill requirements: a survey. *MIS Quarterly,* pages 35-43.

CSAB (1987). Criteria for Accrediting Programs in Computer Science in the United States. Computing Sciences   Accreditation Board, ACM, New York.

Deans, P., Karwan, K., Goslar, M., Ricks, D., and Toyne, B. (1991). Identification of key international information systems issues in U.S. based multinational corporations. *Journal of Management Information Systems,* 7(4):1-24.

DPMA (1990). Information Systems: The DPMA Model for a Four Year Undergraduate Degree - Draft. Data Processing Management Association, 505 Busse Highway, Park Ridge, IL 60068.

Eliot, L. B. (1991). The top ten issues in information systems. *Decision Line, 22.* Decision Sciences Institute, Atlanta, Georgia, USA.

Fielding G. D. (1989). Improving curriculum and assessment through a school-university partnership. *NASSP Bulletin, 35:*63-74.

Freedman, D. H. (1986). Harvard MBAs could be hazardous to IS managers. *Infosystems, 33:*26-28.

Gibbs, N. and Tucker, A. (1986). Model curriculum for a liberal arts degree in computer science. *Communications of the ACM,* 9(3):202-210.

Gordon, C. L., Necco, C. R., and Tsai, N. (1986). Education and training for software development personnel. *Interface,* pages 29-33.

Gries, D. (1991). Teaching calculation and discrimination: A more effective curriculum. *Communications of the ACM,* 34(3):44-55.

Gupta, J. and Seeborg, I. (1989). The graduate MIS course in the schools and college of business. *Journal of Management Information Systems, 5*(4):125-136.

Kraemer, K. L., Bergin, T., Bretschneider, S., Duncan, G., Foss, T., Gorr, W., Rubin, B., Wish, N. B., and Northup, A. (1986). Curriculum recommendations for public management education in computing. *Public Administration Review, 46:*595-602.

Lindmeyer, R. C. (1987). Making IE student field projects work for everyone's benefit. *Industrial Engineering, 19:*48-56.

McLeod, R. (1985). The undergraduate MIS course in AACSB schools. *Journal of Management Information Systems, 2*(2):73-85.

Miner, J. B. (1980). *Theories of Organizational Behavior.* Macmillan, New York.

Mulder, M. and Dalphin, J. (1984). Computer science program requirements and accreditation-an interim report of the ACM/IEEE computer society joint task force. *Communications of the ACM, 27*(4):330-335.

Raths, D. (1991). Software upgrades are more complex than ever. *InfoWorld,* 13(39):S62-S64.

Rifkin, G. (1988). The schooling of MIS: Are you meeting the needs? *Computerworld,* 22:61-65,67-70.

Ruiz, J. and VanderMeer, S. (1989). Internships: high returns on low investments. *Public Management, 71:*16-17.

Tamir, P. (1985). *The Role of Evaluators in Curriculum Development.* Croom Helm,

Australia.

Taylor, M. S. (1988). Effects of college internships on individual participants. *Journal of Applied Psychology*, 73:393-401.

Tosi, H. L., Rizzo, J. R., and Carroll, S. J. (1986). *Managing Organizational Behavior.* Pitman Publishing Inc., Marshfield, Ma.

Tucker, A. B. et al. (1991). Computing curricula: A summary of the ACM/IEEE-CS joint curriculum task force report. *Communications of the ACM, 34*(6):69-84.

UCLA (1990a). MoIS Summary Report. UCLA Information Systems Research Program, Anderson Graduate School of Management, Available in May 1990.

UCLA (1990b). MoIS Syllabus Book. UCLA Information Systems Research Program, Anderson Graduate School of Management, Available in February 1990.

Yaffe, J. (1989). MIS education: A 20th century disaster. *Journal of Systems Management, 40*:10-13.

5 Globalization of Information Technology: Here to Stay or a Passing Fad?

Tor J. Larsen
Norwegian School of Management

At the Norwegian School of Management, near Oslo, we are rethinking the scope of our undergraduate and graduate programs for 1992. Internationalization of business has been singled out as a critical element to be incorporated into every relevant course. The chosen philosophy is to integrate internationalization into traditional courses.

The introduction of the issue of globalization of information technology invited us to rethink not only course content, but also the basic premises of our Management Information Systems (MIS) education program. We began by examining who we were educating and for what purpose. Were we educating application specialists, system development specialists, or line managers (as users and custodians of information systems)? We concluded that the mission of a business school is to educate (future) managers.

Information technology represents a formal means of communication, which is a major part of a manager's work. The concept of formal communication is complex, since it requires the integration of organizational, group, and individual systems that also span organizational boundaries. External (to the organization) communication may introduce the need for global systems. Managers need to understand what may be communicated for-

*mally and the innovative processes that may need to be created
to meet information needs.*

*MIS programs on the undergraduate level should address
the needs within the organization and expand to the international
scene. The graduate level should introduce more flexibility. The
globalization of information technology must be integrated with
other MIS issues.*

The use of information technology has increased sharply
over the last decade. Information technology is now regarded as
a necessity for conducting business and as a vehicle for creating
strategic business advantage (Keen, 1991; Keen, 1988). A
natural consequence of this development is the need to update
our education of future managers to increase their ability to
effectively and efficiently create and use information technology
in the global business setting.

Throughout the forty-year evolution of information technology, we have seen a plethora of concepts hit the headlines only
to be returned to the grab bag of concepts and issues: in the 60s
hardware, software, and programming were important topics; in
the 70s systems development, user participation, and decision
support systems drew our attention; and in the 80s we struggled
with end-user computing, strategic use of information systems,
telecommunications, and expert systems.

We may wonder whether the concept of globalization will
suffer the same fate. That is, in the long run, will globalization
require special attention in its own right within our Management
Information Systems (MIS) educational programs? To answer
this question, we at the Norwegian School of Management looked
at the globalization of information technology in conjunction
with other critical issues of MIS. This required a basic analysis
of what is needed within our curricula and how that material
could be delivered. The following material highlights the principal issues that were considered in the fundamental reorganization of the MIS education at the Norwegian School of Management.

BACKGROUND

Norway is a country with a population of a little more than
four million people. We export approximately 50% of our gross
national product. Therefore, we are highly dependent upon

international trade. In many ways, knowledge is a critical factor for maintaining our competitive stand in international markets. Business education in Norway is responsible for educating future managers to assist us in this process.

Public and private institutions offer MIS education on the university level. In Norway, there is no accrediting organization with the mandate of securing a minimum common platform. The institutions are free to choose their own focus. Consequently, there is no systematic curriculum development trend among them.

The Norwegian School of Management, situated near Oslo, is a private business school. Approximately 85 percent of our gross income comes from student fees and research funds. Fifteen percent is governmental support. At present, the Norwegian School of Management is undertaking a major revision of its educational programs. Two events initiated the drive for change. First, business is becoming increasingly internationalized. The implementation of the common market of the European Economic Community in 1993 has highlighted the need for synchronization and adaptation. Second, a new dean took office at the Norwegian School of Management in 1989. He was elected on a program highlighting internationalization and strategy as two critical elements in all future research and educational efforts.

Therefore, internationalization is at the forefront of all our efforts. Globalization will be integrated into every relevant aspect of business education. Not only has this dimension become the responsibility of every faculty member, the dean's office has taken on a particular responsibility in acting as a discussion partner with faculty members to ensure quality implementation of subject matter and pedagogical form. The new strategy has so far lead to the introduction of an executive Master of Business Administration and a Master of Science program in which students may specialize in European Management, International Shipping, and Energy Management. In the Fall of 1992, a revised four-year, full-time, undergraduate and graduate program will be implemented.

To carry through these changes, the business school has a staff of approximately 70 academicians. Faculty members received their degrees from many countries, with the largest number holding degrees from Norway, the United States of America, and Great Britain. Faculty participate regularly in international conferences, publish in leading international journals, and work in other countries as visiting professors.

Regarding Management Information Systems, we have, over the last five years, experienced waning interest among students, faculty, and the administration for the traditional undergraduate course work emphasis on computer use and systems development. On the graduate level, the number of students attending specialized courses dropped catastrophically, down to the level where the future need for indepth studies was being seriously questioned.

Some MIS faculty sought comfort in the view that the decrease in interest is an international trend and, therefore, unavoidable. This might be true. The consequence of this view might easily be demise of separate MIS courses. For us, the moment of truth was the revision of our undergraduate program. We had to convince our dean, administration, and colleagues that there will be a continuing business need for MIS. We understood the role of information technology in the internationalization of business to be part of the answer. However, we soon came to realize that we needed to address other fundamental issues, such as: What is the focus of MIS education, and, How can information technology be used to integrate organizational and individual roles.

The remainder of the chapter explains our basic thinking and our solutions. The new form and content of our MIS undergraduate and graduate program has been accepted and is under implementation.

BASIC PREMISES, SOLUTIONS, AND RECOMMENDATIONS

The section contains two parts. The first subsection presents the basic issues, controversies, and problems we evaluated to determine our MIS curriculum. In the second subsection, we present our solution for the undergraduate program and our recommendations for graduate education.

Issues, Controversies, and Problems

Knowing where to start often puts you halfway to success. We began by considering three basic dimensions. First, we needed to clarify the market for our educational efforts. Second, we needed to answer the question: what are the theoretical foundations of MIS. Third, we needed to clarify whether what we claimed to be our field within business administration was really a uniform phenomenon within organizational settings.

When we returned to the foundations of what we thought we should be doing in our educational efforts, we kept in mind John Naisbitt's words on the evolution of information technology (1984, p. 11):

> New information technologies will at first be applied to old industrial tasks, then, gradually, give birth to new activities, processes, and products.

This principle also applies to education.

When we began considering how to add the aspect of the globalization of information technology to our existing educational programs we had the opportunity to critically evaluate our platforms. There are two compelling reasons for this. First, the introduction of globalization gave us the opportunity to innovate; we could avoid using old solutions for new challenges. And second, it is our opinion that the globalization of information technology, in most cases, is not a stand-alone issue. Global uses of computer systems will coexist with other information systems used for internal organizational needs or domestic markets. Therefore, we saw the need to evaluate existing internal and domestic usage to get the global picture right and to evaluate the impact on the two because of globalization. For these reasons we took some time to reconsider the fundamentals.

The Market - For Whom Do We Educate

It would seem obvious that the mission of a business schools is to prepare people for careers in business. When we consider what we do in reality, perhaps that statement is no longer so obvious. There is a difference between public and private organizations. The two may not benefit equally from one common program, since they may differ on issues such as:

(1) The way in which income is generated and used:
Private organizations earn their money in the market from customers and are relatively free to spend their resources according to their own considerations. Public organizations

are in many cases allocated resources through a political budget and planning process.

(2) The decision process within the organization:

Private organizations are oriented toward hierarchical decision making. Public organizations may have to include committees composed of representatives from groupings within as well as outside the organization in their decision making processes .

(3) The professional structure:

Private organizations often have a clear division of responsibility between managers and specialists. In public organizations one profession may dominate (for example, medical doctors in public hospitals).

The differences between public and private organizations warrant considerable thought, but it is not the emphasis of our discussion. The following material is related to organizations in the private domain. This does not mean that the arguments forwarded here have no bearing on public sector organizations, but rather that we will not attempt to evaluate what the differences and similarities may be here.

In principle, we may choose between three distinct foci for information technology education. First, we may elect to educate specialists in functional areas, such as marketing, finance, accounting, or production. This alternative would call for indepth studies within one or more of these fields. The objective would be to ensure that students would be competent users and, possibly, creators of data and software. They would also learn about expert systems and decision support systems within their chosen specialization.

The second choice is to design a general program for people who will participate in the process of creating information systems. Programs of this nature will include the elements of computer hardware and software, data structures, electronic communication, programming, systems analysis, and the management of MISs. The focus of this type of program is information rather than technology (as is the case in computer science). It mixes the business view with technological considerations. That is, the program spans the systems life cycle from eliciting information requirements from users to methods and techniques of information analysis and programming. This approach to MIS has dominated the basic education on information technology in undergraduate as well as graduate programs. Also, many specialization programs within Master of Business Administration (MBA) or Master of Science (MSc) studies have adapted this profile and it may be said to color the recommendations of the American Association of Collegiate Schools of Business (AACSB).

Our third choice is to focus on the manager in the line organization (the line is defined as the hierarchy of managers from the Company Executive Officer to the level of manager above the foremen on the job floor). Regarding information technology, managers carry a dual role. They are responsible for the processes needed to develop and run information systems in the organization. In this regard, managers should be knowledgeable about business needs and ways in which information technology may support the business. They must plan for and control the projects and computer usage of their subordinates. The second role managers have is that of the user. Managers may use computers to support their own jobs (for example, determining requirements for the user interface to increase the likelihood of use, deciding what applications may be of help, and deciding how data will be used). Managers also allocate execution of computer tasks among staff, and act as discussion partners in computer-related matters.

Theoretical Foundations

We debated the theoretical foundations of MIS as a stand-alone program within business schools. In research, the often expressed view is that MIS has become a field in its own right because publications build on previous research within MIS rather than on the disciplines of organizational theory, behavioral theory, sociology, or psychology - some of its supporting fields (Culnan & Swanson, 1986; Orlikowski and Baroudi, 1991). Yet even in cases where researchers build on research within MIS, there is no common theme among the multitude of research findings published in the journals. At best, they deal with some dimension of information systems and organizations, groups, individuals, or technology. However, we are hard pressed to identify a common denominator.

The proposition put forward and accepted at the Norwegian School of Management is that what we are dealing with is communication. Communication has been called the glue that holds organizations together (Zmud, Lind, and Young, 1990).

Porter (1990) claimed that communications infrastructure is one of the critical advanced factors that will determine international comparative business advantage in the future. When we take information technology into account, we are talking about formal communication. Fundamentally, computer systems accept, store, manipulate, refine, transmit, and present data. We select data to input and store because we think that they may be of use for somebody at some point in time. We manipulate, refine, and transmit data in an effort to communicate.

The communications paradigm does not impose a straightjacket on the field. It would allow for a multitude of views, just as we find within other academic areas, for example organizational theory (Morgan, 1986; Van de Ven & Joyce, 1981). The communications paradigm allows for all types of communication: oral, pictorial, or traditional written data. The added dimension of information technology is that the communication occurs through an electronic channel with certain functional capabilities and that the communication may be delayed.

Organizations consist of the five interrelated components

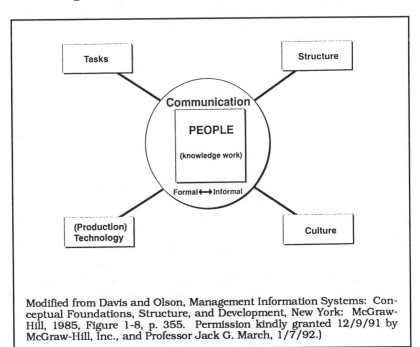

Modified from Davis and Olson, Management Information Systems: Conceptual Foundations, Structure, and Development, New York: McGraw-Hill, 1985, Figure 1-8, p. 355. Permission kindly granted 12/9/91 by McGraw-Hill, Inc., and Professor Jack G. March, 1/7/92.)

Figure 1: Organizational Subsystems

of people, tasks, technology, structure, and culture (Leavitt, 1965; Davis & Olson, 1985). We believe that communication is an additional component necessary for making organizations work. In principle, organizations function through people. Therefore, the model Leavitt forwarded needs elaboration, as shown in Figure 1.

The position taken here is that communication is a phenomenon that occurs among people and that organizational behavior cannot be explained without knowledge of communication patterns. We choose to believe that organizational structure, partitioning of tasks, technological arrangements, and culture are results of how human action or inaction is communicated. Therefore, we disagree with Leavitt's view that, for example, technology and structure directly influence each other. The fundamental difference is the one that academics in the field of systems thinking make between purposeful and purposive systems (Checkland, 1981). Purposeful systems are formed according to the free human will. Purposive systems develop according to nature, or unintentionally. That is why, for example, technology and structure should only be related through people. If the two evolve because of some purposive force, they are beyond human intervention and the need for management is nullified. Of course, it may be that phenomena are purposively related. However, the best way to think about them is to adapt the view that people organize with a purpose in mind, since we then create the basis for shaping our environment according to need.

The are two principal questions we have to ask regarding communication: What is it we want to communicate? and, How should we proceed to ensure that we create the communication systems we need? A long standing slogan within the MIS field says that information systems should deliver the right information to the right person in the right format at the right time at the right cost. Traditionally, we have tried to achieve this is through the elicitation of user requirements (Wetherbe, 1991; Olle et al., 1988). The danger of this approach is that we easily get lost in technical issues related to methods and programming. To counteract the technical dimension, we need to adapt concepts that tie us more strongly to the ultimate function of information systems, that is, that the system delivers data that the receiver understands. An example of an approach of this nature is the concept of service management in marketing. Service manage-

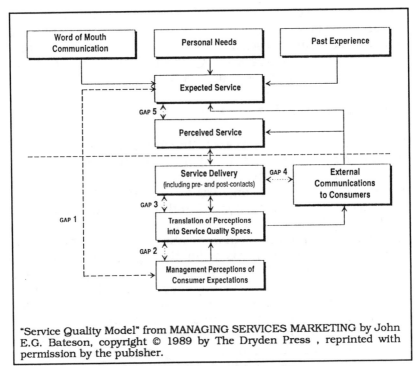

Figure 2: Service Quality Model

ment has risen to the forefront among marketers as a way in which a firm may tie its sales function more strongly to the requirements of its consumers. A typical model within this school of thought is shown in Figure 2.

The benefits of models of this nature are their emphasis on differences in perceptions between those responsible for creating products and the users; gaps that may explain the existence of inferior delivery.

The process of creating the information systems we need is intrinsically a question of innovation. Innovation encompasses the issues of creativity and implementation (Couger, 1990; Schultz & Ginzberg, 1984). Innovation theory also includes the organizational and individual level (Kanter, 1983; Van de Ven, 1986). Regarding information systems, the organizational level includes all activities where the end result is an information system that is used by many (for example, the creation of transaction systems through systems development). The individual level includes issues such as idea generation through change champions (Beath & Ives, 1988) and individual use and development of information support in the context of end-user computing (Nelson, 1988). The organizational and individual level systems are developed and controlled as a totality by means of strategic planning and control (Keen, 1991).

A Taxonomy of Information Systems

The view developed here is that formal communication in organizations occurs through information systems in unique ways. Two dimensions need to be considered to understand how communication works in organizational settings. First, there is an interaction between informal and formal communication. Formal communication does not happen in isolation but in interaction with informal communication. Second, communication occurs on different levels within the organization (levels are defined by the constellation of people). Consequently, we have three levels, that is, the individual, the group, and the organization. Each of the three levels benefit from the specific theories that help us understand the interaction between formal and informal communication.

The foundation of this model requires understanding the relationships on the two dimensions of information and level within the boundaries of a specific organization. Building on that, the concept of interaction among organizations within a relative homogeneous area, such as a nation, are introduced. Finally, the phenomenon of collaboration among organizations on the global scale is added. Surrounding these notions is the concept of management of information systems. And the total formal communication system is based on information technology. Figure 3 summarizes these dimensions.

Simply put, the baseline for our educational efforts is what happens within an organization. When we add the domestic and global aspect, we should at each step look for genuine differences that need to be addressed. This is a totally different approach from starting at the global level and looking backward toward the organization. The main arguments for the inside-out approach are integration and knowledge. Information systems function as a whole. We may say that the quality of information systems is no better than its weakest link. Therefore, if the internal systems do not work, there is little hope that external applications will function in a satisfactory manner. Knowledge

Managerial issues

ORGANIZATION SITUATED ----- ABROAD -----

ORGANIZATION SITUATED ---- DOMESTICALLY ----

----- HOME ORGANIZATION -----

LEVEL	INFORMAL INFORMATION	FORMAL INFORMATION
ORGANIZATION	Communication Innovation Process versus structure, for example: organic versus mechanistic organizational forms	Planning and control systems Transaction systems
GROUP	Communication Innovation Formal and informal groups Group processes	Presentations software Collaborative groups Information systems Group decision support systems
INDIVIDUAL	Innovation Psychology Behavioral theory Knowledge work	End-user computing Decision support systems Executive Information systems

Technical issues

Figure 3: The Taxonomy of Information Systems

about the effective use of information technology must be based on the appropriate application of information technology within the organization. Of course, this does not mean that we may remain ignorant of the additional challenges of moving computer power into the larger environment. Understanding opportunities and possible stumbling blocks have always been prerequisites for successful use of information technology. The conclusion is, simply, that in educational terms it seems more appropriate to start with the internal view. The globalization issue is an important dimension that should be integrated into other elements of information systems. Finally, and most basically, it will be the integrated knowledge about formal communication that constitutes the basis for success. Our thinking has also been influenced by Porter's (1990) view that a strong international stand is based on excellent business performance in the domestic market. Therefore, we argued that the appropriate use of information technology on the global scene builds on the quality of internal information systems.

The Issues of Globalization of Information Technology

The use of information systems on an international scale has resulted in the need to introduce additional themes into our educational programs. The themes range from technical issues (standardization of hardware, software, data, telecommunication equipment, and applications) to people problems (differences in culture, education, religion, and languages). Also, national governments impose challenges through differences in regulations and mandates of legislation to protect their own industries.

The way in which we may systematize the various aspects of globalization is to use the framework in Figure 3 as the baseline. An additional worry in education is the availability of literature about the globalization of information technology. Fortunately, textbooks are forthcoming (for example; Palvia, Palvia, and Zigli (Eds), *Global Issues of Information Technology Management*, Harrisburg: Idea Group Publishing, 1992), as are publications in popular and academic journals, and articles in proceedings from major conferences. Figure 4 shows examples of global use of information technology and illustrations of literature that may be of use.

Managerial issues		Literature reference
LEVEL	FORMAL INFORMATION	
ORGANIZATION	Transaction systems: - Electronic document Interchange - International banking and financial systems Planning and control: - Financial planning and control - Product development and manufacturing	Ives & Jarvenpaa, 1991 Keen, 1991 Keen, 1990 Lee, et al., 1991 Mareschal, et. al., 1991
GROUP	Tele-conferencing	Kraut, et al. 1990 Fulk, et al., 1990
INDIVIDUAL	Electronic mail International negotiations preparations	Zmud, et al., 1990 Rangaswamy et al., 1989
	Technical issues	Numerous articles in: - Business Week - Datamation - Computer World

Figure 4: Examples of Global Use of Information Technology on the Organization, Group, and Individual Level.

The information technology theme has two dimensions. First, we need to understand the prerequisites for communication. Students should know who the major producers of hardware, software, and telecommunication equipment are and what efforts they have made and are making to standardize their products. It is equally important to examine why they do not standardize; that is, the issue of proprietary solutions. We must also spend time on the role of protocols (for example, ISO, X.25, EDIFACT, or X.400), who the major international standardization organizations are, and what they are trying to achieve. The standards the computer manufacturers develop (for example, IBM's SNA under SAA or DEC's NAS) and how these relate to the work of standardization institutions should be an integral part of the curriculum. Legislative efforts, such as the standardization efforts of the European Economical Community for Europe of 1992 (Cecchini, Catinat, & Jacquemin, 1988), need to be included into curriculum material.

The managerial challenge is one of integrating ever more diverse views, participants, and technological considerations into the decision processes. At present, the four most critical issues in regard to globalization of information technology are thought to be (Ives & Jarvenpaa, 1991):

(1) Linking IT and business strategy.
(2) Development of information technology platforms.
(3) International data sharing.
(4) Cultural environment.

We conclude that the globalization of information technology is an area that contains multiple genuine issues, ranging from technological issues to managerial considerations. However, globalization is to a large extent integrated into the information processing that occurs within the firm. In reality, global use of information systems may, in some instances, be developed as an extension of the information systems for the domestic market. We most probably have reciprocal relationships where the nature of the business will decide the relative impact of these areas of use of information technology. What is certain is that the appropriateness of the system will depend upon the degree to which the global, domestic, and internal information systems are integrated.

SOLUTIONS AND RECOMMENDATIONS

Success depends on the quality of the implementation. First, we considered the requirements for the bachelor and graduate level. Second, we determined who should be responsible for the training. Third, we evaluated the life-cycle of knowledge; that is, whether to adopt a pedagogical model that encouraged "learning how to learn for life" or gave immediate technical competence. These considerations formed the background for evaluating how the issue of globalization of information technology was to be introduced into our curricula.

Requirements at the Undergraduate and Graduate Level

Regardless of level, education within MIS is a balancing act among theory instruction, case illustration, student work, and evaluation. In principle, the four elements should develop in parallel to ensure a natural progress. The main differences between undergraduate and graduate programs are the extent of specialization and the degree to which students are responsible for their own education.

The undergraduate program. The objective of an undergraduate program is to ensure that students get a basic education in the central issues of MIS. In this context we have to ensure that future managers understand the issue of formal communication since we cannot guarantee that students will continue to the graduate programs or choose MIS as a part of their portfolio at that level.

A natural sequence in learning is to start with the concrete and use references to the "natural world" as a baseline for abstraction. Although guidelines of this nature cannot be taken literally, it indicates what the chain of MIS issues should be. We start with practical examples of what formal communication means and why it is of importance to us. Next follows instruction of the basic elements of information technology. Students learn about the principal elements of computer hardware, operating systems, data organization, and telecommunications. The next thing to do is to illustrate applications in more depth. In this regard, the most critical element is to help students understand how these various elements are interrelated.

Many MIS programs at the undergraduate level include computer literacy training. The Norwegian School of Management is of the opinion that this is a totally inappropriate use of our resources. Learning how to use word processing programs, spreadsheet packages, and the like, is a vocational skill. This type of training is best undertaken in short intensive courses administered prior to or in the first few weeks of the undergraduate program. The existence of this type of training as part of our regular education is a waste of time, at best, and a red herring, at worst. The more vocational training is included into our curriculum, the less the communication imperative is understood among our own staff, our colleagues in other faculties, and university administrators. In addition, an increasing number of students are computer literate when they enter the undergraduate program. For this reason alone it would make more sense to require completion of computer literacy crash courses only for those who lack the experience.

Following the material on communication and information technology, we introduce the issues of what information systems are supposed to deliver and how to create them. The focus here is on service management, information requirements elicitation, and innovation.

The third and final theme consists of managerial considerations. We end on this note because managerial issues cannot be meaningfully discussed until students have a working knowledge of the information technology issues and are able to generate workable ideas. Students become aware of the challenges to management of the line organization, to computer experts, and the nature of interactions between the two.

The undergraduate program needs a very strict structure. It may be well served by traditional mass lectures to present theories and examples, but the critical element is the volume and quality of student assignments. Assignments should be an integral part of the entire program. The nature of the assignments should be twofold: they should act as vehicles to ensure that students understand basic theoretical issues; and equally important, some assignments should be of the nature of cases where the students analyze practical business questions. The cases must not be overly simplistic. That is, they should not focus on problems that require limited analyses based on computer tools. For example, in parallel to lectures on communication and information technology, a case study might require the student to evaluate a complex business situation and develop a framework for a computer infrastructure.

The graduate program. In many business schools the program of MIS at the graduate level is a replication of the course in the undergraduate program. Often, the major difference is only that the readings package used for the graduate students is three times as thick as the one used for undergraduates.

The typical reason for this state of affairs is that the students have bachelor degrees in areas other than business. Evidently, there is little we can do about this; however, it is problematic. A graduate program should provide students with the opportunity to take more responsibility for their own education. The best way to achieve this objective, we believe, is to run graduate courses as seminars. A seminar is a pedagogical form where the instructor determines the basic literature but students do the work. Consequently, there is very little traditional lecture. The classroom should be a place for interaction, where students present the result of their work and where critical issues are debated. In fact, turning the graduate level education around to this form may well be a critical success factor in the process of creating knowledge workers rather than copy-cats out of our student body.

Apart from the pedagogical structure, basic knowledge is a prerequisite for success in adapting the seminar form. The class cannot have meaningful discussions if the instructor regularly has to get to the blackboard to explain basic information.

The Placement of the MIS Education

Computers are used everywhere for all sorts of purposes. The question is whether MIS should include education on how computers should be used in finance, marketing, or the other disciplines within business schools. We think that the issue may be settled by thinking of information technology as business support.

Most organizations are in the business of producing and selling products other than computers. In this context, computers are regarded as a support tools, albeit critical ones. If we believe this - and make ourselves consciously aware of the criticism that information systems professionals have exhibited a technical rather than business orientation - it would follow that other disciplines should be made responsible for determining how computers are used within their field. This is nothing more than capitalizing on a well established view that as much as possible of the ingredients needed to conduct business should be integrated into the line organization rather than be put in staff units.

For this reason financial applications are best taught in finance, marketing applications in marketing, etc. If this is not the case, MIS faculty should initiate the transfer of responsibility for these application-oriented uses of computers from MIS to their logical department. Many MIS faculty feel threatened by this prospect, fearing that nothing will be left for MIS. We would suggest that if all there is to MIS is the use of computer technology in other areas, then business schools might just as well do without us. If this were the case, the best contribution we could give our business schools would be our own demise. It would, in any case, just be a matter of time.

However, it is precisely the adoption of the communications paradigm (of which MIS is the natural custodian for the common interest of all) that justifies our existence. The adoption of this umbrella rids MIS of computer applications training, and the removal of this type of training from MIS courses frees time that may be used for issues that are critical to the organizations we serve. In conclusion, the strategy of funding MIS on the basis of computer application use in other fields is not proper. The focus for this part of MIS is distribution rather than centralization.

Lifelong Learning

One thing is certain: any specific computer technique we teach to students becomes obsolete within a few years. Consequently, if an educational program consists largely of tool training, its value is a short term one. Yet, businesses very often require that prospective employees have a working knowledge that can be utilized immediately upon employment.

We put forward the argument that requirements of this nature are short-sighted. First, focusing on techniques causes the overall picture to suffer. Second, businesses will have to provide tool training sooner or later in any case. In principle, we think that the objective of business schools is to educate managers (though of course, we may give our students the opportunity of specializing within areas).

However, educating systems analysts - or even more problematic, programmers - can hardly be said to represent training of managers. The dilemma for MIS is that while training students in specialization programs as systems analysts has a clear career identification, the education of managers that understand integrated information technology has not. Although this type of competence is highly appropriate and asked for, students and business are very slow to accept it.

Today's emphasis on the education of systems analysts within MIS was, from a historical perspective, a natural evolution from the focus of programming in the early days of our field, and it was a career for which nobody else had educational programs. However, the time has come to realize that we need to educate line managers to understand the opportunities and requirements of integrated information technology. This may create an extended platform for people who earlier saw a career in organizational development or similar positions. Understanding how to develop and use information technology is very much a question of organizational and individual development. The marriage between information technology and organizational development should make for an interesting and highly desirable mix of knowledge.

Making the education of managers our goal may save us from the limitations of vocational training, however, this shift of focus does not guarantee lifelong learning if the new program becomes a stew of relevant but loosely connected elements. In our opinion, the basis for lifelong learning, in addition to relevant knowledge, is problem solving. The way in which this element is integrated into our MIS curricula may vary between undergraduate and graduate programs.

In the undergraduate program students should have training in solving practical problems in context. One way in which this may be done is to ensure that students can use a method that integrates business needs with technological possibilities. A method of this nature may contain elements such as:

(1) business situation analysis
(2) critical success factors for the market and organizational planning and control
(3) description of applications that will support (2)

(4) technological scenarios for (2) and (3)
(5) evaluation of the quality of present applications and hardware/software in light of (2), (3), and (4)
(6) identification of projects that must be initiated to develop new applications or substitute old ones
(7) a budget for an investment period of the next five years where economical constraints are taken into consideration

Some would argue that this is too much for undergraduates. In our experience it is not. The key to success is that the faculty believe it is doable, that we take the time and effort to develop good cases, and that we require students to work on problems like these.

In addition we must ensure that undergraduates have an appreciation for the literature. It does not suffice to run courses based on a single textbook. Readings packages must also be put together for areas missing in the textbook or for areas in which an indepth knowledge is necessary. Examples of the latter would be the issue of globalization, managerial use of information technology, or the centralization versus decentralization of EDP departments. The effective way to ensure that students acquire this knowledge is to have them write a paper on the subject matter using the literature.

On the graduate level we think that the scientific approach to problem solving is the appropriate method. That is, graduate students should be well acquainted with central theories of MIS, the concept of hypotheses, and how to operationalize variables, collect, and analyze data. It is disconcerting to see how afraid many business schools are of science. However, we can see no conflict between science and practical life. We would strongly advocate that there is nothing as practical as applied research.

We must hasten to say that MIS programs at the graduate level may also contain technological matter and other material. We simply underpin the need for the strong presence of the elements that foster lifelong learning. And of course the material whether of a scientific or practical nature, should have a managerial orientation.

Globalization in Our Curricula

MIS is not the only area where academicians turn to the issue of globalization. For example, the Strategic Management Journal as recently as the Summer of 1991 ran a special issue on global strategy (Bartlett and Ghoshal, 1991).

The inclusion of the globalization angle may vary at the undergraduate and graduate level. At the undergraduate level, we think that the principle of integration should be followed throughout. This is another example of integrating into the line organization as much as possible, rather than creating staff units.

The issues of globalization should be integrated into their natural frame of reference. This means that when we, at the initiation of our courses, present examples of the use of formal communication, global applications are one ingredient. We cannot avoid talking about international issues when we discuss who the vendors of computer equipment are, or for that matter, telecommunications. Consequently, most issues within our undergraduate curriculum will have a natural sequence of development from definition of basic terminology, organizational use, the domestic scene, and globalization.

The place where the undergraduate program should capitalize on globalization as a specific issue is under the heading of management. The objective would be to understand the threads that may impact the global issue. Internationalization of information technology is a good opportunity to illustrate the need for a business-to-technology coupling and the demand for an integrated approach to MIS.

The degree of freedom is greater at the graduate level. In cases where the business school runs one course on MIS or implements a general managerial oriented specialization, we think that the integrative approach should be applied. The graduate level also invites the opportunity for the implementation of specialization. MIS may be invited to offer courses under specializations in other topic areas, either as an obligatory or as an elective course. Obviously, the permutations here are numerous. Courses offered may be technical (examples of expert systems or decision support systems) managerial, or a mix of these.

Specialization within MIS at the graduate level again

contains possible numerous variations. If we keep our focus on educating managers, examples of courses for the globalization of information technology include:

(1) The alignment of global business with information technology
(2) Information resources management from the global perspective
(3) Network organizations and service management
(4) The impact of legislation, culture, and education on the global use of information technology

A means for increased student awareness of differences among nations is to require that students spend some time studying abroad or do their thesis in firms operating internationally. Collaboration with universities abroad requires, in most cases, that the business school see internationalization as important enough to establish contacts and implement rules for the transfer of credits for courses taken. Most probably, such arrangements would apply to the business school in general and not to MIS specifically. These concerns would also apply to the thesis.

Naturally, it would be just as appropriate to send faculty abroad to other universities or have them conduct research in multinational or international firms. There is a vast difference between doing it yourself and reading about it. Anyone who has tried to learn another language or adapt to another culture has gained a much richer insight into the kinds of problems internationalization imposes on us. Globalization is a cultural phenomenon.

The Structure of Our Educational Programs

Programs that are run at the Norwegian School of Management main campus will, from the Fall of 1992 follow a three quarters per year model. Students who have little or no experience with computers are required to take a crash course before the start of the first quarter in the first year of study. Additionally, computers are used extensively in other disciplines and students are required to purchase their own PC at the start of the program.

The undergraduate level course structure. Our four year program, leading to the degree of Master of Management, is divided into two parts: the undergraduate program (three years) and the graduate program (one year). Students do not earn a degree on completion of the first three years but must finish four years of study. MIS at the undergraduate level is offered at the second year of the program and consists of three consecutive courses. The reason for the placement of MIS in the second year is that students have been exposed to basic issues in mathematics, statistics, accounting, and organizational and behavioral theory in their first year of study. The details of the curriculum are still under development. The overall model for the MIS courses is shown in Figure 5.

The structure of the graduate program. We offer a specialization at the graduate level of the four-year program. The approach taken here is to combine the two discipline areas of information technology and logistics. The principal reason for the combination of the two areas is that information and logistics are two of the main elements that bind the organization together internally and externally. We have suggested three obligatory and a set of elective courses. Their principal focus and content are shown in Figure 6. In some courses the issue of globalization is integrated into the material. In other instances, such as network organizations, globalization is the core element.

Finally, we also offer two elective MIS seminars as part of our executive MBA program. The first seminar is on the issue of service management and information technology. The focus of the second seminar is information resource management. Since a Master of Business Administration is an international degree, the instruction takes place in English. We have used the integrated approach to the globalization of information technology here also.

We are currently in the initial stages of discussing the need for a specialization in Strategic Management and Formal Communications for our MSc program. Globalization will be one of the major themes here. Apart from the fact that the language of the specialization will be English, it is too early to say exactly what the structure will be like.

We are of the opinion that the basic principles we have discussed for the development of undergraduate as well as graduate programs are of a general nature and not specific to Norwegian needs or the special interests of the faculty at the Norwegian School of Management. The line management focus and the integration of globalization issues into formal communi-

COURSE 1: BASIC FOUNDATIONS

Communication:
- Why is formal communications important?
- Definitions of communication, information, and data.
- Theories of formal communication on the:
  - Organizational level
  - Group level
  - Individual level

Technology:
- Hardware
- Operational software
- Data and data storage
- Electronic communication

Applications:
- Organizational level
- Group level
- Individual level

COURSE 2: INNOVATION AND IT

Theoretical Foundations:
- Service management
- Innovation

Innovation on the Individual Level:
- End-user computing
- Individual needs and collective requirements

Innovation on the Organizational Level:
- Systems development
- Project administration

Strategic Planning and Control:
- A phase model of strategic planning
- Strategic planning of IT and strategic planning in other business areas
- Building platforms to support organizational and individual innovation

COURSE 3: INFORMATION RESOURCE MANAGEMENT

Management, Planning, and Control:
- Managing the individual level in the line-organization
- The management of the EDP-department
- Strategic management

Globalization of IT:
- The use of IT in a global context on the levels of:
  - Organization
  - Group
  - Individual
- Managerial issues regarding the globalization of IT

Future Trends:
- Expected technological development
- The strategic possibilities, where are they?
- The future challenge facing managers

Figure 5: The MIS Curriculum at the Undergraduate Level.

OBLIGATORY COURSES:

Strategic logistics:
- Customer service and logistics strategies
- Partnerships with vendors and distributors
- Production and logistics
- Organization of logistics

Networks as organizational design:
- Principles of network organizations
- Network organization analysis
- Task differentiation and coordination of networks
- The management of network organizations

Service management and quality control:
- Service and total quality
- Information technology and quality control
- Market segmentation
- Internal and external communication
- Cultural aspects and innovation management

ELECTIVE COURSES:

Information systems innovation and organizational entrepreneurship:
- The individual's role in innovative processes
- Organizational evaluation of new innovations
- Implementation considerations
- The management of innovations

Business development and strategic information system:
- Information technology development trends
- Inter-organizational systems and competition
- Information technology strategy development
- Integration of information technology
- Governmental regulations

Companies unlimited - business telematics:
- Electronic communications technology
- Electronic data interchange, theories and practice
- Governmental policies regarding electronic communications

Executive information system (EIS):
- Executive communication and decision behavior
- Informal versus formal communication and decision making
- Implementation and continuous development of EIS

Purchasing management:
- Objectives and management of purchasing
- Collaboration with vendors
- Purchasing negotiations and strategies for contract development

Transport and physical distribution:
- Transports and governmental regulation and deregulation
- Carriers
- Distribution systems
- Strategic alliances and third party contracts
- International distribution

Figure 6: The MIS Curriculum at the Graduate Level

cation, service management, innovation, and management of information technology is a platform that would benefit innovation of the MIS curriculum in most business schools.

On the undergraduate level, the underlying structure shown in Figures 3 and 4 and the principal topics exhibited in Figure 5 are generally valid. Implementation may vary among business schools. Programs may emphasize some aspects more than others. Often, MIS has only one course on the undergraduate level. Also, the level of information technology diffusion and expertise may be quite different from nation to nation. The recommendations put forward in this chapter mirror the needs of a highly industrialized nation. We are of the opinion that our principles apply to most cases where a managerial focus is adopted. Consequently, if fragmented, the vision may be lost. But we hasten to add that the details regarding basic foundations, innovation, and management must take into account specific interests of the faculty, the general level of managerial experience, the use of technology in the local society, and the need for globalization. History has taught us that we cannot transplant a complex structure from one place to another. Local reformulation and ownership are required to achieve success.

We are of the opinion that a common graduate course for students who do not have a MIS background may benefit from adapting the principles put forward for undergraduate education. We are much more uncertain about the general applicability of our solutions for specialization. Business schools develop focus to position themselves in the educational market and programs may mirror the research interest of their faculty. At present, logistics and information technology are two areas in which Norwegian industry needs to perform better. However, we could think of many other marriages (for example; marketing and information technology, strategy and information technology, or global use of information technology). Our solution is as much a result of organizational facts and politics as rational selection.

FUTURE CONSIDERATIONS

One thing is certain: the use of information technology will continue to increase in all areas of business. In our opinion, the most important consequence of this is an increased need for integration. Our challenge is to educate line managers who understand the coupling between business and information technology support that will determine the structure of the technical integration. The fundamental problem we have is that many managers still have a lukewarm attitude toward MIS. We believe the main reasons for this is that we have oversold information technology capabilities. In the 60s we advocated that the capabilities of computers were almost limitless. Since then we have tried to save the business world by virtue of decision support systems, office automation, end-user computing, and strategic use of information technology. The relationship between the true capabilities of computers and managers' interpretations of its relevance is illustrated in Figure 7.

Line management initially overestimated what computers could do. As a consequence, line management perceptions became pessimistic. Although the line management has become increasingly aware of what computers can do, their perceptions have never quite caught up with actual potential. One reason is that we have oversold computer functionality. Another reason is that the field has been moving so fast that line management cannot keep abreast of the development.

We would argue that it is the combined effect of computer use in all its facets that, finally, will bring line management into synchronization with the actual potential of information technology. In this regard, the globalization of information technology can be used as one vehicle for convincing line management of the importance of information technology. What we, in the capacity as experts, need to do is to sell our field by sober example of the benefits and loss-of-opportunity that may occur because of information technology.

However, information technology is not only an issue of isolated gains and losses. Information technology will be a prerequisite for planning and control of markets, production, finance, and human resources. Organizations cannot hope to handle the complexity and diversity of information needed to run businesses in the time available for decision making unless line management proactively engages themselves as custodians of idea generation and the use of information technology. Most line managers will, in the process, find that they also have to become users of computers.

It is the responsibility of the MIS profession to lay the foundation for line managers who exhibit this orientation. We do this by presenting a managerial education that incorporates the major elements of MIS, with globalization as an integral part.

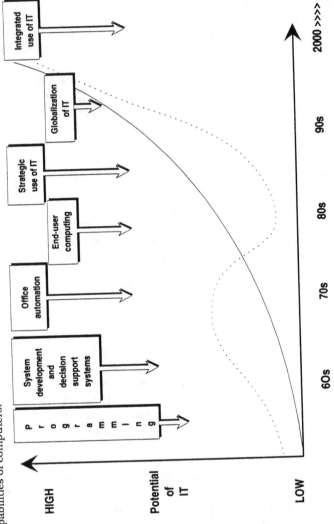

Notes:
Thick line indicates the evolution of computer capabilities.
Dotted line indicates the perception line management has
of the capabilities of computers.

Figure 7: The Relationship Between the Capabilities of Computers and Line-Management Perceptions

CONCLUSION

The introduction of globalization into our MIS programs is a good example of the increasing complexity of our field. We cannot simply expand our present curricula. We need to make some tough and hard choices to bring curriculum development into sharper focus. Otherwise, we risk the demise of MIS as a self-defined unit within our business schools and we will see our colleagues in other areas grab the leftovers.

At the Norwegian School of Management, the challenge has been to rethink the basic premises for MIS. The new base for MIS has two major components. First, we have defined the line manager as our customer. Line management has, traditionally, carried the responsibility for innovation, planning, and control regarding product, production processes, money, and people. In many cases, the active managerial responsibility for the development and use of information technology has been the missing ingredient. We need to convince line managers of the need to incorporate formal communication as a critical factor. This may be achieved by indicating the benefits to be derived from integrating information technology into their areas of responsibility. Simultaneously, we need to help line managers see the negative effects of avoiding information technology.

Second, we have developed an integrated approach to help line management see the interaction among the organizational, group, and individual levels within as well as among organizations. Integration, with information becoming available to organizational members, is a prerequisite for harvesting the true benefits of information technology. Perhaps most important of all, the integrated approach enables effective time management. Time from opportunity or problem definition to implemented solution becomes increasingly shorter. Information technology may support managers in every step of this problem-solving process. We also know that timely supplies and delivery of finished goods cannot occur without efficient use of information technology.

We need to redefine our MIS education to ensure that future, and present, managers understand these interrelated aspects of information technology. At the closure of our courses we may ask students the simple question of the degree to which they think the development and use of information technology is part of their responsibility. A low rating would imply that we, as academicians, still have much work to do.

APPENDIX

Currently Used Undergraduate and Graduate Programs

Four year, full-time program in business administration:

Undergraduate program, obligatory courses:
(1) Basic Foundations:
Definitions of formal communication, information, and data. Hardware, operating systems, data and data storage, electronic communication. Examples of applications on the organization, group, and individual level.
(2) Innovation and Information Technology:
Theories of service management and innovation. Innovation on the individual and organizational level. Strategic planning and control.
(3) Information Resource Management:
Line management planning and control. Management and the globalization of information technology. Future trends.

Graduate program, title: Quality and productivity in management processes
Obligatory Courses:
(4) Strategic logistics:
Customer service and logistics strategies.
Partnerships with vendors and distributors.
Production and logistics. Organization of logistics.
(5) Networks as organizational design:
Principles of network organizations. Network organization analysis. Task differentiation and coordination of networks. The management of network organizations
(6) Service management and quality control:
Service and total quality. Information technology and quality control. Market segmentation. Internal and external communication. Cultural aspects and innovation management.

ELECTIVE COURSES
(7) Information systems innovation and organizational entrepreneurship: The individual's role in innovative processes. Organizational evaluation of new

innovations. Implementation considerations.
The management of innovations.

(8) Business development and strategic information systems:
Information technology development trends.
Interorganizational systems and competition. Information technology strategy development. Integration of information technology. Governmental regulations.

(9) Companies unlimited - business telematics:
Electronic communications technology.
Electronic data interchange, theories and practice.
Governmental policies regarding electronic communications.

(10) Executive information systems (EIS):
Executive communication and decision behaviors. Informal versus formal communication and decision making.
Information technology support of managers.
Implementation and continuous development of EIS

(11) Purchasing management:
Objectives and management of purchasing. Collaboration with vendors. Purchasing negotiations and strategies for contract development.

(12) Transport and physical distribution:
Transports and governmental regulation and deregulation.
Carriers. Distribution systems. Strategic alliances and third party contracts. International distribution.

Executive Master of Business Administration:
Elective courses (based on other courses, but with more emphasis on case studies):
(13) Information Resource Management
(14) Service Management in the Field of Information Technology

REFERENCES

Bartlett, Christopher A. and Ghoshal, Sumantra (Eds). (1991). Global Strategy (special issue). *Strategic Management Journal, 12*(Summer 1991).

Beath, C. M. & Ives, B. (1988). The Information Technology Champion: Aiding and Abetting, Care and Feeding. *Proceedings from the 22. Hawaii International Conference on Systems Sciences.*

Cecchini, P., Catinat, M. & Jacquemin, A. (1988). *The European Challenge 1992 - the Benefits of a Single Market.* England: Gower.

Checkland, P. B. (1981). *Systems Thinking, Systems Practice.* England: John Wiley & Sons.

154 Larsen

Couger, J. D. (1990). Ensuring Creative Approaches in Information System Design. *Managerial and Decision Economics, 11*, 281-295.

Culnan, M. J. & Swanson, E. B. (1986). Research in Management Information Systems, 1980-1984: Points of Work and Reference. *MIS Quarterly, 10*(3), 289-302.

Davis, G. B. & Olson, M. H. (1985). *Management Information Systems: Conceptual Foundations, Structure, and Development.* New York: McGraw-Hill Book Company.

Fulk, J., Scmitz, J. & Steinfield, C. W. (1990). A Social Influence Model of Technology Use, in Fulk, J. & Steinfield, C. (Eds), *Organizations and Communication Technology*. England: Sage Publications.

Ives, B. & Jarvenpaa, S. L. (1991). Applications of Global Information Technology: Key Issues for Management. *MIS Quarterly, 15*(1), 33-49.

Kanter, R. M. (1983). *The Change Masters: Innovation and Entrepreneurship in the American Corporation.* New York: Touchstone.

Keen, P. G. W. (1991). *Shaping the Future: Business Design Through Information Technology.* Massachusetts: Harvard Business School Press.

Keen, P. G. W. (1990). Telecommunications and Organizational Choice, in Fulk, J. & Steinfield, C. (Eds), *Organizations and Communication Technology*. England: Sage Publications.

Keen, P. G. W. (1988). *Competing in Time: Using Telecommunications for Competitive Advantage.* Massachusetts: Ballinger Publishing Company.

Kraut, R. E., Fish, R. S., Root, R. W. & Chalfonte, B. L. (1990). Informal Communication in Organizations: Form, Function, and Technology, in Oskamp, S. & Spacapan, S. (Eds), *People's Reactions to Technology*. England: Sage Publications.

Leavitt, H. J. (1965). Applying Organizational Change in Industry: Structural, Technological and Humanistic Approaches, in March, J. G. (Ed), *Handbook of Organizations*. Illinois: Rand McNally.

Lee, R. M., Dewitz, S. D. & Chen, K. T. (1991). AI and Global EDI. *Proceedings from the 24. Hawaii International Conference on System Sciences, IV*, 182-191.

Mareschal, B. & Mertens, D. (1991). Financial Analysis of the International Banking Sector: the BANKS Multicriteria Decision Support System. Proceedings of the Decision Sciences Institute, 33-36.

Morgan, G. (1986). Images of Organization. California: Sage Publications, Inc.

Naisbitt, J. (1984). Megatrends: Ten New Directions Transforming Our Lives. New York: Warner Books, Inc.

Nelson, R. R., (Ed), (1989). End-User Computing: Concepts, Issues and Applications. New York: John Wiley & Sons, Inc.

Olle, T. W., Hagelstein, J., MacDonald, I. G., Rolland, C., Sol, H. G., Van Assche, F. J. M., & Verrijn-Stuart, A. A. (1988). *Information Systems Methodologies: A Framework for Understanding.* England: Addison-Wesley Publishing Company.

Orlikowski, W. J. & Baroudi, J. J. (1991). Studying Information Technology in Organizations: Research Approaches and Assumptions. *Information Systems Research,* 2(1), 1-28.

Palvia, Shailendra, Palvia, Prashant, and Zigli, Ronald M. (Eds), *The Global Issues of Information Technology Management,* Pennsylvania: Idea Group Publishing, 1992.

Parasuraman, A., Zeithaml, V. A., & Berry, L. L. (1989). A Conceptual Model of Service Quality and Its Implications for Future Research, in Bateson, J. E. G. (Ed), *Managing Services Marketing.* Illinois: The Dryden Press.

Porter, Michael E. (1990). *The Competitive Advantage of Nations.* New York: The Free Press.

Rangaswamy, A., Eliashberg, J., Burke, R. R. & Wind, J. (1989). Developing Marketing Expert Systems: An Application to International Negotiations. *Journal of Marketing,* 53(October), 24-39.

Schultz, R. L. & Ginzberg, M. J. (1984). *Applications of Management Science, Supplement 1: Management Science Implementation.* Connecticut: JAI Press Inc.

Van de Ven, A. H. (1986). Central Problems in the Management of Innovation. *Management Science,* 32(5), 590-607.

Van de Ven, A. H. & Joyce, W. F. (1981). *Perspectives on Organization Design and Behavior.* New York: John Wiley & Sons.

Wetherbe, J. C. (1991). Executive Information Requirements: Getting it Right. *MIS Quarterly,* 15(1), 51-65.

Zmud, R. W. (1990). Opportunities for Strategic Information Manipulation Through New Information Technology, in Fulk, J. & Steinfield, C. (Eds), *Organizations and Communication Technology.* England: Sage Publications.

Zmud, R. W., Lind, M. R. & Young, F. W. (1990). An Attribute Space for Organizational Communication Channels. *Information Systems Research,* 1(4), 440-457.

Assessment of Global IT Education in the United States

6

Prashant Palvia
Memphis State University

Business school programs are being slowly and steadily internationalized in the United States. While international courses have been introduced into most business disciplines, incorporation of a global perspective into the management information systems curriculum is a relatively new phenomenon. The need for such globalization of MIS programs is paramount, as evidenced by the growing use of information technology by businesses for global expansion.

This chapter provides a comprehensive view of the status of global information technology education in the United States. Business schools with programs in international IS (IIS) at all three levels: undergraduate, master's and Ph.D. are identified. Also the structure of these programs is reported as well as faculty interests in IIS. Finally, a thorough topic analysis of IIS courses is provided, both at undergraduate and graduate levels, and an outline syllabus of an IIS course is included. The final message is that the internationalization of MIS programs in the U.S. is growing, and more and more faculty is getting involved. In a nutshell, the future of international information systems in the United States business schools is bright and promising.

Today's world has become what Marshall McLuhan (1964) once envisioned as the global village, and out of sheer necessity, many corporations are realizing the importance of globalizing their businesses to remain competitive. These corporations and governments are increasingly using information technology (IT) for conducting international business and commerce activities. Information technology not only has become an "enabler" in the globalization of business, but in many ways has also replaced the traditional ways of conducting business with new and innovative applications.

While the corporate world is rapidly employing the use of information technology for global expansion, universities and business schools have generally not kept up with the challenge of providing education on the global issues related to the use of IT. Providing this education and training to information system professionals, IT managers, and executives is of paramount importance if IT is to be properly exploited for global application. Given the increasing emphasis on technology and globalization in businesses, in fact, it would seem that providing education on Global Information Technology Management (GITM) will soon become prudent and necessary.

The purpose of this chapter is to review the status of Global Information Technology Management education in the United States, and provide directions and guidelines for such education. Specifically, the chapter addresses the following topics:

1. General information on the current status of, and the need for, internationalization of business school programs.
2. Identification of the status of current undergraduate and graduate education in Global IT in the United States.
3. Structure of the programs that teach global IT topics.
4. Motivation for internationalizing MIS programs in business schools.
5. Topic analysis of required courses in global IT at both the undergraduate and graduate levels.
6. Doctoral programs focusing on global IT issues, and dissertations in the area.
7. Faculty interests in Global IT education and/or research, both

in terms of the number of faculty and their specific interests.

Note that the terms Global IT (GIT) and International Information Systems (IIS) will be used interchangeably in this chapter.

INTERNATIONALIZATION IN BUSINESS SCHOOLS

A recent study by Porter and McKibbin (1988) sponsored by the American Assembly of Collegiate Schools of Business (AACSB) examined the state of business education in the U.S. As reported by Evangelauf (1988), Porter and McKibbin identified six undernourished areas in the curriculum. Three of these areas relevant for this chapter are:

1. External Influence on Business: More attention should be devoted to external forces, such as international development, changing demographics, and legal trends.
2. International Dimensions: Business schools should rigorously incorporate a global perspective into the curriculum.
3. Information Orientation: The business school curriculum should focus on the management of information to better serve the economy's information and service sector.

As a promising note, the AACSB has been making a continuous effort to internationalize the curricula of business schools. According to a survey by Nehrt (1987), a majority of AACSB member schools have taken steps to internationalize their curricula at both undergraduate and MBA levels. It is not uncommon to see courses listed in International Accounting, International Economics, International Finance, International Management, and International Marketing in most business school catalogs.

The one academic discipline that stands out which generally does not explicitly list courses in the international area is Management Information Systems (MIS). As a matter of fact, the current as well as proposed ACM and DPMA curricula do not specifically list an International MIS course. The preliminary ACM 1991 curriculum courses are shown in Table 1 (the revision has not been completed; the courses shown in the table are included in the deliberations). Note that the structure of the proposed curriculum is very similar to the earlier curriculum recommendation (Nunamaker et al, 1982). The preliminary DPMA 1991 curriculum courses (Information Systems: The DPMA Model, 1990) are shown in Table 2. Both of these curricula lack explicit references to international MIS, although it is anticipated that there may be some international issue coverage in the specific course descriptions. What is also surprising is that an international MIS course is not listed even among the DPMA electives.

What the above suggests is that concerted formal approaches have not been universally adopted to internationalize the MIS curriculum. This is exactly what provides the motivation for this chapter, which is to examine the individual efforts made by various business schools in the United States. These individual efforts have been driven by the growing realization within the MIS academic community of the importance of incorporating a global dimension into the MIS programs. For example, some recent major MIS conferences have focused on the global theme. To name a few, the 2nd International Conference of the Informa-

Code	ACM Curriculum
ISO1	Computer and Programming Concepts
ISO2	Data and File Structures
ISO3	Systems and Information Concepts in Organizations
ISO4	Database Management Systems
ISO5	Fundamentals of Information Systems Development
ISO6	Computer Communication Networks and Distributed Processing
ISO7A	Decision, Executive, and Cooperative Work Support Systems
ISO7B	Knowledge-Based and Expert Systems
ISO8	Information Systems Development Tools and Techniques
ISO9	Information Management
IS10	Information System

Table 1: Preliminary ACM 1991 Curriculum Courses

Code	DPMA Curriculum
CIS-01	Fundamental Concepts of Information and Computer Technology
CIS-02	IS Concepts
CIS-03	Computer Concepts
CIS-04	Application Development
CIS-05	Application Design and Implementation
CIS-06	Systems Development 1 (Single User Systems)
CIS-07	Systems Development 2 (Multi User Systems)
CIS-08	Systems Project
CIS-09	Management of IS

Electives

Code	
CE-01	IS Professionalism and Ethics
CE-02	Information Center Concepts and Management
CE-03	Audit and Security Management
CE-04	Telecommunications
CE-05	Distributed Processing
CE-06	Implementation of PC Network Systems
CE-07	Office Automation Systems
CE-08	GDSS/Electronic Meeting/EIS
CE-09	Decision Support/Expert/Neural Net Systems
CE-10	Software Engineering
CE-11	Alternative Analysis and Design Methodologies
CE-12	Computer Graphics
CE-13	Systems Simulation
CE-14	Software and Hardware Architecture
CE-15	Advanced Database Concepts
CE-16	Human-Computer Interaction

Table 2: Preliminary DPMA 1991 Curriculum Courses

tion Resources Management Association held in May 1991 in Memphis, Tennessee had the theme: "Global Information Technology Management;" and the Eleventh Annual International Conference on Information Systems, held in December 1990 in Copenhagen, Denmark had the theme: "The Role of Information Systems in the Globalization of Business." Such trends are corroborated by the study cited earlier by Porter and McKibbin (1988) and the Landmark MIT Study (1989). According to the MIT study sponsored by Arthur Young and others, information technology has a significant role to play in the 1990s due to the continued globalization of businesses and increasingly competitive markets.

GLOBAL IT EDUCATION IN THE UNITED STATES

Much of the information presented here and in subsequent sections comes from a recent comprehensive survey, conducted by the author, of MIS departments of Business Schools in the United States and Canada. The survey was undertaken as a "needs assessment" study to assess the teaching and research needs in International Information Systems in business schools. The survey questionnaire was prepared after an extensive review of the MIS and International IS literature. The questionnaire was refined and finalized using a two-stage process. In the first stage, the instrument was tested with MBA and doctoral students, and in the second stage, it was pilot-tested with twenty MIS faculty in the U.S. with specific interests in International IS.

The finalized questionnaires were mailed to all MIS department chairs, as listed in the 1989 *Directory of MIS Faculty in United States and Canada*. Note that over 90% of schools listed in the directory are from the U.S., so our results are representative primarily of United States schools. Either the department chair or his designee provided a response. There are 445 schools listed in this directory. A total of 96 responses were received (21.5% response rate). Considering that schools of all sizes and emphases are listed in the MIS directory, and many of them had no interest in Global IT, we believe that the response rate achieved was quite high. In fact, we got responses from most schools that had an interest in Global IT. Consequently, it is fair to assume that most schools that did not respond either had no International IS programs currently or had no immediate or short-term plans to do so.

Because of the above observations on response patterns, the results are reported three-ways for a better understanding: first in absolute numbers, second as a percent of the total 96 responses received, and as a percent of the total 445 schools listed in the MIS directory.

It appears that Global IT is receiving increased attention in many MIS programs. Many schools are teaching International

	Total Number	Percent of Responding Schools	Percent of All Schools
1. In graduate programs	36	37.5%	8.1%
2. In undergraduate programs	30	31.3%	6.7%

Table 3: Global IT Education in North America

University of Arizona
Fordham University
University of Hawaii
Memphis State University
University of Texas

Table 4: Universities with Graduate Courses in IIS

University of Arizona
Auburn University
University of Baltimore
University of Detroit
Fordham University
Georgetown University
University of Hawaii
Memphis State University
New Mexico State University
Pennsylvania State University at Harrisburg
University of Pittsburgh
University of San Diego
University of South Florida
University of Texas
U. S. Naval Post Graduate School

Table 5: Universities with Plans to Offer Graduate Courses in IIS

IS topics in some manner in both undergraduate and graduate programs. As per Table 3, 36 schools are currently teaching International IS topics at the graduate level, and 30 are teaching at the undergraduate level.

Very few schools actually have separate courses in International Information Systems. Of the ninety-six responses, none indicated having exclusive IIS courses at the undergraduate level. The five schools shown in Table 4 reported having graduate courses in IIS.

What is more interesting is the indication of plans to offer separate IIS courses in the next five years. A total of seventeen schools indicated having (tentative) plans for graduate IIS courses in the next five years, and five indicated having such courses at the undergraduate level. This is a clear indication of the rapid recognition of the importance of Global IT issues in Business school Information Systems curriculum. A listing of the schools that identified themselves by names as having plans to offer graduate IIS courses is provided in Table 5. Based on the author's professional network, it is believed that there are more universities, not on this list, that are considering the introduction of such courses.

From the above statistics, it is apparent that Global IT is steadily becoming part of graduate MIS education. At this time, based on our survey, there are no separate courses in Global IT at the undergraduate level; however, international topics are taught as part of other undergraduate MIS courses.

STRUCTURE OF IIS PROGRAMS

Three alternatives for teaching IIS were considered in the questionnaire, and educators were asked to rank their preferences both for undergraduate and graduate education. The alternatives were:

- A separate IIS course
- IIS integrated into the core IS curriculum
- IIS incorporated in selected IS courses

For both undergraduate and graduate education, the majority preferred the alternative of incorporating IIS in selected IS courses, followed by integrating IIS into the core curriculum. A separate IIS course was the last choice (more so for undergraduate programs than for graduate programs). This is not a surprising result due to the comprehensive nature of our sample. As discussed earlier, while there is a trend towards increased emphasis on globalization of MIS in business schools, the majority still does not have, or have plans for, globalized MIS program.

It is more reflective to examine each alternative and its responses in terms of the characteristics of the schools opting for that alternative. For graduate education, there were fourteen schools that ranked the "separate IIS course" alternative as number one, and seven more that ranked it as number two. However, more than 90% of these twenty-one schools are either currently teaching IIS, or have plans to do so in the next five years. Again for graduate education, thirty-two schools ranked "the IIS integrated into the core" option as number one and thirty-eight ranked "the IIS in separate courses" as number one. Schools preferring these two alternatives generally had no current programs or no future plans for introducing global IT into the curriculum.

For undergraduate education, only three schools indicated having a separate IIS course as their first choice. Forty-six preferred the choice of including IIS into separate courses, and thirty-three wanted them integrated into the IS core.

The above results can thus be summarized as follows. There does not seem to be a perceived need for a separate IIS course at the undergraduate level. There is almost a consensus that international IS topics may be integrated into the entire IS

Course	Frequency	Percent
Introduction to MIS/Computers	38	66%
International Business	11	19%
Databases	3	5%
Management of MIS	2	3%
Telecommunications	2	3%
Systems Analysis and Design	2	3%
Other	10	17%

Table 6: Prerequisites for the IIS Course

core or into specific IS courses. For graduate education and for schools currently teaching IIS or seriously contemplating teaching it in the future, a separate IIS course seems to be the most desired option. For the rest of them, the option is to teach IIS topics in the core curriculum or specific IS courses. In other words, the educators are suggesting an evolutionary path in graduate IIS education: start out with teaching IIS in the core or specific courses, and once the momentum and the critical mass is built, go to a full separate course.

Educators were also asked to list the prerequisites for the International Information Systems course. Generally, the schools currently teaching IIS topics or anticipating to do so responded to this question. There were 58 faculty who answered this question, and they were allowed to list multiple prerequisites. Table 6 lists the courses cited as prerequisites, their frequencies, and percentages (of the total 58 responses).

Note that the other category includes courses such as: "General Management," "Financial Management," "Marketing,"

Reason	Percent
Increasing global competitiveness among corporations	87%
Emergence of global markets	68%
Advances in information and computer technology	48%
Role of information technology in development	35%
Academic/college influence and requirements	23%
Interests of your faculty	20%
Government influence and requirements	20%
Other	8%

Table 7: Reasons for Internationalizing MIS Programs

"Technology Management," and "Cultural Relativity." From table 6, a conclusion can be made that an introductory MIS/Computers course is the minimum prerequisite requirement for the IIS course. In addition, a prerequisite course on international business, if it can be offered, can significantly expand the student's outlook to the broader horizons of global activity. Beyond these two courses, individual focus and strengths of schools will drive prerequisite requirements.

MOTIVATION FOR IIS PROGRAMS

It is enlightening to examine the underlying reasons for the surge of interest in IIS programs in the United States. Such an examination provides clues to the future trends in IIS education and also whether this accelerated activity is transient or of a long-term nature. Table 7 lists the major reasons for internationalizing MIS programs in the U.S., and the percentage of respondents citing a particular reason. Note again, that each respondent could indicate multiple reasons.   It is heartening to note that in the educators' views, the globalization of MIS programs is occurring primarily due to the changing global business scene, with its requirements for conducting business worldwide and staying globally competitive. Secondarily, the rapid advances in information technology and computers are making such globalization possible, thus also driving the internationalization of MIS programs. These trends in business and technology are not transitory or reversible. The more situational and circumstantial factors are rated low by the educators. In other words, the internationalization of MIS programs is not a passing fad; therefore, it should enjoy sustained existence and growth.

TOPIC ANALYSIS FOR GLOBAL IT EDUCATION

Given the newness of International Information Systems in academics, the subject matter is largely untreaded territory and potentially vast. A literature search was conducted to identify useful topic areas for inclusion in an International IS course. The following "main" areas emerged from the literature search:

Information Technology Environment: Typically traditional Information Systems operate in a single country, and only the environment of the country affects the development and management of information systems. In the new era of Global Information systems, one has to contend not only with the country issues, but also with regional issues, as well as with global worldwide issues. In terms of regional issues, the world can be divided into several regions according to different classifications, e.g., by the level of development, by culture, by political philosophy, etc. While specific country issues may be too many to deal with, it would be possible to address regional and worldwide issues. Some examples of studies dealing in country/ regional issues are [Palvia and Palvia 1992, Wilder 1989, Sircar and Rao 1986, Roby and Rodriguez-Diaz 1989, Dhir 1992].

Models and Frameworks: Many frameworks and models are available to methodically study and organize MIS literature (e.g., [Ives et. al. 1980, Gorry and Scott Morton 1971, Mason and Mitroff 1973]). However, all of these models are typically (by default) designed to study domestic issues. It would be appropriate to develop new models, adapt existing models, and enlighten students with these models and frameworks for proper perspective on global issues.

Planning and Management Issues: Planning and management of global information systems is inherently more complex, and requires a whole set of new issues and skills. Some concerns to be addressed in the class room include: relating global business strategy to global IT strategy [Ives and Jarvenpaa 1991], impact of globalization on IS management and IS organization, management and planning for global information systems [Kefalas 1990], and new roles for the chief information officer.

Development of International Information Systems: Traditional system designs and development methods and strategies need not be directly applicable in a global environment. Students must learn some basic fundamentals of global information systems, e.g., technological components of such a system, architectural alternatives for data centers [Palvia and Sankar 1990], systems analysis and design for IIS [Kefalas, 1990], managing the development in an international context, addressing a multitude of implementation problems, and evaluation [Palvia, et. al. 1992], and maintenance.

Technology: Information technology, different technology requirements in developing global information systems, and the vast differences in the state of technology in different countries can have serious impact on global applications, and need to be discussed in the a global IT course. Issues to be addressed include hardware, software, telecommunications [Harper 1989, Stallings 1990], standards and compatibility, distributed processing and databases, data integrity, security and control.

International Data Flows: Transborder data flows (TBDFs) [Carper 1989] and electronic data interchange (EDI) [Hansen and Hill 1989] raise some interesting issues in an international context. For example, while many countries have laws controlling the flow of sensitive security, financial, or personal data, it is very hard to enforce the laws and control such "undesirable" data transfers.

Types of Systems and Applications: While most of the above concerns relate to traditional transaction-oriented information systems, the more decision- and management-oriented systems may have a different set of problems and ramifications in a global context. Some examples of such systems are: decision support systems [Sauter 1991], executive information systems, expert systems, and strategic information systems [Palvia et al 1990]. While such global systems are not prevalent yet, a few have begun to appear and lessons can be drawn from them.

Country Differences: Again major differences between nations can be studied either from regional perspective or major country perspective. Many of these differences can be classified under cultural/societal differences (e.g., work ethics, management style, time orientation, individual versus group orientation, internal motivation, etc.) and affect the design and management

---

MIS issues in advanced countries

Global issues of IIS

Impact of globalization on IS organization

Impact of globalization on IS management

Role of IT in Global Competitiveness

International telecommunications

Table 8: Important Educational Items for Undergraduate Education

MIS issues in advanced countries
Frameworks and models for IIS
Global issues of IIS
Impact of Globalization on IS organization
Impact of Globalization on IS management
Planning for IIS
Management of IIS
New challenges for CIO
Role of IT in global competitiveness
Elements of a Global IT strategy
New organizational forms due to IT
Managing the development of IIS
Implementation of IIS
Internationally distributed databases
International telecommunications
International standards
Security and control
Transborder data flows
International EDI
Global strategic information systems
IT related laws and policies of nations

Table 9: Important Educational Items for Graduate Education

of global information systems. In addition, there are a myriad of other country specific issues which impact information systems. Some examples are: accounting and financial practices, laws and policies on software, hardware, and information systems, language barriers, labor markets, political climate, economic resources, etc. Some examples of studies relating to cultural, political, societal differences between countries are: [Couger et al 1990,   Couger 1986].

Several specific items were identified for each of the above topic areas and listed in the study questionnaire. There were a total of 56 items, and each respondent rated the importance of each item for graduate and undergraduate education on a 4-point likert scale. Table 8 lists the items that received average ratings between "important" and "very important" for under-graduate education. Table 9 contains a similar list of items for graduate education. Comparing the two lists, there are only six items listed for undergraduate education, while there are twenty-one items listed for graduate education. Further, the under-graduate list is a subset of the graduate list. The very short list for undergraduate education may imply that at this time, the U.S. educators do not feel a strong need for international IT education at the undergraduate level. What the undergraduates need is a basic understanding of some fundamental global issues related to information technology, but not necessarily a detailed examination. It is therefore recommended that such issues be incorporated in existing undergraduate MIS courses. Given the nature of the items, the two likely undergraduate courses for such limited coverage of topics are: "Management of IS/IT" course and the "Telecommunications" course.

On the other hand, a broad range of items is identified for the graduate IIS course. These relate to international issues on organization, management, strategy, telecommunications, data flows, standards, databases, and the international environment.

Given the variety and breadth of the international IS topics, an independent and separate IIS course is the first recommendation of the author. An outline of a one-semester course in International Information Systems, based on the author's teaching such a course in Fall 1991 at Memphis State University, is provided in the Appendix.

   In the event a full course is not feasible at a given institution, we offer the following model for fully integrating the international dimension in the existing curriculum (see figure 1). We believe that most IIS topics can be integrated into the

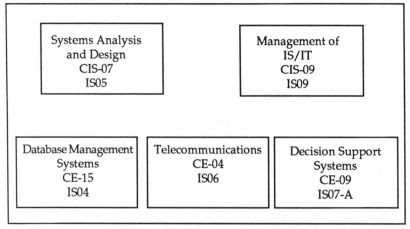

Figure 1: Integration of International Information Systems into IS Curriculum

following five courses. The corresponding ACM and DPMA codes for these courses are also shown in the figure. Three of these courses were also recommended by Eom (1990). Note that individual constraints and preferences may dictate the selection of only a subset of these courses for integration.

Systems Analysis and Design

Many new dimensions are added to the whole process of the system development life cycle. International issues to be included in this course are regulations on international data flow, systems compatibility, social and cultural influences on system requirements, level of technology in other countries, user sophistication and acceptance, different perspectives on cost-benefit analysis, technology transfer process, etc.

Management of IS/IT

This course will perhaps include the bulk of the international IS issues. Possible topics to include are the role of the Global Information Officer (GIO or the multinational CIO), linking IS strategy with global business strategy, global IS planning, global IS management, stages of IS development in other countries, etc.

Database Management Systems

Included in this course should be guidelines (Eom, 1990) for managing and integrating databases scattered between foreign subsidiaries and the parent company. Potential alternatives between centralization and decentralization need to be discussed. Other critical elements to be included are the issues associated with transborder data flows (TBDF), country policies related to security and privacy of data, and special problems in globally distributed databases.

Telecommunications

Telecommunications is a vital link to the establishment of a global network and the development of a global information system. Several issues that need to be discussed in the telecom-

Electronic Data Interchange (EDI)
Information Systems and International Trade
Transborder Data Flows
International Standards
Group Decision Support Systems
Electronic Contracting with EDI
Global Information Systems
IT for Global Competitiveness
Global Telecommunications
Global IT Marketing
Globally Distributed Systems
Legal Issues in IIS
Technology Transfer
Architecture of IIS
Privacy Issues
Security Issues
Common Global System Strategy
Organizational Coordination across Transnationals

Table 10: Current and Potential IIS Dissertation Topics

munications course include international standards (or lack thereof), telecommunications infrastructure in host countries, vendor support, telecommunications equipment (e.g., terminals, phones, FAX machines), the role of local state-owned PTTs (post, telegraph and telephone agencies), public versus private telecom systems, and the costs of telecommunications.

Decision Support Systems

Because of the diversity and the breadth of information sources, decision makers in an MNC need more systematic support from computer-based information systems (DSS). The DSS course should examine the unique problems of providing large-scale decision support for global decision making, the impact of cultural and social factors on the design, development, and use of these DSS, and finally the impact of different financial, economic, and accounting systems on the design and development of the DSS (Eom 1990).

Note: All areas are in the context of international environment.

IS for global competitiveness
Strategic information systems
Global IS strategic planning and policy
IIS planning and management
Issues, models, and frameworks
Behavioral/organizational impacts of information
        technology
Implementation of IIS
Evaluation of IIS
Operational global information systems
MIS for emergency and crisis management
Global information technology
Telecommunications
Networking
Transborder data flows
Electronic data interchange
Databases/distributed databases
Expert systems
Decision support systems
Executive information systems
Environmental scanning systems
Financial systems
Computer supported cooperative workgroup systems
Systems analysis and design
Software engineering and development
Offshore software development
Security
Audit & control
Performance and measurement
Laws and legal issues
Cross-cultural comparisons
Ethics in other nations
Third world/developing countries' issues
Communist block country issues
Technology transfer
End user computing
Research by other IIS researchers
Global IT education

**Table 11: Faculty Interest Areas in International
Information Systems**

DOCTORAL PROGRAMS IN IIS

Nine universities in our sample indicated having IIS dissertations in progress. In fact, there have been several dissertations already written (or near completion) in IIS topics (e.g., out of University of Arizona, University of South Carolina, and University of Pittsburgh). What is remarkable to note is that twenty-two universities anticipate having IIS doctoral dissertations in the next five years. A list of current and potential dissertation topics, as indicated by the responding MIS faculty, is identified in Table 10.

FACULTY INTERESTS IN GLOBAL IT

The IS faculty is the principal resource for providing instruction and promoting research in International Information Systems. It is therefore instructive to examine both quantitatively and qualitatively faculty interests in International Information Systems. First, the quantitative results are very encouraging. Our response pool of 96 schools identified 125 faculty who had a teaching, research, and/or general interest in IIS. Of course, many smaller schools did not identify any faculty interested in IIS, while some larger schools had as many as three, sometimes four professors with active interest in IIS.

Now, qualitatively, in terms of the specific interests within IIS, a multitude of interest areas/topics were identified. These are listed in Table 11. This listing generally corroborates the topics listed under the "topic analysis" section of this chapter. Such a wide range in interest areas also suggests that, on an overall basis, there should not be major obstacles in implementing IIS programs and preparing faculty for delivering IIS education.

CONCLUSION

This chapter has described some important aspects of Global IT education in the United States, and some schools in Canada. The general observation and inference is that global IT education is being considered seriously in many of the U.S.

business schools, and several schools have already begun to offer International Information Systems courses, especially at the graduate level. This trend bodes indeed very well for the future of Global Information Technology education. The chapter also provided a topic analysis for topics to be addressed in an International Information Systems. The topic analysis brings out a wide range of issues to be included in the IIS course. An outline of an IIS course is provided in the Appendix as a starting point for those contemplating the introduction of a similar course. On the supply side, faculty interests in IIS were assessed both quantitatively and qualitatively. Again, a wide variety of interests were noted.

Given the above needs assessment of global IT education, the following implications emerge for Global IT education:

1. Initially, there will be a single IIS course in most schools. However, with more activity in the area and given the breadth and diversity of the field, multiple courses in IIS may be required.
2. Currently, books in the IIS area are very few (some new and promising books are (Kefalas 1990, Palvia, et. al. 1992, Roche 1991, Deans and Kane, 1992)). The large body of knowledge is contained in journal articles, unpublished research papers, and simply in the heads of practitioners and researchers, yet undocumented. Given the growing need for IIS education, more books need to be published. Even books which focus on special topic areas in IIS may find a niche.
3. As per our study, there is at least a critical mass of educators in MIS who are currently teaching, conducting research, or generally interested in IIS. However, many of them, as well as additional faculty, will require formalized training in IIS in order to be proficient in teaching IIS in the class room. It is recommended that educators be provided such training opportunities in short-seminar (one week to several weeks) settings.

APPENDIX
Outline of a One-Semester Course in International Information Systems

Course Description:Information technology's impact on globalization of businesses; International information technology environment (West and East Europe, Pacific rim countries, third world countries); models and issues in International information systems; planning and managing global systems; components and development of such systems; technology transfer; case studies and applications.

Text:
1. Global Issues of Information Technology Management, edited by Shailendra Palvia, Prashant Palvia, and Ronald Zigli. Idea Group Publishing, 1992.
2. Assigned Journal Readings.

General Objectives
1. To underscore the importance of information technology for the globalization and competitive posturing of businesses.
2. To examine the state of information technology in different parts of the world.
3. To study the various managerial and technical issues associated with developing and operating global information systems.

Specific Objectives:
1. To develop an understanding of the role of information technology in the development of global and competitive businesses.
2. To address the technical and managerial problems, issues, and challenges in management information systems in different parts of the world, i.e., in advanced, developing, and under-developed countries.
3. To examine/develop the various models and paradigms for understanding and analyzing global information systems.
4. To study the technical aspects of global information systems.
5. To study the methods and problems in developing global information systems.
6. To examine the planning and management issues related to global information systems.
7. To study and evaluate the various models and methods for technology transfer, and discuss their pros and cons.
8. To draw inferences from various applications and case studies related to the development and management of global information systems.
9. To identify research areas within "global information technol-

ogy management", and focus on high-need, high pay-off sub-areas.

Course Content & Weekly Outline

Week 1: Information Technology (IT) and its role in globalization of businesses
History of IT evolution
Types of Information Systems
Strategic and Executive Information Systems
IT's impact on business and increased competitiveness.
Key MIS issues
Currents trends in IT

Weeks 2 and 3: Global Information Technology Environment

IT Environment in West and East Europe
IT Environment in Pacific Rim countries
IT Environment in Third World countries
Technological challenges for advanced, developing, and under-developed nations.
Key MIS issues and priorities in above nations
Technical, Economical, Societal, and Cultural Problems of IT implementation in different countries.

Weeks 4 and 5: Models, Paradigms, and Issues of Global Information Systems
Frameworks for classifying and understanding such systems
Stages of IS/IT development in other nations
Types of global systems
Impact on management practices due to global IT
Technical, management, behavioral issues of global IS

Week 6: Planning and Management for Global Systems
Multinational CIO (GIO) Challenges
Strategic, tactical, and operational planning for global Information Technology strategies
Managing Information Technology in Multinational Corporations and international agencies.

Week 7: Technical components of Global Information Systems
Hardware
Software

Telecommunications
Databases (distributed)
Architectural alternatives
Mid-term Examination

Weeks 8 and 9: Development of Global Information Systems

Creating Global Software
System Development Life Cycle issues
Behavioral/cultural issues in development
Management and execution of life cycle
Cost-benefit analysis of global systems
Evaluation/return-on-investment of global systems
Maintenance of global information systems

Weeks 10 and 11: International Technology Transfer
Models/paradigms for technology transfer
Transborder Data Flows
Impediments to technology transfer
Strategic Information Technology Transfer
Data communications and storage methods
Electronic data interchange (EDI)

Weeks 12 and 13:   Applications and Case Studies
Based on:
>   different types of systems
>   different country environments
>   different types of technologies
>   development/implementation problems.

Week 14: Global IT Research
Research areas of greatest need and potential
Theory Building in Global Information Technology Management
Research methods and their suitability
Descriptive/analytical/empirical/model-based research
Anticipated problems in conducting research and countering
>   strategies

Week 15: Final examination

REFERENCES
1989 Directory of Management Information Systems Faculty in the United States and Canada. MISRC/McGraw Hill, 1989.

Carper, W.B. Transborder Data Flows in the Information Age: Implications for International Management. *International Journal of Management*, Vol. 4, No. 4, December 1989, pp. 418-425.

Couger, J.D. Effect of Cultural Differences on Motivation of Analysts and Programmers: Singapore vs. the United States. *MIS Quarterly*, Vol. 10, No. 2, June 1986, pp. 189-196.

Couger, J.D., Adelsberger, H., Borovits, I., Zviran, M., and Motiwalla, J. Commonalities in Motivating Environments for Programmers/Analysts in Austria, Israel, Singapore, and the U.S.A. *Information & Management*, Vol. 18, No. 1, January 1990, pp. 41-46.

Deans, P.C. and Kane, M.J. International dimensions of Information Systems and Technology. PWS-Kent Publishing Co., Boston, 1992.

Dhir, K. The Challenge of Introducing Advanced Telecommunication Systems in India. *The Global Issues of Information Technology Management*, Edited by Palvia, Palvia, and Zigli, Idea Group Publishing, Harrisburg, PA, 1992.

Eom, H.B., Integrating International Dimensions into MIS Courses: A New Challenge to Information Systems Educators. *The Journal of Computer Information Systems*, Spring 1990, pp. 11-14.

Evangelauf, J. Success Has Spoiled Business Schools, New Study Charges. *The Chronicle of Higher Education*, Vol. 34, No. 31, April 13, 1988, pp. A21, A20-A21.

Gorry, G.A. and Scott Morton, M.S. A Framework for Management Information Systems. *Sloan Management Review*, Vol. 13, No. 1, 1971, pp. 55-70.

Hansen, J.V. and Hill, N.C. Control and Audit of Electronic Data Interchange. *MIS Quarterly*, Vol. 13, No. 4, 1989, pp. 403-412.

Harper, J.M. *Telecommunications Policy and Management*. Pinter Publishers, London, 1990.

Information Systems: The DPMA Model for a Four Year Undergraduate Degree, Draft, 1990, Data Processing Management Association.

Ives, B. and Jarvenpaa, S.L. Applications of Global Information Technology: Key Issues for Management. *MIS Quarterly*, Vol 15, No. 1, March 1991, pp. 32-49.

Ives, B., Hamilton, S. and Davis, G.B. A Framework for Research in Computer-Based Management Information Systems. *Management Science*, Vol 26, No. 9, September 1980, pp. 910-934.

Kefalas, A.G. *Global Business Strategy: A Systems Approach*. Cincinnati, South-Western Publishing Company, 1990.

Mason, R.O., and Mitroff, I.I. A Program for Research on Management Information Systems. *Management Science*, Vol. 19, No. 5, 1973, pp. 475-485.

McLuhan, Marshall. *Understanding Media: The Extensions of Man.* McGraw-Hill New York, 1964.

Nehrt, L.C. The Internationalization of the Curriculum. *Journal of International Business Studies,* Vol. 18, No. 1, Spring 1987, pp. 83-90.

Nunamaker, J.F., Couger, J.D., and Davis, G.B. Information Systems Curriculum Recommendations for the 80s: Undergraduate and Graduate Degree Programs. *Communications of ACM,* Vol. 25, No. 11, November 1982, pp. 781-805.

Palvia, P. and Palvia, S. MIS Issues in Indian and a Comparison With the US. *International Information Systems,* April 1992, pp. 100-110.

Palvia, P., Palvia, P., and Zigli, R.M. Models and Requirements for Using Strategic Information Systems in Developing Nations. *International Journal of Information Management,* Vol. 10, No. 2, 1990, pp. 117-126.

Palvia, S., Palvia, P., and Zigli, R.M. *The Global Issues of Information Technology Management.* Idea Group Publishing, 1992.

Palvia, P. and Sankar, C.S. Architectural Alternatives and Issues in Designing Global Information Systems: Frameworks for Design and Research. *Proceedings of National Decision Sciences Institute,* San Diego, 1990.

Porter, L.W. and McKibbin, L.E. *Management Education and Development: Drift or Thrust into the 21st Century?* Hightstown, NJ: McGraw Hill Book Company, 198

Robey, D. and Rodriguez-Diaz. The Organizational and Cultural Context of Systems Implementation: Case Experience from Latin America. *Information & Management,* Vol. 17, No. 4, November 1989, pp. 229-240.

Roche, E.M. *Managing Information Technology in Multinational Corporations.* MacMillan Publishing Company, 1992.

Sauter, V. Cross Cultural Aspects of Model Management Needs in a Transnational Decision Support System. in *The Global Issues of Information Technology Management,* edited by Palvia, Palvia, and Zigli. Idea Group Publishing, 1992.

Sircar, S. and Rao, V. K. Information Resource Management in Singapore: The State of the Art. *Information & Management,* Vol. 11, No. 4, November 1986, pp. 181-190.

Stallings, W. *Business Data Communications.* Macmillan Publishing Company, New York, NY. 1990.

The Landmark MIT Study: Management in the 1990s. Arthur Young, 1989.

Wilder Clinton (CW Staff). (1989, May 22). Foreign and US executives see eye-to-eye on the top IS issues. *Computerworld* and *Proceedings of the CIMS conference in Babson College,* Wellesley, MA.

Information Technology Education in Japan: Problems and Approaches

7

Osam Sato
Tokyo Keizai University

This chapter discusses information technology (IT) education in Japan, and the problems that have occurred in its development. IT education has achieved national importance, and the system for its development extends throughout governmental agencies, academic institutions (which include many varieties of schools), and industrial firms. First, the current IT educational system in Japan is introduced. Second, based on some government surveys, problems with IT education in both academic organizations and private firms are discussed. Next, immediate solutions to those problems which include general directions, new curricula, new courses of both academic and industrial sectors, and new media applications, are presented. The chapter concludes with a future course for IT education in Japan which includes a global perspective on IT education. The importance of Japanese government in the development of the IT educational system is stressed throughout this chapter.

IT Education and Business

Many firms in Japan have been informatizing or becoming IT oriented as their managers come to appreciate the strategic importance of IT in the business environment. Strategic applications of IT, such as Strategic Information Systems, enable Japanese businesses to gain cost effectiveness, to achieve product differentiation, and to exploit market niches. These strategic benefits have resulted in increased investment in IT. Expenditures for IT are reaching $8,900 per employee in the manufacturing industries and $23,400 per employee in the service industries (Central Academy of Information Technology, 1990a, p.68).

Naturally, education and training in IT concepts and IT skills are also considered very important to Japanese firms. For the last three decades, the Japanese government, academic institutions, and industries have worked hard to develop a direction for IT education in Japan. These efforts are discussed in this chapter. However, Japan has also experienced many problems in implementing its educational program for IT. These problems have resulted in too few software engineers to meet the demands of the industrial sector, and a growing need for basic computer literacy in employees.

Japan's IT educational problems can be classified into two broad groups. The first group consists of the universal problems faced by every industrialized country that heavily employs IT. These problems include a lack of well designed software packages, a backlog of applications waiting to be developed, and a shortage of skilled engineers. The second group consists of problems specific to Japan and come from the country's history, culture, politics, and value system.

Goals of IT Education in Japan

The IT educational program in Japan has as one of its goals the achievement of the basic IT literacy level that is needed by all people living in an information society. Instructional courses in basic computer concepts are needed as a foundation for wordprocessing, data entry and retrieval, electronic mail, and computer aided instructions. This basic IT literacy education is becoming an important background component of education. And by reflecting a new view of learning, IT-based education has increased in significance (Resta, 1989).

A second goal of IT education is to provide the technical knowledge needed by professional IT engineers. This knowledge includes an understanding of computer languages, algorithms, data modeling, system analysis and design methodologies etc.

Faced with the new information society, it is impossible to neglect the increasing need for professional IT engineers. The competitive strength of Japanese firms depends on the quality and quantity of high-level professional IT engineers available to them.

THE CURRENT IT EDUCATION SYSTEMS IN JAPAN

General View

The Japanese government establishes the national policy for IT education, including research and development agencies and academic organizations. Academic organizations beyond the high school level include vocational schools ("Senshu gakko"), technical schools ("Koutou senmon Gakko"), junior colleges ("Tanki Daigaku"), universities ("Daigaku"), and academic societies for researchers. Since an overview of the Japanese educational system has been given elsewhere, this chapter concentrates on just IT education.

Private companies also educate their employees, and the information systems department of each firm usually has this responsibility. Information systems departments educate IT engineers, IT engineer candidates, and employees engaged in end user computing. Some companies not only educate their own employees, but also provide educational services to customers.

The government, academic organizations, and private firms jointly engage in IT education to satisfy Japan's industrial need for IT. The next few sections describe the Japanese IT education system, and later sections discuss the problems and future trends for internationalization of IT education.

Higher Academic Organizations

Vocational schools. Vocational schools provide high school graduates with another one to four years of training. A strong need for IT graduates caused the number of vocational schools providing IT education to double in the period from 1985 to 1989. In fiscal year 1989, there were 287 vocational schools offering IT programs and 88,700 students enrolled in those programs (JIPDEC, 1991, p.241). In the past, vocational schools produced only operators and programmers by one or two year educational programs. However, in an effort to meet industry demand for higher level software engineers, the vocational schools are now lengthening their programs to three and four years of training. The greatest advantage of vocational schools is their ability to focus only on IT education.

Technical Schools. Technical schools accept high school graduates who aspire to be high level systems engineers. Many technical schools have reorganized and expanded their IT curriculum. According to Ministry of Education, Science, and Culture (MESC; discussed below), the number of students enrolled yearly in an IT related course of study has increased from 1736 in 1985 to 2893 in fiscal year 1989 (JIPDEC, 1991, p.242).

Junior Colleges. Same as in the United States, junior colleges in Japan offer two-year courses of study. This short time frame prohibits a complete IT education, so the IT course of study is usually limited a basic level such as office automation skills. Practical rather than theoretical skills are stressed.

Universities. Universities have four-year programs that range from basic IT literacy (such as office automation) to rigorous, theoretical knowledge (such as computer sciences). This diversity is due in part to MESC's efforts at increasing and expanding the IT curriculum in universities. The number of students enrolled yearly in IT related courses of study were estimated by MESC to have increased from 17,268 in 1985 to 27,852 in 1989 (JIPDEC, 1991, p.242).

The content of a student's IT education depends on whether they are enrolled in a technical or business oriented department (see appendix A for examples of courses found in a technical program and appendix B for examples of courses in a business orientated program). The technical programs are attempting to produce engineers while the business schools are producing business systems analysts. MESC has decided that a course in management information systems is required in every business administration department.

Industrial Education

Firms that use IT have also made an effort to improve the quality of their system engineer through education. An Informatization White Paper (1991) gave the following three reasons why firms engage in the training of their employees:

1. An absolute shortage of software engineers means that it may not be possible to purchase the necessary talent in the labor markets.

2. It is more difficult to outsource system analysis and design than it is the actual writing of code.

3. With the increasing strategic importance of information systems, firms need high quality software engineers.

The Supply of IT engineers. Many Japanese firms have experienced a shortage of IT engineers and this has resulted in a heavy software backlog. The shortage of high-level systems engineer is worse than that of programmers. While only 10% of the firms have enough programmers, only 5% of all firms feel that they have a sufficient number of systems engineers. (CAIT, 1990a, p.90).

The academic organizations mentioned earlier are the main source of IT engineers in Japan. They supply firms with more than 85% of the new programmers and 50% of the systems engineers. However, new IT employees rarely have the specific skills needed by firms, and resources must therefore be devoted to their education. This lack of entry level skills has been caused in part by an absence of a standard curriculum in higher level schools discussed above.

Firms that can't get a sufficient number of IT engineers from schools must look elsewhere. It is difficult for firms to purchase talent from other organizations because of the lifelong employment system. And although this practice is gradually changing, it must be considered a factor in the short run. Many firms not in the IT industry retrain existing employees for the programmer and system engineer vacancies. Some firms get 10.8% of their programmers and 25.6% of their systems engineers from this shift of personnel. Outsourcing is another possibility and 91.7% of firms with programmer or system engineer shortages take this route (CAIT, 1990a, p.109).

Education Within Firms. A report by CAIT (CAIT, 1990a) reveals that most firms have their IT employees spend two weeks a year in training and 18.2% of IT user firms give their employees three or more weeks of training. The most common method of training is lectures, but some firms also use practical exercises, on-the-job training, and self-teaching methods (CAIT, 1990a, p.95). Some large companies have established internal schools to handle the training of IT employees. For example, in 1989 Kao Corp. established Kao System Technology School which provides a two-year course for systems engineers and Matsushita Electric Industrial Corp. Ltd. established a Software Engineers' Laboratory. Since not all firms have the resources necessary to train employees internally, other methods have also been used:

1. Paying tuition to send employees outside the firm for education. This might include either government sponsored courses, such as those held by CAIT (discussed below), or courses held at privately owned companies. Conducting IT training courses has become a popular venture for firms with experience, and firms such as CSK Corp. have entered this new market.

2. Dispatching engineers to other IT manufacturers for on-the-job training.

National Policy

The growth in IT education stems from both educational and industrial needs. Therefore, the national policy of IT education is defined by both the Ministry of Education, Science, and Culture (MESC), which supervises the Japanese educational system, and the Ministry of International Trade and Industry (MITI), which is in charge of the industrial sector.

MESC focuses on the fostering of young IT engineers and on the improvement of IT literacy education in schools. MITI handles more pragmatic industrial problems, such as the shortage of IT engineers and the reformation of the Japanese industrial structure into a high-technology orientation. Although there is an intimate relationship among these objectives, MESC and MITI often tackle IT educational problems independently because of their different points of view and specific goals.

Policy of MESC. Based on a report from the Curriculum Council of 1987, MESC introduced a "New Course of Study" to take effect in the fiscal year 1993. The new curriculum will include both IT education itself (such as "The Basics of Information Processing") and the application of IT to education.

The Education Reformation Office in MESC issued a

report in 1988 called "Training and Securing Information Processing Engineers." This report was aimed at academic institutions and, according to Emura (1991), proposed four guidelines:

1. Expanding the number of information related courses and the number of faculty members able to teach IT courses.

2. Establishing "Graduate Schools in Frontier Science and Technology" for high-level IT engineers.

3. Development of a standard curriculum.

4. Improvements in educational quality.

Based on these guidelines, a number of actions were taken and these actions are discussed later (see General Direction in this chapter).

Policy of MITI. MITI's objective is the development and control of the Japanese industrial sector. Based on a recognition that we have already entered into an informatization society, MITI considers IT support for industry very important. MITI's practical objective is to help satisfy the industrial sector's need for IT engineers in terms of both quantity and quality.

MITI's perspective on informatization is well documented in a report called "Software Engineers in Japan by the year 2000" (Industrial Structure Council of MITI, 1987). This report predicts a "software crisis" in Japan with a shortage of 966,000 of IT engineers by the year 2000 (422,000 for software engineers and 544,000 for programmers). This report also warns about a shortage of high-level engineers, whose scarcity may be a bottleneck for the future informatization of industry and may lessen the competitive power of Japanese firms. There are three possible methods of averting the shortage of IT engineers. First, it is possible to improve the productivity of software development by computer aided software engineering, computer aided design, and other software engineering technologies. A second solution is the enlargement of the education system for software engineers. The last solution is the active education and training of employees in other functional business areas to be software engineers and programmers.

JIPDEC. In addition to direct control of industry, MITI has also implemented its policies through the activities of the

Japanese Information Processing Development Center (JIPDEC) since 1967. JIPDEC is a non-profit organization whose objectives "are to promote information processing by computers throughout not only industry but also the entire society and thus to contribute to the overall economic and social development of Japan" (JIPDEC, 1990b, p.3).

The activities of JIPDEC include:

1. Research & Development of expert systems, CASE tools, software engineering, parallel processing, distributed processing, and the social impacts of IT.

2. Surveys and studies of the IT marketplace with an aim towards international information exchange for market research.

3. Promotional activities such as publications, conferences/ symposia, and the exhibition of IT advances.

4. Development of Information Processing Systems for the government, and the private sector.

5. Conducting training programs, and researching the application of a CAI system called "CAROL".

6. Administering the Information Processing Engineers Examination.

These activities are conducted either by JIPDEC or one of its three affiliated organizations: Center for the Informatization of Industry (CII), Central Academy of Information Technology (CAIT), and Japan Information Technology Engineers Examination Center (JITEC) (JIPDEC, 1990b).

CAIT. CAIT is an affiliated organization of JIPDEC, and acts as its education and training division. CAIT's current form was established in June 1987, when the old Institute of IT (IIT) was reorganized and renamed. The task of CAIT is to act as a core organization for executing the educational projects which originate from MITI.

Through MITI's support, CAIT performs the following activities (JIPDEC, 1990b, p.11):

1. Development and promotion of information processing education.
2. Training information processing technical instructors and high-level information processing personnel.

Information Processing Engineers Examination. The Information Processing Engineers Examination (IPEE) is a system of national examinations whose aim is "to provide the technologies level to be acquired and educational target for information processing engineers and an objective criteria for evaluating their skill and qualifications" (JIPDEC,1990b, p.12). Although JIPDEC was designated by MITI to run the IPEE, JITEC actually conducts the twice yearly examinations. The first IPEE was in 1969.

The IPEE consists of five levels of examination: (a) programmer examination, (b) senior programmer examination, (c) on-line systems engineer examination, (d) system engineer examination, and (e) system auditor examination. Since 1969, there have been 3,397,594 applicants and 323,057 successful candidates (JIPDEC, 1991, p.251-252).

Vocational schools often let students concentrate on IPEE preparation as their course of study. According to a survey by CAIT, 96% of vocational schools recommended that their students attempt the examination, and 98% offer a special class for IPEE preparation (CAIT, 1990a, p.27). Many technical schools also let their students concentrate on preparing for the programmer portion of the examination. Because of their short two years study course, junior colleges are less aggressive in the examination. Students in universities also take the programmer portion of the IPEE examination, and about 44 percent of successful candidates of IPEE are university students (JIPDEC, 1991, p.255).

Many firms encourage their IT engineers to pass the examination, but incentives vary across firms. In some firms passing the IPEE is required to be ranked as an "engineer," while in other firms successful completion boosts the salary of the employee. Generally speaking, the IPEE works as a motivational tool, and this is especially true in the software industry where prospective customers often evaluate the technical ability of a software firm by the percentage of successful candidates in its staff.

As both a standard for IT knowledge and a target for IT

education in Japan, the IPEE is an important part of the internationalization process.

PROBLEMS IN JAPANESE IT EDUCATION

Although the Japanese government, academic organizations, and industries have all been working hard to improve IT education, many problems remain. In 1990 and 1991, CAIT conducted surveys to uncover IT educational problems in both schools (from high schools to universities) and industry. Typical problems in both sectors are discussed below.

Education Problems in Academic Institutions

The problems faced by schools seemed to fall into four general categories: (a) educational environment, (b) curriculum, (c) teachers, and (d) students.

Educational Environment.
1. A lack of sufficient budgetary funds means that every type of school cannot purchase enough hardware, software packages, and even books to support the number of students enrolled in classes. The shortage of hardware is the most frequently cited problem in universities. Although almost every school in Japan has at least one classroom which is dedicated to IT education, usually about 40 personal computers which may be connected by a local area network (Jacobsen, 1989, p.10), improving the facilities beyond this point is difficult because of a lack of funds. This is a learning bottleneck, because not all students have access to computers to do their work.
2.   Rapid technological innovation causes classroom materials to become quickly obsolete. A related concern is that teachers must constantly upgrade their skills and, without funds for seminars and books, this training either does not occur or is paid for by the teacher.
3.   A lack of interaction between schools and industry means that teachers are unsure of industrial needs and thus have a difficult job teaching correct topics.
4.   A lack of teaching assistants forces professors to devote more of their valuable time to mundane tasks. Only 27% of all programming language classes have a teaching assistant,

and on average, there is only one teaching assistant for every two classes taught (CAIT, 1991b, p.71). This deficiency comes not only from budgetary problems, but also from bureaucratic restriction which prohibits part-time employment of Ph.D students in national universities.

5. Devoting more hours to IT education means that the time students spend studying other subjects must be decreased. Thus there is a practical limit to the amount of educational time that can be devoted to IT.

Curriculum.

1. Although there are some well-known IT educational goals (e.g. IT literacy, problem solving ability, and technical skill), most goals are so vague that it is impossible to find a clear means of achieving them. This lack of focus is caused by rapid changes in the discipline and the newness of the field, and is one of the main causes of non-standard curriculums across the country. These same characteristics also make many of the IT courses very unstructured and difficult to teach.

The lack of a standard curriculum for IT education has caused teachers in a variety of schools to feel unsure about what they must teach students. Firms that recruit freshmen do not rely totally on school education, because the level and content of IT education across institutions is so varied that firms can not find a common baseline knowledge in graduates.

Teachers.

1. Academic institutions suffer from a lack of experienced teachers, and universities view this as their second worst problem. The need for IT teachers continues to grow, but the IT field is so new that an appropriate teacher education system has not yet been established (Sakamoto, 1989). This lack of teachers is impairing the quality of education, especially in the area of practical programming. It is not unusual for one teacher to have forty to one hundred students without the aid of a teaching assistant. The lack of teachers has also reduced the variety of IT courses that can be offered.

2. Generally speaking, teachers are so busy teaching and doing administrative work that they do not have enough time to keep abreast of the latest IT developments, learn new educational techniques for IT, and keep informed of industry needs. Although other disciplines face these same issues, the rapid

progress in IT make the issues more difficult to solve. CAIT offers some courses for IT teachers, but more has to be done in this area.

3. Since most IT courses are either new or have to be continually updated, teachers must spend a lot of time and effort preparing to teach a course. They may have trouble finding an appropriate textbook and often have to make up their own handouts, exercises, and cases because previously accumulated material is not available.

4. Many teachers have a lack of industry experience and thus have trouble giving their students practical knowledge and techniques for use in the private sector. The lack of practical experience seems to be more of a concern at vocational and technical schools than at universities (CAIT, 1990a, p.28).

5. A difference of opinion between old and new faculty members may be partly the caus of the lack of a standard curriculum. The older generation wants to teach traditional procedural languages (such as FORTRAN and COBOL), while the newer faculty members often promote more modern tools such as spreadsheet or fourth generation languages (e.g.,IFPS, SAS).

Students.

1. Almost all students lack practical business experience, so they often have a difficult time imagining what their career will be like. This absence of experience may cause a lack of motivation with respect to the students' school work, especially in courses like systems engineering, database management, and project management. More interaction between schools and industry, such as apprenticeship programs for students or faculty exchange programs for teachers, would help alleviate this problem.

2. As in all disciplines, students enter the classroom with different initial levels of knowledge and experience, and these differences often make it hard to determine the content of the class. This is especially true with respect to programming languages, since some students own personal computers and write programs as a hobby.

Other Problems in Universities

Other problems often cited in universities include:

1. A lack of compatibility between operating systems, software, data, diskette formats, and peripherals.

2. A lack of understanding about the needs of IT educa-

tion among the administrative staff of universities. For example, a budget may be assigned for hardware, but no funds allocated for software.

3. IT advances are so rapid that it is difficult to keep teachers well informed.

4. The hardware infrastructure may not be adequate. For example, the response rate for some university mainframe computers may go down radically if all students use a terminal during class.

5. Lack of good textbooks and materials (e.g. software, VCR tapes, and readings).

Industry Education Problems

A lack of good mentors disturbs the internal diffusion of IT knowledge and experience within many firms. The best mentors are usually excellent systems engineers and the need for systems development is often so high that firms can not spare them to help educate young systems engineers.

What we should teach software engineers is also largely an unanswered question in many firms, and educational quality depends to a great extent on the individual instructor. New educational medias are emerging (computer aided instructions and audio/video materials), but firms do not yet know how to best utilize them. In general, education within firms tends to be ad hoc and opportunistic. Many firms do not have enough resources for an educational program. This includes the ability to spare IT engineers from their current projects in order to attend classes. Emerging educational programs should be able to address the role of IT in business and end user issues.

Since many firms do not have a consistent method of evaluating software engineers, the design of their educational program is difficult. The lack of a clear career path for software engineers also makes planning for their long range educational needs difficult.

Many firms use external educational programs, but the content is often too broad to have real practical benefit. Many programs are not organized very well and there is no guarantee that the content will match the corporate standard. These courses are also expensive, difficult to evaluate, and usually only available in metropolitan areas. It may also be difficult to match the availability of the engineer with the time period of the class.

IMMEDIATE SOLUTIONS OR RESPONSES TO PROBLEMS

General Direction

The expansion of IT departments within academic organizations is one method of increasing the availability of IT engineers, and this has been the direction in Japan for the last few years. Based on a request by Education Council, the Educational Reformation Office in MESC published a mid-term report in June 1988 entitled "Training and Securing Information Processing Engineers." This report (according Emura, 1991; JIPDEC, 1991) called for the expansion of IT faculty and courses on both the undergraduate and graduate levels. This includes the establishment of new IT related courses in a variety of schools, the reorganization of old courses, and increasing the number of students admitted into IT related courses of study. The development of a standard curriculum and the establishment of graduate schools are important parts of this process. Two new graduate schools in "Frontier Science and Technology" were established in 1990.

The report also called for general improvements in education quality, such as the establishment of organizations for information exchange about teacher education, establishment of courses for teacher re-education, and the dispatch of inland researchers of IT education to advanced schools and firms.

New Curriculum for Education

Since the lack of a standardized curriculum is one of the biggest problems in the Japanese IT educational program, Japan has developed some prototype curricula based on the standards produced by the Association of Computing Machinery (ACM) and Data Processing Management Association (DPMA). MESC, working to develop a curriculum for academic organizations, appointed the Information Processing Society of Japan (IPSJ) to carry out "Research Studies to Improve Information Processing Education at Universities and Other Educational Organizations."

MITI entrusted CAIT with the design of a standardized curriculum for IT education in industry. CAIT published the *Primary Educational Guideline for Information Processing Engineers* in March 1986, and the *Secondary Educational Guideline for Information Processing Engineers* in March 1989. Appendix C summarizes general framework and necessary hours from *Primary Educational Guideline for Information Processing Engineers.*

CAIT has published a new series of textbooks for IT education based on the *Primary Educational Guideline for Information Processing Engineers* report. While these textbooks have been adopted and used in some vocational and technical schools, the widespread distribution of these materials remains a future consideration. The Committee to Reform Information Processing Education, a department within CAIT, is still studying this material. The proposed guidelines offer advice on curriculum design, but it appears that they expect too much of a student's time to be devoted to IT education at the expense of other subjects.

A report entitled *Toward Systematization of Information Engineering* (Nihon Gakujyutsu-kaigi Dayori, 1991) outlines a curriculum that is more computer science oriented. The Division of Management in Japan's Committee of Academician presented a report entitled *Report from Division of Management* in November 1990. While this report suggests a curriculum for an undergraduate management information systems course of study (see Appendix D), the details of the plan have not been specified yet.

Many universities are trying to establish appropriate curriculums for management information systems departments, and a pioneering example is the Department of Management Information Systems at Shizuoka Prefectural University. According to Hayashi (1991), its curriculum is built around the areas of administration and accounting, mathematics and model-building, and computer and communication. Tokyo Keizai University is planning an management information systems course in its department of management that is used as a prerequisite for other classes in programming, information processing, systems sciences, accounting information systems, management information systems, and IT applications. Although these efforts at establishing curricula seem haphazard, it is through a trial and error process that a standardized curriculum may finally emerge.

New Course of Academic Education

The Educational Reformation Office in MESC published a mid-term report in June 1988 calling for expanded IT faculties and courses within academic institutions.   Since then the educational capacity of universities, junior colleges, and vocational schools have increased more than 10% annually. The most difficult aspects of supporting this growth are (a) the obtainment of sufficient numbers of teachers and (b) the acquisition of hardware and software. Private universities have been especially aggressive in expanding their facilities to entice new students, and having excellent IT facilities is a strong selling point of many universities.

Since keeping current faculty members informed of IT developments is crucial, CAIT and other organizations have opened re-schooling classes for teachers at vocational and technical schools. The Association of Computer Education for Private Universities in Japan also hosts an annual conference to exchange materials, information, and experiences. They have established an electronic mail network to help with this process. The national universities system is a data communication network called "N1 network" for electronic mail and remote batch computing to share computing resources.

While there are some ad-hoc cooperative projects between academic institutions and industry, there is a need to establish a system for interaction between these two parties for research and employee education.

New Course of Industrial Education

The future of within-firm education includes:

1. An emphasis on designing a general educational plan that is coordinated with the firm's business and information system plans.

2. An expansion of end user education to give office workers a basic level of IT literacy. To attain this objective requires determining of the company's overall end user comput-

ing strategy (Keen and Woodman, 1984), and then designing an educational program to fulfill the strategy.

3. Since the lack of capable teachers is critical, it is necessary to establish systematic technical and educational programs for teachers. One idea to add social status to the IT educational position is the establishment of a national examination that all prospective IT teachers would have to pass.

4. Telecommunication engineers are in the most demand within industry, so increasing their numbers is a high priority for most firms.

5. Although new methodologies for system analysis and design (e.g. data flow diagram and structured analysis and design) are gradually diffusing through out Japan, they are not integrated enough to be a usable in all stages in system development.

New Media for IT Education

New educational media are emerging which make use of IT itself ; (a) package, (b) broadcast, and (c) network (CAIT, 1990a). "Package" technology includes video cassette, audio cassette, flexible disk, CD-ROM, CD-I, OHP, computer aided instructions (CAI), and Intelligent CAI (ICAI). The "broadcast" media includes TV, radio, and CATV. The "network" media includes VAN, satellite network, teleconference, and E-mail.

These new media can streamline IT education by providing teachers more effective class materials. Off-the-shelf educational software has recently appeared in the market. CAROL, a series of software packages by CAIT, is a typical example (CAROL had sold 15,000 sets by the end of 1990). By using standardized CAI software, it is possible to make economical use of IT know-how and the standardization of IT education is attainable. Intelligent CAI technology uses artificial intelligence technology to combine PCs and VTRs into an interactive video system.

A satellite network is used for long distance education (CAIT, 1991a). One type broadcasts pictures and text from a teacher to a student, and the student can talk to the teacher over a telephone line. JISEN by Japan IBM is an example. The other type is a two-way satellite transmission. NESPAC of NEC and the HITachi satellite Communication Aided education network System (HITCAS) of Hitachi are examples of this type.

FUTURE DIRECTION: THE NEXT ERA

What is "Global IT Education?"

"Global IT Education" has two significant parts. One is the actual process of internationalizing IT education where a standardization across cultures emerges. IT engineers from all countries would share common concepts and definitions. By exchanging information, know-how, and experience across national boundaries, the IT curriculum in each country has the potential to reap unexpected benefits. This exchange of information could be facilitated through (a) the establishment of a recommended curriculum by an authority such as ACM or DPMA, (b) the exchange of faculty members among countries, (c) the absorption of information and knowledge through adoption of textbooks from other countries, (d) the exchange of information and knowledge through international journals, conferences, and newsletters.

The second part of "global IT education" includes specific education about the international applications of IT such as international information systems networks, transnational data flow, and satellite telecommunication networks. These issues are complicated by country specific aspects such as (a) legal restrictions, (b) restrictions imposed by religion, ideology or social systems, and (c) economic or technological constraints on infrastructure. Thus it is important to make a distinction between knowledge which can be applied across countries and knowledge which is specific to individual countries.

The inclusion of international IT concepts into curriculums is assumed to be important, but it is still far from being a reality. For example, Nehrt (1987) reports that in the United States many students have not studied international issues as part of their business education. Tanopoulos and Vernon (1987) report that when international business material is incorporated into curriculums it is often through functional courses such as finance and marketing. This general picture is also true in Japan (Keieigaku Kenkyu Renraku Iinkai, November, 1990). The only inclusion of international IT concepts in Japanese curriculums has been in the area of international telecommunication, such as CCITT, OSI, Ethernet, and BITNET. The real internationalization of Japan's IT curriculum is a future concern.

Internationalization of IT Education

The internationalization of IT education in Japan will consist of both an absorption of knowledge from other countries and a presentation of Japan's IT knowledge to the international community. The absorption of foreign knowledge and technology includes the adoption of technology, know-how, tools, materials, and information from other countries. This adoption process is not necessarily easy in Japan. Although research findings often have universal applicability, such findings are often not universally disseminated.

Most research on IT has been published in the United States and Europe. For Japan to make use of this knowledge it must be translated into Japanese and diffused as IT education to domestic users. Even though the quantity and quality of Japanese IT research is improving, there is still a need for Japan to absorb leading edge knowledge from abroad. New IT knowledge published in American and European journals is passed along by both academic and industrial researchers through many paths to software engineers and software engineer candidates. Both researchers and software engineers are eager to absorb new IT knowledge to help solve their problems, and it is this desire for new knowledge that is leading to the internationalization of IT education in Japan.

The other half of internationalizing IT education in Japan is the presentation of knowledge and research results to other countries. This has been done through researchers presenting results at international academic conferences and submitting papers to international journals. This method of dissemination has been especially popular in the computer sciences and telecommunication areas. The Japanese government and its agencies also publish introductory journals and newsletters which could help present domestic findings and issues to other countries. Mass media has given wide-spread but superficial coverage of some issues.

This process of absorption and exchange of information is part of what UNESCO calls "cooperative international research on the utilization of computers in education" (Jacobsen, 1989, p.8).

Course of Japan

As the strategic importance of IT increases, IT education becomes critical to the continued success of Japan's industries. This chapter has described the problems and efforts of IT education within the Japanese government agencies, academic institutions, and industries.

Generally speaking, the Japanese IT education policy has been internally established under the leadership of the government (Jacobson, 1986). Educational materials and IT knowledge have been adopted from other industrialized nations, especially the United States, but in general Japan has pursued a policy of domestic development of curriculums and materials.   One reason for this path is a language barrier. The international accumulation of IT knowledge and experience tends to be in English journals and a lack of translations means that this material has not been made accessible to large sectors of Japanese society.

A second reason is the considerable involvement of the Japanese government in determining the course of IT education. Since the government may be less progressive and internationally orientated than academic institutions, its involvement may be a major reason for the primarily domestic development of the IT educational system.   This has resulted in a system and problems of IT education different from most other industrialized countries.

Appendix A

Examples of Classes Held in Technical Oriented Schools in Universities.

Computer architecture	Computer in general
Compiler	Programming
Micro computer	Software
Numerical computing	Hardware
Information retrieval	Telecommunications
Knowledge engineering	System design
Voice data processing	Data base
List processing	System engineering
Computer engineering	System science
Electronic control	Simulation

Algorithms
Mechanical recognition
Programming
System programming
Graphics
Assembly language
Information engineering

Information processing
Information science
Program design
Data structure
Robotics
Artificial intelligence
Operating systems

Appendix B

Examples of Classes Held in Business Schools in Universities.

Computer in general
Information processing
Information management
Programming
Information technology applications
Management information systems
System engineering
Information science
Accounting information systems
System science

Appendix C

Subjects and Hours in information technology Education Plan Designed by CAIT.

Necessary Subjects	Hours	
	Lecture	Exercise
Basic knowledge	140	
Information processing and computer	20	
Hardware	40	
Software	40	
Information processing systems	40	
Practical knowledge [a]	186 or 166	174 or 194
Program flow chart	37	53
File	29	1
COBOL	90	110
FORTRAN	70	130
System development and operation	30	10
Related knowledge	300	
Information processing		

202 Sato

miscellaneous	10
Electronics	90
General knowledge of service sector	110
General knowledge of manufacturing sector	90

Note. From "Time allocation" by CAIT., 1986, Shotou Jouhou Shori Gijyutsusha Ikusei Shishin, 14. adapted by permission.
a Depends on selection of language (FORTRAN or COBOL)

Appendix D

Prototype Curriculum for MIS Field.

Year	Freshman	Sophomore
	Information sciences [a]	Information processing [a]
	System sciences [a]	Information management [a]
	Managerial math [b]	Data base [b]
	Organization sciences [b]	MIS [b]
	Managerial sciences [a]	

Year	Junior	Senior
	Marketing information	System design
	Manufacturing information	Networks
	Distribution information [b]	
	Accounting information [b] systems	Office automation
	Financial information systems	Factory automation

Note. From Keieigaku Kenkyu Renraku Iinkai Houkoku [Report from Division of Management] (p.13) by Nihon Gakujyutsu-kaigi Keieigaku Kenkyu Renraku Iinkai, November 1990, adapted by permission.

[a] Compulsory,   [b] Selective compulsory

Author of this chapter thanks Detmar W. Straub Jr., and Russell S. Littlefield for their help in preparing this manuscript. Author also thanks CAIT for providing information and materials for this chapter.

REFERENCES
Central Academy of Information Technology. (1986). *Shotou jouhou shori gijyutsusha ikusei shishin [Primary educational guideline for information processing engineers]*. (Available from Central Academy of Information Technology, World Trade Center Building. 7F, 2-4-1 Hamamatsu-cho, Minato-ku, Tokyo 105, Japan.)

Central Academy of Information Technology. (1990a, March). *Jouho shori kyoiku jittai chousa houkokusho [Information processing education report]*.

Central Academy of Information Technology. (1990b, March). *News letter. 1*.

Central Academy of Information Technology. (1991a, March), *Enkakuchi kyouiku no tame no jouhoushori sistemu no jitsugen housaku ni kansuru chousa kenkyu houkokusho [Report of information processing education systems in distant area]*.

Central Academy of Information Technology. (1991b, March), *Jouho shori kyoiku jittai chousa houkokusho [Information processing education report]*.

Central Academy of Information Technology. (1991c, March). *News Letter. 2*. (Available from CAIT)

Cowen, R., & McLead, M. (Eds.). (1984). *International handbook of education systems* (Vol.III) (pp.209-250). John-Wiley and Sons.

Emura, J. (1991, March). Current trends in the training of personnel in Japan: Present situation of education in information, *News Letter, 2*, 1-13.

Hayashi, S. (1991). Jitsumu-kei gakka ni manabu igiwo dou kangaerubekika [How should we think the meaning of studying in practical department ?], *Keiei to Jouhou, 3*(2), 1-77.

Industrial Structure Council of Ministry of International Trade and Industry. (1987). *2,000 nen no sofutouea jinzai [Software engineers in Japan by the year 2,000]*. Tokyo: Computer Age Press.

Jacobsen, E. (1989). An International Perspective. *SIGCUE Outlook, 20*(2), 6-14.

Jacobson, W. J. (1986). *Analyses and comparisons of science curricula in Japan and the United States*. (Report No. NIE-P-85-3062). Washington D.C.: Office of Educational Research and Improvement. (ERIC Document Reproduction Service No. ED 271395)

Japan Information Processing Development Center (1990a). Jouhouka hakusho [Informatization white paper]. Tokyo: Computer Age Press.

Japan Information Processing Development Center. (1990b). *JIPDEC: The organization and activities*.

Japan Information Processing Development Center ed. (1991). Jouhouka hakusho [Informatization white paper]. Tokyo: Computer Age Press.

Kanaya, T., (1988). Japan. In N. T. Postlethwaite (ed.), *The Encyclopedia of comparative education and national systems of education* (pp.403-408). Pergamon Press.

Keen, P. G. W. & Woodman, L. A. (1984). What to do with all those micros. *Harvard Business Review*, 142-150.

Nehrt, L. C., (1987). The internationalization of the curriculum. *Journal of International Business Studies, 18,* 83-90.

Nihon Gakujyutsu-kaigi Dayori *[Communications from conference of Japanese academician]* (1991, August), Jouho Shori, 32(8), 1003-1006.

Nihon Gakujyutsu-kaigi Keieigaku Kenkyu Renraku Iinkai. (1990). *Keieigaku Kenkyu Renraku Iinkai Houkoku [Report from division of management],* (November 1990), Nihon Gakujyutsu-kaigi Keieigaku Kenkyu Renraku Iinkai.

Resta, P. (1989). Education change and computers: an international perspective, *SIGCUE Outlook, 20*(2), 3-5.

Rogers, E. M. (1983). *Diffusion of innovation* (2nd ed.). The Free Press.

Sakamoto, T. (1989). Asian perspectives. In M. Eraut (Ed.), *The International Encyclopedia of Education Technology* (pp.54-59). Oxford: Pergamon Press.

Thanopoulos, J., & Vernon, I.R. (1987). International business education in the AACSB schools. *Journal of International Business Studies, 18,* 91-98.

Yourdon, E. (1982). *Managing the Systems Life Cycle.* Yourdon Press.

Educating IT Professionals for Work in Ireland: An Emerging Post-industrial Country

8

Eileen M. Trauth
Northeastern University

During the past three decades Ireland has been undergoing a significant societal transformation. It is moving from a traditional society emphasizing farming and domestic markets to one whose economy is heavily dependent on inward investment by multinational information technology firms. As it moves toward a post-industrial society, Ireland has identified information technology education as a key factor in this societal transformation. In order to provide a qualified work force, certain changes in the content and structure of Irish education were necessary. Among these were: making secondary education freely available; establishing technical colleges throughout the country; placing greater emphasis on science, engineering and business in the existing universities; and creating two technologically-oriented universities. To help upgrade the skills of working adults, evening degree programs and government training programs were created. Three recommendations result from examination of Ireland's efforts to educate IT professionals. First, labor force requirements must be monitored against student demographics. Second, the universities must broaden their mission to incorporate greater linkages with industry. Finally, class-based barriers to IT educational attainment must be addressed.

During the second half of the twentieth century, Ireland has been undergoing a societal transformation. It is changing from a traditional, agrarian society with an inward focus to a post-industrial society and a full participant in the world economy. This change is occurring in the context of directed national planning. The plan is based, in large part, upon the development of an employment sector founded upon information technology work and information services. This is largely being accomplished by attracting foreign industries to Ireland. The long term effects of this effort are still to be felt. But it is already clear that this transformation is affecting not only the Irish economy, but its societal institutions as well.

This chapter examines the role of education in a country that is in the process of transforming its labor force from agriculture to information work. It does this by first describing the role of education in Ireland's agricultural society. This is followed by a description of the new industrial policy and the educational changes which are required to make it successful. In doing so, issues and recommendations are highlighted. Finally, the Irish situation is brought into the larger context of international IT education.

The objective of this chapter is to answer two basic questions with respect to countries such as Ireland. The first question is: What are the issues related to educating the indigenous population for work in an information economy[1]? This question is concerned with the educational preparation of individuals for work in the IT sector. It is also concerned with the type of educational infrastructure that must be in place in the country.

The second question is: What are the issues related to educating individuals in advanced industrialized countries for work in countries with emerging information industries? This question is concerned with the knowledge, perspectives and orientations of employees of multinational firms who will be working in or establishing offices in countries such as Ireland. This question extends the educational consideration beyond the borders of the newly post-industrial country to societies which will supply the personnel to establish work sites in these countries.

The data for this chapter are from the results of a study of the emerging information economy in Ireland. There are two purposes of this study. One is to document Ireland's route to a post-industrial society. The other purpose is to argue that information economies are not monolithic. They do not emerge according to fixed, immutable laws. Rather, each post-industrial society is shaped by the cultural, economic, and political factors present in that society[2]. The data come from both primary and secondary sources. Primary sources include interviews with employees and managers at multinational and indigenous IT firms. These interviews are supplemented by interviews with representatives of relevant societal institutions: unions, universities, and government agencies charged with supporting Ireland's industrial policy[3]. Secondary sources include published books and periodicals, public policy documents[4], and agency literature.

While the data used in this paper are specific to Ireland, the issues are not. Ireland is representative of a type of society today, one which is "leap frogging" from an agrarian to a post-industrial society by emphasizing work in the information economy. Such countries have traditions and values associated with an agrarian life style, are often post-colonial, and are geographically peripheral to the global economic powers. For Ireland, as for other similar countries, the challenge is not simply one of attracting foreign investors. It is also to establish linkages between the societal infrastructure and the industrial policy. Key among these linkages is education.

THE ROLE OF EDUCATION IN IRELAND'S SOCIETAL TRANSFORMATION

In examining the role of education in the societal transformation of Ireland it is first necessary to consider what the phrase "educating IT professionals" means for Ireland. For an emerging post-industrial society, this phrase has two components: content and infrastructure. Content refers to *what* future IT workers need to learn. Infrastructure refers to the societal *structures* which disseminate that content. Since the role of education in agrarian societies is quite different from that of post-industrial societies, the educational infrastructure is likewise very different. Thus, the task of educating a labor force for information technology work is not simply a matter of curriculum design. The larger, and perhaps more difficult, challenge is that of changing the educational infrastructure. This chapter considers both aspects of the educational challenge.

Traditional Irish Society

Few societies have changed as much as Ireland in the past thirty years. Ireland, prior to its transformation, has been described as "... a rural, conservative and Catholic backwater of post-war Europe." (Breen, Hannan, Rottman, and Whelan, 1990, p. 1). In order to understand the dimensions of the transformation that has occurred, it is necessary to understand the type of society from which the new Ireland emerged. Ireland was one of the first nations to obtain its independence from colonialism in the twentieth century. The Anglo-Irish Treaty of 1921 divided the island into the independent Irish Free State and Northern Ireland. In 1949 the Free State left the British Commonwealth and the Republic of Ireland was born.

Partition of the island resulted in the absence of an industrial base in the new republic. O'Malley (1989) argues that the industrial revolution did not flourish in Ireland for three reasons. First, it lacked many of the natural resources needed to support heavy manufacturing industry. Second, its colonial status interfered with its participation in the industrial revolution occurring elsewhere. Finally, what little industrialization existed in Ireland at the turn of the twentieth century was in Northern Ireland. Hence, the way in which the Irish Republic was established caused it to regress along the agrarian, industrial, post-industrial continuum.

During its early years, the new Irish nation was isolationist. In an effort to reestablish political and cultural sovereignty, economic policies were directed at creating national self-sufficiency through protectionist policies. The operating assumption was that Ireland would prosper by promoting the interests of small farmers and native industry serving local markets. During this period of economic isolationism there was little motivation for involvement in international affairs. In such a society there was also little need for highly developed societal infrastructures associated with an industrialized society such as telecommunications, transportation, and education.

Agriculture was the dominant economic and societal organizing principle. In the 1920's, farmers accounted for nearly half of the labor force (Rottman, Hannan, Hardiman and Wiley,

1982, p. 46). These farms were family owned, generally small, and passed down from one generation to another. Society was organized around the activities and values associated with a stable, unchanging agricultural society. Land was the basis of social status. One's life chances depended on the prospect of inheriting a family-owned business or farm.

Role of Education

A strong emphasis on learning is part of the Irish character. This is expressed in the value placed on general literacy, language facility and "mental alertness." Until quite recently, however, extensive formal education has not been available to the general population. Since the nineteenth century, primary education has been provided through the free National School system. Until 1968, post-primary education was available in two forms. Free vocational schools were established in the 1930's. Their mission was practical training in preparation for employment in the trades, manufacturing, agriculture, and commerce.

The alternative form of post-primary education was the secondary school, a private, academically-oriented institution, generally run by priests and nuns. The role of the secondary school was not to provide a skilled labor force. Rather, the focus was on

> ... religious, moral and intellectual construction, and the products of this form of education were (if male) destined for jobs in   professional and other white collar occupations, achieved in some cases via third level education. (Breen et al., 1990, p. 126).

Clearly, education beyond primary level was the province of the middle class and wealthy farmers. Formal education was not viewed as a vehicle for enhancing one's position in society, nor was it linked to employment prospects. Rather, it was a refining process for those who were already members of the privileged classes (O'Toole, 1990a).

The Emerging Post-Industrial Society

The late 1950's marked the end of the post-independence search for a national identity and economy based on conceptions of traditional, rural Ireland. The first of several industrial development plans to follow (see Endnote 4), the *Programme for Economic Expansion* represented a significant turning point in Irish history. It was a rupture from the past as it reversed the protectionist policy then in place. The assumption that Ireland would prosper by promoting the interests of small farmers and native industry serving local markets was cast aside. It was replaced with an agenda which opened wide the doors to foreign investment as Ireland began to participate fully in the world economy.

There were two key aspects of this new plan. The first was the mechanization and consolidation of farms in order to be more competitive in the European food market. Increased agricultural production at the expense of agricultural employment resulted. Between 1961 an 1981 the number of males employed in agriculture declined from 34% to 17.4% (Rottman et al., 1982, p. 46). The second aspect of the plan was replacing jobs lost in agriculture with industrial employment. This was to be accomplished by attracting foreign export-oriented manufacturing firms to Ireland. A semi-state agency, the Industrial Development Authority (IDA), was responsible for overseeing the implementation of this aspect of the industrial policy. (See Endnote 3.)

In considering which foreign industries to attract, Irish policy makers identified three high growth industries that were not heavily dependent upon the natural resources that Ireland lacked. They are pharmaceuticals, chemicals, and electronics. Electronics meant the manufacture (usually final assembly for the European market) of computer hardware. It was the decision to attract firms in the electronics industry that set Ireland on its path toward an information economy. It is important to note, however, that during the 1960's and 1970's Ireland did not think of itself as moving toward an information economy. To Irish policy makers, the computer industry was simply a form of manufacturing. But the combination of policy decisions and other infrastructural and societal changes resulted in the emergence of a diverse information economy that has become crucial to Ireland's economic future.

Among the infrastructural changes that were needed to support the new industrial policy was the upgrading of Ireland's telecommunications system. As an agrarian society emphasizing small farming and local markets, sophisticated telecommunications was not an important priority. But the multinational firms Ireland was courting required the ability to move information quickly and efficiently. Consequently, during the 1970's and 1980's Ireland significantly upgraded its telecommunications network with the use of satellite and fiber optic technologies. An unintended consequence of this action was the multifaceted information economy that resulted. In addition to computer hardware manufacture, Ireland subsequently identified other employment opportunities which are based upon a sophisticated telecommunications capability. One of these is remote software development. Multinational companies such as Wang Laboratories and IBM, for example, located software development groups in Ireland. By taking advantage of time differences and cheaper real estate, Ireland was also able to develop a third type of information work: off shore data processing. Today, the data entry and information processing activities of many American and European insurance, publishing, and financial services firms are located in Ireland. Ireland currently has a robust information economy which includes technology manufacture, software development and information processing.

This industrial development policy has brought about a transformation in Irish society. Ireland has moved from a being a nation of small farmers to one which emphasizes employment in targeted high tech industries, key among these being the information technology and services sectors. These new industries now account for a significant part of Ireland's labor force and Gross National Product. Nearly a third of the industrial employment in Ireland is accounted for by the metals and engineering sector (Institute of Public Administration, 1989, p. 388). Electrical, electronic, chemicals and pharmaceuticals industries increased output by an average of 15% per year between 1975 and 1990. In contrast, the traditional, labor-intensive, low value-added industries suffered a decline in output of 2%. Ireland is noteworthy within the European Community by having half of its total manufacturing output accounted for for these fast growing new technology sectors (Power, 1990).

Educating IT Professionals

The successful implementation of this plan hinges on the availability of a qualified labor force. Thus, Ireland's industrial development policy has been the driving force behind the development and growth of IT education in that country. Examining Ireland's approach to educating IT professionals involves considering aspects of the existing educational system which were consistent with the new industrial plan. It also involves identifying those changes in both educational content and infrastructure that needed to occur in order for the industrial policy to succeed.

Access to Secondary Education. An important feature of Irish culture which is consistent with a society emphasizing information work is the high value placed upon learning. However, prior to 1968, secondary education was only available from "fee paying" (private) schools. Therefore, children of poor farming or working class families generally received no more than a primary education. In some cases, they also attended a vocational school.

In conjunction with Ireland's societal transformation, however, greater equality of educational opportunity was desired. It was pursued by making secondary education freely available to all. Religious orders which operated the secondary schools continued to do so in an arrangement whereby the State paid the fees for the students. The influence of nuns and priests has resulted in two noteworthy aspects of Irish secondary education. There is a strong emphasis on a well-rounded liberal arts education and it is carried out in a structured and disciplined environment. The result has led American managers in Ireland to comment on the quality of the overall education and, in particular, the analytical and communication skills possessed by workers who have the Leaving Certificate[5].

Making secondary education free was a first step toward providing a work force compatible with the new industrial policy. It ensured the availability of a workers who would be well-educated in a general sense. Free secondary education also opened the door to greater participation in third level education. It has been at this level that the most significant changes in Irish education in support of the new industrial policy have occurred. The concerted effort to provide education appropriate for information technology work has involved five significant changes in post-secondary education.

Changing the University. When implementation of the new industrial policy began, the only form of third level education in existence was the traditional university. These were traditional in that their focus was classical not vocational. Courses of study were directed at producing a well-rounded individual, not responding to labor force requirements. Therefore, in order to have an appropriately educated work force, one area that was addressed was the university itself. Changes were needed in both content and in orientation. They needed to place greater overall emphasis on science and technology, and specific emphasis on computer science, engineering and business. Along with changes in content, universities also needed to change their perception of the role of university education to include preparation for employment and linkages with industry. But no matter how much or how quickly these schools could have changed, they would not have had sufficient resources to accommodate the number of students who now needed access to higher education.

Technical Colleges. In a sense, Ireland has benefitted from not having had a period of traditional industrialization prior to moving into the post-industrial economy. This is because it has not been encumbered by work patterns suited to manufacturing and assembly line work. It also has not been burdened with an educational system oriented toward traditional, heavy industry. Therefore, Ireland could start from the beginning to create educational programs and institutions to support an information economy. One way it did this was by establishing additional types of third level institutions to supplement the universities. Consequently, a series of technical colleges were established. The Dublin Institute of Technology was located in Dublin and regional technical colleges (RTC's) were located throughout the country. In this way, IT education was brought to the people so that they were not forced to come to the quickly growing cities.

New Universities. Besides adding technical courses of study to the traditional universities and creating technical colleges, a third effort was to create two new universities with the specific mission of providing IT education. One was established in 1972 in Limerick; the other in 1980 in Dublin. These schools were originally called National Institutes for Higher Education and did not have full university status. In 1989 that situation was changed. The University of Limerick and Dublin City University have rapidly progressed from being perceived as vocational schools to enjoying the prestige of a full university. They are distinctly different from the traditional universities, however, in several respects. First, their focus is exclusively technical and professional education. They offer degrees in subjects such as computer science, business, communications and engineering. Second, they have adopted the cooperative education model whereby students incorporate periods of work placement into their courses of study. Finally, these schools have close ties with industry. For example, the managing director of the Digital Equipment Corporation plant in Galway sits on the Advisory Board of Dublin City University and Wang Laboratories is located adjacent to the campus of University of Limerick, a symbolic indication of the close ties between that university and the IT industry. A description of the types of IT education provided by these two universities is provided in the Appendix.

Government Training Programs. Technical education provided by the universities and technical colleges was supplemented by the efforts of government agencies which provide training and employment services. In 1988 several agencies were amalgamated into a single agency Foras Aiseauna Saothair (FAS), the Irish Training and Employment Authority (see Endnote 3). FAS training facilities are located throughout the country to provide specific job training to young people following their formal education and to offer retraining to the existing labor force.

Adult Education. The final component of the changed educational infrastructure relates to adult education. While FAS provides technical skills training, working adults also needed access to higher education. As competition for jobs has grown and new entrants to the labor force increasingly have third level degrees, educational credentials have become more important in Ireland. Many individuals who had been able to obtain positions with only the Leaving Certificate now need a third level degree for career advancement and mobility. To provide for this, the universities have begun to offer both undergraduate and graduate degrees through evening school. Some multinational companies have helped further this educational goal by paying the third level fees of their employees.

While evening degree programs are a common occurrence in America where education has long been linked to employment, the development of "night school" represents a significant societal change in Ireland. In this culture, higher education had been the purview of the privileged. It was for young people who had the financial resources to attend school full-time before embarking upon their positions of leadership in society. Therefore, providing evening degree programs to working adults was truly opening education up to the masses.

In the past twenty years the educational infrastructure in Ireland has undergone a transformation no less dramatic than that occurring in the society as a whole. Many more students are now obtaining a third level education. In 1986 25% of those who had obtained the Leaving Certificate entered institutions of higher education. There has been a significant shift from an emphasis on traditional arts subjects like language, history and geography to science and technology. In 1986 41% of new entrants were studying science and technology, and 22% were studying commerce (Clancy, 1988).

IRISH IT EDUCATION: ISSUES AND RECOMMENDATIONS

The process of examining the transformation of Irish education accompanying the society's rapid migration from an agricultural to a post-industrial society highlights certain issues. The resolution of some will take place with time; others will be much more difficult to resolve.

Labor Force Requirements and Educational Preparation

One significant challenge for both educators and policy makers is maintaining a balance between the kinds of IT jobs available and characteristics of the labor force emerging from the schools. An important motivator for the current industrial policy was to stem the tide of emigration which has long been a feature of Irish society. Historically, the ones who have emigrated were those without employment options, the classic example being the sons who did not inherit the family farm. However, during the 1980's the emigration of Ireland's "best and brightest" became a cause of concern. In 1981, 8.1% of Ireland's graduates had emigrated; by 1987 the proportion had risen to 25.6% (Higher Education Authority, 1988). These individuals emigrate for a variety of reasons. Some want to gain work experience abroad while they are young. Others leave to avoid the high tax burden. However, many leave because there are not sufficient jobs suited to the type of education they have received. A common complaint of electronic engineers is that the multinational companies do not locate the research and development function in Ireland,

thereby limiting their employment prospects following graduation. The country looses out in several respects when its well-
educated graduates emigrate. First, Ireland looses the contribution that these young people could make to its IT industry.
Second, the return on the investment of money spent by the State
on a student is lost when graduates ago abroad to work. Finally,
many of the scarce spaces in the universities are being taken by
students who do not remain in Ireland.

For a country such as Ireland, where the industrial policy
and its supporting infrastructure were enacted in the context of
an overall plan, it would be consistent to recommend that
national monitoring of employment trends and close coordination between industry and academe be undertaken. A further
recommendation and one which is currently being pursued, is to
attempt to attract firms requiring the kinds of skills that graduates possess. Over the past twenty years, high tech employment
has migrated from lower level, minimally skilled jobs to more
sophisticated work. This is evidenced in companies such as Intel
which came to Ireland in 1990 to produce its newest line of
microprocessors.

Vocational Role of the University

Part of the problem of matching educational qualifications with available employment has been attributed to the
reluctance of the universities to accept their new role as the
bridge between education and employment. Several examples
point this out. One executive from an indigenous IT firm com-
plained about his experience in trying to recruit engineers from
one of the universities. Because of the placement office's failure
to adequately advertise the positions in his firm, all the available
graduates took positions with foreign firms not knowing about
employment opportunities at home. Irish IT workers have com-
plained that traditional universities didn't introduce information
technology courses soon enough. As a result, some of them had
to turn to programs such as those provided by FAS following their
formal education in order to acquire the needed skills. Others
have commented that they didn't receive adequate assistance
with job seeking such as help with resume writing and interview-
ing skills.

One Irish IT executive believes that there *are* enough jobs
for graduates with technological degrees. In his view, the prob-

lem is an insufficient number of young people with both education *and* experience. His recommendation is to emphasize cooperative education programs which are ideally suited to provide
this dual form of credentialing. Yet, some of the schools have
been reluctant to incorporate what they perceive to be a blatantly
vocational element into their curricula.

This same individual, in describing his own work history,
told of how he had to leave his university position after his start-
up company was established. The concept of the "incubator" did
not exist in the early 1970's when he began his company. Such
close ties between formal education and industrial application
were resisted by universities who saw these linkages as somehow
contrary to the educational mission. (This situation has since
been rectified; incubators now exist, though usually in the more
technological institutions.)

While progress is being made, there is still evidence of
resistance within universities to adopting this broader view of the
educational mission. The tradition of the university as the locus
of classical education is a long and cherished one. It would be
unrealistic to expect that perceptions and orientation will change
overnight. However, the addition of IT and other technical
subjects to Irish education will be undercut if the traditional
universities are not supportive of this effort. The success of the
University of Limerick and Dublin City University in providing
professional skills within the context of a university education
can serve as both a model and a motivator for the other
universities in Ireland.

Class-Based Barriers to IT Educational Attainment

The issues raised thus far are, to a large extent, a function
of the speed with which Ireland has implemented changes in its
educational curricula and infrastructure. As such, it can be
anticipated that they will be resolved over time. Indeed, some of
the issues that have been cited refer to situations that existed
more in the 1970's and 1980's than today.

Theory vs. Reality of a Meritocracy. A much more
difficult issue to address, and one which is woven into the fabric
of Irish society, is the gap between the theory and the reality of
a meritocracy. When the multinational IT firms first came to
Ireland in the 1970's, the labor force was not adequately prepared for the type of work to be done. Consequently, the firms

received grants from the State to provide the necessary IT training. Thus, in the early years of the IT industry in Ireland, workers from diverse social class and educational backgrounds were able to obtain IT employment. Today, the situation is much different. A combination of greater competition for jobs and a change in the nature of the work has required formal credentials for employment. At a minimum, the Leaving Certificate is required; for many forms of employment, post-secondary credentials are required. This current situation raises the question of whether there are class-based barriers to equal IT educational attainment in Ireland.

In his classic work on the subject, Daniel Bell (1973) describes the post-industrial society as a meritocracy. In the agricultural society, power and status are largely fixed and out of one's control. This is because they are based upon the ownership of land and characteristics such as birth order and gender. In the industrial society, power is in the hands of those with control over the means of production: the capital and the raw materials. While social mobility is not as fixed as in the agrarian society, a clear division between the managers and the proletariat exists. In contrast to both of these societies, the post-industrial society with its emphasis on meritocracy and credentials allows for greater social mobility. If one believes that intelligence is not a function of family background or income and if educational opportunity is available to all, then theoretically everyone has an equal chance of succeeding in the post-industrial society.

The logical conclusion of this line of thinking is that all workers have an equal chance of benefitting from Ireland's movement into a post-industrial society. Data from a variety of sources, however, suggest that members of the middle class[6] have received disproportionate benefits from this societal transformation. In his study of who attends higher education in Ireland, Clancy (1988) observed that in 1986, 55% of the entrants to higher education were children of professionals, managers, and salaried employees, yet this group accounted for only 30% of the relevant cohort. In contrast, 24% of new entrants came from working class backgrounds despite the fact that they represented 55% of the target population. This data is consistent with the author's field data on the class origins of IT workers. It is further reinforced by O'Toole's observation (1990b) that the social class of one's parents is a predictor of one's own social class in Ireland more than in any of the western European societies with which it has been compared.

The implication of this data is that children of working class and marginal farming families do not have equal opportunity for success in IT employment. This claim is controversial and not everyone would agree with it. Many informants have described Ireland as a classless society. In fact, a characteristic of the Irish culture is disdain for displays of class pretensions. Nevertheless, the evidence in support of this claim justifies its consideration among educational issues related to the transformation to an information economy.

Equality of Access to Higher Education. The issue is more subtle than simply making secondary or third level education available to all. The argument is that there is unequal opportunity to obtain a third level education based on social class. This issue exists in the context of a very limited number of available positions in the Irish universities. Acceptance into these courses of study is based upon a highly competitive "points system." These points derive from scores on each subject examined for the Leaving Certificate. Degree programs within the universities vary in the points they require and the number of subjects that must be taken for admission. The more prestigious and desirable the course of study and the school, the greater the number of points the student must have for admission.

While it is true that secondary education is freely available to all, differences in secondary schools, nevertheless, exist. First, children of middle class families have the financial means to send their children to "fee paying" schools—private, college preparatory schools which emphasize the subjects in which one must do well to attain admittance to the university. Second, among the state financed secondary schools, differences exist as well. Wide discretion is given to the schools regarding the subjects which are emphasized. This variation affects not only social class but gender as well. One female informant observed that the computer applications program she wished to enter required having passed the Leaving Certificate exam in Honors Maths, a course of study which many girls schools didn't offer when she was in secondary school. Finally, parents in middle class communities often provide additional financial assistance to the schools. For all of these reasons, one could argue that in light of the limited number of university places, it is more difficult for the underclass to obtain a university education.

Value Placed Upon Higher Education. Another barrier to advanced IT education derives from parental attitudes about higher education. To parents who were able to obtain employment without much formal education, the notion of a child remaining out of the work force until the age of eighteen or twenty-one might seem wasteful, a loss of income to the family. These semi- or unskilled workers have historically worked as manual laborers on farms or in the cities. However, the need for this type of work in Ireland is sharply declining. Children of these workers will be much less likely to find similar employment. Indeed, much of the impetus for a new industrial policy was to respond to this decline. The jobs which are replacing them require brain power rather than muscle power. As such, some form of post-secondary education is increasingly being required.

Symbolic of this change in employment qualifications is the transformation of the Customs House Docks area in Dublin. Long a source of employment for manual laborers, the Docks area is being transformed into a financial services center which emphasizes off shore data processing services for financial companies based in America and Europe. Children of generations of dock workers will no longer be able to look to manual labor on the docks as the source of their livelihoods.

Class-Based Differences in the IT Industry. As a consequence of these factors, class divisions can be witnessed in the IT industry. In the multinational firms which are primarily engaged in information technology manufacture, there is a wider range of social class background. Though, even here, the minimum credentials are rising. The social class gap is most dramatic, however, upon examination of the labor force in Irish IT firms. These firms tend to emphasize the software rather than the hardware aspects of the field. This is because of the low start up costs, limited capital resources required, and the availability of a young, skilled work force. However, this type of work requires significantly more educational background than assembly work for computer manufacture. Consequently, the workers at indigenous IT firms are predominantly middle class.

It is important to note, however, that attitude as well as credentials plays a role in employment opportunities. Information technology work, insofar as it is skilled, pays well, and requires credentialing, can be defined as middle class work. In America, if one possesses the credentials, he or she is likely to find suitable employment. In Ireland, however, credentials are often not sufficient. Several informants working at indigenous IT firms reported that while they have university degrees, they had little or no IT credentials when they were hired. The reasons they gave for having obtained IT employment were related to social class: having the proper accent, living in the "right" neighborhoods, having attended a certain school.

Greater opportunities to attend universities will perhaps make it easier for working class individuals to obtain IT employment. But in order to ensure that this occurs, both concrete and attitudinal changes are needed. Characteristics of secondary schools which serve as a barrier to university admission must be addressed. Greater availability of third level courses at night is another recommendation. But changes in the attitudes of some parents and employers must change as well. Working class parents need to understand the relationship between post-secondary education and employment opportunities. The attitudes of some IT managers must also change. In order to overcome the class-based barriers to IT employment, employers need to understand that individuals from any social class are capable of being productive workers in the IT industry.

Making the fruits of the transformation to an information economy available to individuals from all social classes will not be achieved overnight. Assumptions about one's life chances which were fixed for generations will take time and conscious intervention to alter.

INTERNATIONAL IT EDUCATION AND THE IRISH CASE

The final section of this chapter adds the international dimension to the discussion of IT education in Ireland. This is done from two viewpoints. The first concerns the international component of Irish IT education. The second concerns the international component of IT education for students in advanced industrialized countries such as the United States, Germany, and Japan. This is relevant to the present discussion because workers at multinational companies from these countries are the ones who come to Ireland to establish operations there.

International IT Education in Ireland

We can begin by considering the reasons for including an international dimension within Irish IT education. There are several reasons. Many graduates will be working for multinational companies in Ireland; others will go abroad to work. Those who will work for indigenous companies have equally compelling reasons to have an international orientation. Ireland is a peripheral country within both the European and the world economies. As a country with a small population and market for its IT products, it is heavily influenced by changes in the world economy. Managers at indigenous software firms observed that a start up company in Ireland needs to enter the international market at a much earlier stage of corporate growth than a similar American company because of the small and limited domestic market. For both types of workers, the Single European Market will bring with it greater mobility of workers: from other countries to Ireland and from Ireland to other countries.

Before considering the form that international IT education has taken in Ireland, it is necessary to consider what is meant by the term "international." For a country which is a member of a political or economic unit such as the European Community, does international mean beyond the country's national borders or beyond the boundary of the political/economic unit? Irish education in general (and, therefore, Irish IT education as well) contains components which incorporate both interpretations of "international" into the educational process.

The implementation of the Single European Market contains educational initiatives in which Ireland is a full participant. One is an exchange program whereby students from one European Community country are able to attend universities in other member countries. There are also a variety of European Community programs to foster cooperation and understanding among students from different countries. In addition to participation in European Community programs, there is also a concerted effort within Ireland to place greater emphasis on foreign language skills at both the secondary and the university level. Certain programs are beginning to add the study of a foreign language to the degree requirements. In addition to the formal mechanisms by which the international component is incorporated into Irish education, there is also a significant informal contribution. Because of the presence of so many multinational firms in

Ireland, a significant number of Irish workers at multinational firms have been to countries such as Germany and the United States, in relation to work. This provides the opportunity for IT workers to learn, first hand, about other countries. What these individuals learn from other countries through their work no doubt filters down to their children. Thus, an international orientation begins at an early age.

International IT Education in Advanced Industrialized Nations

As with IT education in Ireland, the question can be raised as to the need for adding an international dimension to IT education in advanced industrialized nations such as the United States[7]. The reasons are different but equally important. Simply put, the world is shrinking. The globalization of companies through mergers, acquisitions, and joint ventures makes it far more appropriate these days to think in terms of a global rather than a national IT industry. In addition, American companies seek to have a presence within the European Community. Finally, labor force costs and requirements are causing many companies to seek employees in countries such as Ireland.

Given this rationale for international IT education, the next question is: What do American IT workers need to know in order to physically or remotely work with people in a newly industrializing country such as Ireland? Both Irish and American managers commented that American workers do not have a sufficiently international perspective. One Irish manager observed that because of the geographical proximity of European countries, American multinational firms tend to think of all of Europe as a single culture. For a cultural "melting pot" nation like the United States, it may be difficult to appreciate the cultural identity issues which are very important to other nations. To respond to this problem, one American manager in Ireland recommended that the study of a nation's culture should be a required part of the preparation of all multinational employees working abroad.

International IT education which will prepare American multinational employees to successfully work in countries such as Ireland needs to emphasize cultural, political and legal issues which have an impact on their work. American IT students need to be aware of regulations governing information practices which are different from those in the United States. Two examples are privacy and telecommunications. American privacy law is fragmented and sectoral (Trauth, 1986). There is no single, comprehensive privacy law. Rather, there are a series of state and federal laws which address record keeping practices in various industries. This is in contrast with much of the world and most of Europe. The Council of Europe, a body larger than the European Community, requires that all member countries enact a comprehensive privacy law. As a member country, Ireland did so in 1988. It is therefore necessary for American IT workers to understand the dimensions of these laws and the impact on the information processing and record keeping practices of companies.

Telecommunications is another aspect of IT which is influenced by state regulation. While a trend toward privatization of telecommunications services is in evidence, most countries are still much more regulated than the United States in this area. This means that an IT worker would need to be aware of the regulatory structure and be prepared to work with the national PTTs (postal, telegraph and telephone companies) in the construction and use of data networks.

But of all the aspects of international education, what is probably the most critical is to acquire an appreciation for cultural pluralism. Interviews with Irish and American workers at multinational firms in Ireland revealed the importance of understanding differences in the work ethic, management style, attitude toward authority, risk taking behavior, and degree of individualism, to name but a few. American IT students need to appreciate that there is more than one way to achieve a corporate goal.

There is clearly a cultural give-and-take when a multinational IT company comes to a country like Ireland, but those which succeed are those which give as much as they take. The implication for the education of American IT workers is an appreciation for cultural differences. One way to accomplish this is to encourage exchange programs between American and foreign schools. Another, for schools with work study components, is to provide opportunities for students to work abroad.

CONCLUSION

This chapter has considered the topic of IT education in the context of a country which is undergoing a rapid transformation from a traditional, agrarian society to a post-industrial one.

Education in general, and IT education in particular are among the key components of the societal infrastructure requiring alteration in order to be compatible with the new industrial policy. Educational changes not only involved additions to existing university curriculum. More importantly, the entire infrastructure for providing IT education was greatly expanded to include new schools, government training agencies, and adult education. Ireland has demonstrated success in its efforts to provide its young people with an education appropriate to an information economy. Nevertheless, the high emigration rate of third level graduates and the influence of socio-economic class on higher education attendance and IT employment are issues which require serious attention.

The topic of international education as it relates to Ireland has two aspects. One is the international component of Irish IT education. It has been observed that IT education in Ireland is inherently international due to its participation in European Community programs and the presence of so many multinational companies. The other aspect of international IT education relates to the education of future employees of multi-national companies, those who will be working in a country such as Ireland. The experiences of those who have done so suggest that an appreciation of cultural, political, and regulatory differences and an understanding of their impact on business practices is the key to success.

This examination of the Irish case of IT education can be summarized in two recommendations regarding the future of IT education in the international context. First, for a country undergoing an economic transformation from agrarian work to information work, IT education should be viewed as but one of the many aspects of society undergoing transformation. For Ireland, as for other newly industrializing countries, constructing the proper educational infrastructure is as important as designing the IT curricula. Therefore, to fully realize the benefits of an information economy, national planners must place as much emphasis on the macro issues related to the educational infrastructure as on the micro issues related to IT curriculum. The second recommendation is that IT workers in both newly and advanced industrialized countries should have an international dimension to their education that reflects their relative positions in the global IT industry. Since the IT industry in countries such as Ireland is heavily dependent upon foreign investment, IT education must prepare Irish students for careers with non-Irish multinational firms and foreign managers. Similarly, as multinational IT firms from advanced industrialized countries increasingly establish offices and plants in countries such as Ireland, they will need managers capable of working with a foreign labor force and in a different regulatory environment. In both cases, IT workers must be prepared to encounter different value systems, work ethics, and management styles. The successful IT firms will those which can acknowledge and accommodate cultural, political, and regulatory differences in the pursuit of corporate goals.

ENDNOTES

[1] The term information economy is used in this chapter as a loose synonym for post-industrial society. It is understood to be that portion of a nation's labor force which is engaged in the manufacture of information technology, the development of software and systems, and the provision of information services. This definition is based on Porat (1977), who included the manufacture of information processing machines within the category of information work.

[2] For a more complete description of the study and its methodology, see Trauth (1991).

[3] The main government agencies responsible for furthering Ireland's industry policy are:
   CTT Coras Trachtala (Irish Export Board): established in 1959 to promote and develop Irish exports.
   EOLAS (Irish Science and Technology Agency): created in 1987 from the merger of the Institute for Industrial Research and Standards and the National Board for Science and Technology to develop, apply, coordinate and promote science and technology in Irish Industry. An additional responsibility is to forge links between higher education and industry.
   FAS Foras Aiseauna Saothair (Training and Employment Authority): established in 1988 from the amalgamation of several existing manpower, youth employment and training agencies to provide training and employment programs, placement services, and advice to industry.
   IDA Industrial Development Authority: originally established in 1949, was reorganized and made an autonomous semi-state agency in 1970 to promote industrial development throughout the country by stimulating job creation in manufacturing, and international traded and financial services.

[4] The industrial policy of the past thirty years has been expressed in a

series of national plans discussed in the following documents:
Programme for Economic Expansion, 1958
Second Programme for Economic Expansion, 1964-70
Economic and Social Development, 1969-72
Industrial Development Act, 1969
A Review of Industrial Policy: A Report Prepared by the Telesis Consultancy Group, National Economic and Social Council, 1982
The Way Forward: National Economic Plan 1983-1987
White Paper on Industrial Policy, 1984
Review of Industrial Performance, 1986
Building on Reality, 1985-1987
Industrial Development Act of 1986
Programme for National Recovery, 1987
Ireland: National Development Plan 1989-1993
A Strategy for the Nineties: Economic Stability and Structural Change, National Economic and Social Council, 1989

[5] The secondary school structure in Ireland is divided into two phases. The Junior Cycle lasts three years and culminates in a series of examinations on specific subjects for which one receives the Intermediate Certificate. The Senior Cycle lasts two years, involves similar examinations, and results in the Leaving Certificate. Attaining certain "points" (exam grades) on the Leaving Certificate is the basis upon which admission to third level education (a university or other post-secondary institution) is determined.

[6] The definition of the middle class in Ireland is somewhat different from that in the United States. Individuals ascribed to the middle class in Ireland would typically be viewed as upper middle class in America.

[7] What is stated in this section about American multinational companies and workers applies to other advanced industrialized nations as well. The United States is used here for convenience and because data collected at American multinational firms has informed much of this chapter.

APPENDIX: IT DEGREE PROGRAMS

Future trends in IT education in Ireland are exemplified in the courses of study offered at the University of Limerick and Dublin City University. Prior to 1989 the two schools were accredited third level institutions but did not enjoy full university status. Before this time their names were the National Institute for Higher Education, Limerick and the National Institute for Higher Education, Dublin, respectively. These two universities were specifically established to provide an appropriately educated labor force in support of Ireland's industrial policy. NIHE Limerick was established in 1972 and NIHE Dublin was established in 1980. The importance of the IT sector in this plan is evidenced in the educational emphasis on IT in these two schools.

University of Limerick

At the University of Limerick, undergraduate IT education is provided through five degree programs offered in two colleges: the College of Engineering and Science and the College of Business. All of the programs described below are four years in duration and include a work placement component ranging from six to nine months (NIHE Limerick, 1988).

College of Engineering and Science
Bachelor of Engineering in Computer Engineering.
This program is designed to provide a broadly based education in computer engineering with an emphasis on software disciplines. It is intended for students who wish to pursue careers in research & design of computer technology and systems, software engineering, computer graphics & computer aided design, and industrial process automation. IT courses required of all students include: Computer Programming; Microprocessors; Electrical Science; Electronic Circuits; Computer Graphics and Simulation; Data Structures and Operating Systems; Microprocessor Engineering and Circuit Design; Signal and System Theory; Computer Hardware Design; Computer Languages; Networks; Operating Systems; Circuit Design.

Specialist courses available in the final year of the program include: Digital Signal Processing; Computer Aided Design; Computer Architecture; Expert Systems and Artificial Intelligence.

Bachelor of Engineering in Electronic Engineering.
This program is intended to equip graduates for the following careers: research into new electronic devices; design of computer systems, robotics, communication systems and networks; and work with satellite communication systems, industrial process automation, software engineering, computer graphics and computer aided design. Following a broadly based education in electronic engineering disciplines, students are offered a choice

of specialization in electronic systems, industrial automation or telecommunications. The common body of material taken by all students includes: Computer Programming; Microprocessors; Electrical Science; Electronic Circuit Design; Signal and System Theory; Computer Software.

Specialist courses available to students in their final year of study include: Computer Science; Telecommunications Systems; Control Systems; Application Specific Integrated Circuits; Computer Vision; Semiconductor Technology; Digital Signal Processing; Robotics; Microwave Electronics.

Bachelor of Science in Applied Mathematics. The aim of this program is to equip students with a range of analytical skills which can be applied to management and industrial problems. Among the careers for which this program prepares students are management information systems, systems analysis & computer operations, engineering or electronics research, and software development. Computer programming is included among the foundation courses for all students in this program. Commercial computing is one of the specializations which students may choose during their final two years of study.

College of Business

Bachelor of Science in Computer Systems.   This program of study is designed for those wishing to pursue a career in software and systems development. Graduates are prepared for employment in programming, systems analysis & design, knowledge engineering, software engineering, and research & development. The subject matter is covered in the following fashion:

Years 1 and 2: Programming; Business Mathematics; Accounting; Engineering Principles; Work Placement (Year 2)

Years 3 and 4: Systems and Program Development; Language Processors; Data Base Management; Computer Graphics; Computer Networks; Industrial Applications; Work Placement (Year 3)

Bachelor of Business Studies.   This program of study is designed to prepare management specialists in accounting & finance, marketing, accounting & economics, personnel management & industrial relations, and agribusiness. As part of the general curriculum all students study computing in the context of mathematics. In addition, students may choose Information Technology as their minor field of study. Among the careers for which this degree prepares students are word processing and information management.

Dublin City University

At Dublin City University undergraduate IT education is provided through five degree programs offered by the Faculties of: Computing & Mathematical Sciences, Engineering & Design, Business, and Communications and Human Studies. All but one of the programs are four years in duration with a six-month work placement during the third year (Dublin City University, 1990).

Faculty of Computing and Mathematical Sciences
Bachelor of Science in Computer Applications. This program is designed to prepare graduates with skills for applying computer technology to the practical problems of business and industry. It does so by providing them with a sound understanding of computer hardware, software engineering, computer programming, techniques of systems analysis and design, and applied quantitative methods as well as emerging technologies. All students take a set of core business courses. The IT content covered in this program includes: Computer Science; Information Systems; Systems Analysis and Design; Programming (COBOL, PASCAL, FORTRAN, Assembler, PROLOG, LISP, C, and a range of fourth generation languages).

Specialization courses in the final year of study include computer applications in accounting, computer real-time systems, and statistics.

Bachelor of Science in Applied Mathematical Sciences. This degree program focuses on the use of computers in the development and application of mathematical models. The emphasis is on the use of these models in business and industry. The first two years of the program emphasize basic mathematical principles and computing skills. During the final two years students   focus on either numerical/analytical methods or operations research.

Faculty of Engineering and Design
Bachelor of Engineering in Electronic Engineering.
The objective of this program is to respond to the demand for professional engineers to work with computer electronics, telecommunications systems, control systems, and semiconductor technology. Graduates are prepared for careers in: design, production and sales engineering; engineering management, research and development; and software engineering. The program has a core theme of electronic system design which includes circuit and system design, mathematics, physics, computing, industrial design, materials science, software engineering, communications, and control systems. During the final year, specializations are available in:Computer Control; Communications; Signal Processing; Power Electronics; Microelectronic Technology; Artificial Intelligence

Dublin Business School

Bachelor of Business in Business Studies. This program is directed at providing graduates with management expertise to respond to the demands of Ireland's industrial development growth. Among the overall objectives of the business degree is the ability to understand and use the tools and techniques of business management. Key among these is data processing. Courses in computing are included among the foundation courses taking during the first two years of the program. Business specialization courses taken during the final two years, however, do not include preparation for a career in management information systems or information technology.

Faculty of Communications and Human Studies
Bachelor of Arts in Communication Studies. This program focuses on information technology as it relates to human communication. Graduates are prepared for careers in media production, public relations, advertising, research, and to work as information specialists. A range of information technologies are studied, including: radio, video, film, photography, and graphics. In addition, part of the basic curriculum includes computer literacy and informatics (study of the effects of the convergence of computing and communications technology on organizations and society).

REFERENCES

Bell, D. (1983). *The coming of post-industrial society: A venture in social forecasting.* New York: Basic Books.

Breen, R., Hannan, D.H., Rottman, D.B., & Whelan, C.T. (1990). *Understanding Contemporary Ireland: State, Class and Development in the Republic of Ireland.* Dublin: Gill and Macmillan.

Clancy, P., Drudy, S. Lynch, K. & O'Dowd, L. (Eds.). (1986). *Ireland: A sociological profile.* Dublin: Institute of Public Administration.

Clancy, P. *Who goes to College: A second national survey of participation in higher education.* Dublin: Higher Education Authority.

Dublin City University. (1990). *Prospectus 1990-91.* Author.

Garvin, T. (1989). Wealth, poverty and development: Reflections on current discontents. *Studies, 78,* 312-325.

Higher Education Authority. (1988). *First destination of award recipients in higher education (1987).* Dublin: Author.

Institute of Public Administration. (1989). *1990 administration yearbook and diary.* Dublin: Author.

Lee, J.J. (1989). *Ireland 1912-1985: Politics and society.* Cambridge: Cambridge University Press.

National Economic and Social Council. (1989). *Ireland in the European community: Performance, prospects and strategy* (No. 88). Dublin: Author.

National Economic and Social Council. (1990). *A strategy for the nineties: Economic stability and structural change* (No. 89). Dublin: Author.

NIHE Limerick. (1988). *Undergraduate courses 1988/89.* Author.

O'Malley, E. (1989). *Industrial development: The challenge of the latecomer.* Dublin: Gill and Macmillan.

O'Toole, F. (April 6, 1990a). A middle class losing its confidence. *Irish Times.* p. 15.

O'Toole, F. (April 2, 1990b). Where all the odds favor the rich. *Irish Times.* p. 17

Porat, M. (1977). *The information economy: Definition and measurement.* Washington, D.C.: Office of Telecommunications.

Power, C. (1990, February). *1992: A new dawn for knowledge-based industries in Ireland.* Paper presented at the Bolton Trust international seminar, 1992: It's impact on technological education. Dublin.

Rottman, D.B., Hannan, D.F., Hardiman, N., & Wiley, M.M. (1982). *The *distribution of income in the Republic of Ireland: A study of social class and family cycle inequalities* (No. 109). Dublin: Economic And Social Research Council.

Trauth, E.M. (1986). An integrative approach to information policy research. *Telecommunications policy, 10*, 41-56.

Trauth, E.M. & O'Connor, B. (1991). A study of the interaction between information technology and society: An illustration of combined qualitative research methods. In H.E. Nissen, H.K. Klein, & R. Hirschheim (Eds.), *Information systems research: Contemporary approaches & emergent traditions* (pp. 131-144). Amsterdam: North-Holland.

Walsh, B.M. (1979). Economic growth and development, 1945-70. In J.J.Lee (Ed.), *Ireland 1945-70* (pp. 27-37). Dublin: Gill and Macmillan.

This research was supported by a Fulbright Scholar Award and by a McNeice Applied Business Research Fund Award from Northeastern University.

Section IV

Global IT Education in Selected Developing Countries

9 Globalization of Information Systems Education: Host Countries' Perspective

Abdulla Hasan Abdul-Gader
King Fahd University

The growth of multinational business has been accompanied by significant increases in international IS operations. In response, IS educators realize the importance of globalizing IS education. Educational efforts have been devoted to imparting certain skills and competencies that will enable multinational corporations' (MNCs) IS professionals/managers to function effectively in an international setting.

Developing nations' IS educators, however, face different challenges when it comes to designing IS educational programs. They are not striving to globalize their IS programs. Their immediate challenge is providing a balanced view of international/domestic issues because of over-internationalization of the educational programs, including IS. Developing nations' students are learning more about international issues, to the detriment of gaining the necessary insight of national aspects. To ensure local relevancy, IS educators realize the importance of several educational corrective strategies, such as developing local cases. At the same time, they view favorably the IS education globalization movement in the developed countries. Such a movement promotes mutual understanding between MNCs and host countries, leading to better working relationships.

*Adopting a host country perspective, this chapter ad-
dresses MNC IS global policy formulation and several implications
for IS management issues in the Middle East. The uniqueness of
the business and IS problems confronting MNCs in the Middle East
countries is illustrated. Insights have been gained from examining
the implications of the pertinent economic, sociopolitical, legal, and
cultural variables that affect MNC IS global policy formulation.*

With the emergence of an expanding interdependent
global economy, information systems (IS) educators need to face
the challenges of internationalization. The growth of multinational business has been accompanied by significant increases
in international IS operations.   It is no longer unusual for
corporations to support significantly high levels of IS operations
in foreign environments.   In addition, a growing number of
corporations have been developing and implementing IS applications outside the country in which they are domiciled.

Research addressing global issues and implications of
information technology is very scanty (Cash et al., 1988). The
problem is more intense when it comes to the globalization of IS
education. Traditionally, the mystique and glamour of computer
technology often lead international business scholars to take a
"hands-off" approach to IS globalization issues.   Moreover,
national orientation of IS educators has widened the gap between
the globalization dimension and IS mainstream learning.

To globalize IS education is to create an awareness of the
environmental variables that have direct effects on business and
IS functions and to impart certain skills and competencies that
will enable IS professionals/managers to function effectively in
an international setting.   To globalize IS education is also to
extend nationally oriented IS education in its broadest sense to:

(1) IS applications development/implementation issues; and
(2) IS operational support issues
    that are unique to multinational corporations (MNCs). Not
    every IS professional/manager needs to be a multinational IS
    expert.

But a well-informed IS professional/manager should know:

(1) what the core problems of international IS operations are; and
(2) in which direction appropriate solutions are being developed.

The problem of globalization of IS education in the developing countries, however, takes on a different shape. Actually, most developing countries suffer from over-internationalization to the degree that many of their education programs are losing local relevance because of three main factors. In many universities in developing countries, it is quite common to find education programs modeled on western universities. Because of a shortage of adequately trained local faculty, many developing countries employ a large number of foreign faculty. Furthermore, many students from developing countries are sent abroad to study in foreign countries.

To cite an example, in a major Saudi university, the Management Information Systems undergraduate and graduate programs follow closely the Data Processing Management Association (DPMA) and the American Computing Machinery's curriculum recommendations. Similarly, other American model curricula are followed closely in engineering and science programs. Realizing the importance of interjecting local relevancy to its adopted curricula, King Fahd University of Petroleum and Minerals (KFUPM) educators work very closely with local businesses to develop local case studies. In addition to using local cases, students majoring in Information Systems are required to spend 28 weeks in a cooperative program prior to graduation.

In 1990, 55.6 percent of KFUPM faculty were non-Saudis (King Fahd University of Petroleum and Minerals, 1990). Additionally, almost all of the Saudi faculty have earned their degrees from foreign countries.

With a built-in international dimension, developing nations have a different need for "globalization" than the developed world. What these nations need is an appreciation of their cultures, especially by those who work on their lands. Mutual understanding between MNCs and host countries can lead to better working relationships. For host countries, development objectives often can only be attained through the MNCs technical assistance. For MNCs, better awareness of the host country's economic, sociopolitical, legal, and cultural dimensions is perhaps the most natural and effective way of gaining goodwill and profits.

Adopting a host country perspective, this chapter addresses MNCs IS global policy formulation and several implications for IS management issues. The objective is to illustrate the uniqueness of the business and IS problems confronting MNCs in developing countries. More specifically, the discussion will stress IS operational and application development issues facing MNCs in the Middle East. Helping MNCs IS executives to understand the differences between their own environment and the one in which they must operate can improve their IS global policies in this region. Moreover, IS professionals working in the Middle East can contribute more effectively if they are aware of the host country culture.

The Middle East region has recently become strategically and economically important to Western business. Strategically, the region holds the world's largest proven oil reserves. Economically, its present and future oil exporting capability is coupled with high dependence on external sources for managerial and technical expertise. MNC presence and influence is clearly evident in the region (Al-Jafari and Hollingsworth, 1983). Although various Middle East nations are somewhat heterogeneous, enough similarities do exist among them. These include a common language, and religious and cultural heritage (Almaney, 1981). Thus, subsequent analysis will focus on Saudi Arabia as a representative Middle East country. Among Middle East countries, Saudi Arabia hosts the largest number of MNCs (Lugmani et al., 1989).

In the following section, MNC global IS policy alternatives are discussed. Saudi business and IS environment characteristics are reviewed next. Then, the influence of the environmental variables on MNCs global IS policy selection is presented. Implications of these variables for IS managers and professionals working in Saudi Arabia are discussed.

BACKGROUND: GLOBAL IS POLICY

The accelerated globalization of business and the importance of IS to the globalization process prompts the adoption of explicit IS global policies. The question remains, however, as to which type of IS global policy is the most appropriate. Should international IS operations procedures and policies and IS applications be the same as those employed in a mainly uninational setting? Should operations procedures and policies, and IS applications be custom-made along with global orientation? Can a balance be struck between these two extremes?

MNC IS operations and applications development policies can best be viewed as an outgrowth of the existing global business strategy (Ives and Jarvenpaa, 1991).   Bartlett and Ghoshal (1989), Levitt (1983), and Perlmutter (1969) have developed global business strategy models for the multinationals. Regardless of their differences, these models share a concern for determining the pertinent balance between a single-country and a global perspective.

One of the earliest global business strategy models is Perlmutter's (1969). He intelligently classifies the setting of MNC global business policy and decision making into three classes: ethnocentric, polycentric, and geocentric.   Building on Perlmutter's work, IS global policies can also be classified into the same classes. An ethnocentric global IS orientation approaches global IS development and operations abroad in the same manner as in the home country.   Home country IS applications development and operations standards and procedures are predominantly imposed on the foreign subsidiaries so that close control is ensured.   Under certain circumstances, it may appear appropriate simply to transplant domestic IS applications abroad. Also in this setting, foreign operations are firmly coupled with, and dependent on, home country management. Among the advantages of such an approach are consistent data dictionaries and possible financial savings due to consolidation. This centralized control can result, however, in poor local responsiveness.

A polycentric IS orientation is a second category into which MNCs might fall. Subscribing to global diversity, polycentric orientation adopts a host-country philosophy.   IS applications development and operations policies permit a substantial degree of local autonomy for foreign affiliates with some degree of centralized coordination. If culturally dependent, IS applications can be developed locally even if economy of scale suggests home country development. These systems can incorporate data maintaining their local attributes (e. g., Arabic) and, at the same time, can be translated to satisfy more global perspectives.

A geocentric IS global policy orientation reflects an idealistic global perspective. There is no such thing as a good-for-all IS application development and universal operational standards and procedures.   Indeed, completely tailor-made approaches to applications development and operations management seem called for here with a global perspective. Despite their different approaches, IS centers all over the globe form an integrated network so that global objectives are optimized. Within the network, IS professionals and other productive resources are interchanged freely in a coordinated manner, moving them from where they are least expensive to where their productivity is greatest. Such integrated IS strategy, however, is still largely a remote possibility (Ives and Jarvenpaa, 1991).

In effect, MNC IS global policies fall into either ethnocentric policies (controlled foreign operations) or polycentric policies (autonomous foreign operations) or somewhere in between these two extremes. Not surprisingly, successful MNC management entails striking a balance between control and autonomy, which should be responsive to the environment in which these organizations are operating (Cash et al., 1988; Reck, 1989). Focussing on the Middle East culture, the following sections detail the contextual variables and their influences on MNC global IS policy.

SAUDI ARABIA: AN EXOTIC INFORMATION SYSTEMS ENVIRONMENT

Different environments experience different types of IS operational and application development problems. As shown in Figure 1, four broad environmental variables can have direct effects upon IS managerial functions: (1) economic (2) sociopolitical, (3) legal, (4) cultural. Insights can be gained by applying this framework to study business and IS environments in Saudi Arabia.

With a highly centralized and a dominant public administrative system, the Saudi business and IS environments symbolize conditions in which IS executives ought to closely evaluate government plans and priorities. Politically, the Saudi government is one of the most stable and openhanded governments in the region. Adopting the principles of Muslim Sharia (Islamic law), Saudi Arabia is one of several Arab monarchies in the Middle East.

Additional characteristics of the Saudi business environment are: its international strategic importance, the tangible presence of MNCs, the scarcity of an indigenous work force and Islamic and Arabic culture. The following paragraphs discuss these issues in detail.

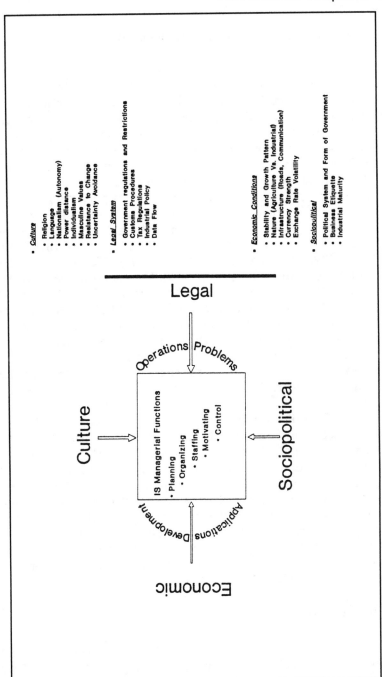

Figure 1

International Strategic Importance

The global economy and, more so, the Middle East countries, have increasingly become interdependent in the world economy. To the world economy, the strategic importance of the region stems from its oil exporting capability, recycled petrodollars, and markets for consumer and capital goods. Possessing the world's largest proven oil reserves, Middle East countries are a significant world economic power. The export of crude oil from the Middle East nations constitutes more than 30 percent of total world oil exports. These nations in turn import a significant volume of capital and consumer goods from the developed world.

Table 1 depicts the size of export markets for the major Industrial Nations as a percentage of their total exports from 1980 to 1986. For example, in 1980, the USA exported 6.2 percent of its total exports to the Middle East countries. In the same year, Saudi Arabia received 2.3 percent of the USA's total exports. It is evident that the size of the Middle East markets is as large as the European Economic Community (EEC) markets. In 1982, Italy sold 23 percent of its exports to the Middle East and in the same year it exported 24 percent to other EEC countries. The results in this table also highlight the importance of the Middle East countries as trading partners for the five industrial nations.

The Saudi economy's involvement in international trade is fairly recent and can only be attributed to two main factors. The first is obviously the oil boom. The second is the development of productive forces based on oil revenue. Before 1973, the beginning of the oil price explosion, Saudi international trade dealings had been fairly limited. With the advent of the oil boom of 1973, its economy entered into a new phase of modernization, leading to the demand for massive capital formation. Since then, a huge amount of capital and consumer goods have been imported from industrial nations. Some economic indicators are depicted in Table 2.

MNC Presence

Encouraged by its lucrative markets, stable political system, and liberal economic policies, a large number of MNCs have been participating in the kingdom's economy (Ali and Al-

		ME* (%)	SA* (%)	EEC* (%)
USA				
	1980	6.2	2.3	8.1
	1982	6.4	3.3	8.5
	1984	6.4	2.8	9.2
	1986	6.0	1.9	9.3
Japan				
	1980	14.1	4.1	14.1
	1982	17.4	5.1	13.6
	1984	14.7	4.4	12.4
	1986	13.2	2.8	11.2
Germany				
	1980	7.3	2.6	9.4
	1982	10.0	4.0	10.2
	1984	8.2	3.5	11.7
	1986	7.2	2.2	8.3
France				
	1980	12.1	4.3	15.5
	1982	17.5	7.2	18.6
	1984	14.3	6.1	20.4
	1986	12.6	3.8	19.4
Italy				
	1980	17.9	6.4	23.0
	1982	23.0	9.5	24.3
	1984	19.2	8.2	27.4
	1986	15.5	4.8	23.8

(*) ME : Middle East   SA : Saudi Arabia   EEC: European Economic Community
Source: Compiled from many statistical tables (Central Department of Statistics, 1985-86).

Table 1: The Size of Export Markets for the Major Industrial Nation as a Percentage of Their Total Export, 1980-86

Shakhis, 1990). To fuel its ambitious development plans, Saudi Arabia has hosted a large number of MNCs and a considerable expatriate work force. Unfortunately, there are no exact statistics on the number of MNCs operating in Saudi Arabia. However, indirect indicators of the ubiquity of foreign corporations do exist. In 1987, the Saudi Arabian Monetary Agency (SAMA) reported that 22.8% of the companies operating in the Kingdom were non-Saudi. As shown in Table 3, these companies hold

Oil production	5,066,300	barrels a day
Oil Reserves	255	billion barrels
Exports	$ 23,736	Million
Imports	$ 21,784	Million
Balance of Trade	$ 1,952	Million
Exchange Rate	$ 0.27	per Saudi Riyal
Gross National Product (GNP)	$ 77,599	Million

Source: The Middle East Review (1990).

Table 2: Saudi Key Economic Indicators (1988)

	Number	**%**	**Capital***	**%**
Saudi	5,406	77.2	45,462,7	66.8
Non Saudi	1594	22.8	22,616.1	33.2
Total	7000		68,078.8	

* Capital in Million Saudi Riyals
Source: SAMA Annual Report (1988)

Table 3: Companies Operating in Saudi Arabia, 1987

33.2% of the capital. The United States alone had almost 300 joint projects with Saudi Arabia in 1987 (Saudi Arabia Chamber of Commerce, 1988).

MNCs have participated actively in making the major infrastructure projects of the seventies and early eighties a reality. With the help of MNCs and foreign workers, the kingdom has progressed from a non-existent infrastructure phase to an environment favorable for business. Some of the achievements of Saudi development plans are (Lugmani et al., 1989):

• a highly regarded communication network (700,000 telephone lines, 15,000 telex lines, packet switch system);

• 15 sea water desalination plants;

• 21 domestic airports and three major international airports;

• seven ports with 107 large capacity berths;

* 23,000 kilometers of paved highways; and

* 1571 hospitals.

Native Work Force Scarcity

Foreign manpower is a very significant component of the Saudi Arabia population. The problem is compounded by the fact that eighty percent of the non-agricultural workers in Saudi Arabia are foreigners. As early as 1962, before the rush for development in the seventies, up to thirty-five percent of the residents of the largest five cities were foreigners (Area Handbook, 1971). This percentage has increased steadily, especially with the injection of petrodollars in the seventies. The number of expatriates was almost three million in 1985, constituting two-thirds of total work force (KFUPM Research Institute, 1987).

With an area of slightly over a million square miles, one-third of the size of the United States of America, the Kingdom of Saudi Arabia encompasses four-fifths of the Arabian Peninsula. Saudi Arabia has only about twelve million inhabitants (KFUPM Research Institute, 1987). Accordingly, its population density was twelve persons per square mile in 1986. In addition to low population density, a lack of indigenous skilled workers to man the ambitious development projects has induced dependence on foreign manpower (Owen, 1986). Looking to the longer term, the Saudi reliance on foreign manpower is likely to persist. For example, Saudi computer and IS education is not coping with the increasing demand for computer professionals. In 1990, the total number of students pursuing computer related university degrees was 2400 students (Mandurah and Al-Orani, 1991). In Saudi Arabia, the percentage of Saudis studying computer

	Saudi	Taiwan
Number of Students	2400	57942
Population (Million)	12	20
Percentage	0.02 %	0.2897 %

Source: Mandura and Bakri (1990).

Table 4: Students in Computer Related Fields

related fields is only 2 for every 10,000 Saudis. In contrast, there are more than 28 students for every 10,000 in Taiwan. Table 4 points to the chronic incapacity of the Saudi education system to graduate IS professionals.

Islamic and Arabic Culture

Another critical dimension in the Saudi business and IS environments is culture. Empirical evidence increasingly conveys the importance of culture to managerial practices (Hofstede, 1980; Inkeles and Levinson, 1969; Muna, 1980; Tricker, 1988). People of each nation have a national character drawn from their culture.   They share a differentiating, enduring pattern of behavior and/or personality characteristics (Inkeles and Levinson, 1969; Hofstede, 1980). Drucker (1986) has stressed the significance of understanding local values, attitudes, and management practices to the effectiveness of MNCs.

As the birthplace of Islam, Saudi Arabia symbolizes a modern state with an Islamic spirit. Almost all Saudis are Moslems. Saudi Society adopts Islam as a way of life. Actually, the influence of Islam and its myriad social prescriptions in everyday life seems to be spreading rather than waning (Al-Ashker, 1987; Dessouki, 1982; Kassem and Habib, 1989). Perhaps the most noticeable facet of the Islamic culture is the Arabic language. Although the Arabic language predates Islam, Islam gave the language a spiritual and sacred significance. To Moslems, the Arabic language is not just a symbol of a common heritage, but also a holy language.

Saudi culture is also characterized by its tribal and familial social structure. The influence of this social structure's traditionalism has lead many researchers to coin the term "Bedoaucracy" when describing Arab organizations (Abdul-Rahman, 1982; Al-Awaji, 1971; Al-Hashemi, 1988; Kassem and Habib, 1989). Derived from "Bedouin", the Bedoaucracy model highlights the importance of Bedouin culture in the Saudi organizational setting. Similar to Max Weber's western bureaucracy model, the Bedoaucracy model delineates several central tendencies within Saudi organizations.   Kassem and Habib (1989, p. 16) have asserted that Saudi organizations tend to have:
1. a moderate degree of specialization;
2. a low degree of coordination because of excessive

personal authority and extensive use of committees;
3. a low degree of formalism;
4. personal preferences and judgments in personnel selection, promotion, placement,...etc; and
5. a high degree of centralization of decision making.

In a well-cited large study of cultural impact, Hofstede (1980) has identified four distinct dimensions of national culture: power distance, uncertainty avoidance, masculinity, and individualism. The power distance dimension reflects the way society distributes the power among its members. It measures centralization of authority. Uncertainty avoidance relates to the society's tendency towards formalism and willingness to take/ avert risks. Masculinity refers to the way society assigns roles between sexes. Masculine societies rate such "masculine" values as aggressiveness and performance higher than such "feminine" values as quality of life and cooperation. Individuals with different cultures may be different in the way they relate to their peers and organizations. An individual in high individualism cultures is more independent. He is less likely to view the organization he works in as his own family.

Hofstede (1980) has shown that the Saudi and American cultures are quite different. Compared to American society, the Saudi society has demonstrated more power distance, more uncertainty avoidance, fewer masculine values, and less individualism.

In another study, Kassem and Al-Modaifer (1987) have reported similar findings. Besides Hofstede's four dimensions, they have added a fifth dimension: "traditionalism". According to Kassem and Al-Modaifer (1987), traditionalism refers to the way society deals with innovations and the extent of particularism (opposite of universalism) and secularism. In comparison to Americans, Saudis are high in traditionalism. They have a tendency to be averse to modernism.

IMPLICATIONS FOR MNC INFORMATION SYSTEMS POLICIES

It is evident from the above discussion that business and IS problems confronting MNCs in Saudi Arabia are different from the ones in their own countries. MNC IS executives/professionals can improve their productivity by understanding these differences. Various implications can be drawn to help MNC affiliates develop such an understanding.

As a single-product economy, MNC business and IS environments in Saudi Arabia are characterized by high levels of uncertainty. Lack of indigenous technology, management, labor and raw materials has also led to a built-in competitive disadvantage. Within such a setting, ethnocentric IS policies can be more pertinent. The high uncertainty factor and the uneconomical factors of production promote more prudent orientation. MNC local IS investments and facilities ought to be minimal. In such a case, headquarters-driven IS application development and operations are favored. Since local IS applications development is very costly, it may appear appropriate simply to transplant IS applications rather than develop them locally.

On the other hand, the uniqueness of the Saudi environment calls for some degree of polycentric strategy. Indeed the Islamic Sharia, language, geographic location, scarcity of IS professionals, IS market maturity and cultural values independently and collectively complicate MNC IS management. Without autonomy, MNC affiliates operating in Saudi Arabia may be incapable of responding to distinct Saudi needs. As shown in Table 5, the implications of these contextual variables are numerous.

Islamic teaching or "Sharia" prohibits some of the things regarded as necessities from a western perspective. Alcohol, interest rates "usury", pork, nightclubs and casinos are blacklisted. Consequently, maintaining adequate non-Moslem systems and programming staff is very difficult. Sharia also imposes the timing of holidays. Unlike most of the world's Saturday/Sunday weekends, the Saudi weekends are Thursdays and Fridays. Communication and coordination between a MNCs subsidiary and the home office is impeded, since four days of the week are official week ends, not to mention other major religious holidays (feasts and events).

Actually, Sharia's influence may go beyond explicit legal authority to more tacit connotations. As Moslems, many Saudis believe that the future belongs to the will of Allah (God) and not to man. Such belief has lead many Moslems to be averse to planning of any sort. A Saudi IS manager/professional with this sort of orientation may resist IS planning. Similar implications can be drawn on concepts such as personal aspiration, helpless-

Contextual Variable	Consequences	IS Management Implications
1. Saudi economy is heavily relying on the outside world to export oil; to import modern technology, labor, management, and raw materials	• High uncertainty; dependence on single money generating product-oil. • Built-in competitive disadvantage because of high cost factors of production.	• IS planning is prone to be ad hoc • IS applications development and operations are costly. Local development and operations are not attractive. MNC may follow a centralized IS development and operation.
2. Dominant government role in the economy	• High uncertainty • Private sector plays minor role • Strict reporting disclosure • Pressure to Saudize jobs	• Evaluate closely government plans and priorities. • Make careful evaluation of emerging technologies. Certain types of technology are not permitted (e.g., radio communication (CB) exept in rare cases.) • Accelerate Saudization programs (recruiting, training, etc.)
3. Islamic "sharia" or teachings	• A ban on "usury," pork, gambling, alcohol, and certain types of entertainment (e.g., casinos, nightclubs). • Misconception about fate and free will. The future belongs to Allah (God) not man. • Different timing of holidays	• It is harder to retain non-Moslem IS professionals • Applications financing has to be internal • Local IS professionals/managers have tendency to resist long range planning. • Harder to coordinate MNC local and satellite operations. Saudi weekends are Thurs. and Fri. not Sat. and Sun.
4. Language: Arabic	• Arabic technical capability is not well developed.	• Applications development software and documentations are basically in English. Local IS professionals must be proficient in English.
5. Scarcity of manual and skilled labor	• High dependence on foreign labor force	• Greater need for IS expatriates. • Possible conflict between local staff and IS expatriates (wage difference, nationalism feelings). • Greater need for staff planning. • Training and development programs are needed.

Table 5: Environmental Variables Affecting IS Management

Contextual Variable	Consequences	IS Management Implications
6. Regional conflict and ethnic sensitivities	• Security consideration outweighs economic considerations. • High shipment insurance rates.	• Limiting MNC options in recruiting certain nationalities. Visa restrictions. • High freight costs.
7. Well developed infrastructure (utilities, transportation, and communication systems).	• Facilitate operations	• Ease of coordinating IS activities • Communication quality, availability and cost make it cost effective to implement on-line applications
8. Thin, small domestic market	• Domestic market is supplier market	• Limited number of competing vendors. Hardware suppliers and external software developers are few. MNCs may have to change their preferred vendors if they do not operate in the Saudi market.
9. Strong and stable currency	• Lower exchange rate fluctuation risk	• Major hardware and software investment decisions are less prone to financial risk.
10. Legal environment	• No import/export restrictions • No labor unions • Favorable tax system • Simple customs procedures	• Free cross national boundary transmission of data. • Opportunity to create an international database. • Ability to import hardware and software freely.
11. Cultural values • Power distance • Uncertainty avoidance • Masculine values • Individualism • Traditionalism	• Centralization and autocratic leadership • Low tolerance to ambiguity • Low cooperation, appreciation of independence and good performance • Prevalence of favoritism and nepotism • Resistance to innovation and change.	• Management policies should be culturally congruent (e.g., motivating IS local professionals is different than Western professionals).

Source: Primary; Similar analysis of the effects of some of the variables appears in Kassem and Habib, 1989, pp. 412-413.

Table 5: Environmental Variables Affecting IS Management (contd)

ness, trust, personal status, and expressions of opinion (see Pezeshkpur, 1978).

Another differentiating factor is language. Since many Saudi government agencies require reports and official communications to be in Arabic, MNC IS departments are forced to either develop Arabic applications or manually translate reports into Arabic. Although there are some scattered success stories, developing large Arabic applications has been very difficult. Practically, non-English IS application development languages/packages are either limited or not available for some applications. However, even if an Arabic application development package is available, securing Saudi IS professionals is not effortless due to the limited pool of local IS professionals.

This scarcity of Saudi IS professionals has led to a spurt of growth in IS expatriates, creating a new set of challenging problems. Firstly, wage and benefit differences and feelings of nationalism can lead to resentment in local professionals. Appropriate personnel policies need to be applied to overcome this deterrent to productivity. Secondly, a greater need for staff planning is in order here. Regional conflict and ethnic sensitivity have resulted in visa restrictions and strict security arrangements. It may take months to get permission for entry. For some nationalities, entry is not allowed at all. Thirdly, training and personnel programs are essential to promote a local supply of IS professionals and to enhance MNC goodwill.

An important factor in effective MNCs IS management is the level of congruence of its policies with the local culture. In contrast to Americans, Saudis have a tendency towards more power distance, more uncertainty avoidance, fewer masculine values, less individualism, and more traditionalism (Hofstede, 1980; Kassem and Al-Modaifer, 1987). Several implications can be derived for IS operations and applications development.

With high power distance value, Saudis have a tendency to centralization and autocratic leadership. Kassem and Habib (1989, p. 18) have maintained that "Gulf Arabs simply expect their leaders to lead them autocratically and to make decisions for them." For IS applications potential users, participative IS applications development project management which has been practiced in the West may not be suitable. Saudi IS users tend to expect an authoritative management style from project developers. Further research needs to be carried to test the validity of involving users in the design of applications. With skepticism toward a participative notion, there is an inherited danger in participative design. Users may view an application developers' quest for their participation as a sign of weakness.

As risk averters, Saudis have a high level of formalism orientation, less willingness to take risks, and a high level of contentment with the status quo. Saudi IS managers/professionals are less likely to allow change if they perceive the remotest possibility of unsound consequences.

Applications users follow this same pattern. The emergence of application resistance may be more than that which has been witnessed in the West.

CONCLUSION

The growth in international IS operations due to increasing multinational business makes IS educators realize the importance of globalizing IS education. They recognize the need for educational efforts to impart certain skills and competencies that will enable multinational corporations' (MNCs) IS professionals/managers to function effectively in an international setting. MNCs IS professionals/managers need to develop an awareness of the environmental variables that have direct effects on business and IS functions in foreign countries.

Unlike their developed nations' counterpart, developing nations' IS educators are not striving to globalize their IS programs. These programs are already globalized. In such countries, IS educators immediate challenge is providing a balanced view of international/domestic IS issues because of over-internationalization of their local educational programs including IS. Developing nations' students are learning more about international issues to the detriment of gaining the necessary insight of national aspects. To ensure local relevancy, IS educators realize the importance of several educational corrective strategies such as developing local cases and increasing industry training.

Moreover, developing nations are basically at the receiving end. Not being able to export technical know-how and skilled labor, the national objectives of developing nations do not necessarily include globalization of education. Rather, developing nations' IS educators view the globalization move in the developed nations as a welcome advancement so that global understanding will come closer. To the developing nations' IS educators, the globalization trend taking place in industrialized western countries, therefore, provides an opportunity to increase awareness of host countries' culture. Such mutual understanding between MNCs and host countries can ultimately lead to better working relationships.

To enhance MNC understanding of IS operations and applications development problems in the Middle East countries, this chapter has described the pertinent economic, sociopolitical, legal, and cultural variables that affect IS functions. Insights have been gained from examining the implications of these variables for MNC global IS policy.

Because of the Middle East's strategic and economic importance, this type of research is vital for the increasing number of MNCs that operate in the region. Middle East companies with IS activities can also benefit from such an analysis.

Acknowledgment: I would like to thank King Fahd University of Petroleum and Minerals administration for financial support. I am grateful to Dr. Karen Loch, Dr. Anthony Herbst and Dr. Ugur Yavas for their comments on earlier versions of this chapter.

REFERENCES

Abdul-Rahman, O. (1982). Oil Bureaucracy and the Development Dilemma. Working paper, Kuwait, National Council for Culture, Arts, and Humanities.

Al-Ashker, A. (1987). *The Islamic Business Enterprise.* Kent, UK: Croom-Helm.

Al-Awaji, I. (1971). Bureaucracy and Society in Saudi Arabia. Doctoral dissertation, University of Virginia.

Al-Hashemi, I. (1988). Management Development in Transition: The Gulf Experience. *International Journal of Manpower, 9,* 3-7.

Ali, A. and M. Al-Shakhis (1990). Multinationals and the Host Arab Society: A Managerial Perspective. *Leadership and Organization Development Journal, 11,* 17-21.

Almaney, A. (1981). Cultural Traits of the Arabs: Growing Interest for International Management. *Management International Review, 3,* 10.

Al-Jafari, A. and A. Hollingsworth (1983). An Exploratory Study of Managerial Practices in the Arabian Gulf Region. *Journal of International Business Studies,* 143-152.

Area Handbook for Saudi Arabia (1971). 2nd edition. Washington, DC: US Government Printing Office.

Bartlett C. and S. Ghoshal (1989). *Managing Across Borders: The Transnational Solution.* Boston: Harvard Business School Press.

Cash J., F. McFarlan, and J. McKenney (1988). *Corporate Information Systems Management: The Issues Facing Senior Executives.* Homewood: Irwin.

Central Department of Statistics (1985). *The Statistical Indicators.* Riyadh, Saudi Arabia: Ministry of Finance and National Economy.

Central Department of Statistics (1985; 1986). *Statistical Year Book.* Riyadh, Saudi Arabia: Ministry of Finance and National Economy.

Central Department of Statistics (1986). *Foreign Trade Statistics.* Riyadh, Saudi Arabia: Ministry of Finance and National Economy.

Dessouki, A. (1982). *Islamic Resurgence in the Arab World.* New York: Praeger.

Drucker, P. (1986). The Changing Multinational. *The Wall Street Journal,* January 15.

Hofstede, S. (1980). *Culture's Consequences: International Differences in Work-Related Values.* Beverly Hills, CA: Sage Publications, Inc.

Inkeles, A. and D. Levinson (1969). National Character: The Study of Modal Personality and Sociocultural Systems. In G. Lindzey and E. Aronson (eds.), *The Handbook of Social Psychology,* Vol. 4. Cambridge, MA: Addison-Wesley Publishing Company.

Ives, B. and S. Jarvenpaa (1991). Applications of Global Information Technology: Key Issues for Management. *MIS-Q, 15,* 32-49.

Kassem M. and G. Habib (1989). *Strategic Management of Services in the Arab Gulf States: Company and Industry Cases.* Berlin: Walter De Gruyter.

Kassem, M. and K. Al-Modaifer (1987). Bureaucracy and Society in Arab World: A Replication and Extension of Hofstede's Value Survey Model. Working Paper, College of Industrial Management, King Fahd University of Petroleum and Minerals.

KFUPM Research Institute (1987). Gulf Cooperation Council (GCC) Main Economic Indicators. Economic and Industrial Research Division, Dhahran, Saudi Arabia: King Fahd University of Petroleum and Minerals (KFUPM).

King Fahd University of Petroleum and Minerals (1990). Annual report, Dhahran, Saudi Arabia.

Levitt, T. (1983). The Globalization of Markets. *Harvard Business Review, 61,* 92-102.

Lugmani, M., U. Yavas, and Z. Quraeshi (1989). Corporate Strategy and Public Policy in Saudi Arabia. *Long Range Planning, 22,* 79-88.

Mandurah M. and S. Bakri (1990). Towards a Saudi Computer National Plan. *Proceedings of the 12th National Computer Conference, Riyadh, Saudi Arabia*, 32-50 (in Arabic).

Mandurah M. and A. Al-Orani (1991). *Status of Computerization in Saudi Arabia.* A report presented at the joint Saudi-Japanese seminar, Riyadh, Saudi Arabia: Saudi Computer Society.

Muna, F. (1980). *The Arab Executives.* London: MacMillan.

Owen, R. (1986). Migrant Workers in the Gulf. *Middle East Review, 18*, 24-27.

Perlmutter, H. (1969). The Tortuous Evolution of the Multinational Corporation. *Columbia Journal of World Business, 4*, 9-18.

Pezeshkpur, C. (1978). Challenges to Management in the Arab World. *Business Horizons, 21*, 47-55.

Reck, R. (1989, August). The Shock of Going Global. *Datamation*, pp. 67-69.

Saudi Arabia Chamber of Commerce (1988). *The Yearly Report of Trade and Corporation*, annual publication, Riyadh, Saudi Arabia.

Saudi Arabian Monetary Agency (1988). Annual Report, Riyadh, Saudi Arabia: SAMA.

The Middle East Review (1990). New Jersey: Hunter.

Tricker, R. (1988). Information Resource Management: A Cross-Cultural Perspective. *Information and Management, 15*, 37-46.

10 Internationalization of Information Systems Education: The Indian Experience

Rekha Jain
Indian Institute of Management, Ahmedabad

A graduate program in Information Systems (IS) and training of teachers for this program has been introduced in India at the initiative of the Department of Electronics, Government of India, since 1983. In India, government bodies play a significant role in the introduction of many programs. The Indian economy is highly protected and the industry has little incentive to be competitive. In such a scenario, the IS curriculum, which must respond both to the rapid technological changes and the globalization of business, is likely to be unresponsive to international trends. This chapter discusses the Indian IS curriculum and the extent of internationalization incorporated in it. Issues related to the implementation of the curriculum, factors influencing the internationalization, the role of industry in influencing IS education and lessons from this experience for other developing countries are examined.

Higher education in India is highly subsidised by the government and is centrally directed. A central government agency, the University Grants Commission, oversees the functioning of all universities. The Department of Education channelizes government funds to these universities. Students are charged only a nominal fee, equivalent of US $ 20-50 a year. Since this income is inadequate, universities are forced to depend on government grants to meet their capital and recurring expenditure. Launching of any new educational program requires scrutiny and approval from a number of government bodies. As a result, new programs are launched, more often than not, at the initiative of government departments than the academic community. Besides the government supported educational institutes, there exist a large number of private training institutes. Their programs, in general, do not have formal recognition. However, since they provide training in areas which are highly valued in the job market, some have acquired informal recognition. A consequence of this regime in education was that, till 1983, India did not have a formal graduate level program specifically targeted to produce Information Systems (IS) professionals.

Even though it had been realized fairly early that India faced a shortage of professionals in IS (Report of the Panel on Computer Manpower Development, Electronics Information and Planning, 18(2), November 1980), concern remained confined to estimating the required number of professionals and the broad mechanisms for bridging the shortfall. For example, at a workshop, estimates of the number of computer professionals in different categories, problem areas for achieving the estimated targets, and recommendations regarding the mechanisms for improving the quality of IS education were discussed (Bhatnagar and Patel, 1985; Jain and Raghuram, 1985). Users of IS in the industry and representatives from the IS industry hardly took any lead in dealing with issues related to IS education. It was at the initiative of the Department of Electronics (DOE) in 1983 that graduate level program in IS and teachers training program were introduced in a number of universities across the country. Elements of professionalization and globalization in IS education were incorporated at the recommendation of the academic committees constituted by DOE.

This chapter describes the Indian model of IS curriculum at graduate level for students and teachers and globalization from the Indian perspective. The role of various agencies in evolving the curriculum is discussed. Internationalization of this curriculum and other issues related to the design and implementation are also highlighted. The analysis brings out steps which could be taken by educators and other concerned bodies in future. In this context, some implications and issues of concern for developing countries are also addressed.

IS EDUCATION IN INDIA

Pre-1986 Scenario

Till 1986, when the first batch of IS graduates completed the program, IS development in India was largely undertaken by the following:

(1) Computer science and engineering graduates from universities and colleges.
(2) Graduates of Masters in Business Administration (MBA)
(3) Trainees from private training institutes
(4) Managers in functional areas who, after developing the requisite skills, design and implement their own systems.

An examination of the IS education component of each of these streams will enable us to understand the IS scenario in India and evaluate the curriculum development efforts.

Computer Science and Engineering Graduates

Students of computer science and engineering usually undergo 4-6 years of formal study. The course focus is highly technical. Students typically study courses in computer architecture, system software, programming languages, data structures, design and analysis of algorithms, linear algebra, numerical analysis, computer graphics, databases, networking etc., and some elective subjects. Usually, the course has a project component requiring students to design some hardware or software component of computer systems. These courses provide strong theoretical foundations. However, these programs lack a business application focus. Graduates from these courses develop the business application viewpoint only during their tenure with business organizations. Many of these graduates join the data-processing department in organizations where they work in the field of IS design and implementation. Most such departments in the organization are perceived as specialists in technology. Applications developed on the initiative of the data-processing department often lack a business perspective. Partly because of the lack of interaction between the data-processing and functional areas in developing applications and partly because of lack of vision for usage of IS, Indian organizations have not exploited the potential of this technology to any significant extent.

MBA Graduates

Students of MBA usually study an introductory course in computers followed by electives in IS. These courses, at least, in leading management institutions, have an appropriate mixture of "science" and management orientation. In terms of curriculum focus, these institutes attempt to provide a balance between techniques and managerial issues in IS design. However, most courses offer limited case studies on software project management, configuration choices and networking strategies, application development methodologies being followed by Indian organizations, etc. Only leading management institutes offer specialization in IS which is somewhat equivalent to an MBA minor in IS in the ACM curriculum (Ashenhurst, 1972; Nunamaker, Couger and Davis, 1982). There are no formal guidelines for specialization in IS. Therefore, depending on the assessment of need, the courses vary from year to year and from institution to institution. Moreover, few organizations have realized the importance of IS and exploited the full capabilities of these graduates. The IS function does not have a central role in most Indian organizations and therefore does not attract the best talent. Also, the number of graduates leaving these institutes and specializing in IS is fairly small to be able to create any measurable impact.

Private Training Institutes

Spurred by the demand for software professionals, a number of private institutes have mushroomed in many Indian towns. They offer training in popular PC-based packages and in programming COBOL, PASCAL, BASIC, FORTRAN, and C. The course duration ranges from a few weeks to a few months. In most cases, there is no process of accreditation of these courses, and consequently, no standardization of quality or range of training. The trainees are expected to start as assistants to data-processing personnel or junior programmers. Over the course of their career they move on to acquire more programming skills.

By the end of 1990, there were about 700 such training institutes across the country, up from approximately 400 in 1989-90. Most of them are ill-equipped in terms of quality of faculty and hardware equipment. The focus is on teaching language-specific programming skills. Few, if any, teach programming methodology, large program development discipline, or the importance of documentation.

Self Trained

Since most Indian organizations have not exploited or realized the strategic importance of IS, generally they do not have a comprehensive, focused training program for their executives in IS. But many users individually have realized the benefits of end-user computing and have acquired the necessary skills to develop their own systems.

A number of IS-based programs focused at functional managers had been developed by many private/autonomous and government organizations by 1990. However, the percentage of people covered, the quality of teaching, and the faculty's lack of understanding of management requirements have left large gaps in terms of program design and implementation. Often, PC-based packages in the context of the functional areas have formed the course content rather than an integrated approach towards IS for the organization or for the department. Only leading management institutes have offered executive development programs in IS integrating the technological and manage-

Category of IS professionals	Requirement	Supply from formal institutions
Ph.D.	250	240
M.Tech.	14,500	2,500
B.Tech.	24,000	7,000
Masters in Computer Applications	40,000	18,000
Diploma in Computer Applications	99,000	80,000
Diploma in Computer Engineering	18,500	7,000
Total	1,96,250	1,14,740
Say	2,00,000	1,15,000

Source: *Report of the Working Group on Electronics*, Eighth Five Year Plan, Department of Electronics, Government of India, 1989, p.134

Table 1: Requirement of IS Professionals

rial perspectives. The programs have been targeted at two major groups: end-users and the system developers. The focus for end-users is on awareness of information technology capabilities and provision of basic computing skills. For system developers, the courses provide an organizational and managerial perspectives.

Post - 1985 DOE Initiative

DOE had estimated in 1980, and subsequently in 1989, the requirement of IS professionals in different categories to meet India's targeted software production till 1994. Table 1 presents a first order estimate as well as the capacity of different training and educational institutes. This exercise showed that there is a large gap between the supply and requirement of IS professionals.

To reduce this gap, DOE has initiated the following steps:

i) programs at undergraduate and graduate levels in computer science to be offered in a large number of engineering colleges
ii) design and development of a graduate program in information systems to be called the Masters in Computer Applications (MCA)
iii) the introduction of a Diploma program in Computer Applications (DCA) and a Diploma program in Computer Engineering (DCE)
iv) plans were laid for training of teachers for teaching diploma and master level program in computer applications and development of video- and TV-based educational programs
v) design of a continuing education scheme for retraining of practicing managers.

Graduate Program in IS

DOE has sponsored a three-year graduate IS program called Masters in Computer Applications (MCA). The program for students is fairly detailed in terms of curriculum design, mechanism for funding, design of entry level criteria etc., whereas that for teachers suggests only broad outlines. The curriculum is based on previous ACM and IFIP reports related to curriculum design for IS (Ashenhurst, 1972; Nunamaker, Couger & Davis, 1982; Buckingham, 1986). It is divided into the following four disciplines:

1) Mathematical Sciences
2) Computer Science and Computing
3) Management Science
4) Analytic Techniques

Under each discipline there are core, allied, and elective courses. Exhibit 1 provides a list of courses and a broad outline of the topics covered in the MCA program. DOE has identified prerequisites, lecture, and tutorial hours for each course. In the first two years students have to take all the specified courses in the curriculum. In the third year, they choose courses from a list of electives and are also expected to work on a "live" project for six months.

The courses have a strong computer science and mathematics bias. The curriculum has only four courses on management/social aspects of IS. The final year has none in management science. Courses on production and marketing are not incorporated into the curriculum even though these courses form the core of the business management curriculum. Further, the majority of the management courses offered in the first two years have a quantitative orientation.

The first-year courses in computer science impart concepts related to the organization and architecture of computers, algorithm design and implementation, representation of data, programming language skills, and file processing. The courses on discrete mathematical structures, linear algebra, numerical and statistical methods are of basic level and cover a wide variety of topics. The course on accounting and financial management is introductory. The curriculum also cover concepts related to the role of IS in organizations, information and decision theory, and evaluation of IS.

The second-year courses too, have a mixture of computer science, mathematical, and management courses. The courses in computer science build on the concepts imparted in the first year, with introduction to data and file management concepts and tools and data communication. The system analysis and design course focuses on application development strategies and the application development process. Optimization models are covered in depth, as is evident from the two courses listed in Exhibit 1. The two introductory level courses which have a management/social science orientation are managerial economics and introductory behavioral science.

In the third year, students are expected to select courses of their choice for the first part of the year. Mostly, these are courses in computer science and engineering or mathematics. In the second half of the year, students work on a project in design and development of IS for an organization. It is expected that the project would involve system analysis and design and considerable programming.

Training for Teachers

The MCA program is administered by the mathematics, operations research, computer science, or engineering department in the universities which were earlier offering undergraduate or short duration training in computers. The faculty in these departments need to upgrade their skills in order to be able to offer the MCA program. The DOE has identified certain centres for training of teachers. The training programs are generally organized during summer and winter breaks to facilitate attendance by teachers. Teachers who have educational background in physical science or mathematics are eligible to attend these courses. The curriculum is offered in 4-5 modules. Each module covers a specific course from among those specified in the MCA curriculum to enable the teachers to have extensive coverage of the subject. There are no pre-specified course contents for the teachers. The program design is finalized by the selected centres in consultation with DOE. The course contents vary across the centres and from year to year.

Implementation of the Curriculum

Between 1983 and 1990, DOE has implemented the MCA program in about 70 centres and teacher's training program in a number of centres across the entire country. Most MCA programs and teachers training programs were offered in engineering colleges or computer science schools.

DOE/University Grants Commission provides initial funding of equivalent of US $ 10,000 - 15,000 for purchase of hardware, provision of infrastructure, and setting up a library. A recurring grant for part-funding of salaries of teachers is also provided. The state government and the Ministry of Human

Resource Development contribute the remaining amount of salary of teachers. About 2000 students graduate every year. Entry is on the basis of entrance examinations. Although the programs are promoted and funded by DOE, universities implement the curriculum and design of the qualifying examination independent of DOE. As a result, there is a wide variation in the quality of graduates and their capabilities.

In 1990, DOE and the Indian Society for Technical Education revised the MCA curriculum. By mid-1991 the revised curriculum had been passed on to only a few centres offering the MCA program.

The revised curriculum is also of three year duration. Exhibit 2 provides a list of courses offered in the revised curriculum. The course format was changed by removing the elective courses and replacing them by a pre-specified set of courses. The number of management courses in this curriculum has been reduced from four to two. The orientation of the computer science courses is now tilted more towards IS design issues. The introduction of new courses on decision support systems, software engineering, artificial intelligence, computer graphics etc., indicates that DOE has made efforts to incorporate emerging technological trends in the curriculum.

As far as the private training institutes are concerned, accreditation is a major problem since there are major variations in programs across the country. DOE announced an accreditation policy in 1991, with four level of examinations called O, A, B, and C. Levels O, A, and B refer to progressively higher levels

Year	Revenue in US $(millions) at 1991 exchange rate		Yearly Growth Rate	
	Hardware	Software	Hardware	Software
1985	93.6	39.2		
1986	138.8	62.0	48.2%	58.2%
1987	204.0	79.9	46.9%	28.9%
1988	269.6	158.0	32.2%	97.5%
1989	360.0	106.8	33.5%	-32.4%

Source: Dataquest, July 1990, Department of Electronics, Annual Report (1989-90)

Table 2: Profile of Indian Computer Industry

of proficiency in programming in COBOL and BASIC. Level C is the "advanced" level test on

- System analysis and design
- Data communication and networking
- OS principles
- Data Base Management Systems
- Data structures and language

Accreditation is based on a minimum level of computing resources (hardware, manuals, software books and journals provided), the percentage of students sent from these institutes for each category of examinations and a minimum pass percentage of students sent for examination.

IS CURRICULUM AND GLOBALIZATION

In order to understand the effect of globalization on the IS education scenario in India, we need to understand the interlinkages between the global environment, the Indian IS environment and role of various agencies related to the development of the curriculum. Indian industry, and the IS industry in particular, is influenced by international trends in business and information technology. In an effort to respond to the emerging global scenarios, the industry could put pressure on the educational and training systems within the country to provide manpower with appropriate skills and educational background. The other mechanism which influences the IS education system is the academic and professional bodies and their perception of different types of skills to be imparted to the students. To appreciate the impact of globalization on Indian industry and Indian industry's influence on IS developed within the organization and the IS curriculum design, we need to understand the Indian business environment.

Industry Profile

The General Business and IS Supply Environment. The Indian business environment was (until recently) characterized by protected markets and therefore limited competition. There are a large number of public or government monopolies (e.g. Airlines, Railways, Television etc.) which generally have little or no customer orientation and very limited scope or imperative to respond to competition. There are high import tariffs on many capital goods and restrictive laws regarding foreign participation. Therefore, the Indian business has been slow to respond to globalization of business and technological developments. Since 1984 there has been a progressive, albeit, slow move towards modernization. Specifically, the policy environment for growth of electronics and telecommunication industry has been very encouraging. The availability of computers in India has increased significantly. Computer hardware is allowed to be imported duty free as long as the importer is able to fulfill a software export obligation of 250% of the cost of hardware. Banks have been instructed to advance loans on easy terms for software development. The government has allowed many software companies to set up datacom links with their clients abroad. On the telecommunication side, the government has allowed manufacture of EPABXs, telephone instruments, and communication cables for the first time in the private sector. Consequently, the computer industry in India has been recording a steady growth rate since 1985. Table 2 shows the growth rates in hardware and software revenue of the Indian computer industry from 1985 to 1989.

From 1986 onward, the market has continuously grown for PCs (including XTs, ATs, 386- and 486-based desktops), minis, 4GLs, networks, and DBMS packages (Dataquest, July 1990). Two organizations, Videsh Sanchar Nigam Ltd. and Computer Maintenance Corporation Ltd., provide access to users to networks in India and abroad through a X.25 gateway. From 1986 onward, the telecommunication infrastructure and services have improved with the setting up of a number of digital exchanges and datacom lines.

IS Environment in Organizations

Even though the Indian computer industry has grown by at least 30% each year during 1983-88, IS in most organizations have remained grooved in traditional uses such as payroll, inventory management, sales accounting, etc. The focus has been largely on computerization of existing manual tasks and report generation. Most commercial systems have been implemented on minis in COBOL.

This state of IS within organizations is due to the insulated and protected environment in which most organizations operate within the country and lack of trained professionals. A large number of applications chosen for computerization are not related to organizational goals. Most organizations automate their manual procedures per se without focusing on developing applications for decision support. Another reason IS has not taken off in Indian organizations is the relative cost of hardware and software. Hardware is 2-3 times more expensive in India than in most western countries. A diffused focus on user-training has turned even the good IS into systems that are not properly used. Senior and top managers in most organizations are not aware of the strategic benefits of IS and hence neither initiate projects which could have potential competitive advantage for the organization, nor aggressively support such applications when they are initiated from elsewhere. Most Indian organizations do not have an IS policy for acquisition of technology, development of applications, or training of personnel. However, the demand for business and information professionals is expected to increase with increasing openness of the Indian economy.

Another area where expertise in IS is in demand is in software exports. The government has viewed this to be an area of importance in helping India achieve a balance in external trade and has, therefore, tried to provide a suitable policy environ-

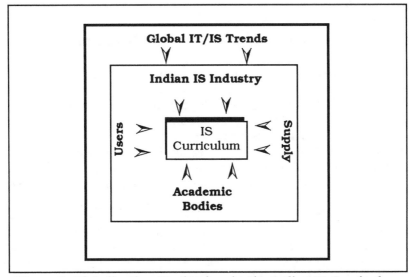

Figure 1: Globalisation Mechanism in the Indian IS Curriculum.

ment. For example, it has liberalized import policy for software exporters, established channels for provision of foreign exchange for import of computers, and simplified procedures for export. The large pool of English proficient, technically trained manpower provides a potential advantage to India in this field. But the availability of reliable high speed datacom links and latest computing platforms are also crucial for raising India's software export revenue. The ability of Indian organizations to build innovative alliances with foreign firms and the government's openness and commitment are other factors which would influence software export revenues. Until 1991, more than 80% of India's software export was in the coding of customized application on mini platforms. The market share of this segment is expected to decrease in future. By limiting the market segment tapped for export to coding of customized application, India has faced constant competition and threat from automatic tools for program generation and higher productivity and skills of programmers in other developing countries. The Indian software industry, therefore, needs to reorient its software export strategy and remove constraints on availability of manpower (Bhatnagar and Jain, 1991). To be able to exploit the IS business potential globally, a clear identification of training and education programs vis-a-vis the market requirements is also necessary. This makes it imperative for Indian IS education to be compatible with worldwide trends.

Industry Characteristic and IS Education

Industry has not put pressure on the academic environment since, possibly, it has met its requirement of software development by drawing on the pool of existing manpower or through upgradation of existing skills. Another reason may have been the on-job training provided to existing personnel which has enabled them to design the usual data processing systems that most organizations have opted for. Such training efforts undertaken by organizations did not have any impact on the educational system. and experience from these programs has remained largely undocumented. In the initial stages of computerization, (say until late 1980s), many users were themselves not sure as to how to evaluate software and therefore were not demanding. Thus, even developers with lower order skills could meet the requirements of such organizations. In addition, due to the isolation of the IS education from global trends, the IS graduates who could have provided skills and training to Indian businessmen in identifying and developing international markets were unable to do so.

Mechanisms for Incorporating International Component

A characteristic of the prevailing economic environment has been its meagre requirement to respond to global influences. Consequently, the Indian IS sector itself has been slow to keep pace with global business and information technology; on the other hand, its impact on the academic institutions has been minimal. Therefore, the impetus for globalization has come largely at the initiative of the DOE committee which has drawn up the curriculum outline and incorporated revisions. Figure 1 represents the mechanism for incorporating global trends in the Indian IS curriculum.

ISSUES

Focus and Design of IS Curriculum

The curriculum adopted by DOE lacks an organizational perspective. Some of the core courses like marketing and production are absent in the DOE curriculum. In contrast, both ACM and IFIP curricula provide adequate coverage to the managerial dimension of IS, besides the techno-economic aspects of such systems. These curricula are clearly focused and application oriented.

Further, the course outlines in the DOE model are so drawn up that they lack a focus on the integration of IS with the functional aspects in organizations. For example, in a course in financial management in the MCA curriculum, students are at most expected to be able to analyze the various financial statements using a spreadsheet instead of being trained in the various features related to financial IS. The latter would have required coverage of issues such as, what are the different components of an financial IS, what kind of interface should such a system provide to other IS in the organisation, what kind of performance should it have and so on. While the DOE curriculum lacks an IS perspective in the management courses, it is also deficient in dealing with the managerial issues in the quantitative and computer science oriented courses. The focus on learning in the latter courses is on imparting conceptual knowledge. It would appear that these courses could have been used as vehicles for demonstrating application areas for use of models and quantitative techniques in organizations.

The initial DOE curriculum did not have courses on software engineering, decision support systems, IS as a competitive weapon, case studies on joint-ventures, use of productivity enhancement tools etc., which would have made the curriculum compatible with other internationally well-known curricula. This absence also left a gap between the coverage provided in the curriculum and emerging global trends.The applications of networking, workstation usage, and public database were still in their infancy in India in the early 90s, though the use of such technology is growing. There is generally low literacy amongst users about the potential of such technology, especially in the business context. Little or no weight is given in the curriculum design to let students use and understand innovative uses of information technology for business. Though subsequent revision of the curriculum in 1990 incorporated courses on networking, graphics, software development, and database technologies, getting the appropriate computing platforms for students to practice on and a lack of well-trained teachers in these subjects is going to be an impediment to the implementation of this change.

Since the curriculum is perceived by the faculty to be based on text-books, no attempt is made by them to integrate the real life experiences of some of the Indian organizations which have implemented networks and large databases etc. In many of the MCA centres it is difficult to get management faculty to teach, as these centres are located in computer science and engineering schools and there is little liaison with the management education group.

The above limitation of MCA curriculum, however, have to be viewed in the light of the fact that it was drawn up by experts in technical education. The design of the IS curriculum and the subsequent revision were not based on a formal feedback from participants, the industry and other educational institutes. On the operational side, the Indian model did not have the flexibility to allow students of other streams like MBA to specialise in IS whereas as early as 1982 the ACM report proposed a mechanism for allowing the MBA and MS students to major in IS by prescribing a set of courses which would complement the learning in other areas. The ACM curriculum also proposed an MBA program minor (area of emphasis) in IS with four courses on Systems and Information Concepts in Organization, Program, Data and File Structures, Information Analysis, System Analysis and Design. Even in the revised Indian curriculum no efforts have been made in this direction.

Funding

The funding mechanism of the DOE allows for one-time purchase of hardware and software. As such, the funds are barely sufficient for the centres to purchase the required equipment. There is no mechanism by which these centres can upgrade their equipment or purchase new software. In this area, where the rate of obsolescence is so high, a recurring grant would have been useful. Further, with the devaluation of the Indian currency since July 1991, the increased costs of hardware are going to substantially effect the availability of hardware in most educational institutes.

Role of Industry

The industry which is a major beneficiary of skilled manpower, could have been asked to play a more active role in funding IS education. Many private organizations the world over had taken such initiative and almost all major software and hardware vendors have opened training and educational institutes in many countries. For example IBM and WANG have such ventures in Singapore and elsewhere. India needs to learn from these examples. Besides support for financing IS education, a major consequence of such an approach would have been greater role of industry in design of IS curriculum and hence greater linkage between IS education and national and international market trends.

Accreditation

The introduction of accreditation could have a healthy impact on the system. Besides ensuring uniform standards, this could encourage setting up of quality private training institutes. The accredited institutes could ensure a minimum level of acceptance for the students in the job market. 1991 was the first year of implementation of this system.

An interesting development that took place in 1991 was the provision of accreditation by the apex industry association of hardware, software, peripheral and training organizations - Manufacturers' Association of Information Technology (MAIT). The MAIT and DOE accreditation were independent of each other. MAIT had started providing accreditation to some private training institutes based on infrastructure, facilities and experience. MAIT accreditation, however, did not take into account the design of curriculum and academic processes. To the general public, the difference between the DOE and MAIT accreditation was not very clear. The DOE and MAIT accreditation need to be dovetailed.

Administration

Given the hierarchical nature of the educational system in India, the decisions regarding course design, duration and implementation are simply passed down from DOE to various universities and centres. There is no formal system to provide feedback to the DOE. For example, even after a year and half, of revising the curriculum, DOE was not able to send the new curriculum to most universities and MCA centres.

Industry's Perception of IS Professionals

The industry as a whole is not aware of the capabilities of MCA graduates. Most employers offer these graduates programmers' job. Partly this is due to the lack of integration across the management and computer science disciplines in this program, and partly because the industry does not perceive the importance of the role of a information analyst. The DOE needs to "market" this program to the industry. But the acceptance of these graduates in the industry will only come about when the educational program is well-developed.

Real-politik of Decision-making

There has been very little public debate either in professional or academic bodies regarding various aspects of this curriculum like duration, subject coverage, internationalization, training of teachers, etc. This may have been due to the general unresponsiveness and lack of openness that is characteristic of most committees, at least in the Indian context. However, issues such as privatization of computer education and accreditation of these institutes have gotten highlighted and discussed in a number of professional meetings. Steps towards accreditation of private training institutes have already taken place. This may have been, possibly, because the training industry has the backing of the powerful manufacturer's association. Any decisions regarding these issues affects the revenues of the training industry.

Teachers' Training Programs

The teachers training program for the graduate IS program was indigenously developed. In comparison to a model developed by the Royal Society of Arts (RSA) jointly with Micro Electronics Education Program (Exhibit 3), (Samways, 1986), the Indian model for training teachers is very restrictive in the selection of eligible teachers for training. It also reveals a "science" bias in the selection criteria. On one hand, this kind of selection process is detrimental to an integrative learning process across courses; on the other, it excludes the management teachers from being trained in the technical components of IS. It is relatively inflexible in allowing teachers to accumulate credits as per their convenience. It would appear that a module on pedagogy would be a useful addition to such a course.

DOE arranged for training of teachers during the summer and winter breaks. Since different universities have vacations at different periods in the year, many teachers who want to attend such courses are unable to do so. Moreover, since the attendance in such courses gives no tangible benefit to the teacher, there is little incentive for them to attend the course. The training of teachers thus remains a weak element in the new IS education system.

IMPLICATIONS FOR OTHER DEVELOPING COUNTRIES

Based on the experience of professionalisation of IS education in India, some generalizations and lessons that may be of relevance to other developing countries may be drawn.

a) It is extremely important to have industry representatives, teachers and administrators all through the process of design, development and implementation of an educational program, especially in one where the underlying technology is changing so rapidly and through which it is hoped to achieve competitive advantage at the national level.

b) The administrative mechanism for implementation needs to be well planned. This should be designed to accept feedback and respond within very short time periods.

c) Since educational institutes in most developing countries have resource shortages, innovative funding schemes, possibly in collaboration with the industry for computing resources, need to be evolved. This would provide for close liaison with the industry and make education more market oriented, besides helping to solve the resource crunch.

d) There should be a clear identification of the role of government and industry in implementing the educational programs. This allows for sharply focused programs in terms of resource availability and course content. The role of the government should be confined to training of the teachers, development of computer-, video- and TV-based teaching materials, whereas the industry should take the responsibility for training of professionals.

e) It may be worthwhile to examine other mechanisms for training of IS professionals, such as a one-year course for existing employees in either the functional areas or in the IS department.

f) In many developing countries it may not be possible for universities to charge high fees from students and, consequently, to provide adequate computing resources. The students, universities and banks should work out a mechanism whereby students could be offered loans for pursuing this course.

The loans could be repaid after the students start working. Since it is difficult for the banks to penalize defaulting students, some ingenious scheme would have to be thought about.

g) The professional bodies should play an active role in promoting development of IS professionals. These bodies should ideally have representatives from academics who have visions and are sensitive to changing market demands and representatives from industry who realize the value of education and not mere training.

FUTURE DIRECTIONS

The DOE has indeed taken some positive steps in formulating and evolving a curriculum for IS education and has provided a policy environment for standardization of curriculum. However, the DOE must recognise the importance of having practitioners and industry representatives on its decision-making panels for curriculum design. It must set up appropriate administrative channels for quick action and design systems for accepting feedback. Focus should also be provided to training at the user level. These courses need to emphasize the strategic uses of IS for Indian organizations. Computer-based training, sharing of teaching material through networks, developing teaching material which is video or TV based are options which the DOE should examine actively. In the future, if IS curriculum in India is to keep pace with emerging international trends, then the DOE, the industry, the universities and professional bodies will have to find innovative solutions to some of the problems discussed in this chapter.

EXHIBIT 1 :
BROAD OUTLINE OF THE INDIAN MODEL OF
THE IS GRADUATE PROGRAM

Courses in the Curriculum
1.   Introductory Programming
      Computer Organization, Algorithm Development and PASCAL
2.   Discrete Mathematical Structures
      Graphs, Groups, Subgroups, Lattice, Boolean Algebra
3.   Logical Organization of Computers
      Representation of Information, Basic Logic Design, Memory,

CPU, I/O, Case Study of PC Architecture

4. Linear Algebra
Vector Spaces, Linear Mapping, Linear Inequalities and Convex Sets, Inner Product and Norms, Quadratic Forms

5. Business Data Processing
Introduction to Business Organization, Data Capture and Validation, System Investigation, Business Files, COBOL (50%)

6. Data and File Structures
Data Structures and Algorithms, File Processing Environment, File Organization, Sorting and Searching

7. Accounting and Financial Management
Principles of Accounting, Assets, Working Capital, Interpreting Accounting and Financial Statements, Standards for Control, Budgeting, Forecasting, Project Appraisal

8. Computer Oriented Numerical Method
Computer Arithmetic, Iterative Methods, Solution of Simultaneous and Ordinary Different Equations, Numerical Differentiation and Integration

9. System and Information Concepts in OrganiZations
Information Systems and Organizations, Representation and Analysis of Systems, Structure Systems, Information and Decision Theory, Information Systems, Application Systems, Evaluation and Selection

10. Computer Oriented Statistical Analysis
Basic Concepts related to Probability Distributions, Statistical Inference, Time Series Analysis

11. Computer System Architecture
Introduction to Computer Systems, Processes, Multiprogramming Systems, Other Concepts.

12. Computer Based Optimization Models
Review, Analysis of Allocation Problems with Mathematical Program, LP, Characteristic of Scheduling Situation, Queuing Theory

13. Introductory Behavioral Science and Organizational Structure
Goals, Objective and Constraints, Human Systems, Socio-technical Systems

14. Data Management
Data Environment, OS Topics, File Organization, DBMS (logical, internal, real world), DBMS facilities, Management and Evaluation

15. Computer Oriented Optimization Models-II
Dynamic Programming, Project Scheduling, Project Management, Sequencing Models and Applications, Replacement Models and Applications.

16. Performance of Computer Systems and Management
Computer Selection Techniques, Performance Measurement

using Monitors, Trends in Cost Performance, Lease vs Purchase Decisions, Software Evaluation.

17. Information Analysis
Application Development Strategies, Application System, Life Cycle, System Development Management, Individual and Group Behaviour in Development, Requirement Analysis and Feasibility Assessment, Information Requirement Determination, Requirement Analysis and Logical Specifications

18. Managerial Economics
Forecasting, Demand Function, Cost Function, Production Function, Breakeven Analysis.

19. Data Communication and Distributed Processing
Fundamental Concepts of Data Transmission, Data Communication Methods, Communication System Network, System Consideration, Concurrency and Cooperation of Dispersed Processors, Analytic Methods and Design Consideration, Software Consideration in Communication Environment, Application Design on Distributed Processes

20. System Analysis and Design
Quality Assurance, Software Make/Buy, Planning to Accommodate Change, Detailed Logical Design, Physical Logical Design, HW/SW Selection, Program Development and Testing, Implementation and Management

21, 22, 23. Electives from the following
(1) Knowledge Base Management (2) AI and Expert Systems (3) Computer Graphics (4) Translator Design (5) Software Project Management (6) Formal Language and Automata Theory (7) Micro Processor (8) Advanced Numerical Methods

24. Project IS design and development

EXHIBIT 2: OUTLINE OF THE REVISED MCA CURRICULUM

Courses in the Curriculum
1) Mathematical Foundations of Computer Science.
2) Computer Programming and Problem Solving Through Pascal.
3) Computer Organization and Assembly Language Programming.
4) Accounting and Financial Management.
5) Combinatorics and Graph Theory.
6) Business Data Processing Through COBOL.
7) Data and File Structures.
8) Computer Based Numerical and Statistical Methods.
9) Organizational Structure and Personnel Management.
10) System Software and C Programming.

11) Database Management Systems.
12) System Analysis and Design.
13) Computer Based Optimization Models.
14) Translator Design.
15) Operating System.
16) Software Engineering.
17) PC Software.
18) Analysis and Design of Algorithms.
19) Decision Support Systems.
20) Computer Centre Management.
21) Distributed Computing, Networks and Applications.
22) Simulation and Modelling.
23) Artificial Intelligence.
24) Interactive Computer Graphics.
25) Project on System Design and Development.

EXHIBIT 3 : SALIENT FEATURES OF THE RSA TEACHERS TRAINING PROGRAM

Teachers either opt for the Certificate, which is a basic qualification, or a Diploma, which is a higher level award. The trainees are expected to develop their own learning objectives and a set of assignments/evidence that would be used for the assessment of learning. The Board's accreditor evaluates both the objectives and the relevance of the assignments for obtaining the Certificate/Diploma. The RSA also provides a resource list of books and learning objectives. The curriculum has been designed to be modular by allowing variable entry points. It is flexible in terms of allowing a wide variety of choice of subjects. Since IS requires understanding of the technical, the social and organizational impact of IS, usage of real-life situations within the classroom context is emphasized. The curriculum is not time bound and certification is based on the level of skills and knowledge acquired - not on attendance at a specific course. The scheme also provides for transfers of candidates between institutions in the country.

REFERENCES
Accreditation of Training Industry. *Computers Today*, 1991, Jan., 42-51

Ashenhurst, R.L. (ed). A Report of the ACM Curriculum on Computer Education in Management. *CACM*, 1972, 15 (5), 363.

Buckingham, R.A. An IFIP-BCS Curriculum for Information System Design.

Computer Education, 1986, 52, (2), 24.

Bhatnagar, S.C., & Jain, R. A Realistic Assessment of India's Software Export : Some Implications For Future Strategy. *Vikalpa,* 1991, 16(3), 35-46.

Bhatnagar, S.C., & Patel, N.R. Developing Computer Professionals: Challenges and Opportunities. *Vikalpa,* 1985, 10 (4), 387-397.

Electronics Industry. Report of the Working Group, Eighth Five Year Plan, Department of Electronics, Government of India, 1989, 127-135.

Jain, R., & Raghuram, G. Strategy for Promoting Computer Literacy. Discussion Paper presented in the Workshop on Computers in Education, 7-8 Dec., 1985, held at Indian Institute of Management, Ahmedabad, India.

Nunamaker, J.F., Couger, J.D. & Davis, G.B. Information Systems Curriculum Recommendations for the 80s: Undergraduate and Graduate Programs. *CACM,* 1982, 25, (11), 781-805.

Pawar, R. On Privatising Computer Education. *Computers Today,* June 1991, 40.

Report of the Panel on Computer Manpower Development, *Electronics Information and Planning,* 1980, 18 (2).

Samways, B.RSA New Initiatives: Information Technology for Teachers and Trainers. *Computer Education,* 1986, 52, 3-4.

Sifting the Chaff, *Computers Today,* June 1991, 35-38.

11 Globalization in IT Education: The Hong Kong Scenario

K.B.C. Saxena and Louis C.K. Ma
Hong Kong Polytechnic

Globalization reveals an imposing future for many organizations in Hong Kong as their purchasing, marketing, and production activities spread across many countries. As more Hong Kong organizations prepare for globalization, their IT capabilities become crucial to their performance. Globalization requires significant changes in organizational structure and locations of activities in the firm, and IT plays a major role in implementing these changes. Globalization is a relatively new concept and Hong Kong organizations seem to have only a limited understanding of its need and other related issues. They, therefore, need to be educated about the global IT issues. This chapter describes the various mechanisms for introducing globalization in IT education in Hong Kong and proposes a framework for assessing the level of globalization in tertiary-level IT education. Further, it conjectures the reasons for the current status of globalization in IT education and recommends a strategy for improving the situation.

GLOBALIZATION AND GLOBAL INFORMATION TECHNOLOGY

Today more and more organizations are becoming increasingly *globalized* in their activities; that is, they are purchasing, marketing, and/or producing products and services in more than one country. The two major catalysts of globalization are (1) the Far East's challenge to just about every aspect of U.S. business, and (2) the European Economic Community (EEC) 1992 Single Market initiative (Keen, 1991). Organizations participating in these new world markets will increasingly be at a serious strategic disadvantage if they are unable to firmly control their worldwide operations and manage them in a globally coordinated manner (Bartlett & Ghoshal, 1989). As a consequence, they must also deal with the issues and opportunities of using information technology (IT) on a multi-country basis. A globally competing organization is influenced by global forces, such as (Manheim, 1991):

- tightly-linked global financial markets

- global sourcing of inputs, marketing and distribution of products, and manufacturing of components and final products

- increased pressures for improved product quality and reduced product price
- evolution of businesses toward more comprehensive and continuous global coordination.

Globalization has affected organizations in Hong Kong as their production facilities move to China and their purchasing and marketing spreads across many countries in different continents. As more Hong Kong organizations prepare for globalization, their IT capabilities become crucial to their performance. Globalization requires significant changes in organizational structure and locations of activities in the firm. The rapid growth of the tertiary and services sector in Hong Kong and the trend of global market competition have led to a higher dependence on the effective use of information as a key to its business success. IT will, therefore, play a major role in facilitating, and in some cases, driving these organizational structure changes. Thus, there is a very strong need to educate Hong Kong organizations about the global IT issues. Unfortunately, the current IT education scenario does not seem to fulfill this need.

In a globally competing organization (GCO), the usual issues in IT exist along with some additional complexities due to operations spread over multiple time zones and political jurisdictions; multiple languages; multiple national practices in work patterns, marketing, production, and distribution; different capabilities for voice and data communication; different availabilities of labour skills; different economic and environmental conditions; etc. (Ives and Manheim, 1991). In such an organization, IT does and will play a critical strategic role. Global information technology (GIT) refers to the theme of a conscious approach in a GCO of using IT for gaining competitive advantage (Manheim, 1991).

The objective of this chapter is to evaluate globalization in tertiary-level IT education in Hong Kong and make recommendations, if necessary, for improving the situation. The next two sections describe the business environment and global information technology in Hong Kong. Following this are the sections describing the role of IT education, tertiary education institutions in Hong Kong, and the IT education programs in these institutions. The next section describes a framework for assessing the extent of globalization in the tertiary-level IT education. The section following it discusses various ways for introducing globalization in IT education and applies the framework developed earlier to the curricula of all the tertiary-level IT courses which are likely to include globalization. It also describes the problems inherent in these approaches and the solutions to these problems are described in the next section. The chapter concludes with a description of future directions of IT education in Hong Kong.

THE HONG KONG BUSINESS ENVIRONMENT

Due to its limited natural resources, Hong Kong is almost entirely dependent on imports to meet the needs of its population of around 6 million and its diverse industries. Hence, it must export on a sufficient scale to generate the foreign exchange earnings to pay for those imports. An effective and efficient economic infrastructure is essential for Hong Kong to maintain its established international centre of finance, trade, and industry.

The most notable changes in the Hong Kong economy over the past decades are characterised not only by a rapid increase in domestic production, but more importantly by a significant shift in economic activities towards sectors with greater sophistication and higher added values such as the sea and air transport, financial and other services, electronics and computers, as well as fashion apparel and upmarket toys which are gradually displacing plastic flowers, cheap radios and the lower end of the textile industry (Kao & Young, 1991). The shifting of economic activities towards the services sectors can also be observed in terms of proportion of employment : the manufacturing sector experienced a continuous decline from 47% in 1971 to 28% in 1990, while the services sectors continued to increase from 41% to 62% in the same period. In terms of contribution to Gross Domestic Product (GDP), the manufacturing sector declined from 31% in 1970 to 18% in 1989, while the services sectors increased from 60% to 67% in the same period (Roberts,1991). Along with the rapid growth of the services sectors, which require neither large capital nor plant, is the increase of small business operations.

Another major factor contributing to the rapid growth of the Hong Kong economy is the increasing economic links with China. With the adoption of an open economic policy since 1978 in support of its modernisation programs, China has the potential of becoming a major international trading partner. This has led to a rapid increase in economic links between Hong Kong and China with a profound impact on the growth and development of the Hong Kong economy. Since 1988 China has been the largest supplier of goods to Hong Kong, the largest market for Hong Kong's re-exports and the second largest market for exports. Along with China's open policy is the abundant supply of "inexpensive" labour, leading to a continual shift of some labour-intensive jobs from Hong Kong to China. The "June 1989" events in Beijing may indicate a significant internal cultural backlash within China which would slow down its progress on both political and economic reforms. However, its dependence on Hong Kong's economy may increase as Hong Kong is a major direct/indirect source of foreign exchange earnings for China. The recent (1991) endorsement of the Accord by the British Prime Minister and the Chinese Premier as a follow-up to the Sino-British Joint Declaration of 1984 and the Basic Law as drafted in 1990 as well as the Port and Airport Development Strategy (PADS) projects, may continue to boost confidence in the future prosperity of Hong Kong through to and beyond 1997, when there will be a change of government from Britain to China.

Hong Kong's Links to the Global Economy

The favourable geographical position of Hong Kong, which provides a bridge in the time gap between North America and Europe, together with strong links with China and other economies in the Pacific rim as well as excellent communications with the rest of the world, has helped Hong Kong to develop into an important *international financial centre*. In 1990, 84 of the top 100 banks in the world had operations in the territory (Roberts, 1991).

The rapid economic growth of China and other Pacific rim countries has created an excellent opportunity for Hong Kong to further expand its *international/regional trade* markets. In particular, re-export trade figures have increased at a compound rate of more than 20% per annum for the past 3 years. However, the trade barriers imposed by some countries may have a serious effect on Hong Kong's export-oriented economy.

The rapid economic growth of Pacific rim countries will pose increased competition for Hong Kong not only in the Pacific region, but also in international markets. These countries have lower land costs and wages than Hong Kong, making Hong Kong less competitive in the labour-intensive industries. A reactive strategy adopted by many manufacturers in Hong Kong is to shift major production operations from Hong Kong to China, in order to reduce the overall production costs. Alternatively, Hong Kong may have to concentrate more on service sectors and light "high-tech" industries.

In addition to being an international centre of finance, commerce, and trade, Hong Kong has the potential to become a cultural centre of east and west as well as the international centre for communication - leading to more business opportunities through these international links.

Globalization in Hong Kong Business

Hong Kong businesses appear to be very globalized in the areas of trade, finance and services sectors, but they are more focused on certain areas of globalization as described below :

- Most local organizations in the areas of trade, finance, and services sectors have global links to overseas customers, suppliers, principals and agents.
- The establishment of off-shore production sites (mainly in southern China) having marketing, financial management, administration, and design/engineering support functions mainly provided by the Hong Kong head-office, are becoming more popular in the manufacturing sector.

- There are many branch offices of multi-nationals in Hong Kong, with global links to their regional or international headquarters.

- Hong Kong is also a popular choice as the regional head-quarter of multi-nationals, with global links to their regional branch offices and head-quarters.
- There are very few multi-national head offices in Hong Kong with global operations. Cathay Pacific Airways, Hong Kong Bank, and Worldwide Shipping are among the more prominent examples.

The world is moving towards growing independence and globalization. Entrepreneurs seek a place where they can deal freely with the rest of the world, and open market-oriented Hong Kong is a favourable choice. There is a good opportunity to further exploit the world trend towards globalization and Hong Kong's established position as a model free market may make it a major provider of IT services for the world. Considering the world trend towards shortening product cycles, Hong Kong's own ability to respond quickly to the needs of global niche markets may offer another opportunity (Kao & Young, 1991).

Effect of the Changing Business Environment in Hong Kong

The change of government of Hong Kong from Britain to China in 1997 may lead to an unstable political environment in Hong Kong through to the 21st Century. The low tax system, free trading port supported by established port and transport facilities, energetic and skillful workforce, entrepreneurial management, and an efficient infrastructure in Hong Kong, along with the increasing economic link with China and other fast-growing countries in the Pacific rim, may further contribute to the economic growth of Hong Kong through increasing international trade and finance. However, Hong Kong will have to overcome both increasing competition mainly from Asian countries and the effect of protectionist policies, mainly from Europe and U.S.A. Furthermore, the decline of labour-intensive manufacturing establishments may have to be replaced by the development of modern technology in the industrial sector for supporting the rapidly growing service sectors both in Hong Kong and Asia. There will be a continual shift towards an information based work environment of both blue and white collar workers. The expected turbulent environment in Hong Kong and the continual growth of the service sectors and high value-added industries, will provide a high level of challenge and reward for those effective managers/professionals who could successfully explore new markets or be able to gain benefit for their organizations or industries through technological innovations. The support by the tertiary education sector for enhancing the effectiveness of our managers/professionals is crucial.

GLOBAL INFORMATION TECHNOLOGY IN HONG KONG

As stated before, global information technology (GIT) refers to the theme of a conscious approach in a GCO of using IT for competitive advantage (Manheim,1991). Obviously GIT requires understanding of basic business strategy issues, which are typically observed by medium and large corporations. Unfortunately, most of the business organizations in Hong Kong are small in size but still compete globally. For example, a small manufacturing organization has its production facilities in China, its management in Hong Kong and its suppliers and customers spread across several countries in Asia, Europe and America. Thus, they do realise the complexity of their international operations but they do not have the vision of "globalization". Most of them do not have even a formal strategic business plan and may not appreciate how IT could give them a competitive advantage in their business (except that it could automate their operations and support production processes). They do understand the need to communicate with their suppliers and customers, but do not understand that global IT applications could provide them competitive advantage. As such, there is very little diffusion of GIT in most Hong Kong organizations. There is, therefore, a very strong need for the tertiary education institutions in Hong Kong to provide IT education which could enrich the focus of GIT.

As the world is moving towards the information age and services sectors, wealth will increasingly come from knowledge rather than natural resources. This will lead to a higher dependence on the effective and efficient application of IT. IT has been dominated by the advanced industrialised countries and large companies. Since Hong Kong does not have a strong R&D base, the choice of technology areas has been differentiated and focused on particular niche markets. However, recent technological innovations are opening up large market sectors and permitting new players to participate (Kao & Young, 1991).

Technological changes will undoubtedly affect the nature of work to a very large extent. In particular, the proliferation of IT into the work environment has created the greatest impact on the nature of work of both white collar (including managers) and blue collar workers. The application of management information systems, data bases, office automation, CAD/CAM, telecommunications and artificial intelligence will allow managers and professionals to benefit from the innovative use of IT, not only in improving the efficiency of information workers and managers, but also in doing some more tasks effectively which would have been impossible without the use of IT. Due to the political uncertainty and the lack of long-term investments, medium or small organizations in Hong Kong are relatively slow in the adoption of new technologies, which involve substantial capital investment.

A direct consequence of technological change is the reduction of some routine and low-skill jobs, such as clerks and routine process factory workers, while some high-skill jobs, such as programmers or CAD/CAM control operators, requiring significant technical background, are created. This has a significant impact on education and vocational training programs. On the other hand, the availability of inexpensive labour in China will slow down the increased use of IT in some organizations, whereby cheap labour is conceived to outweigh the benefit from IT. These organizations may be hit if inexpensive labour become more expensive or even unavailable.

Most large computer installations are in the services sectors, which employ around 70% of IT professionals with around 40% in banking and finance. The average ratio of personal computers (PCs) to all employees ranges from around 3% in banking/finance to a low 2% in construction with an overall average of 4.4% (VTC, 1990). Most systems are on-line and communication intensive with links from mainframe/mini computers to local area networks and PCs. Large corporations tend to install more sophisticated on-line and database systems with global communication links, while medium and small organizations often use data management software in PCs. According to a survey in 1989, IT applications were focused on transaction processing systems (55%) together with some management information systems (25%), but very few (18%) decision support systems, executive information systems or expert systems (Burn & Ma, 1990).

ROLE OF IT EDUCATION

Hong Kong has a very skillful and energetic workforce of around 2.8 million comprising 64% males and 36% female (Roberts, 1991) with virtually no strikes. A productive workforce has been one of the significant contributing factors to Hong Kong's prosperity. Taking the effect of the government's 9-year free education scheme together with increased family income, it is expected that most of Hong Kong's teenagers would at least complete secondary school (Grade 11) prior to joining the workforce in the mid 1990's. Furthermore, the ratio of the number of degree openings to the number of eligible candidates would be among the highest in Asia. A better educated workforce is essential for supporting the growth of the services sectors and the trend towards information-based work environment.

Education programs, therefore, have to be responsive in reflecting environmental changes, such as government systems, regional and international competition, and trade protection. Professionals/managers should understand the technology appropriate to the work they perform/manage and be capable of supporting and facilitating the innovative applications of technology and be more sophisticated in decision-making.

In particular, tertiary education institutions are traditionally the fountainheads of "high-tech" industries. This process has been most successful in the US, such as the Silicon Valley, spawned by the developments at Stanford University. The tertiary institutions in Hong Kong have served the community by educating undergraduates (degrees and diplomas) and postgraduates. As the needs of the community shift with the upgrading of the economy, the tertiary institutions are now providing more research and consultancy support. The six tertiary education institutions are planning to set up a joint company to provide technical services type research for both the private and public sector (Kao & Young, 1991).

Tertiary Education Institutions in Hong Kong

The Hong Kong tertiary education system follows the British pattern and predominantly has two types of institutions - universities, which are centres of academic excellence and research, and polytechnics, which used to be responsible for vocational education, generally at the technician level. In addition, there are also post-secondary colleges mainly catering for academic sub-degree programs. However, because of the increasing demand of degree-level graduates, these polytechnics as well as some of the post-secondary colleges have emerged as degree- and higher degree- granting institutions like universities. Polytechnics, however, have two constraints:first, they have to retain some of the sub-degree courses, and second, unlike universities, their degree programs require academic accreditation.

There are three universities at present in Hong Kong : (a) University of Hong Kong (HKU) established in 1911, (b) Chinese University of Hong Kong (CUHK) which started in 1963, and (c) the Hong Kong University of Science and Technology (HKUST) which opened for classes in October 1991. All three universities have undergraduate courses and three kinds of higher degrees, two of which, the Master of Philosophy (M.Phil.) and the Doctor of Philosophy (Ph.D.), are awarded on the basis of original research, and another Master's degree is obtainable by coursework.

There are two polytechnics - the Hong Kong Polytechnic (HKP) and the City Polytechnic of Hong Kong (CPHK) established in 1972 and 1984 respectively. Initially the polytechnics were created as centres of vocational education and awarded mainly certificate and higher certificate, diploma, higher/professional diploma, and associateship courses in a number of technical and industrial disciplines. The role of the polytechnics, however, changed in the early 1980s when they were permitted to offer degree level courses and were asked to slowly transfer their certificate, higher certificate and diploma courses to technical institutes (TIs). As a consequence, they were permitted to offer undergraduate degree courses in 1983, Master's degree by research (M.Phil.) in 1987, taught Masters programs in 1988, and doctoral (Ph.D.) programs in 1989. However, to ensure that the standards of degrees awarded by the polytechnics were comparable to those of internationally recognized degrees, all degree courses offered by the polytechnics required academic accreditation by the U.K.'s Council for National Academic Awards (CNAA) until 1989, and later by the newly created Hong Kong Council for Academic Accreditation (HKCAA). Another tertiary education institution, the Hong Kong Baptist College, has also started offering degree programs in 1986 and, as from 1989, offers only degree and higher degree courses which are accredited by CNAA/HKCAA. Similarly, another college, the Lingnan College, offers a three-year Honors Diploma, and Hong Kong Shue Yan College offers a four-year diploma course.

In order to promote distance education, a seventh degree-granting institution, the Open Learning Institute of Hong Kong (OLI), was established in 1989, which offers a second chance for those who have been unable to go on to further education after leaving school as well as opportunities for workers and managers to update their qualifications.

IT Education Programs in Tertiary Education Institutions

IT is a relatively new term that means different things to different people in different situations. IT, as understood within the Hong Kong Polytechnic, is "the discipline combining the technology of computer systems, software engineering, electronics and telecommunication, and being applied to such diversified areas as management, accounting, information retrieval, office automation, computer-aided engineering, computer-aided manufacturing, computer graphics, artificial intelligence and expert systems" (Saxena, 1987). In contrast, the Information System (IS) discipline provides the analytical framework and the methodology to analyse, design, implement, and manage complex information/decision systems (Nunamaker, 1981). It integrates systems analysis, statistics, management, management science, accounting, economics, finance, marketing, production, and computer and communication technologies to accomplish these tasks. Thus, IS are the ends and IT is the means (Earl, 1989). The issue of *what* should we do with the technology constitutes the IS strategy, whilst the question of *how* do we do it constitutes the IT strategy. Thus the terms IS and IT are very closely related and will be used interchangeably in this chapter.

In Hong Kong, there is generally a distinction between *Computer Science* (which is usually associated with mathematics, science and engineering) and *Computing Studies* (which generally refers to computer-based information systems or data processing). The term *Information Systems* (or Management Information Systems, Computer Information Systems, etc.) was until recently used only in the context of a business curriculum, and was not very popular in commerce and industry. This is because the polytechnics provided vocational education necessary for producing systems analysts, which subject they called computing studies (or computer studies). With the change in the role of polytechnics, the situation has, however, changed and is now similar to U.S.A. (Davis, 1987), where the terms used are Computer Science and Information Systems (or MIS, CBIS, CIS, etc.).

Education in computer science and electronics is offered by all the universities and polytechnics. However, as we are interested in the globalization in IT education and not in the technology alone, we need to focus our attention on courses in computing studies, information systems and management which are more likely to have a significant coverage of all the key areas identified in the proposed framework for globalization of IT educational programs. Undergraduate programs in computing studies are offered by the two polytechnics whereas masters programs in information systems, information technology, and management are offered by a number of tertiary institutions. A summary of these programs is given in the Appendix.

A FRAMEWORK FOR GLOBALIZATION IN IT EDUCATION

Globalization is a relatively new concept which requires understanding basic business strategy issues and resolving them through global IT applications. Most organizations in Hong Kong do not seem to have this vision for various reasons and need to be educated.

The shift to a globally competing organization (GCO) raises a number of new issues for IS/IT management. It is widely recognized that successful use of IT will provide competitive advantages to GCO's. Manheim (1991) distinguishes between a *sustainable competitive advantage*, which is being more effective than any competitor for a sustainable period of time, and *competitive necessity*, which is that part of an organization's strategy which must be adopted if an organization is to remain at least equally competitive with other similar organizations. Using these concepts, he proposes a framework for an effective IT strategy consisting of four basic elements:

1. *Base:* elements to build a sound IT foundation
2. *Parity*: elements to maintain competitive equality
3. *Incremental initiatives*: focused actions which, by targeting on specific segments of the organization's markets, seek to achieve an incremental lead over competitors
4. *Breakthrough*: actions which seek to achieve a restructuring of the market and the organization's role in it such that a sustainable advantage is achieved.

Using this framework, we can identify IT elements to support the base and parity and call it "basic global IT". We may similarly call other IT elements which support the incremental initiatives and breakthrough as "advanced global IT". According to Manheim (1991), the IT elements falling in these two categories are:

Basic global IT

Base: transaction processing systems, management information systems.

Parity

> operations decision support systems (DSS), basic electronic mail, basic telecommunication infrastructure, executive information systems (EIS), basic electronic data interchange (EDI), basic value-added networks (VAN), basic applications development process, end-user controlled application development process

Advanced global IT

Value-added and intelligent EDI, individual work support systems: personal information managers, location-independent computing; group work support systems, intelligent work support systems: electronic messaging, learning, active DSSs, task-team support systems, IS management process.

Ives & Jarvenpaa (1990, 1991) suggest five broad areas for global IT research. These are:

1. Linkage of IT and an organization's global business strategy.

2. Issues related to development of global business applications of IT. A global IT application contributes to achieving an organization's global business strategy by using IT platforms to store, transmit, and manipulate data across cultural environments.

3. Centralization, standardization, and trans-border flow of corporate data.
4. Impact of global issues on the development and operation of IT infrastructure and delivery platforms.

5. Economic impact of IT on national politics and culture.

We can combine the two frameworks to define another framework for assessing globalization in IT education. Thus, the following seven elements may be considered as indicators of globalization in IT education:

1. Basic global IT
2. Advanced global IT
3. Global business strategy and IT linkage
4. Global business applications of IT
5. Global storage and flow of corporate data
6. Global IT infrastructure and delivery platforms
7. Impact of IT on national economy and culture

Globalization in IT education then refers to the exposure, knowledge and understanding of global IT and related issues indicated above through IT courses, experts, and/or personal or organizational experiences. The more the exposure or knowledge/understanding gained, the higher the level of "globalization" in IT education.

GLOBALIZATION IN IT EDUCATION: ISSUES AND PROBLEMS

Globalization can be introduced in the IT education in many ways, some of these are described below.

1. Through curriculum design. This is a direct approach for introducing globalization as the relevant subject material is formally taught within the course.

2. Through institutional collaboration.   This is an indirect approach in which institutions in two or more countries enter into collaborative education programs. Globalization is introduced through sharing of knowledge, expertise, curricula and/or instructional materials from other countries.

3. Through overseas education. This is also an indirect approach in which students go to an educational institution overseas for the study. Globalization
is introduced through their exposure to IT education in a different country, which may have a better coverage of the globalization in its IT education programs. This approach is similar to the second because in both cases an external institution is instrumental in exposing the students to the globalization aspects.

Introducing Globalization through Curriculum Design

A quick look at the IT courses included in the Appendix shows the following:

1. Undergraduate programs in computing studies and masters programs in information technology cover "basic global IT" and

may shed some light on "advanced global IT," but they do not cover the remaining five areas described in the framework.

2. Masters programs in information systems cover "basic global IT" as well as some "advanced global IT" and "global business strategy and IT linkage," but they also mostly miss the remaining areas.

3. Masters programs in management (M.B.A.) cover the "basic global IT" area only partially and provide a low coverage of "advanced global IT", "global business strategy and IT linkage", and "global business applications of IT". They, however, still miss the other three areas.

In general, five out of the seven areas (identified as indicators of globalization) are not covered comprehensively in almost all the tertiary level IT courses in Hong Kong. It clearly points out that these IT courses are very much deficient in the coverage of globalization. This may appear strange in view of the importance of globalization for Hong Kong. In the absence of any research base covering these issues, we may only conjecture several reasons for this state of affairs:

1. Most organizations in Hong Kong are small in size and, therefore, tend to have a good IS/IT foundation but lag behind in having a strategic focus for defining their IS/IT applications portfolio. Globalization is a concept of significant strategic impact which is often overlooked in the absence of long-term IS/IT strategic planning. It seems that the short-term view of IT has been carried into the curriculum design process itself.

2. A government-level IT policy may help address the strategic issues affecting globalization. Unfortunately, the *laissez-faire* policy of government is a definite handicap in this matter. There are a number of bodies related to IT (such as Hong Kong Computer Society, Hong Kong IT Federation, Hong Kong Productivity Centre, etc.) which can help in shaping an IT policy for Hong Kong but, to make matters worse, each one of these is working on its own in a fragmented manner. They, as a consequence, have so far failed in planning an appropriate direction for the IT industry and its impact on other associated industries (Burn & Ma, 1990).

3. Technological areas included under "advanced global IT" provide a value-added perspective of IT as these applications may be difficult to cost-justify using the conventional cost justification methods. Often, the short-term focus on IS/IT hampers the development of this "value-added" perception of IT applications, and they are given a low priority due to their seemingly high cost.

4. As the "advanced level global IT" seems to be a neglected area in the IT courses, the graduates of these courses do not have sufficient expertise in developing or managing the development of such applications. As a consequence, even if an organization happens to decide in favor of one or more of such advanced applications, they are discouraged by the lack of available expertise and, therefore, seemingly high success risk. This lack of expertise also affects the curriculum design process as subjects for which teaching staff may not be available are often left out or covered superficially.

Introducing Globalization through Institutional Collaboration

Institutions may collaborate in many ways. Overseas institutions may offer their courses in Hong Kong through a local educational institution which provides human and other resources for running the course as part of collaboration. An example of such an arrangement is the M.B.A. programme offered by the University of Warwick, U.K. in Hong Kong through collaboration with the Hong Kong Polytechnic. As the curriculum and instructional material used for the course is provided by the University of Warwick, globalization is introduced through case studies and other instructional material designed initially for the students in U.K. The problem with this arrangement is that the staff teaching on the course may not be familiar with the instructional material used, especially the case studies, which may affect the quality of instruction. The University of Warwick does send their staff to monitor the instruction quality, but that may be of limited help.

To overcome this problem, some overseas institutions send their own staff members for teaching all or part of the course. An example of this is the Curtin University of Australia which runs their course in collaboration with the Hong Kong which runs their course in collaboration with the Hong Kong University. Still, the problem that remains is that the case studies and the instructional material used are not designed for the Hong Kong students and may not be relevant to the local environment and culture.

Some institutions, therefore, provide only faculty exchange as part of collaboration and the visiting faculty members either select or develop their own teaching material or adapt themselves to locally developed material. The Department of Management at the Hong Kong University of Science and Technology is an example which collaborates with the University of California at Los Angeles (UCLA) business school for exchange of faculty members. This arrangement is better and is beneficial to both the collaborating institutions in terms of learning and experience. Still the problem with this arrangement is that often the faculty exchanged is the one who could be spared by the parent institution rather than the one who is most appropriate for the job !

Introducing Globalization Through Overseas Education

The demand for IT and management courses is very high in Hong Kong and remains unsatisfied in spite of so many tertiary institutions. As a consequence, a number of students go to universities in U.S.A., Canada, Australia, and U.K. for studying these courses. During their stay overseas as a student, they are exposed to the local IT infrastructure and global applications in use by the organizations there, either through case studies or through their course-work, projects, dissertations, etc.

This mechanism has all the advantages of institutional collaboration. In addition, it also has the advantage of giving a first hand experience to the students, who may be provided a better understanding of the issues. However, overseas education is quite expensive and many potentially good students are unable to afford it.

OVERCOMING PROBLEMS TO GLOBALIZATION IN IT EDUCATION

Globalization seems to be a relatively neglected area in the tertiary-level IT courses in Hong Kong. The main reason for this could either be lack of awareness of its significance or a deliberate negligence. Collaborative ventures between educational institutions, too, have not been of much advantage, perhaps because collaboration was not specifically aimed to provide a "focus for globalization." It seems that the situation could be improved only by designing *specific approaches* for introducing globalization. This section describes four such approaches and then describes how a specific institution uses a mix of these approaches for introducing globalization.

"Conversion" Courses

There has been an acute need for non-computer professionals like engineers, accountants, managers, etc., to use IT in their own professions and/or to become involved in the decision making which surrounds IT and to play an active role in the development of strategies for its effective utilisation. Many small businesses in Hong Kong are now using computers and need someone with adequate knowledge to manage this use effectively, while at the same ime not being able to afford a full-time computer professional. There is, therefore, a need for courses for professionals and managers who wish to gain maximum impact from the application of IT in their own environment. Such courses have been called "conversion" courses as they convert other professionals/managers into an *information technologist*, i.e. someone who is knowledgeable in IT and can apply or help in applying it within his/her own environment.

Existing IT courses are either strong on basic global IT and weak on its strategic aspects or strong on strategic aspect and weak on technology. In any case, they do not cover either the technological or the strategic aspects of globalization to a level of depth which may actually help managers and professionals to plan for introducing globalization in their organizations. Conversion courses, such as MSc in Information Systems and MSc in Information Technology offered by the Hong Kong Polytechnic and the MA in Information Systems programme offered by the City Polytechnic, provide the coverage of basic global IT and some areas of the advanced global IT and the strategic aspects of IT. These courses could, however, be revised easily to include more of globalization.

Use of Case Studies

Case studies provide a valuable source of knowledge in business, management, and social sciences. Globalization may be a new concept in Hong Kong but many organizations in U.S.A. and Europe are already into it and a number of case studies describe some of their success stories. Global coverage of IT issues and practices to widen the intellectual horizon of Hong Kong managers and professionals could be provided mainly through case studies and site visits. Relevant foreign cases (in fact more Asian cases in addition to traditional USA/Europe-based cases) may be incorporated in IT courses, especially "conversion" courses, to support the teaching or management development programs.

Education in Strategic Thinking

The integration of IT strategies in management development programs is essential so that managers are more capable of not only linking IT plans to business goals, but also in exploiting technology driven opportunities in addition to the traditional business requirements driven opportunities. There is a need to recognise the contribution of value-added systems (such as DSS, EIS, expert systems, etc.) because tangible benefits based on cost-reduction and manpower savings are not applicable to strategic systems. They provide more intangible (value added) benefits and are, therefore, difficult to cost-justify using conventional approaches (used for transaction processing and operational systems). Hence, managers should be made aware of these implications. In fact, effective managers ultimately must be their own management development specialists and the impact of IT on business and management should be an integral part of management development education.

Modular Technology Transfer

Value-added systems such as decision support systems (DSS), executive information systems, expert systems, group work support systems, etc. are an integral part of basic as well as advanced global IT (Manheim, 1991), and are collectively referred to as "management support systems" (MSS) (Benbasat & Nault, 1990). Recent developments in MSS applications and technologies are well-known to us and have gained strategic importance for many organizations in United States and Europe (Earl, 1989, p.15). However, surprisingly enough, the MSS technology has not permeated through Hong Kong as revealed through a number of surveys on use of such systems by managers and professionals in Hong Kong. These studies also revealed that there were mainly two reasons for this lack of MSS utilisation: (a) lack of awareness regarding the potential of MSS applications among end-users, MIS and general management; and (b) lack of expertise in building such systems among system developers. We, therefore, developed a three-tier educational strategy for promoting MSS technology transfer. The essence of this strategy is to provide two different types of teaching modules for the same subject - MSS in our case - one for the users and IT planners, and the other for the system builders. The user- and planner-level module should create demand for these systems over a period of time, and the system building-level module should enable a matching supply of such systems through freshly trained system developers. Specifically, according to this strategy:

• provide *knowledge* of MSS technology to IT planners so that they could evaluate its role in their strategicIS/IT plan;

• provide *understanding* of MSS technology to IT users (managers, engineers, professionals, etc.) so that they can demand for MSS applications; and

• provide *skills* to IT providers (systems analysts, designers, etc.) so that they can build sophisticated support systems.

This modular technology transfer strategy is a general strategy which can be applied to any strategically critical area for promoting its demand as well as supply.

Introducing Globalization in IT Education at the Hong Kong Polytechnic

The Department of Computing at the Hong Kong Polytechnic is the main department responsible for offering courses in computing studies, information systems, and information technology. The staff in the Department have been using a variety of strategies for introducing globalization, though perhaps not specifically as part of the department's educational strategy.

The Department offers two "conversion" programs at the masters level - a masters in information systems (MScIS) and a masters in information technology (MScIT). As both of these courses are aimed at working professionals and managers, they are offered in a part-time evening mode and take about 2 years or more to complete. The MScIS focuses more on global IT and strategic aspects whereas the MScIT focuses only on global IT (see Appendix).

Case studies are used extensively in many subjects within the information systems area, e.g. systems analysis and design, information resource management, strategic information systems planning, management support systems, etc. A number of case studies based on local organizations have been written by the staff, which are used in conjunction with the more popular American and/or European case studies. This helps students to understand global IT in the local context.

The staff in the Department organizes a large number of extension (i.e. extramural) courses on various aspects of IT. Lately, courses on information resource management, strategic IS planning, etc. are also being organised by the staff. Further, the two masters programs are modular in nature, and people may enroll in individual modules of MScIT as well to meet their specific needs. Visitors specialising in various aspects of global IT regularly visit the Department and offer seminars which are open to outside professionals. As an example, Bob Synott, a leading authority on IS/IT strategy, visited the Department in 1991 and taught a course on IS strategy formulation as well as offered an open seminar on globalization of communication networks. We believe that all these activities contribute significantly toward the education of IT professionals and managers in strategic thinking.

Modular technology transfer as a strategy was developed by one of the authors of this chapter for promoting MSS technology in Hong Kong. The outcome of the strategy is not visible yet, but the students in the MSS courses seem to be very satisfied with the learning strategies used.

It is true that all these approaches were introduced as appropriate educational strategies for various subjects within the IS/IT area without any specific goal of introducing globalization. However, lately globalization has been an area of interest for some of the staff members in the Department including the authors of this chapter. We are reviewing our strategies and hope to improve our coverage of globalization in the future. The evaluation framework developed in this paper is an attempt in this direction.

FUTURE DIRECTION OF IT EDUCATION IN HONG KONG

The future development of business opportunities as well as employment in Hong Kong will concentrate on the services sectors, which have a higher dependence on the effective application of IT. The most important move is a well-defined IT direction and strategy; a technical strategy where the focus is to enable the achievement of business goals through a flexible technological framework and defined standards; and a vision of the essential technologies for the future (Burn & Ma, 1990). This should be reflected in IT education.

Distance Learning as a Popular Mode of Education

Due to the limited supply of land in Hong Kong and the budgetary constraints imposed by the Hong Kong Government on tertiary education, it is becoming very expensive to increase the number of degree openings by traditional classroom type education. Furthermore, the limited social security in Hong Kong makes it financially more difficult for most working adults to go back to full-time studies. Hence, evening studies and open learning programs are very popular in Hong Kong. For example, the Open Learning Institute attracted some 60,000 applications for its 4,000 places in 1990. The OLI adopts a multi-media approach to instruction, broadcasting many high-quality programs on public television. There are some other distance learning programs offered by overseas universities to Hong Kong students. The trend of this type of cost-efficient distance learning education is likely to become popular in Hong Kong. Furthermore, a large portion of the course materials for distance learning programs are developed by foreign universities, which indirectly provide a more global perspective for Hong Kong students.

Higher Level of IT Literacy through IT Education in Schools

Introduction of IT education in secondary schools has improved the IT literacy in the society and should be further supported by the Education Department. Furthermore, the enrichment of IT subjects in tertiary institutions for non-computing students (e.g. through well-planned service-teaching, double-majors and conversion courses) is also needed so that there will be more "hybrid" managers/professionals who are more proficient in applying IT to their specialised areas (Ma, 1991).

Comparative Analysis of Globalization in the Region

After two decades of high economic growth, Hong Kong has the highest per capita GDP (US$12,000) in Asia except Japan (US$23,600). This is followed very closely by Singapore (US$11,600), then Taiwan (US$8,000) and Korea (US$5,600). However, it appears that in the traditional areas of technology-based industries, Hong Kong has lagged behind its neighbors. Japan is the most developed country and has several large companies, which depend on many small companies to supply the niche products and technology. Singapore competes with Hong Kong in many similar industries/markets, its strength lies in comprehensive government planning and control. Taiwan flourishes with a relatively large number of small companies. Korea derives its industrial strength from having several large dominating companies (Kao & Young, 1991). Technological innovations not only allow traditional needs to be fulfilled more efficiently, but more importantly also create novel needs, which may lead to exciting business opportunities. This trend demands that future technology needs and opportunities be anticipated and the necessary technology infrastructure identified and put into place now in a planned and coordinated manner. This need is urgent, because competitive neighbours, especially Taiwan, Korea and Singapore, are directing vast public resources to the development of a broad range of technologies. This continuing threat to Hong Kong's competitiveness is a matter of alarming concern.

Another strategy is to further exploit the world trend

towards globalization and Hong Kong's established position as a model free market, and prepare Hong Kong as a major provider of IT services for the world. Systems integration and service vendor sector of the IT industry, which involve much smaller R&D efforts, are typical examples (Kao & Young,1991).

Better Links between Industry and Education

More active links between industry and education (Burn & Ma,1991) are required so that an appropriate balance between theoretical and practical aspects of IT could be incorporated in education. This may lead to a better acceptance of new technologies by the industry. Joint research and consultancy as well as placement of staff from educational sector to industry (and vice-versa) should be encouraged.

Appropriate continuous education programs as well as refresher or re-orientation courses are required for IT professionals, not only to meet their current job requirements, but also to prepare them for their career (Burn & Ma,1990). Organizations should take a long-term view in developing their staff with the appropriate IT skills to look after the organization's needs as it grows. The development of an appropriate perspective on strategic systems, competitive advantage and globalization are important considerations.

CONCLUSION

Finally, there is a need to review IT education programs from time to time in order to reflect not only the rapid changes in IT, but also the globalization of the Hong Kong business environment as well as their relevant contributions to the society. We hope that our observations and experience in globalization and respective support from IT education and other parties are useful for the readers (senior executives, IT managers, training managers, and academics in particular) in planning and running IT education programs.

APPENDIX :
COVERAGE OF GLOBALIZATION IN IT BY SOME DEGREE AND TAUGHT MASTERS PROGRAMS IN HONG KONG

(a) Areas of Global IT Education Courses/Institutions	1	2	3	4	5	6	7
Undergraduate programs)							
B.Eng in Computer Engineering							
Chinese Uni.	H	L (b)					
City Poly	H	L					
Uni. of Sci. & Technology	H	L					
HK Poly (Electronic Eng.)	H	L					
Uni. of HK	H	L					
B.Sci. in Computer Science or IT							
Chinese Uni. (Comp. Sci.)	H	L					
City Poly (Computer Studies)	H	L					
City Poly (IT)	H	L					
HK Poly (IT, from 1992)	H	L					
Uni. of HK	H	L					
B.A. in Computing Studies or IS							
City Poly (IS)	H	L					
HK Poly (Computing Studies)	H	L					
B.A. in Business							
Chinese Uni.	M	L		L			
City Poly	M	L		L			
HK Poly	M	L		L			
Open Learning Institute	M	L	L	L			
Uni. of HK	M	L		L			
(Masters programs)							
Master in Computer Science							
City Poly	H	L					
Uni. of Sci. & Technology	H	L					
Uni. of HK	H	L					
Conversion Masters in IS/IT							
City Poly (MA in IS)	M	L					
HK Poly (M.Sc. in IS)	M	L	L	L			
HK Poly (M.Sc. in IT)	H	L					
MBA							
Chinese Uni.	M	L	L	L			
City Poly	M	L	L	L			
Uni. of Sci. & Technology	M	L	L	L			
HK Poly	M	L	L	L			
Uni. of HK	M	L	L	L			L

Note(a) Areas of global IT education :
1. Basic global IT
2. Advanced global IT
3. Global business strategy and IT linkage
4. Global business applications of IT
5. Global storage and flow of corporate data
6. Global IT infrastructure and delivery platforms
7. Impact of IT on national economy and culture

(b) Extent of coverage : Low (L), Medium (M) or High (H)

REFERENCES

Bartlett, C.A. & Ghoshal, S.(1989). *Managing across borders:The transnational solution.* Boston, Mass.: Harvard Business SchoolPress.

Benbasat, I. & Nault, B.R. (1990). An evaluation of empirical research in managerial support systems. *Decision Support Systems, 6,* 203-226.

Burn, J.M. & Ma, L.C.K. (1989). Computing careers in Hong Kong - The problems of training. *Hong Kong Computer Journal, 5*(12), 30- 35.

Burn, J.M. & Ma, L.C.K. (1990). Computing careers in Hong Kong: Short-term solutions for long-term problems. *Hong Kong Computer Journal, 6*(7), 34-38.

Burn, J.M., Ma, L.C.K., Couger, J.D., & Tompkins, H. (1991). Motivating IT professionals - The Hong Kong challenge. *Proceedings of the 24th Hawaii International Conference on System Sciences, 4,* 524-529.

Davis, G.B.(1987). A critical comparison of IFIP/BCS information systems curriculum and information systems curricula in the USA. In R.A. Buckingham, R.A. Hirschheim, F.F. Land, & C.J. Tully (Eds.), *Information systems education : Recommendations and implementation* (pp. 134-145). Cambridge, U.K.:Cambridge University Press.

Earl, M.(1989). *Management strategy for information technology.* Hertfordshire, U.K.: Prentice Hall International.

Ives, B. & Jarvenpaa, S.L.(1990). Global information technology: Some conjectures for future research. *Proceedings of the 23rd Hawaii International Conference on System Sciences, 4,* 127-136.

Ives, B. & Jarvenpaa, S.L.(1991). Application of global information technology: Key issues for management, *MIS Quarterly, 15*(1), 32-49.

Ives, B. & Manheim, M.L.(1991). Global information technology. *Proceedings of the 24th Hawaii International Conference on System Sciences, 4,* 171.

Kao, C.K. & Young, K. (Eds.). (1991). *Technology road maps for Hong Kong: An in-depth study of four technology areas.* Hong Kong: Chinese University of Hong Kong.

Keen, P.G.W.(1991). *Shaping the future: Business design through information technology.* Boston, Mass.: Harvard Business School Press.

Ma, L.C.K. (1991, February). Integration of IT in business and accountancy education. *Proceedings of the International Conference on IT in Training and Education.* Brisbane University, 97-100.

Ma, L.C.K. & Tsang, Y.H. (1991, February). Preparing MIS executives for the 1990s. *Proceedings of the International Conference on IT in Training and Education.* Brisbane University, 101-105.

Manheim, M.L.(1991). Global information technology: Issues and opportunities.

Proceedings of the 24th Hawaii International Conference on System Sciences, 4, 172-181.

Nunamaker, J.F.(1981). Educational programs in information systems, *Communications of ACM, 24*(3), 124-133.

Roberts, D. (1991). *Hong Kong 1991:A Review of 1990,* Hong Kong: Government Information Services.

Saxena, K.B.C.(1987, January 22-February 4). The Teaching of Information Technology at Hong Kong Polytechnic. Paper presented at the Commonwealth Workshop for Trainers in Information Technology and Management, Bombay, India.

VTC - Committee on EDP Training. (1988). *1987 Manpower Survey Report on the Electronic Data Processing Industry,* Hong Kong: Vocational Training Council.

VTC - Committee on EDP Training. (1990). *1989 Manpower Survey Report on the Electronic Data Processing Industry,* Hong Kong: Vocational Training Council.

Section V

Strategies for Teaching Globalization

12 Issues in Teaching Globalization in Information Systems

Sue Conger
Baruch College, City University of New York

In fifty short years, business organizations worldwide have evolved from national to multi-national to global enterprises. As with all trends, there are forces that both ease and inhibit movement into global markets. In general, information technologies enable globalization; and, in general, cultural differences and history inhibit globalization. In this chapter, we discuss information technology enablers and historical and cultural inhibitors to provide a view of the issues of implementing applications in a global business environment. The technology enablers include application and communications technologies. Communications technologies remove the barriers of geography and time, while providing equal access to multi-media applications. The historical and cultural barriers inhibit cross-cultural exchange of ideas, technologies, and methods of work. Dealing successfully with both the technological and cultural issues is a challenge to information systems professionals and business managers. Preparing information systems students for globalizing technology is the challenge to information systems programs. This chapter first defines each of the technical, historical and cultural issues. Then, approaches to teaching each issue are related to specific information systems courses.

In the decades of the 1970's and 1980's, Eastern and European companies merged with businesses in the Americas and each other to become industrial combines. In the decade of the 1990's, major political and social changes are occurring in much of the world. These changes will result in further merging of Eastern European, Asian, African and Latin American organizations with these new industrial combines. The global economy, which has been talked about in news programs and businesses for years, is a loose coupling of nations. Globalization of businesses actually cements the economic ties between all nations of the world.

Globalization is an important issue because it will continually evolve, certainly for our lifetimes. Globalization of business presents an opportunity to equalize international relationships in ways that governments have not done. Globalization also highlights cultural aspects of doing business that American businesses traditionally ignore or minimize. In a global economy, we cannot continue to do 'business as usual'. Rather, we must broaden our horizons both organizationally, for performing and coordinating different tasks in different parts of the world, and philosophically, for how we relate to people in different cultures and organizational contexts.

As the world changes, it is the duty of educators to help business students understand the complexities of global organizational life. While there is little historical precedent to guide educators, we can draw on experiences from other settings to develop student (and our own) understanding of these topics.

Globalization issues are not new. We, in the United States, have many cultures living and working in relative harmony. In our national multi-cultural climate, however, we expect people from different parts of the world to conform to our 'protestant work ethic'. If they cannot, or choose not to conform, we relegate them to low level positions, or we 'out-place' them from the business. While it may appear easier to ignore cultural differences, what we are finding at the national level is that many social program, economic and political messes result from this ignorance.

Globalization is a difference in degree as well as a difference in kind from having a multi-national work force in one country. For differences in degree, one national segment of an organization cannot simply impose its work ethic on another; the imposed-on segment will fail. Further, when future survival depends on cooperation, coercion becomes a less tenable tactic. Coercion invites retaliation at some later date, and organizations strive for stability, not instability. Maintaining whole cultures at a low level or eliminating them from the global economy is a short-term possibility (short here meaning 100 years); but doing so will make the eventual changes more unsettling. This situation is more true now than in the past because of the computer and the integrated technological enablers that simplify true equalization across the world.

Globalization is also a difference in kind. The issues we must deal with cooperatively, expand from technical and social to also include historical, political, and cultural differences. These additional issues act as inhibitors to change, cooperation, and global integration. In information systems, all five of these issues are paramount to the success or failure of the applications development, deployment, and technological innovation that support globalization.

In this chapter, we review the technological enablers and social inhibitors to globalization. In the next section, we introduce application and communications technologies in a fairly technical discussion. In the third section, we turn away from technical issues to deal with the human side of globalization — the social factors that act as inhibitors to globalization. Even though the two topics appear unrelated, in fact, they are closely related. Technology cannot be successfully deployed without attending to the human issues. Attention to human issues, without computer technologies, will not bring about globalization. Finally, for each topic, we identify the related information systems courses, the level of discussion, and possible approaches to the topic.

INFORMATION TECHNOLOGIES

Two basic classes of information technologies enable and support globalization: application technologies and communication technologies. The application technologies include object-orientation, data base software, and new storage technologies that all support business needs for distributed, multi-media work. Communications technologies include communication media and telecommunications.

Application Technologies

An application is a set of programs that automates some business function. Application types support one of the three information process levels in organizations: strategic, management, or operations.

Strategic applications include surveillance and decision oriented systems. A strategic application might include data from internal and external information sources. The internal data might summarize corporate manufacturing, marketing, and sales information. The external data might be product and industry projections from, for instance, Dow-Jones, New York Times, and Compu-Stat (historical business statistics) information services. The data are integrated in a data base environment for easy access. An executive using a strategic application might look for trends that identify the future industry environment.

Managerial applications are knowledge based and decision oriented. They focus on problem recognition and analysis. Applications at this level are somewhat more structured and have more accurate data than at the strategic level. Examples of managerial applications are overnight funds investment analysis systems and manufacturing problem analysis.

Operational applications support day-to-day transaction processing of organizations. These applications are highly structured and oriented to accurate, known data and its transformation to support basic business functions. For instance, order entry, inventory control, payroll and accounts receivable are all examples of transaction processing applications.

Today, each of these application types is ordinarily packaged as a stand-alone, centralized technology. By integrating and distributing applications, emerging and mature technologies will fundamentally alter computing and the way we view applications in organizations. The technologies which allow application integration are object orientation, data bases, and storage equipment technology.

Object Orientation

Object orientation [Conger, forthcoming] is a method of developing applications which packages data and the allowable processes on that data together in *encapsulated objects*. Objects are entities from the real world about which an application maintains information. Processes are operations on data that transform it in some way. For instance, a high-level object might be an order. Orders are allowed to change status in addition to being created, modified, shipped, used to create an invoice, and closed. These actions are the order processes.

Objects are grouped into *object classes* which describe like objects that have *exactly* the same properties, attributes, and processes. Object classes are arranged in *hierarchic lattices* of relationships. Within a hierarchy, objects at lower levels *inherit* the data and processes of the superior classes. Objects in a lattice arrangement may have *multiple inheritance*, that is, they can inherit data and processes from more than one superior object in a hierarchy.

Figure 1 depicts a hierarchic lattice showing employees, with two subsets: exempt and non-exempt. A further subset of exempt employees are managers, with a subset of managers - members of the management committee. Exempt and non-exempt are called sub-classes of the class Employee. Manager is a sub-class of the class Exempt. Management Committee is a sub-class of Manager. The sub-class Management Committee, in addition to having its own data and processes (for instance, bonus program processing), inherits the data and processes of managers, exempt employees, and employees.

Objects' only legal means of communication are *messages*. Messages are requests from some *client object* to some *supplier object* for some *service*. The service is a process that is

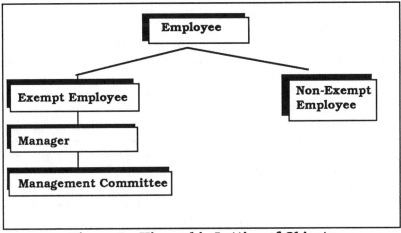

Figure 1: Hierarchic Lattice of Objects

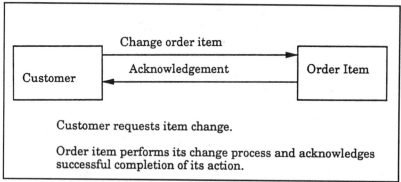

Figure 2:   Object Communication Example

executed (See Figure 2). There is usually a message back to the client to give the result of the process or to acknowledge its completion.

Object orientation is fundamental to multi-media because it allows *everything* in an application to be defined within the class structure as an object. So, at a high level, an order is an object. At a very low level, an integer number that is a value for an item quantity on an order is also an object. The abstraction of anything into an object definition allows us to define hardware equipment objects, software program objects, and data objects, to name a few.

Hardware objects will be used to define, for example, video, facsimile, and audio storage devices to applications. The resulting hardware objects are 'plugged in' to applications to support access and interaction. Any equipment that can be connected to a computer can be defined and integrated more easily using an object orientation than by traditional methods of uniquely defining each device.

Data Base Repositories

Data bases and their dictionaries are currently repositories for the basic business information of an enterprise. For instance, most organizations have customer, inventory, accounting, personnel, and other data bases.

The type of information businesses want to store in a data base is becoming more complicated, so the data bases themselves must change to accommodate that complexity. Data bases are beginning to incorporate object orientation to support the definition of data, hardware, software, and all of their interrelationships in one integrated environment. This shift from a *data*-orientation to an all-encompassing orientation has led to a renaming of data bases to *repositories*.

As a repository, the data base is the storage place for all objects in a given computer environment. Repository objects might include software, computer, storage devices such as video-disks, compact disks, diskettes, video recorders, and so on. Data bases are integral to multi-media because the media will be defined and accessed through some data base repository that maintains an object-oriented view of applications.

Storage Technologies

The storage technologies used in multi-media applications will provide for billions of characters of storage for text, graphic, paper image, still-motion video, full-motion video, audio, and audio and video combined. The number of bits of information in full-motion video images is orders of magnitude larger (on the order of 10^6 more information) than traditional data. Current technology supports write once-read many (WORM) laser disks. These disks provide a cost-effective means of storing gigabytes (i.e., billions of bytes) of information. Write many - read many (WMRM) laser disks are becoming more common, and by 1995 will become standard devices in most computing environments. NeXT, Steven Jobs' current company, already includes one implementation of this technology in its offerings.

Compact/laser disk technology enables the storing of large numbers of text, graphic, and/or video images. The resolution of stored images can be raised substantially with higher density storage facilities. Large companies, like insurance companies, will be able to store electronic versions of forms permanently. Paper-intensive organizations will create electronic images of their paper-work (See Figure 3). The images will be passed from one work station to another with requested processes, automating organizational work flow. United Parcel Service already uses an electronic receipt *form* with the capability of storing an electronic image of a signature to verify receipt of a package.

Multi-Media

Multi-media is a term that describes the integration of object orientation, data base and storage technologies in one

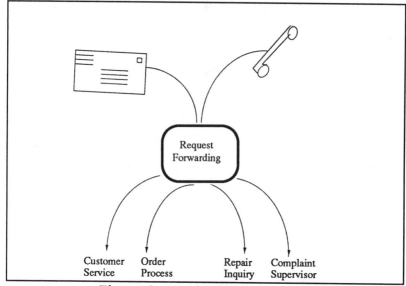

Figure 3: Work Flow Processing

environment. By the twenty-first century, multi-media will transform both applications and the way we interact with them. All these new technologies must be incorporated into traditional application processing to be useful in business organizations. By defining the equipment as objects and storing the object definitions in a data base repository, integrating new equipment and technologies in traditional applications becomes not just possible, but fairly easy.

The educational challenge of these technology areas, as they relate to globalization, is first, to use the new technologies, and second, to relate the use of the technology to effective business decision making *about the use* of the technology.

Object orientation is a fundamentally different way of thinking that is by no means mature. Every language that supports object orientation has its own non-standardized method of defining objects, their processes, and the messages by which they communicate. The current commercial object oriented data bases are regarded as exploratory; they cannot support the volume of traffic needed for most basic operational-level processing. In addition, the hardware technologies are also in their infancy. Each has its own interface standard and requires custom developed computer communications. Training, for both students and faculty, requires equipment, software, and understanding of how the technologies can be used. Some information will have to come from vendors, other knowledge will result from basic research that matures enough to develop applied research, which, in turn, matures enough to be used in classrooms. This process has a long lead time of two to five years or more.

In a global environment, we want to teach not just technology, but the effective use and deployment of technology. Truly distributed applications will be a reality. The issue will become: Where do we most effectively place data, data base software, software objects, storage media, and personal computers? Distribution of data and functionality will require new decision criteria. Before distributed applications, decisions were based on what the software and hardware could do. Constraints drove the decision process. Now, we can have anything anywhere. The decision criteria shift from being technologically driven to being business driven. *Why* do we need data *x* for *y* PC's in location *z* if we can have *a* data for *b* PC's in location *c*? *What business requirements* demand *this* placement of data, hardware, etc.? The extent of distributed multi-media access and enabling of peoples in far off locations that takes place will become a conscious business decision. Ethical, political and practical issues inform distributed media placement decisions. These issues are explored more in the next section.

Multi-media applications, because they support data, graphics, photos, audio, and video images, can have a significant cultural component. Design of culture-free or culturally rich applications becomes a decision. Is it truly possible to design culture-free applications? My feeling is no, all applications have cultural assumptions at least implicit in their design. Multi-media will make obvious our assumptions about appropriate words, pictures, and ideas for users. Biases that surface will relate to information system developers, user designers, and manager approvers. When applications go global, assumptions that survive in the United States, in all likelihood, will be inappropriate globally. The assumptions will require development of the same application with different media components to fit the using culture. Systems Analysis and Design courses and Introductory MIS courses should discuss the assumptions of application developers and how they carry over to the finished product. Techniques must be taught for making assumptions explicit and for designing cultural diversity into applications.

Communication Technologies

Communication technologies include media for communicating and integrated networks linking people for communications. In this section, we define nine media and types of networks. Then, media and networks are related to globalization and teaching of globalization.

Communication Media

Video conferencing equipment integrates television, computer, and communication technologies to transmit audio and video signals in an attempt to simulate face-to-face meetings [Johansen, 1984]. A video conference is a pseudo-face-to-face meeting using interactive television technology.

Audio conferencing supports group meetings using telephone equipment. Several people at separate locations can be connected for a multi-person conversation.

Telephone technology supports conversations between two participants with the technology that we all grew up with. Conversations are between two people in different locations, or even different time zones.

Audio messaging (usually called voice-mail) is a technology that allows verbal messages to be recorded in lieu of a paper telephone message for, for instance, an unanswered telephone call. Some systems include capabilities for message editing, indexing, storing, and forwarding [Rice and Bair, 1984].

Electronic messaging systems (usually called e-mail) provide the capability of creating, sending, saving, archiving, and replying to messages communicated via computer. Storage of messages on a computer means that communications can be asynchronous, and e-mail conferences can span several weeks [Hiltz and Turoff, 1978]. Current technology requires that message input be typed, but as our use of alternative forms of input matures, voice input, fax input, or other forms of input will be supported.

Shared data bases are one or more interrelated files accessible, in a read-only manner, by multiple departments or organizations. Allowable operations may include off-loading data, ad hoc inquiry, personal analysis or reporting. Data bases are either corporate or private. Corporate data bases are owned by the company using the data (e.g., Accounting Data Base). Public data bases are owned by companies which sell subscription access rights to subscribers (e.g. New York Times Information Service, Quotron).

Just as not all face-to-face and video meetings *need* face-to-face contact, not all interactions require a conversation. Frequently, information sharing is the reason for initiating a communication. An example is the broadcasting of stock trades of the New York Stock Exchange by the Securities Industry Accounting Corporation (SIAC), in response to the implicit desire of brokers and others to know current trade activity. If this information were not made available, less efficient decisions would be made because of the absence of information.

There are currently over 200 publicly available data bases on a wide variety of topics [Meltzer, 1981; Strassmann, 1985]; over 100 public data bases on the stock market and financial services [*Wall St. Computer Week*, 1987]. Public data base access on a regular basis can supplement or replace telephone calls, paper-based document research, and memo requests for information.

Shared applications automate detailed sequences of actions (i.e. procedures) required to complete a certain task. One or more procedures are embodied in a program with clusters of related programs comprising an application system (e.g., Accounts Payable). A shared application is one for which more than one unit is responsible for the information managed in the system. Typically, in a shared application, one or more units perform data entry, a different unit integrates, analyzes, and massages the information, then, one or more units use the final information to monitor and control their portion of the business.

A **wire transmission** is conducted via TWX, telex, or cable networks. A message is recorded in the electronic format for the specific network, then transmitted via "point-to-point, dial-up telegraphic services without intelligence in the system" [Rice and Bair, 1984, p. 190]. Similarly, *facsimile* transmissions use telephone technology to electronically transmit paper-based documents that can include graphic images from one location to another.

All of these technologies have two traits in common: they eliminate the constraints of geography and time, and second, they support some level of interactivity of the communication. The implications for global offices are that not only limitations of time and geography are removed, but that man-made social and political organizations can also be transcended. A person in

Hong Kong, where it is 7 a.m., and another person in New Jersey, where it is 7 p.m., can communicate via several of these methods as if they were nearby and in the same time zone. Using these media should improve decisions because the more information available, the more informed the decision.

There are two challenges and opportunities in teaching these technologies,

1. Teaching the technology and it use.
2. Teaching imaginative application development that uses the technologies appropriately.

The first challenge is similar to that for multi-media supporting technologies. The second is slightly different. As any programmer can tell you, any language can be used for any application; but, not all languages do the same job equally well. The same analogy holds for communications media. All media *can* be used for any communication, but not all media can be used equally well for all communications. As humans, we tend to use what we know and disregard the disadvantages of the familiar. With computer-mediated technologies, business relationships might suffer with the use of an inappropriate technology. Especially in a global environment, sensitivity to cultural differences both for communications and for the use of communications media is important. While we have some clues about the technology, much more research and practical experience using the technologies globally is required to provide a basis for teaching cultural sensitivity in using communication media.

Telecommunications Standards

Networking technologies have been in organizations for over 20 years. Only in the last five years have compliance with international standards and integration of existing network types matured sufficiently to support global communications across organizational boundaries. First, we define the current state of each trend, then we discuss its relevance to teaching information systems globalization.

The hurdle to networking has been the lack of communications standards describing how messages are packaged, routed, and identified, and rules by which computers actually communicate (i.e., protocols). The International Standards Organization (ISO) and the United States government initiated the major developments in architectures and protocols.

The ISO developed the Open System Interconnect model

(OSI) in 1978 to define a layered approach to intra-computer and inter-computer communication. Groups of OSI layers comprise standards that can stand alone to provide a level of inter-connection without requiring total change to existing networks. The sets of rules for packet switching (ISO standard X.25) and electronic mail processing (ISO standard X.400) are two such stand alone standards (Rowe, 1991).

The X.25 standard operates at the computer interface level to guarantee inter-computer communications. It can work as part of an entire OSI system or as part of a different system that can communicate to it.   Some of the different systems that support X.25 connection include Novell networks, IBM's System Network Architecture (SNA), and Digital Equipment's DECnet architecture.

As an example, the X.25 standard defines the type of character strings that identify a 'packet' of information. A packet is a variable size message that might be part of a larger message. Each packet includes header and trailer information to say 'here is what is coming', and 'that is all' in addition to the actual message. Some of the functions performed by the three layers of the standard that are part of X.25 are:

- Activate/deactivate physical connections
- Transmit bits over physical connection
- Detect and recover from errors
- Address messages
- Maintain sequential order of packets.

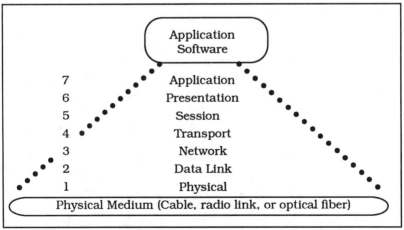

Figure 4: OSI Communications Architecture

The other major advance to communication standards resulted from the United States Department of Defense's interest in connecting many computers of different manufacturers using different protocols and different code standards. To provide this service, the transmission control protocol/internet protocol (TCP/IP) was developed to connect networks from different vendors.

TCP/IP overlaps some of the X.25 functions but also includes functions at the higher layer of the OSI model for network management. TCP/IP is viewed as a temporary solution to the problem of multi-vendor mainframes, each of which has its own proprietary network architecture. Eventually, all vendors on all sizes of machines will support the OSI model and the need for TCP/IP will disappear. In the intervening years, TCP/IP supports the interconnections of networks mixing equipment from many manufacturers.

The United States leads the world in networking networks. The US Army established the Advanced Research Projects Agency Network (ARPAnet) in the 1960's to link researchers and to provide super-computer access to researchers who would not otherwise have access. The Computer Science network, CSnet, and National Science Foundation network, NSFnet, added facilities to support electronic mail and computing resources to participating educational institutions. These networks form the backbone of Internet, which currently links over 40,000 computers worldwide with ties to commercial, government and educational organizations.

Network Integration Technologies

Internet forms a computer network that is limited because it can only transmit information that originates and concludes in computers. Other communications technologies - voice and video - require more integration with computer networks to support a full-range of communications signals and equipment. The Integrated System Digital Network (ISDN) and cable television industries are maturing to support that integration.

ISDN is an "integrated telecommunications system for providing a variety of voice, text, data, and video-based services" [Brancheau and Naumann, 1987]. Though the individual technologies comprising ISDN are available today, ISDN makes them accessible over a unified, fully digital network. In addition, these diverse services will be accessed through a small set of highly standardized interfaces widely distributed throughout the world [Brancheau and Naumann, 1987]. At its most basic level, ISDN provides enhanced communication capabilities through "basic bit transport" facilities [Leakey, 1988]. Enhanced capabilities such as reduced error rates and faster exchange routing are possible without necessarily modifying the basic network structure of telephonic systems.

More intelligent levels of service are also enabled through ISDN: intelligent network services, generic data communications, and value-added applications. These services differentiate ISDN from plain computer communication networks because of the *value-added* programs imbedded in the service. Intelligent networking capabilities will provide new services such as time-dependent call routing, store-and-forward electronic and voice messaging, enhanced monitoring of network performance, customer services (e.g., on-demand bill preparation), and enhanced network administration [Leakey, 1988].

Cable television is a technology that supports the transmission of real-time video images via coaxial cable to individual homes. The next major expansion of cable television will be to businesses using ISDN capabilities for two-way, interactive video-conferencing and telecasts of, for example, stockholder, staff, or coordination meetings, between geographically dispersed people. While this technology is partially available today in video-conferencing facilities, usage is limited to large organizations that can afford the high cost of renting and/or maintaining the facilities.

Generic data communications services will take place using enhanced broadband ISDN services which will provide services for conversing, messaging, and retrieving information. Cable TV will enable the individual in remote areas of the world to participate in the global networks of tomorrow. Video conferencing, an historically expensive technology that has been available for over 20 years, should finally become standard and inexpensive. Messaging will be greatly expanded from simple text e-mail to include audio, video, and even moving video pictures. Retrieval services will enable communications between high speed and high resolution television, computer aided design (CAD), videotex and color facsimile. These last services begin to define the customer applications capabilities, and also include at-home banking, grocery shopping, ticket purchase for events and travel, etc.

The challenge in teaching these technologies as they relate to information systems comes not only through telecommunications courses, but also through information systems management courses. Telecommunications courses deal with how to interconnect, when to select which type of service, and planning for change that will be even more constant than in the past.

Management courses develop the business, political and social issues of networking. For instance, What are the ethical issues in deciding when and where to install communications capabilities? How do you decide when to visit a location and when to simply communicate electronically? What organizational hierarchical changes should be expected from the use of these technologies? How do telecommunications and integrated distributed computing relate to business down-sizing, 'right'-sizing and re-engineering? How do you train and develop social skills for using, for instance, video conferences which require a different verbal protocol than face-to-face communications? Some of these issues are further developed in the next section on the historical and political barriers to globalization. As we understand the context in which we work, identifying the issues and how to deal with them becomes somewhat more manageable.

SOCIAL BARRIERS TO GLOBALIZATION

There are three main social barriers to globalization of businesses: infrastructure differences, technology transfer differences, and political and cultural differences. Each of these are discussed in historical context and today's world.

Infrastructure

Infrastructure usually refers to the installed base of equipment and services for communications, transportation, and services of a geographic entity (i.e., a country). Infrastructure relates to computers, telecommunications, and supporting software, including, for instance, data base and networking software. Historically, the separation between developed and developing countries has divided on political lines to define the capitalistic-*have's* and the socialistic/communistic-*have not's*.

The decade beginning in 1990 has seen radical change for many countries around the world. Russia has decentralized and disbanded the socialist union it so carefully built. Eastern bloc countries are struggling with democratic-like, capitalistic-like reforms, redefining their own realities in the process. The changes in Russia are sparking similar self-examination and sometimes radical change throughout the world.

New political managers in Eastern bloc countries desire to change overnight from infrastructures that are state-of-the-art for 1915 to those that meet the challenges of 1990. Reality is not that simple. The countries have few 'old' applications, telecommunications, or sophisticated transportation to learn from. They start from close to ground zero in computing, but wish to be internetworked, with multi-media, integrated application and database environments, by the year 2000. At the same time they implement the technology, they are collecting the information to populate this technical environment. The goals cannot be met without radical and improbable change throughout the societies trying to effect the changes.

Support and transfer of technology from the remainder of the world is required to effect the changes being sought throughout Eastern Europe and the Soviet states. Support in the form of money, capital equipment, and software worth billions of dollars is also needed. Given the economic realities of the 1990's, massive, free support from governments is unlikely. Support with strings attached is too constraining. So, the only choice left is for the newly capitalized countries to go alone - slowly, falteringly, and over many years. The history of African and Latin American countries that have followed the same path neither foretells nor assures success for Eastern Europe.

The issue of infrastructure is important in teaching overviews of information systems, communications, analysis and design, and even program development. For survey courses, awareness of problems and differences is the goal. Altruism in business organizations is not dead, but imaginative, practical, cost-effective solutions take time and effort to sell to bottom-line oriented managers. The issues, alternatives, and trade-offs of promoting a risky foray into the third world must be developed and presented. Students cannot be left on their own to develop these lines of thought. Survey courses need to focus on the differences and hurdles to be overcome when working in a low infrastructure country. Expectations of future managers and information systems professionals need to be realistic about both the challenges and opportunities of working in a technologically constrained part of the world.

In analysis and design, infrastructure is important because applications cannot be built when the hardware and software do not exist. If they are installed, they must work and be supported by knowledgeable professionals. Those professionals must be able to perform all aspects of system development and must be capable of communicating freely in a common technical language with their compatriots in other parts of the world. In the southern hemisphere and in Eastern Europe, equipment is scarce, software is arcane, professionals, as westerners know the term, do not exist, no analysis and design methodologies, tools, or techniques beyond those in use in the 1960's are in use, and the technicians who build systems do not talk with users or communicate *freely* with anyone.

Systems analysts and designers need to be trained to deal with the inequities of third world computing. How do you integrate an obsolete system into a network and still get it to work? Besides giving students an appreciation of the difficulty of making obsolete equipment fit into state-of-the-art, the challenge can be made fun. In addition to the challenge, they have an opportunity to learn something about early computing life that books cannot teach. From the 1950's through the 1970's, computing professionals had to be jacks-of-all-trades with a pioneering attitude that has been lost to the increased specialization and complexity of 1990's computing environments. Those 'jacks' (and jills) are now running many computing organizations. Doing well in both modern and old-fashioned environments gives a perspective on change and integration that could well boost many careers.

Infrastructure is a natural topic in communication courses. Discussion of telephone communications leads to discussion of computer communications, distributed processing, and inter-networking — all topics depending on a cabling infrastructure, communications switching infrastructure, and computing infrastructure that third world countries simply do not have. Nor, based on history, will they have it any time soon. Building a network to include Guyana and Hungary, for instance, will require expenditures and infrastructure knowledge far beyond what is required in the western world. Again, for those professionals working in this environment, the experience is worth all the headaches.

Finally, infrastructure is a natural discussion topic in information systems management courses. The philosophical and political decisions which commit organizations to computing in developing countries (DC's) are made by managers. There are enormous risks both to companies and to individual careers at stake from these decisions. The rewards of a successful integration of DC's into a multi-national application might be beyond individual lifetimes. So, what is the motivation? Should we integrate DC's because it is the *nice* thing to do? How much should our organizations be expected to pay for infrastructure, training, and support? There are no easy answers, no silver bullet. These issues are among the ethical dilemmas of our time and should be approached within the context of ethical computing as it relates to globalization of computing.

Technology Transfer

Technology transfer is a large-scale introduction of a new technology to some previously non-technical environment. Transfers of computing and communications technologies to all DC's in Eastern Europe, Asia, Latin America and Africa are needed. History leaves me pessimistic about such transfers taking place easily, smoothly or soon. Broad-scale transfers for such disparate technologies as farming methods, birth control, building of dams, and water purification have failed simply because technologists fail to contend with cultural differences and resistance [Hirschman, 1967; Morrison, 1966].

Technology transfer suffers from the same bias that diffusion of innovation theory in general suffers — if the technology is not accepted, there is something wrong with the intended user, not the transfer agent or the technology. Naively, we think our way of implementing and using are the right way as if no other way is as good. The concept of equifinality - many paths lead to the same goal - eludes most westerners. We fail to evaluate the technology *within the context* of the intended cultural structure. We assume stupidity on the part of the users and also assume this stupidity can be corrected by sufficient education. What we forget is that projects fail when planning is incomplete, potential difficulties are not assessed or are miss-assessed, and cultural impacts of projects are insufficiently analyzed. With oversimplification of both the project and the circumstances of its implementation, we alienate the intended users and reduce the probability of successful technology transfer for generations.

Hirschman [1967] examined over twenty large-scale projects undertaken by the United Nations around the world to transfer a variety of technologies. He discusses, for example, a paper mill in Bangladesh, railroads in Nigeria and Italy, electric power systems in Uganda, a telecommunications system in Ethiopia, water management projects in Brazil, Mexico, Columbia, Iran, India, and Thailand, and agricultural projects in Uruguay, Brazil, and El Salvador.

Hirschman concluded that successful transfer of technologies depends on correct assessment of potential difficulties, plus a good measure of luck, which he calls the "Hiding Hand" [Hirschman, 1967, p. 1]. The hiding hand is a force beyond human control that contrives for some projects to fail that should succeed, and some to succeed that should fail. Even with the 'hand', Hirschman advocates realistic planning and management to increase the probability of success. Planning relates to the uncertainties, problems, and management difficulties inherent in the project.

Uncertainties and problems inherent in any project relate to availability and understanding of input, process and output ... not unlike any information system. Input assessment should address personnel, technology, skills, time, environment (including social, work, cultural, and physical), local management, political structure, and cultural ethics of work, motivation, and reward systems. Process assessment evaluates both technical and managerial implementation duties and activities. Output assessment identifies intended and unintended outcomes and their impacts. Planning on all levels (strategic, tactical, and operational) should be used continuously to assess the application environment.

Administrative difficulties increase exponentially with the presence of inter-group conflicts due to:

- regional, ethnic, or religious rifts

- nationwide projects requiring harmony and co-operation

- projects requiring large numbers of people

- low levels of technical skills when proficiency is required.

Projects with conflicts in all four categories tend to fail [Hirschman, 1967]. Projects with conflicts in no more than two of the categories may be successful.

Hirschman's lessons can be applied without change to teaching of information systems globalization.   In addition, computer-related technology transfer should apply the theories of diffusion, politics of application development, and systems analysis to maximize success [Rogers, 1983;   Markus, 1983; Robey, 1981]. In particular, courses on management of information systems can teach the following collective wisdom:

- Start with a small project with high visibility ...

- Pick the project based on a *need* for its function.

  Try to find a project that does not disturb the political, social or bureaucratic status quo. Specifically manage any status quo disturbance resulting from the project's development.

- Ensure a local champion who will effectively manage the project to completion;   defer to the champion's superior understanding of local politics, culture and ethics.

- Ensure substantive user involvement throughout the entire project.

- Choose local personnel (including users) to actually *develop* the project carefully. Try to identify desirable traits such as: willingness to innovate, desire to change, desire to improve skills, desire to advance in the organization. Train them thoroughly and act as advisors only.

- Select a methodology for guiding and documenting the life cycle of development that *fits* the organization and culture.

- Keep to the background as much as possible.

These guidelines do not guarantee success; they only minimize the chance of failure. In any technology transfer project, it is imperative that the sensitivity to local differences is maximal. Teaching and training in a different culture does not mean making the target audience the same as you. Equifinality must be allowed. Technologists' roles change from doer to facilitator, with less control than usual over outcomes.

Politics and Culture

Above, we mentioned projects that disturb the political or cultural status quo. For each of these types of disturbance, instability in the sub-culture can further damage a project. Threats to an organization's political structure also threaten the potential success and future continuation of information systems projects. Equifinality is again required — we do not necessarily need an exact clone of the United States form of government or of organizing to ensure success of innovations in information systems technologies. In this section, we discuss several kinds of political and cultural threats to implementing new technologies and how to minimize them.

Problems with political structures are minimal when the problem is wholly new in the country or the problem being solved is spatially isolated from other problems. Politicians tend to be less disturbed when they, along with everyone else, have little understanding of the project, its potential impact on politics, and the technology involved in the project. If the project, for instance, installs the first networking capabilities for one centralized mainframe computer, both technological newness and spatial isolation are present. If, however, the project installs networking among 5,000 personal computers throughout the capital city in numerous organizations, it may be new but it is not isolated. If the politicians perceive threats to their authority with such a massive sharing of information, the project will have less chance of success.

Applications to be avoided to minimize political problems include projects that withhold and dispense jobs and/or money, projects that affect a large number of people, especially ruling classes, and projects that threaten existing political agencies.

Applications to be sought include:

- Technically complex projects that introduce new technology

- Projects whose success will result in massive increases of local competence and morale

- Projects that will result in massive losses (e.g., face, prestige, or money) to the local backers if the project is not successfully completed

- Projects for which all funding is available at the outset

- Projects with a high demand

- Projects that can cheaply develop reliable, loosely coupled, cohesive, flexible, and reusable components.

Once political stability is effectively dealt with, social and bureaucratic stability must be evaluated. Both of these are subsets of the political aspects of application development. So, in some part, dealing with the political aspects also deals with these. But, social aspects of computing are subtle and pervasive, requiring additional thought and care at several levels. Inattention to social issues can be equally devastating in ensuring failure of a project. The project team, user environment, and technologist role all have social environments for attention.

Aspects of social culture include:

- Male-female work roles

- Work ethic, including the meaning of *work*, motivation, achievement, and management, in this culture

- Time commitment, for instance, how are due dates perceived: as absolute deadlines, as goals but not critical, or as something managers need that do not affect daily work?

- Goal versus process orientation

- Project technologist versus user social roles

- Structure of classes, management hierarchy and work.

Inattention to these issues again reduces the probability of project success. In the eastern cultures, for instance, it is suicide to place a female as project manager, simply because they come below dogs and cats on the social scale and will not be attended to. Further, deliberate flaunting of a known social custom, such as placing a female manager in an eastern country, loses great face for the flaunters, and further reduces the probability of success by reducing both user and project team respect for the entire sponsoring organization.

Does that mean that women should never be used as project managers? No, only that to maximize prospects for project success, you must include sex as a criterion for selection of key personnel whose respect and seniority must be recognized.

Social change is frequently brought about by computers, which can enable both coming together of work groups or separation of work groups, depending on the way technology is installed. If the social aspects of computing run counter to the social work culture, the application has a reduced probability of success. Even in the West, there is ample evidence of this problem. Applications are frequently installed and work technically, but they are unused because they run counter to the social culture of the work place [Pressman, 1985]. This type of attention means that designers, programmers, and all technologists involved in multi-cultural projects should think in terms of local *versions* of applications that are tailored to the social work environment.

These political and social stability issues impact management of information systems, project design and programming. Managers must be taught to deal with political realities of both the country and the organization(s) affected by the application. Project designers and programmers must learn that local customizing of applications to fit the social aspects work may be required.

Governments and Computing

In most countries, the postal service includes control

over telegraph and telecommunications. The PTT's (for post, telephone and telegraph), as these organizations are known, personify government control by controlling both the growth and types of telecommunications and telecomputing within a country. Like other technologies, regulated PTT's both enable and disable depending on the philosophy of the group in charge.

At one extreme, for example, is Canada. Canada aggressively built and supported its data network, financing continuous upgrades. As a result, Canada has one of the most highly developed telecommunications infra-structures in the world.

At the other extreme, for instance, is Brazil. Brazil enacted two sets of laws: one that controls telecommunications and one that controls computing. The telecommunications laws kept the country in the dark from an information perspective. The laws restricted trans-border data flow so much that people coming into or leaving the country had diskettes confiscated if they were found. Brazil became increasingly isolated in an increasingly open world.

In addition, Brazil's 'Law of Similars' forbade the importation of any equipment that was similar to that manufactured in-country. Only personal computers built within Brazil's borders have been available. Because of financial and other constraints, the Brazilian technical industry has not kept pace with the rest of the world. Consequently, the personal computer industry in Brazil cannot compete in the world market, thus rendering the country again to a backwater position.

When the Brazilian government changed in 1990, the new regime vowed to change the closedness of the country, but it has a long history to overcome. The Law of Similars has been repealed and the trans-border data flow laws are under review for sweeping change.

The issue of trans-border data flow is a real one. The concerns range from national defense to personal privacy to fear that a loss of information will translate into a loss of jobs. Most countries have had some sort of trans-border data flow laws for the last decade, and most are currently reviewing their policies again to further open their borders electronically. Fears about job loss due to trans-border data flow have diminished as job loss appears more related to cost per hour of work, quality of labor, and governmental incentives to keep (or not keep) work at home, than it does to laws about trans-border movement of business information.

On the other hand, laws about national security and personal privacy are becoming more strict, both for within country usage and trans-border movement of related information. Internal measures, coupled with laws, can deter the loss of national defense secrets only to a small extent. Clifford Stoll's, *Cuckoo's Egg* showed that without completely fool-proof computer telecommunications systems, laws alone will not stop a determined espionage effort.

Data Politics

Information is power. To ignore this thought is to ignore a central truth of the information society. Enabling previously disabled societies, or segments of societies, takes place by providing access to global information sources, This type of enabling changes forever the informational status quo. Computer-based data are a political battleground because ownership implies control over access, and access implies perfect information which in turn implies perfect decision-making. Both ownership and access of data have micro and macro issues. At the macro level, trans-border data flow and regulatory laws are government attempts to limit information movement and innovation. At the micro level, organizational pecking orders are determined in part by who has critical information.

Ownership of data is one aspect of data politics. Any rational person will admit that the organization *owns* the data, but, in reality, some sub-unit acts as the surrogate for the organization in performing ownership functions. Owners are responsible for creating, maintaining, and backing up data.

This discussion is simple when the data in question are owned and used by a single department. The problems arise in interdepartmental situations using data bases and the integrated technologies discussed in the first section. The situation is further complicated when a technical organization, such as Data Base Administration (DBA), is responsible for guaranteeing the integrity of the contents and for providing backup and recovery capabilities. An added wrinkle occurs when one or more of the departments is remotely located from the others claiming ownership. Then, ownership is shared by different departments whose managers have their own perspectives, goals, and aspirations for their organization. One owner may try to gain control over the data in order to also control access to the data. Regardless of whether the strong organization is a user or DBA, the ownership problem must be dealt with.

Ownership issues can be dealt with in an introductory information systems survey course, systems analysis and design, and in management of information systems. All three courses can deal with the basic issues of responsibility for application, computing facilities, data bases, and, ultimately, data. As with social and political issues, there is no one right answer to ownership questions. Awareness of the problem and the potential for creating organizational tension must be discussed first. Role playing, especially by international students who use their native perspective, can be useful to bringing out regional and cultural differences as well as organizational self-interests.

Students can discuss ways to minimize ownership problems, for instance, having a set of policies explicitly defining responsibilities and ownership roles before an application is ever implemented. But it is important that students recognize that pre-planning may not work in all situations. The need for creative problem solving in dealing with multi-organization, multi-geographic, and multi-cultural politics of ownership and access must be stressed. Ad hoc steering committees of key senior managers, pre-defined policies, negotiated access, and using departments all reporting to the same senior manager who arbitrates disputes are all possibilities.

Many application environments evolve over years. Each evolution brings new organizational shifts in data power and interest. So, each major version of an application should include an assessment of ownership issues and should attempt to define and negotiate access, ownership, responsibilities, and rights *before* any changes are made. These points can be made in all levels of classes from a survey through management.

TEACHING GLOBALIZATION IN INFORMATION SYSTEMS COURSES

Like it or not, technology is *not* neutral because it is implemented by people who have motives. With that notion in mind, the challenge is to develop a sense of ethics and raised consciousness about the role of technology and the role of technologists in developing global applications. Consciousness requires awareness of philosophy, history, political science, and economics in addition to computer-related issues. The role of technology, in general, should be supportive of globalization and non-partisan in its support. The role of technologists is more complex: to provide the technological base for global work while promoting equality and enrichment through the technology supported. Each of these roles is explored in this section.

The Role of Technology

The technologies discussed in this chapter all enable people in different parts of the world to interact as if they were in the same location. The term for this enabling capability is *fungibility*. Fungibility is the removal of geographic and time constraints such that any one point in space is considered equal to any other point in space. Fungibility is important because with the removal of constraints, all peoples in the world are enabled as equal actors in business and social transactions. This enabling does not mean that all people will become equal, simply that technology makes the equality more possible than the non-technological state.

The technologies also enable any organizational form that is managed by any form of management. There are no preconceptions imbedded in technology about the *right* way to organize or manage. Decentralization, centralization, distribution, management grids, and oligarchies can all be sustained. Theory X — people are stupid and lazy, and Theory Y — people are smart and motivated, are equally feasible, as are all points of management orientation in between the two extremes.

When used to equalize, integrating technologies can remove social barriers, transcend organizational hierarchic lines of authority, and provide more accurate information about the state of the world to its users. Conversely, when used to subjugate, integrating technologies can erect and highlight social barriers, disintegrate work groups, and make users less trusting, open, and motivated. In summary, technologies do whatever the men and women implementing them want them to do. This simple fact leads us to the role of technologists.

The information systems courses and technical topics for discussion are summarized in Figure 5. Information systems survey courses and management courses are usually taught with as much emphasis on using technology as on managing technology. In each of these courses, storage technologies,

Course	Technical Topic
Introduction to MIS	Introduction to Multi-media capabilities Communications technologies, technical aspects, implementation trade-offs
Database	DBMS Aspects of Multi-media Object oriented DBMS Intelligent DBMS components Technical issues in media-culture sensitivity -- designing and managing data bases for same meaning/different data manifestation.

Management of MIS	Overview of IS development process and issues.
	
	Similarities and differences between applications for
	    single-user,
	    multi-users,
	    multi-organizations,
	    multi-cultures.

Systems Analysis and Design/ Software Engineering	Designing multi-media applications -- Object orientation Intelligent DBMS Hardware/software design, standards, integration Infra-structure: applications cannot be built when the hardware and software do not exist. Develop knowledgeable professionals who can perform all aspects of system development and communicate freely in a common technical language with technologists in other parts of the world.

**Figure 5: Summary of Technical Topics and Related
IS Courses**

Course	Technical Topic

Telecommunications/ Networking	Service offerings -- what technologies are available
	
	When to select which type of service
	
	Planning for change
	Hardware/software design, standards, and integration
	for centralization,-
	         decentralization,
	         distribution,
	         client/server, etc.
	
	Communications technologies implementation, i.e., how to interconnect
	
	Developing and managing multiple versions of networks, applications, communications structures

Communications	Hardware/software design, standards, integration for centralization, decentralization, distribution, sharing, etc. Communications technologies and their implementation Implementing an organizational communications infra-structure

**Figure 5: Summary of Technical Topics and
Related IS Courses** (Contd.)

communications media and networking should all be discussed and used in lab sessions to show the different effects. Multimedia applications are perfect for demonstrating the effects along with summarizing the technology in text that accompanies a full-motion video demonstration. Students should be taught how to use e-mail and encouraged to communicate with each other and the instructor to get practice and first-hand knowledge of the issues and limitations of e-mail.

In systems analysis and design, a shift to object orientation is taking place. Object orientation will become the predominant methodology taught within ten years. For now, it is taught as a technique to monitor until it matures a bit more. Also in systems analysis courses, designing for new media and storage technologies is discussed. This discussion differs from that in the survey and management courses because it emphasizes analysis and design issues rather than usage issues. It is not enough for application developers to simply know the techniques of analysis and design for software. They must also know some graphics design for human interfaces, effective media use for integrating multiple media into applications, and knowledge-based application techniques for integrating artificial intelligence in applications. Seemingly innocent uses of technology, such as computer-based training (CBT) sessions are an example of this point. Computer-based training will require the same careful cultural and technical analysis with culturally designed presentation to avoid offensive or repugnant video presentations that are every day occurrences in western culture. Ensuring that hand motions, direction of gaze, tone, pitch, cues and text imbedded in video and audio frames are culturally acceptable requires a different way of thinking and training.

Data base courses discuss object orientation as it relates to data base design, management and software. New data base software that supports object orientation should be implemented and used for classroom demonstrations and exercises. Finally, storage technologies are discussed in the most technical detail for deciding how to design the data contents and map from a logical to a physical design when using new storage devices.

Finally, communications courses focus on telecommunications issues, but include communications media and the role of media in deploying telecommunications systems. Telecommunications issues include standards, types of networks, differences between protocols, differences between network standards, and interconnecting different types of networks. Communication media related topics include definition of the media, how they are physically connected to a network, and the types of applications for which they are used.

Teaching the technical topics is fairly straightforward, but it is incomplete without also discussing the social issues and contexts of their use. For this discussion, we turn to the role of technologists in developing global applications and networks.

The Role of Technologists

The role of technology is to support the social, political, and organizational goals of its users. Finding an implementation that is ethical and moral in meeting the users' goals is the task of technologists and all people in business organizations. Technologists are singled out here because they are uniquely central to implementing the equalizing technologies discussed. Managers are also important because of their decision roles.

The main courses in developing these roles are introductory information systems survey, systems analysis, and management of information systems (See Figure 6). The discussion is essentially the same in each course, with the most depth and time spent on topics in the analysis and management courses.

In systems development, organizations decide which applications to build through apparently rational decision making processes that focus on risk/return and cost/benefit trade-offs. When resources are scarce, portfolios of applications with different risk and cost profiles are recommended. Since systems developers (the 'technologists') rarely take part in these decision processes, it is important to raise the awareness of general managers who do. Awareness raising takes place through case studies and role playing exercises in management of information systems courses and, possibly, in introductory information systems survey courses.

In addition to the rational decision means, it is equally important to imbue a need for ethical and moral evaluation of projects on management students. We cannot tell people what to do in advance of a specific context, we can only help them learn to evaluate all aspects of a problem and all potential solutions. Consideration of all issues raises the likelihood of more considerate decisions; non-consideration of ethical, moral, social, or cultural issues almost ensures inequitable decisions. Inclusion and exclusion of organizational groups for purely monetary motives may be morally unacceptable as well as financially short-sighted. The "big picture" and long-term thinking need to be emphasized. Separation of infra-structure decisions from incremental growth decisions should be considered. Creative financing and tax advantages of including developing countries and other remote parts of the world should be explored. Non-monetary gains that might occur and possible positive and negative unintended side-effects of doing versus not doing a project should be considered. Awareness, evaluation, and conscious decision making are the goal. Students learn this reasoning process through case analyses, by evaluating with guidance, both acceptable and unacceptable situations. When a case is found to have problems, the students need to analyze what is wrong, why it is wrong, what are the possible motivations of all players in the situation, and how to correct the situation.

For example, after technical data base details are discussed, the design and deployment of data bases is introduced first, for a simple, one location environment. Then, a distributed

Course	Social Topics
Introduction to MIS	The role of technology and the role of technologists
	Data Access
	Data Ownership
	Communications technologies and their use
	Infrastructure: awareness of problems and differences
	Issues, ethics, alternatives, risks and trade-offs of promoting entry into Third World business computing
	Presenting globalization issues and risks to management
	Differences and hurdles to be overcome when working in a low infrastructure country
	Importance of realistic expectations about infrastructure and risk of Third World computing
	Issues in trans-border data flow.
Database	The role of technology and the role of technologists
	Data Access
	Data Ownership and politics
	Responsibility for application, computing facilities, data bases, and ultimately, data - political issues
	Trans-border data flow and how it relates to database applications
	Deployment of multi-media data base and data base applications in a multi-cultural environment

Figure 6: Summary of Social Topics and Related IS Courses

Course	Social Topic
Management of MIS	The role of technology and the role of technologists
	Data Access
	Data Ownership
	Responsibility for application, computing facilities, data bases and, ultimately, data
	Communications technologies
	Effectiveness and efficiency of communications technologies and their use
	Ethical issues in deciding when and where to install communications capabilities?
	How do you decide when to visit a location and when to simply communicate electronically
	What organizational hierarchical changes should be expected from the use of these technologies? How do you train and develop social skills for using.
	Philosophical, fiscal, and political decisions involved with a commitment to computing in less developed countries...ethical dilemmas of third world computing
	Cultural differences (in, for instance, social definitions of work, motivation, and success), western biases and equifinality.
	Guidelines to maximize technology transfer success and to minimize political impacts.
	Social change and IS implementation
	Issues in transborder data flow, privacy of data and job migration.

Figure 6: Summary of Social Topics and Related IS Courses

Course	Social Topic
Systems Analysis and Design/Software Engineering	The role of technology and the role of technologists
	Communications technologies
	Effectiveness and efficiency of communications technologies and their use
	How to design and integrate systems when equipment is scarce, software is arcane, professionals do not exist, no analysis and design methodologies, tools, or techniques beyond those in use in the 1960s are in use, and communications is never *free*.
	Develop positivie perspective on change and integration
Telecommunications/ Networking	The role of technology and the role of technologist
	Organizational issues in distributed applications—choices and tradeoffs
	Communications technologies— effectiveness, efficiency, and use
	Infrastructure: Discussion of telephone communications leads to discussion of computer communications, distributed processing and inter-networking—all topics depending on infrastructures for cabling, communications switching, and computing
	Assessing risks and costs for infrastructure development
	Need for multi-cultural *versions* of applications
	Legal issues in transborder data flow
	Risk/return, cost/benefit, tangible/ intangible outcome analysis in evaluating global applications

Figure 6: Summary of Social Topics and Related IS Courses

Course	Social Topic
Communications	Effectiveness and efficiency of communications technologies and their use
	Organizational trade-offs and alternatives for developing a communications infrastructure
	Designing an organizational communications infrastructure
	Globalization issues in communications media deployment
	Cultural sensitivity in using communication media
	Effectiveness related to cultural differences
	Ethical issues in deciding when and where to install communications capabilities?
	How do you decide when to visit a location and when to simply communicate electronically
	What organizational hierarchical changes should be expected from the use of these technologies?
	How do you train and develop social skills for developing multi-cultural applications
	Opportunities for organization and enlarged job design
	Legal issues in trans-border data flow

Figure 6: Summary of Social Topics and Related IS Courses

environment in the same country is developed. Finally, lectures and exercises on distribution of software and data across country boundaries should be discussed. Technical courses should stress that there is no one right answer, but there are solutions that are better than others, and there are bad solutions. Students need to be taught how to analyze a solution, by evaluating both good and bad designs, to determine a solution's organizational, technical, cultural, and social acceptability.

Experiential role-playing exercises, like one called 'analysts and users', can be adapted to each situation and acted out. In analysts and users, the class is divided into teams and each team is divided into two groups: analysts and users. The users leave the room for 10-15 minutes while the analysts decide how to solve a problem: to walk the users through a puzzle completion problem. One successful use of this exercise is described. Before the exercise begins, everyone is told that groups can communicate during the time they are separated, but that communication must be in writing, through the teacher. The results, in my experience, are that users initiate all contacts; analysts barely answer them. By the end of the time, users are furious and disgusted by the insensitive behavior of the analysts. The analysts' attitudes are invariably that time pressure and a need to complete the decision task were much more important than talking to the users. This exercise raises everyone's awareness of the boxes we draw around ourselves, and the need to break out of our boxes in a more effective, lasting way than any lecture could ever demonstrate. In developing cultural sensitivity, the need for 'out of the box' thinking is even more important.

Systems developers, the technologists, also have a special role in developing and evaluating alternatives to computer implementation projects. Frequently, the technologists decide which aspects of a problem should be highlighted and which ignored. For this reason, the above discussion applies equally well to the technologists' training in systems analysis. In addition, they need to be taught how to unobtrusively teach managers what they need to know in evaluating non-technical aspects of computerization projects.

Senior technologists have taught managers the technical aspects of project decisions for years. The technologists are frequently successful in obtaining their goals because the manager's they teach only know what they are told. Thus, by filtering or not filtering information, technologists influence the process. In the same way, technologists can be taught to deal with the global aspects of computing in different countries and cultures. Multi-cultural aspects of applications must become as much a part of the systems culture as logging onto a system to create a program specification. The first place to begin learning this role is in the systems analysis classroom. Role playing, case studies, and class discussions can all be used to highlight the importance of the human aspects of computing.

To a lesser extent, infra-structure, technology transfer, and data politics are discussed in data base courses to provide a context for discussing global issues. Similarly, in telecommunications courses, infra-structure, technology transfer and stability are discussed in raising student consciousness about related global computing issues. Students can be given cases to analyze and discuss that demonstrate the ethical and practical difficulties of introducing new technologies into developing countries.

Barriers to Globalizing Information Systems Courses

Two major stumbling blocks to achieving globalization of information systems curriculum are the lack of globally aware faculty and a continuing lack of equipment due to funding problems.

Faculty need to either consult in global organizations to learn first-hand about the issues and pitfalls, or go back to school themselves to learn about globalization. Being a citizen in a global environment does not qualify anyone for teaching the issues. Time, money, and faculty interest are all required. One approach to initiating a globally oriented curriculum is to treat it as an organizational innovation. Identify a 'champion' for the project among the faculty. Send that person to school, or fund a learning internship with a company, to get the person educated about global issues. The global champion then reviews and suggests revisions to course outlines. The champion holds one or more seminars to bring other faculty up to speed on the critical issues, types of technological differences, social awareness, etc. This approach works best in an environment that is already multi-cultural and multi-national, because there is internal motivation for globalizing courses; but, it can work in any motivated environment.

The second issue is more difficult. Education continually lags industry in its installed base of information technologies and lack of access to emerging technologies. Access to some technologies through, for instance CSnet, is possible. But access to multi-media, distributed data bases, and mainframe and micro networks which are required for globalization, is difficult, if not impossible, in most academic institutions. Educational grants through federal governments are one potential source of funding for modernizing facilities. Another possibility is 'adopt-a-school' programs in which local business organizations work with faculty and administration to assist in funding, faculty training, internship programs for students, etc. Funds availability is the first major problem to overcome.

Second, many colleges and universities have arcane rules and practices that inhibit any bold initiatives, like globalizing the curriculum. For instance, the deans of colleges typically have budget responsibility for faculty computing budgets; computing facilities are frequently divided into academic, administrative, and library fiefdoms. In addition, many college fiefdoms have no hardware/software acquisition budget; they obtain windfalls, grants, or other unplanned monies, frequently with several minutes to spend whatever money they get. (You might say, no, this is so stupid it cannot be this way. I personally was in two meetings in which the manager of academic computing was called out, and returned to say that we had to spend 'extra' money. The amounts were $6,000 and $15,000. For the first, we had 15 minutes, for the second, we had two days to decide how to spend the money.) This is **NOT** the best way to manage any institution. But changing historical sources of power in any institution is not easy, and schools are probably worse than businesses in this respect because they do not have to answer to stockholders for poorly managed resources.

In short, the changes required to initiate globalization of an information systems curriculum vary in difficulty. Minor difficulties include changing syllabi, selecting books, and preparing course material. Medium difficulties are training of faculty in global issues and sensitivity to cultural differences, and in the design, planning, and management of applications technologies for ethical, culturally sensitive computing. Major difficulties are obtaining resources (hardware and software) and organizational support (from deans and computing managers in the institutions) for the educational change process.

CONCLUSION

This chapter identifies technical and social issues relating to teaching business globalization in information systems courses. For each course, a practical method of discussing issues was proposed. As globalization increases and evolves, so must information systems education if it is to enable the globalization. Globalization of businesses provides an opportunity for business people, including both managers and information systems professionals, to positively impact our global environment. To incorporate a global perspective in information systems education, both technical and social issues must be discussed together. Faculty must be re-trained, new types of equipment must be acquired. If we can successfully raise student consciousness to all aspects of global issues, those students will be better prepared to effectively participate in the new world.

REFERENCES

Brancheau, J. C., and J. D. Naumann, "A Manager's Guide to Integrated Services Digital Network", *Data Base*, 18, 1, 1987, pp. 20-32.

Conger, S., *Software Engineering in the 1990's*, Belmont, CA: Wadsworth Publishing, forthcoming.

Hirschman, A. O., *Development Projects Observed*, Washington, D.C.: The Brookings Institution, 1967.

Hiltz, S-R. and M. Turoff, *The Network Nation: Human Communication via Computer*, Reading, MA.: Addison-Wesley, 1978.

Johansen, R., *Teleconferencing and Beyond: Communications in the Office of the Future*, New York: McGraw-Hill, 1984.

Leakey, D. M., "Integrated Services Digital Networks: Some Possible Ongoing Evolutionary Trends", *Computer Networks and ISDN Systems*, 15, 1988, pp 303-312.

Markus, M. L., "Power, Politics, and MIS Implementation", *Communication of the ACM*, 26, 6, 1983, pp. 430-444.

Markus, M. L., *Systems in Organizations: Bugs and Features*, Marshfield, MA.: Pitman Publishing, 1984.

Meltzer, M. A., *Information: The Ultimate Management Resource: How to find, use, and manage it*, New York: AMACOM, 1981.

Morrison, E. E., *Men, Machines, and Modern Times*, Boston, MA: MIT Press, 1966.

Pressman, R., *Software Engineering: A Practitioner's Approach*, 2nd Ed., NY: McGraw-Hill, 1985.

Rice, R. E., and J. H. Bair, "New Organizational Media and Productivity", in Rice & Associates, *The New Media: Communication Research and Technology*, Beverly Hills, CA: Sage Publications, 1984, pp. 185-216.

Robey, D., "Computer Information Systems and Organizational Structure", *Communications of the ACM*, 24, 10, 1981, pp. 679-687.

Rogers, E. M. *Diffusion of Innovation*, Beverly Hills, CA: Sage Publications, 1983.

Rowe, S., *Telecommunications in Business*, New York: MacMillan Publishing, 1991.

Stoll, C., *The Cuckoo's Egg*, New York: Doubleday, 1989.

Strassman, P. A., *The Information Payoff: The Transformation of Work in the Electronic Age*, New York: Free Press, 1985.

Wall St. Computer Review, 4, 1987.

13 Educational Implications of Multimedia Computing's Effect on Global Information Systems

Sorel Reisman
California State University, Fullerton

Graphical user interfaces (GUIs), embellished by multimedia computing (MMC), present a stage in the evolution of the user/computer interface. The new interfaces stem from the evolution and convergence of the technologies of 1) instruction, 2) computing, and 3) audio/video media, as well as from extant experience in MMC application development. Coupled with other technologies such as telecommunications, MMC has the potential to drastically alter the nature of information systems and the cultures within which they can be used.

Educators responsible for training information technologists must change traditional curricula and address issues related to the development and use of the new information systems. California State University, Fullerton (CSUF), a traditional, budget-constrained university, initiated such changes. Based on CSUFs experience, recommendations for both educators and systems developers are presented. The development of MMC applications will require developers to consider the multicultural diversity of a global community of information system users. Such sensitivity can only be acquired through interdisciplinary curricula that focus upon the technical aspects of MMC system development as well as the cross-cultural dimensions of MMC system use.

End user computing began more than 15 years ago, but was really legitimized at the end of 1981 with IBM's announcement of the Personal Computer. Today, advances in technology are bringing about such dramatic changes in information systems that we may be witnessing the onset of the next generation of end user computing. Many of these changes can be seen in the multimedia computing (MMC) enhancements to graphical user interfaces (GUIs) such as Apple's Macintosh desktop, Microsoft's Windows, and IBM's Presentation Manager. MMC extends the functionality of GUIs to include audio, still-images, and full motion video. As MMC becomes an integral part of interface evolution, information technologists will develop new computer-based information systems that capitalize upon the full power of MMC. Coupled with advances in technologies such as telecommunications, the new systems, characterized by human-friendly interfaces and instant electronic access to worldwide markets, will provide small and mid-sized companies with trade opportunities that have traditionally been the province of large multinational corporations.

But how will these systems develop? How will systems developers learn about the new technologies? Who will devise the design methodologies that integrate MMC into system development processes? And finally, how will future generations of knowledge-workers use these new systems in the electronically linked, global business community of the future?

This chapter discusses a variety of strategies that can assist instructors and information technologists in creating the educational infrastructures that will help to answer these questions. The first section describes the evolution of multimedia computing, beginning with MMC's historical roots in instructional technology, and concluding with a description of some current MMC application trends. The second section describes a case study of MMC projects and activities at California State University, Fullerton (CSUF). Section 3 builds on the tactics discussed in Section 2, and describes the challenge of introducing MMC instruction into a traditional instructional environment (Reisman, 1991). Section 4 presents a number of issues and concerns regarding international and cross-cultural implications of multimedia computing application development and use. It concludes with a set of recommendations for educators who are responsible for training the system developers and end users of the future. For readers interested in developing multimedia applications, Reisman (in press) provides a guide by describing MMC application development projects at CSUF.

THE EVOLUTION OF MULTIMEDIA COMPUTING

MMC is not really new, but only recently has a traditionally diverse and unrelated set of technologies and methodologies evolved to the point where MMC has become feasible. The convergence of the technologies of a) instruction, b) computing, c) audio/video media, and d) MMC application development, has initiated the emergence of the phenomenon of Multimedia Computing.

Instructional Technology

The process of education has traditionally focused upon the delivery of instruction to groups of learners. Since the early 1950's, however, advances in instructional design methodologies have allowed the educational process to also focus on the individual learner. Group instruction continues to be used where it is cost effective, but if individualized instruction can be justified, it too is now available.

Reisman and Carr (1991) describe five forms of individualized instruction that have evolved since the 1950s. These are 1) self-study, 2) programmed instruction, 3) computer assisted instruction, 4) computer managed instruction, and 5) multimedia instruction. Self-study occurs when a learner uses a textbook in a self-directed manner, and solves problems related to the subject matter of the text. Programmed instruction (PI) is characterized by the use of a specially designed text that guides the student from one learning objective to another, soliciting structured or unstructured student responses to carefully constructed questions and problems. (The guiding mechanism may be the text itself, or it may be a mechanical device such as a teaching machine.)

Computer assisted instruction (CAI) takes the notion of PI a step further by adapting the branching and input (response) processing power of the computer to PI. The availability of computer power also enables the use of more extensive and complex instructional design strategies than were possible with programmed instruction. Computer managed instruction (CMI) capitalizes on the data management functions of computers by using the computer to direct the learner to variously prescribed learning materials or media. Materials and media such as film, tape, or video equipment might be used to supplement any of the previously described forms of individualized instruction. Finally, multimedia instruction is the computer based delivery of individualized instruction using integrated, on-line, "multimedia equipment."

Computer Technology

Reisman and Carr describe multimedia instruction in terms of technologies that have only become available within the last 15 years. However, some would argue that multimedia instruction is not quite so recent. IBM was the first company to put multimedia equipment on-line with the IBM 1500 System. Promoted in the mid 1960's, the IBM 1500 consisted of special purpose workstations controlled by a conventional, timeshared IBM 1800 minicomputer. Locally-attached to each workstation were analog audio and slide projection devices providing users with individualized, multimedia, computer-based learning. Although only a small number of 1500's were shipped, the product was a model for two other prominent, competing, NSF-funded systems. These were PLATO, a mainframe-based system developed at the University of Illinois, and TICCIT, developed by MITRE Corporation (Anastasio, 1973). A limitation of these systems was that they used unreliable and slow mechanical devices for their audio/video (a/v) storage sources. Despite this and despite the systems' lack of market success, through the 1970's they served as models for the ongoing development of other multimedia instructional systems (Reisman & Martin, 1977; Reisman, 1978), many of which were models for the multimedia computing systems of today.

By the early 1980's, the availability of optical laserdisc players and personal computers provided the practical foundation for instructional multimedia computing. Reisman and Carr (1991) assert that "the technology behind [instructional multimedia computing] is the hybridization of the microprocessor and the videodisc player" (Pp. 281-282). This hybridization gave rise to the development of interactive video (IVD) wherein laser optical videodisc players could be controlled by programmable embedded microprocessors, or by attached personal computers. The advent of interactive video enabled the development of applications that were characterized by varying degrees of multimedia complexity. Simple applications included basic start/stop audio and video control (functionally similar to the page turning of teaching machines); very complex interactive audio and video applications were functionally similar to the multimedia instructional mini/mainframe applications of the 1960s.

Applications in which the laserdisc player simply presented sequences of audio and video from start to end (i.e., with little or no user intervention) were classified as Level I applications. Applications built around embedded processor-based multiple choice-like programmed logic were classified as Level II applications. Level III applications were those in which the amount and degree of control of presented audio, video, text, and graphics was a function of a complex computer program executing in an attached personal computer. Level III interactive videodisc applications were the precursors of the MMC applications of today. It is the physical "compaction of the system" and the establishment of de facto Level III hardware standards such as the IBM 4055 InfoWindow System that were the impetus for today's MMC systems and applications (Reisman & Carr, 1991). However, system compaction and hybridization alone were not sufficient factors for IVD to evolve into MMC. Significant advances in audio/video technology proved to be another key element.

Audio/Video Media Technology

The term "multimedia" is not new. Educators and trainers have long been familiar with multimedia equipment, including projectors and recorders for 16 mm films, 8 mm film loops, 35 mm slides, and audio tape. In a computer sense, instructors used this equipment in an off-line mode to enhance and supplement instruction. Such equipment has typically been used for traditional, group oriented instruction. Computer managed instruction courses, however, often prescribed the use of off-line multimedia equipment for individualized instruction.

Early mainframe multimedia systems provided direct, on-line control of a/v devices such as slide projectors or audio tape players, but the mechanical nature of the devices was not well-suited to the environment of electronic computing. Furthermore, if a course required the integration of audio, still images, and video motion, each of those effects had to be provided from a separate mechanical device. Consequently, early multimedia systems were nightmares to maintain, consisting of a myriad of incompatible electronic and mechanical devices interconnected with countless, dissimilar wires and cables. The first practical integrated a/v technology that solved these problems was the laser optical videodisc, the laserdisc.

Although the specifications for laserdiscs can vary, in the context of interactive video, a single-sided laserdisc is a read-only medium that can contain combinations of up to 54,000 color still images; 30 minutes of interruptible, variable speed color video motion; and 30 minutes of dual track audio. In summary, laserdiscs have become an integrated electronic substitute for earlier media such as film, slides, tape, etc.

One of the drawbacks of laserdiscs is that audio and video are encoded on the disc in analog form. Although laserdisc players are readily controlled from a digital computer, the analog a/v data format does not easily lend itself to the kinds of media manipulation (e.g., deliberate and creative image distortion or electronically induced special audio effects) desired by IVD application developers. Furthermore, laserdisc players were designed to use standard television and audio devices as output "peripherals." Such consumer electronics products are generally incompatible with digital computer peripherals. These incompatibilities have given rise to a host of hardware products that attempt to integrate analog and digital outputs so that they may be (dis)played together on a standard computer and/or consumer electronics output device. Unfortunately, there is no standard among these products and, in general, most of them do not really meet the needs of IVD applications. They are difficult to use, functionally inflexible, and produce lower quality audio and video than IVD application developers desire. The solution that has emerged to these problems is the CD-ROM.

CD-ROM technology is functionally comparable to laserdisc technology except that the former is digitally based. A CD-ROM is a read-only medium that can contain approximately 600-700 MBytes of digital data; CD-ROM drives are conventionally accessible DASDs (Direct Access Storage Device) that can be easily and naturally integrated with existing personal computer systems. CD-ROM data files can contain data that represent any traditional media that can be digitized (i.e., text, graphics, audio, still images, and video). The amount of text, graphics, video, etc., depends on the data compression technique employed prior to recording the data on the disc. When digital data are retrieved, they can be electronically decoded to produce output that can be formatted for computer displays and/or analog audio or video equipment. Unlike laserdisc technology, the digital data stream output of a CD-ROM drive can be directly processed by an executing program to more easily produce the kinds of special effects that are so difficult to achieve in IVD applications.

Multimedia Computing Application Development

Early MMC application development systems were derived from "course authoring" systems that were designed to facilitate the development of CAI and CMI courses. IBM's Coursewriter and Interactive Training System (ITS) were models for many early mini/mainframe-based, multimedia instruction authoring systems.

By the early 1980s, when more reliable and cost effective optical-based storage products replaced earlier mechanical a/v devices, and PCs had made computing more affordable, application developers had learned a great deal about the do's and don'ts of developing MMC applications. Much of the expertise that had accumulated over the years was reflected in features that had become incorporated into IVD application development software.

During the 1980s, as developers standardized on the laserdisc as a primary a/v storage medium, the experience-base for multimedia application generation surged. Much of that progress resulted from the availability of more user friendly development tools that took the principles of Fourth Generation Languages and object oriented programming and integrated them with a/v function available in IVD hardware. Examples of IVD application development software include Apple's HyperCard, AIM Tech Corporation's IconAuthor, and IBM's Audio Visual Connection.

When CD-ROM products were first introduced, there were relatively few tools available to facilitate the development of a new generation of MMC applications. The first tools consisted of hardware manufacturer-supplied rudimentary assembly or C language routines designed to control the new CD-ROM MMC function. The emergence of standards for CD-ROM platforms and operating systems has only recently begun to result in a proliferation of tools that can really capitalize on MMC technology. As CD-ROM products become less expensive and more user-friendly, MMC application development should become more profitable for developers, with MMC applications becoming more affordable for end users.

Applications of Multimedia Computing

Education has historically played a key role in the evolution, development, and application of multimedia systems. Systems such as Plato and TICCIT were used to test and improve upon theories and practices of programmed instruction. These activities eventually led to industry's widespread adoption of computer based training (CBT), a concept little different from CAI. CBT has become a popular and highly successful training practice among many cost conscious businesses. Much of the popularity of CBT has been based on reports describing the benefits of the technology for a broad base of learners in many different subject areas (DeBloois, et al., 1984; Maher, 1988). Companies often find CBT especially attractive because they are able to demonstrate cost-benefits that can be realized from its use (Boeing, 1981; Brandt, 1987).

Within the last few years, CBT courses have greatly improved as a result of advances in course design techniques, course authoring software, and courseware delivery hardware. Many of those improvements are attributable to the evolution of multimedia, particularly based on interactive videodisc methodologies and products (Graham, 1986; Comcowich, 1989). Personal computer-based CBT courses, embellished with the multimedia effects of IVD, have made CBT courseware more appealing and popular than ever before. This can be seen in the use of an increasingly large number of courses advertised in commercial IVD catalogues (Pollak, 1989).

As CD-ROM-based MMC systems become increasingly popular, it is inevitable that IVD-based courseware will be converted to run on the newer platforms. And as instructional application developers become familiar with the newer function of CD-ROM-based systems, older applications will be embellished by newer features. For example, Comsell Corporation, an Atlanta-based developer and provider of industrial IVD training courseware, has converted many of their IVD courses to newer MMC platforms.

Although the instructional community again seems to be taking the lead in developing MMC applications, in fact, a variety of different applications of MMC is emerging. Many of the newer applications focus on information presentation. Early efforts to extend text-based computer presentations were severely hampered by the high cost of computer memory as well as by the inadequate processing power required to display color, graphics, and still and video-motion images. These costs have decreased, processors have become more powerful, and high density optical storage devices have become available. Consequently, today, traditional computer output can more easily be enhanced visually and audially. For example, inquiries to multimedia database management systems can now result in the output of traditional textual and numerical data supplemented by audio, graphics, single images, and/or full motion video. Meghini *et al.* (1991) describe such function in their experimental multimedia document-retrieval system Multos. Other examples include information kiosks that provide on-line product information in large retail outlets, or location directory information for tourists and site visitors.

The emerging multimedia applications are not limited to the standalone workstation usage that characterized the first PC business applications. As peer-to-peer and client-server networking environments evolve, they too will be affected by the complexity of multimedia. For example, networked, public interactive information kiosks (housing multimedia workstations) can upload consumer access information, or can receive up-to-date data used in the kiosk's displayed information. In the future, more complex networked, multimedia applications will require the transmission of voice and video as well as conventional data (Little & Ghafoor, 1991).

Other, less conventional PC applications have also been improved upon by combining networking technology with multimedia. The effectiveness of computer technology to facilitate group decision making and brainstorming has been widely reported (for example, see Gallupe, *et al.*, 1991). One of the drawbacks to these traditional, text-oriented decision support systems is that their use is often predicated upon the direct involvement of a human facilitator. From both a cost and convenience standpoint, this requirement somewhat limits the full potential of these systems. With an expert-system-like, multimedia-based, computer controlled, video recorded facilitator, such limitations can be overcome. Now, standalone or networked multimedia-enhanced brainstorming systems can be used by teams of decision makers on an as-required basis. This can be done without concern for the logistical complexities required to secure specially trained facilitators, or for the scheduling of specially designed decision support centers (Reisman, *et al.*, in press).

As MMC-based information applications become more widespread, innovative managers will propose innovative ways to use the new technology. It is unlikely however, that this will occur overnight. While organizations will have to be convinced that there really are cost-benefits to be derived from these new systems, an even more difficult barrier will be the natural inclination to resist change, particularly in tradition-bound industries.

CHALLENGING TRADITIONS

MMC is a technology well-suited for individualized user/machine interactions, whether at retail kiosks or at instructional workstations. Consequently, the introduction of MMC into a conventional computing environment should address the potential conflict presented by a technology whose characteristics may be completely at odds with the environment into which it is to be introduced. Educational institutions, steeped in decades and even centuries of tradition are often the most reluctant to change and therefore can present the greatest challenge, particularly when change to time-honored activities is proposed.

The time-honored business of colleges and universities is teaching and research. The relative importance of these functions varies from institution to institution, depending on local or state policies. In view of the evidence of the value of MMC in industrial CBT, it seems obvious that the instructional component of colleges and universities can benefit from this new technology. However, given the nature of instruction in most of these schools, the introduction of MMC poses a unique challenge. This section describes some of the characteristics of traditional universities that cause them to be resistant to the introduction of MMC.

The Problem of Lecturing

Most post secondary institutions accept as the norm that a teacher prepares a lesson and "speaks" it to a large audience. The amount of real time instructor/student interaction largely depends on the instructor's inclination. Where such large group lecture-mode practices have been taking place for years, it is very difficult to introduce the methodologies of individualized instruction. In general, in institutions where lecturing is the preferred instructional mode, lecturers have large investments in the process, both in terms of prepared materials, and also in terms of their own egos. Most full time instructors consider themselves to be outstanding communicators whose teaching skills are exemplary, and most do not perceive a need to introduce new instructional techniques regardless of their proven worth. Even in cases where this is not so, instructors understand that change, particularly that which involves technology, can require a significant investment in time.

Traditional universities and colleges do not reward instructors for curriculum development. Teaching is often considered a minimum condition of employment, with rewards of promotion or tenure based on research, publications, and professional service and committee work. The development of innovative or unique classroom teaching materials, however impressive, is usually a matter between the instructor and the students, none of whom is very influential in matters of tenure and promotion.

In the event that instructors can be convinced, or are sufficiently enlightened to recognize the value of individualized instruction, the reality is that the design, preparation, testing, and implementation of individualized learning materials is a complex technical undertaking whose demands on instructors can exceed their expectations. The process is very time-consuming, and often the results are disappointing, eliciting few accolades for the designer. In fact, one of the biggest drawbacks to creating such materials, and one that is difficult to find documented in "the literature," is that the final result will probably receive less than rave reviews from the instructor's peers. Such material, especially if it has been developed outside of a commercial enterprise, is often the subject of the NIH ("not invented here") syndrome. Critics of these materials are not in short supply, each proclaiming the ability to do a better job if he/ she

were to undertake a similar project. (Evidence of this phenomenon can be seen in the proliferation of introductory level
textbooks that abound in every discipline. Presumably these
exist because of authors' beliefs that no existing introductory
text is as good as the one they can write.)

Traditional colleges and universities present another
drawback to the introduction of individualized technologies in
the classroom. Usually, these institutions do not have facilities
designed for individualized learning workstations. Conventional
classrooms and laboratories are ill-equipped for the physical
requirements of such sites, and the scarcity of space and funds
often precludes the possibility of easily building new technology
centers.

The Problem of Cost/Benefits

The benefits of MMC-based CBT training are well documented. These benefits, at a minimum, include reduced training
time and improved learning levels. In addition, the value of these
benefits is amplified when factors of cost avoidance are used to
weigh off the costs of the technology. The actual benefits and the
related accounting advantages used to justify the industrial use
of CBT are usually irrelevant in publicly funded post secondary
institutions. For example, there is virtually no value in undergraduates' completing a course any sooner than the end of the
conventional semester or quarter. In most traditional instruction environments, cost avoidance arguments such as the elimi-
nation of instructor travel expenses are simply not a consideration. Funding and expenditure policies of educational institutions are also completely different than those of commercial
enterprises. This is particularly true in terms of depreciation of
capital equipment, as well as in the private sector's motivation to
save rather than spend at the end of a fiscal year.

Finally, in traditional college and university environments the cost per student contact hour is usually measured in
terms of class size. The procedure often used to optimize on this
variable is to increase class size, and at the least, to try to hold
the quality of learning (however it may be measured) constant.

Meeting The Challenge at California State University, Fullerton

In December, 1986, the Dean of the School of Business
at California State University, Fullerton issued a Request For

Proposals (RFP) from full-time faculty regarding the use of multimedia computing technology in the curriculum. At that time, CSUF's experience with personal computing had been limited mainly to the use of mainframe timesharing terminals, and more recently to student and faculty use of micro computer laboratories. The RFP requested that all responses contain an overall conceptual strategy including a multi-stage plan for implementation. Proposals were judged on the basis of the qualifications of the respondents, the practicality of the plan, and the benefits to the students and faculty of the School of Business and the University.

California State University, Fullerton is one of 20 universities within the California State University (CSU) System. The mandate of the more than 600 faculty of CSUF is to provide high quality instruction to its 25,000 students. For the most part, this instruction has been carried out through traditional lectures taught to relatively small classes of fewer than 40 students. While in many ways this process has been a strength of the university, from the standpoint of introducing MMC into this environment, CSUF's philosophy of instruction presents many challenges.

Because it was impossible to ignore these factors at CSUF, it was decided that an evolutionary rather than revolutionary strategy be proposed. The plan was to introduce MMC in a manner that would not conflict with existing patterns, but would demonstrate the benefits of the technology to the broadest base of users. The ultimate objective of the proposal that was funded was the establishment of an MMC learning center that would serve as the focal point for MMC instruction-based activities as well as for the development of new MMC applications.

Overcoming Fears. To many people unfamiliar with it, MMC is often perceived as another manifestation of computer technology whose value, if there is any at all, can mainly be derived in traditional, computer-oriented disciplines such as mathematics, science, or engineering. Therefore, it was decided that a few interested faculty members from a broad range of disciplines needed to be recruited to help "spread the message." A project team of four professors, one from the School of Business, two from Chemistry, and one from Foreign Languages was organized for this project. This group provided the manpower required for the project and also represented the multi-disciplinary aspects of MMC. Except for the business professor, none of these people had previous experience in this field.

Introducing a New Technology . Although IVD-based MMC has been available for years, many faculty and administrators were completely unaware of its application, particularly its widespread use in training. A series of campus-wide seminars and tutorials was organized for faculty and administrators, to sensitize them to the existence and benefits of commercially available IVD products. Seminars were held throughout the year and were targeted towards potential users (professors) and potential funding benefactors (administrators). The seminars did not focus on the physics or engineering of the related technologies; instead, companies were invited to present their hardware and courseware products and to focus on the successful use of those products.

Demonstrating Statewide Interest. In the Autumn of 1987, it was determined that there was sufficient MMC activity within the CSU System to justify an information exchange meeting. The CSU Chancellor's Office granted a funding request for such a meeting to be held on the CSUF campus. Invitations were sent to the Vice President of Academic Affairs at each of the CSU campuses requesting that two delegates be sent from each campus to attend a CSU Symposium. Although funding had been provided for approximately 40 attendees, actual attendance exceeded 140. One third of the audience was composed of those actively involved in IVD-based MMC, one third were planning to become involved, and one third wanted to learn more about the technology's potential for their campus.

The first day's schedule consisted of presentations by CSU faculty who described MMC projects at each of their campuses. On the second day, invited executives from IBM, Apple, Pioneer, and TEAC described each of their company's MMC philosophies and plans. In the afternoon of the second day, the audience broke off into work groups, each assigned the task of defining the requirements for a California State University Consortium. Each group later presented its recommendations to the main body and the results were consolidated into a plan to create a statewide MMC consortium. Unfortunately, severe cutbacks in California State funding for post secondary education have resulted in that plan's having been put in abeyance for the foreseeable future.

CSUF's Next Phase

At the end of the first year, all the objectives of the initial phase of the CSUF MMC project had been met and surpassed. Successful implementation of an extensive set of commercially available applications had been demonstrated to a broad range of university personnel. Evidence of widespread interest in MMC, within the California State System, at other universities, and in industry, confirmed the utility and even cost effectiveness of MMC in a broad range of disciplines and industries. Most of the early objections to the technology had been refuted and the value of MMC was no longer in question.

A proposal to create a 10 workstation MMC learning center was prepared and submitted to internal CSUF funding committees. At the same time, financial assistance was sought from hardware and software vendors. Funds and support were forthcoming and resulted in the approval of an interdisciplinary MMC learning center that was established on the main floor of the university's central library.

THE LEARNING CENTER

Shortly after funding for the center was approved, planning for the operation of the new facility began. Because most of the related technology that was then available was based on interactive videodisc products, the center was named the Interactive Videodisc Learning Center (IVLC).

The IVLC was conceived as a facility to provide students, faculty and staff with access to multi-disciplinary MMC learning materials. The mission of the Center was (a) instructional - to provide a facility that would deliver MMC-based instruction, and (b) developmental - to provide a focus of expertise to enable the creation of new MMC applications. These goals are consistent with the State of California's Master Plan for Higher Education which sets as a first priority for CSU campuses, the delivery of high quality instruction. The second priority for CSU member institutions is research. Despite the IVLC's lofty mission, a primary consideration was to determine how to offer as much instructional access as possible, to as many students as possible, as effectively as possible, all at the lowest expense possible. While the experiences and models developed by others provided a measure of advice (Parkhurst & Grauer, 1989), few had focused on how to accomplish similar goals on a shoestring budget.

Two categories of issues were considered in planning of the IVLC. The first concerned pragmatic and logistical matters related to the day-to-day operation of the facility; the second focused on instruction-related issues. A formal study was undertaken to evaluate instruction-related matters. Within the framework of the study, it was also possible to address operational matters of concern in the first category.

Operational Issues

Selection Of Workstations. CSUF, like many other universities provides students with access to several personal computer laboratories. Each of these PC centers contains 30 to 40 personal computers, enough machines to meet the demands of student computing on the basis of seven day, 24 hour access. These labs are staffed by graduate students who oversee the security of the facility, provide their clientele with assistance if needed, and lend out various computing-related materials. These labs are established by departments that require personal computing to support their curricular needs.

The IVLC had been established as an interdisciplinary center with the goal of providing instruction to any department in the university. It was this mission that resulted in the Center's having been established in the main library. Additionally, an interdisciplinary mission implied the availability and utility of a larger selection of already-produced videodiscs than might be available for a single discipline.

One of the major disadvantages of the interdisciplinary mission however, was that the IVLC had no particular academic department acting as its source of support and funds. The consequence of this was limited funding for staff and equipment. Nevertheless, it was decided that the budget allocated to the purchase of hardware be used to acquire IBM InfoWindow System workstations. The main reason for this was that the InfoWindow System had become the *de facto* standard for the delivery of IVD-based MMC instruction. Although it was possible to acquire a greater number of less expensive workstations, the IBM products were chosen to avoid the expensive problems that might later arise due to hardware unreliability, poor maintenance, or a lack of vendor support. Available funding permitted the IVLC to begin operation with 10 of these workstations.

Daily Operating Schedule. A graduate assistant was required to oversee the Center, both to provide assistance when it was required, and for purposes of security. Budgetary considerations limited the Center's schedule to Monday through Thursday from 10:00 AM to 4:00 PM, and Friday from 10:00 AM to 1:00 PM. These hours (27 per week), together with the 10 workstations, limited the total amount of available student contact time to a maximum of 270 hours per week.

Instruction Related Issues

Despite the increased interest in MMC-based CBT, primarily in training and secondarily in education, it is not clear that the process is as effective as many believe. Often, reports of effectiveness do not include thorough descriptions of the nature of the conducted research. In a review of the effectiveness of 16 IVD training studies, DeBloois *et al.* observe "that many of the studies use inadequate research models, too few subjects to generate statistics of any power, non-randomized approaches, inadequate controls, and so on" (1984, p. 52). In a similar review of effectiveness studies, Maher notes "the generally poor quality of much of the research [though] some of these studies are illustrative of the way videodiscs are being used in industrial training" (1988, p. 9).

Probably one of the most popular forums for the presentation and dissemination of MMC-related information are the annual conferences on Interactive Instruction and Delivery sponsored by the Society for Applied Learning Technology. A review of the proceedings of those meetings reveals that in 1988, of the 36 presented papers, only four contained a description of research methodologies used to assess MMC effectiveness (SALT Proceedings, 1988). The situation was relatively unchanged in 1989, when only three of the 35 papers contained a discussion of methodologies used to assess effectiveness (Salt Proceedings, 1989). Certainly this does not mean that well designed studies are not being conducted. It does mean however, that fewer reliable data exist than one would surmise.

To confirm the largely anecdotal benefits of MMC-based learning as well as to affirm its utility within CSUF, a study was conducted to use the IVLC to formally assess the effectiveness of

MMC and to determine if the technology could be practically and effectively used by CSUF students in their everyday instructional program. From a practical standpoint, the study was intended (a) to address the instruction related issues listed above; (b) to assess the practicality of providing MMC-based individualized instruction in an environment accustomed to traditional instructional methods; and (c) to initiate instructional use of the IVLC. From a learning outcomes standpoint, the study was designed (a) to compare the achievement of students using MMC technology with students who received their instruction in a traditional manner, and (b) to assess students' perception of MMC as an instructional medium.

Courseware and the Curriculum. Students enrolled in a three unit, one semester course entitled *MS265: Introduction to Information Systems and Programming* were selected for this study. This course, prerequisite to the undergraduate business program at California State University, Fullerton, consists of three major topics. These are (a) principles of information systems, (b) introductory computer programming, and (c) basic principles of productivity software. The productivity software is a spreadsheet (Lotus 1-2-3), a word processor (Wordperfect 5.0), and a database manager (dBase III+). The learning objectives for all sections of MS265 are determined and approved by department and business school curriculum committees. All sections are coordinated by a department-elected course coordinator who, among other things, is responsible for ensuring that the course objectives are met, in a consistent fashion, by all instructors in all the sections

From the 15 sections of MS265 that were offered during the semester, five were randomly selected for this study. Two of those five sections were randomly assigned to receive MMC-based instruction (MMC); for comparison purposes, the remaining three sections received instruction in a traditional lecture format (TI).

One of the purposes of this study was to establish and assess procedures for running an IVLC. Hence, to avoid confounding issues it was decided that new or experimental instructional course materials would not be used. Instead, instructional videodiscs that had been developed and tested elsewhere were obtained. One of the main reasons for selecting MS265 as the target course for this study was the existence of a large selection of commercially available videodiscs that relate to the productivity software aspects of the curriculum. It was decided that such discs could be used to replace the lecture approach normally used to teach those three packages.

Catalogues of suitable discs were surveyed and a number of vendors' courses were reviewed to assure their operation on the IVLC's workstations. Although many software vendors make claims about the compatibility of their products with different hardware configurations, not all those claims have been well tested. It was necessary to ensure that any instruction that was initiated during the study would not be interrupted because of technical problems with untested course material.

Budgetary considerations precluded the acquisition of one copy of each set of materials for each workstation for all three software packages. While that strategy would have permitted each software product to be presented on all 10 workstations at any time, the approximate total cost of 30 sets of course materials would have been US $60,000 (Lotus, dBase, and Wordperfect on 10 workstations, each costing approximately US $2,000). Consequently, three copies of each set of materials were acquired from Atlanta, Georgia-based Comsell Corporation (three each of Lotus, dBase, and Wordperfect) for an approximate cost of US $18,000. These financial considerations influenced the manner in which the treatment instruction had to be administered in the study. The students in each of the MMC classes were randomly assigned to one of three subgroups (Table 1). Each group received a different sequence of instruction in the three packages. Table 1 indicates, for example, that during Period 1, Group A learned Lotus, while Group B learned Wordperfect, while Group C learned dBase. In this way, nine of the 10 workstations could be allocated to three each of Lotus, dBase, and Wordperfect

SUBGROUP	SEQUENCE		
	PERIOD 1	PERIOD 2	PERIOD 3
A	Lotus	Wordperfect	dBase
B	Wordperfect	dBase	Lotus
C	dBase	Lotus	Wordperfect

Table 1: MMC Sub Group Assignments

instruction. The tenth workstation was set aside as a backup.

Individualized Learning Environment. Most classes at CSUF are taught in a traditional lecture format. The material selected for this study is normally taught in regular lectures supplemented by hands-on work in a PC laboratory. This was the first time that the productivity software part of the course had been taught entirely in an individualized instructional setting.

There were implications of this both for faculty and for students. This study allowed instructors to reallocate their lecture time to the IVLC. Hence, during their regularly scheduled lecture time instructors could be present and assist IVLC graduate assistants. For the students, the "come when you like" nature of individualized instruction provided an opportunity not generally available at the university, receiving instruction at times that were convenient to the student.

Time constraints implicit in offering this kind of material within a traditional university environment in a single semester imposed restrictions on the preferred instructional strategy. Normally, individualized instructional materials are used in a self-paced learning environment in which students proceed through the lesson materials, from objective to objective, at their own pace. When a student completes an objective, the student is tested and either proceeds to the next objective (if successful), or receives remediation (if unsuccessful).

Self-pacing results in some students' completing instruction sooner than others. The university environment demands that all students complete a course by the end of the semester. This requirement imposed time limitations on the MMC students in the study, forcing them to complete all the instruction within a prescribed time frame. Because of this, the semester was divided into three, three-week time periods, one time period for each software package (Table 1). MMC students were required to complete the instruction for each package within each assigned period.

This scheme provided a maximum of 810 workstation-hours for each period (3 weeks @ 270 hours/week). For each of the 70 MMC students in the study, this allowed for approximately 11.5 hours of workstation contact time with each package. The duration of instruction for each set of instructional MMC materials, quoted by the vendor, was seven hours. This implied a factor of safety of almost 70%.

To maintain a uniform rate of workstation usage, students were not permitted to use a workstation for longer than one hour at a time. This rule served two purposes. If all the workstations were being used, it prevented newly arriving students from being kept waiting for an excessive time. Secondly, workstation sessions longer than one hour serve no useful purpose. From a learning standpoint, multiple sessions, each of shorter duration, are more beneficial than fewer and lengthier sessions. Students were not permitted to reserve workstations.

   Attendance and Testing. In keeping with the benefits of self-paced instruction, students were advised that they could attend and use the facility any time within each three week period. The only caveat was that all instruction and a posttest had to be completed within an assigned period. Classes that had been originally scheduled to provide the MMC students with traditional instruction in the packages were canceled and replaced by access to the IVLC. Because one of the objectives of the study was to determine workstation usage, an on-line log was developed and maintained to record each student's use of the MMC materials. At the onset of the study, approximately 70 students were assigned to one of the three MMC groups (A, B, and C). By the end of the semester, normal attrition reduced this number to approximately 54 students.

   The use of self-paced (criterion-referenced) individualized instruction implies that all learners will reach criterion, the only variable being the time it takes for instruction to be administered. However, the norm-referenced nature of final grade assignment in traditional (university) learning environments dictated that a posttest be administered to all students at the completion of their instruction.

   For each set of MMC materials, multiple choice and true/false paper and pencil tests were created. The items were selected from a test bank that accompanies the SRA textbook, Information Systems, A Problem-Solving Approach (McLeod, 1989). MMC students were advised that they must complete the test for each package within one week of completion of the instruction for that package. The same tests were administered to the traditionally taught, instructor-led sections of MS265. The test grades partially contributed to students' mid-term grade. Tests and assignments on other curricular material contributed to the balance of the final grade.

   After the third and final posttest, all MMC students were reconvened to anonymously complete a two-part questionnaire.

| | WORDPERFECT | | LOTUS | | dBase III | |
	MMC	TI	MMC	TI	MMC	TI
N	53	68	54	68	53	49
MEAN (%)	78.7	72.8*	79.7	73.4**	80.6	77.7
S.D. (%)	10.0	11.4	13.0	13.3	12.3	12.3

* p < .004
** p < .01

Table 2: Treatment Comparisons

In the first part, respondents were asked to rate the overall quality, flexibility, and ease of use of the MMC materials that were used in this study. In the second part, respondents were asked to state their positive or negative attitude regarding general issues related to MMC.

Results Of The Study. Table 2 summarizes the results of ANOVA's that were performed on the posttest scores of the MMC and TI groups. In all three cases, MMC students' scores were higher than those of the TI students. For the Lotus and Wordperfect modules, MMC scores were significantly better than TI scores. (Lotus: $F(1,120) = 6.9$, p< .01; Wordperfect: $F(1, 119) = 8.82$, p <.004.) While the dBase posttest scores of the MMC students were also higher than those of the TI students, these results were not statistically significant.

An examination of the relative results shown in Table 2 indicates that the MMC test scores were between approximately 6% and 10% higher than the TI posttest scores. In an undergraduate university environment, such numerical differences are not only statistically significant, they are also significant in a practical sense. Where subject grades are reported as letter scores, a 1% - 9% difference is equivalent to a full letter grade, e.g., the difference between a grade of B and a grade of A.

A comparison was done of the completion times for the MMC versus TI modules. The total average time for all three MMC modules was 18.00 hours, each module requiring approximately 6.0 hours. This compares with the officially prescribed lecture time of nine hours plus the estimated nine hours necessary for traditionally taught students to complete their assignments.

This analysis indicated that with approximately the same investment in learning time, MMC students outperformed the TI students.

A calculation of Pearson coefficients of correlation between posttest scores and module completion times indicated that there was no correlation between the time learners spent using an MMC module and their subsequent achievement scores (Lotus: $r = -.03$, $p > .05$; Wordperfect: $r = -.236$, $p > .05$; dBase: $r = .098$, $p > .05$). This result tends to validate the design of the criterion-referenced and self-paced nature of the MMC materials. Even in the time-constrained environment in which this study was done, learners were able to complete the modules with "better than average" achievement scores without the remediation normally associated with these kinds of learning materials.

Responses from each part of the questionnaire were analyzed to determine MMC subjects' overall attitudes regarding (a) their

FACTOR	SECTION 1 (N=23)	SECTION 2 (N=22)	Overall (N=45)
Quality of Instruction	3.09	3.55	3.31
Flexibility of Instruction	3.43	3.41	3.42
Ease of Use	3.35	3.68	3.51
Overall Section Mean	3.30	3.55	3.42
Rating scale: 4 = Excellent, 3 = Good, 2 = Fair, 1 = Poor			

Table 3: Questionnaire Ratings About Courseware

FACTOR	SECTION 1 (Affirmative) (N=23)	SECTION 2 (Affirmative) (N=22)
1. Was the facility easy to use?	100%	100%
2. Were assistants helpful?	96%	100%
3. Would you recomend MMC?	87%	91%
4. Offer more MMC business courses?	88%	86%
5. Offer MMC in other disciplines?	87%	87%

Table 4: Questionnaire Responses About MMC

experience with the MMC materials used in this study, and (b) MMC in general. In the first part, using a four point rating scale (4= Excellent, 3 = Good, 2 = Fair, 1 = Poor), subjects were asked to rate three factors specifically related to the MMC materials used in this study. Respondents' overall opinion about all the modules was determined by calculating the mean rating for each factor, and the overall mean. As Table 3 indicates, with a mean rating of 3.42 respondents were overwhelmingly positive about the MMC materials used in this study.

In the second part of the questionnaire, there were two questions about the use and operation of the IVLC and its workstations (Table 4). Respondents' unanimously positive responses indicated a high degree of satisfaction with the operation of the IVLC. However, while responses to the last three questions about MMC in general were still very positive, they were somewhat more qualified.

Observations Regarding Workstation Resource Utilization. Individualized instruction can be a two edged sword. On one hand, for students and instructors there are many benefits that can be realized from its use. On the other hand, because of the freedom that it allows learners, it can present major problems regarding the planning of resource utilization. During the design of this study, one of the main concerns was the paucity of resources, particularly with regard to the number of available workstations. Every effort was made to ensure that the IVLC would be open enough hours to provide sufficient workstation hours for all students for all the learning materials. No amount of planning could solve the problems that might arise if student usage was not uniform throughout each time period. If a disproportionate number of students elected to receive their instruction during the last week of each period, there would not have been enough workstations available to satisfy the demand.

This situation did not materialize. It should be noted, however, that students were warned that this could happen and that failure to complete a posttest within an allocated period would result in a grade of F. (Even in individualized instructional settings, sometimes fear is the best motivation!)

Despite these warnings, student attendance was noticeably low in the first week of a period, picked up in the second week, and was very high in the last week. Though there were sometimes occasions in the third week when students had to wait for a workstation, the wait times were not excessive. It is probably for that reason that this weekly attendance trend was consistent in all three periods. If there had been fewer available workstation-contact hours, students who procrastinated until the last week would probably have learned from their first experience to use the facility sooner in subsequent periods.

Because availability of workstations was one of the concerns of this study, it is important to consider the effect of this variable on the number of students that could be accommodated in the IVLC. Based on the observed pattern of usage, it seems that there is a linear relationship between the number of available workstations and the number of classes that can be offered instruction such as that provided in this study. If the IVLC had 30 MMC workstations, six sections of MS265 could use the IVLC. Thirty workstations is the same number of PCs usually found in department computing laboratories.

Doubling the number of hours that the Center was open, however, would probably not have doubled the Center's utility. Students cannot and should not be expected to receive instruction late at night or on weekends. Based on the experience of this study, it could probably be expected that extending the Center's operating hours would have produced diminishing returns, depending on when those extra hours of operation were scheduled. For example, opening two hours earlier and closing two hours later Monday through Thursday would probably significantly increase usage. Similar but not as much extra usage might be expected for Friday, the last day of the week. Much less usage would be expected for weekends. However, rules of thumb such as these could probably be easily affected by a "strategically announced" testing/exam schedule.

Recommendations

Much has been learned from studies and activities such as the one conducted at CSUF. The following is a list of suggestions and recommendations that should be considered by anyone planning to initiate an MMC facility similar to the IVLC.

a) Acquire industry standard hardware in order to have the broadest possible selection of generic courseware from which to choose if you decide to use commercially available materials.

Try to have at least one complete workstation available as a backup should a workstation become inoperable. Purchase the best hardware that you can afford.   End users will be very unhappy if hardware keeps breaking down. If two workstations become inoperable and they cannot be repaired quickly, try to replace components of one system with components of the other. That way, at least one of the systems may be made operable.

b)   If your facility will have as primary goal the delivery of instruction (as opposed to the development of instructional materials) use commercially available courseware.   Although this courseware is costly, for the sake of the publicity, many vendors are willing to negotiate substantial discounts, especially for universities.

Be sure that the courses that you select have been tested for educational utility in other instructional environments. Test them thoroughly in your own environment to be sure there are no technical problems.

c)   Although it is surely possible, with a limited budget, to undertake a single, well-defined project, try to obtain a specific department's ongoing support (i.e. funding) for the project and for subsequent projects. It is inadvisable to undertake projects on the basis of "Let's see how it all works out before we commit any of next year's funding." Realities being what they are, you probably will have to accept such conditions, as undesirable as they are.

d) Establish your center as a separate entity, not as part of an existing computer laboratory.   MMC learning centers have different needs than conventional computer labs and should be perceived as library-like facilities. De Marco and Lister (1987) have shown that computer programmer productivity is significantly higher if the programming workspace is aesthetically pleasing, quiet, and private. Your center should provide similar conditions for its learners.

e) Ideally, a center should be managed by a full-time director. In the early stages of development this may not be (fiscally) possible. Planning and managing such a facility is very time consuming and will affect the time available for teaching, research, etc.

If it is not possible to employ a "professional" director, hire/select/obtain one senior graduate assistant who can be responsible for the day-to-day management of the facility. That person's responsibilities should include managing other student assistants, enforcing guidelines and rules, ensuring that student testing policies are enforced, etc. That graduate student must report to a faculty or staff member who is ultimately responsible for all aspects of the center.

f) It may not be necessary to justify your project with studies to determine the effectiveness of its inherent technology. Like IVD, there may have been countless studies that have already done this. Your first consideration should be the provision of a service to end users. Although testing of procedures and rehearsal of activities will definitely yield interesting, if not useful data, the real test is in providing a service to satisfied end users.

g) Be sure to collect achievement and opinion data. Ultimately, a center provides a service for its "customers." If it is not serving its customers satisfactorily, changes will be in order. Data that you collect will point to changes that may be required.

Collect comparative data as well. Your greatest accomplishment will be to show that your customers are more satisfied and performing better than your competition - in the case of CSUF, that was lecture format.

h) Start slowly. Select one subject area for the first project. Gain experience based on the simplest case. As your experience-set grows, incrementally add new courses and new disciplines.

GLOBAL IMPLICATIONS OF MULTIMEDIA COMPUTING

The Challenge For System Developers

The evolution of the human/machine interface has brought with it many new challenges for users and developers of end-user applications, some of which have become evident in the work that has taken place in CSUF's multimedia learning center. This section discusses some of the problems and solutions that have been addressed in the last decade of evolving user interfaces, focusing on trends that have implications for international aspects of multimedia computing.

Since the early 1980's, personal computer software companies have sought to gain a competitive edge by promoting their wares in international markets. The success of those efforts has varied, depending both on the selected market as well as the complexity of the software adaptation (referred to as "localization"). In non-U.S., English speaking countries, much of the work required to localize a software application focuses on changing the spelling of words (such as "honor") to their non-U.S. (British) equivalents ("honour"). In some cases, American idioms may also require changing. Software developers have learned to plan for the possibility of these levels of localization in the original application design process, for example, by separating program logic files from screen message files.

As the PC marketplace expanded beyond English speaking countries, the need to provide for foreign character sets led to standardization on the 8-bit, 265 character, ASCII character set. Prior to that, many CP/M-based application developers had become accustomed to using the "high" bit of ASCII characters as proprietary attribute bits that only had meaning within their own applications. For example, within a word processor text or document file, if the eighth bit of the 7-bit character "$" (ASCII 036) were turned on, that might have meant that the "$" should be boldfaced. However, using the 256 ASCII character set, that boldfaced "$" would have been in conflict with the Extended ASCII 8-bit character "n" (ASCII 164).

Entry into foreign marketplaces has also required developers to consider the structure of foreign languages. For example, many applications contain input data entry fields that are displayed within graphical menu boxes. These menu boxes are designed with fixed lengths and widths, stored in separate files, and called upon by program logic as they are required. However, fixed length data fields that are sufficient, for example, for the input or output of English words may be insufficient for the input or output of lengthier German text.

Another software "internationalizing" practice that has become common is the provision of application installation options that allow users to select and use different formats for dates (e.g. - mm/dd/yy versus dd/mm/yy) and currency (e.g., - $, £, ¥, etc.).

Until recently, all these practices have focused less on substance and more on localizing the form of the applications. With the inevitable shift to the inclusion of audio, and still- and video-images in the multimedia interface, localization of software will become even more difficult. From the standpoint of form, it will be necessary to continue to develop new techniques and processes to efficiently plan, produce, store, and execute different versions of multilingual audio and video, each depending on the country in which the application is to be used. From the standpoint of substance, the challenge will be even greater. For example, will a multimedia application script developed for use in one culture, be useful, even in translated form, in other cultures? As we have heard countless times, "A picture is worth a thousand words." But will pictures developed for use in one culture convey the same thousand-word message in another culture, or will it be necessary to completely redevelop different multimedia application interfaces for different countries and cultures? Consider for example, cultures in which the left hand must not be used for certain social behaviors, and where it is an affront to display the soles of your shoes. It is possible that an MMC vignette featuring a Nike-wearing, left-handed long ball hitter sliding into second base could create an international incident!

As our knowledge and experience with new multimedia applications grows, we may also discover that the applications themselves may not be as transportable among countries and cultures as we might wish. For example, the models upon which computer based training are based have largely been derived from Skinnerian and Crowderian learning theories and practices culled from Western European and North American experience. Despite their success in the "west," can we be confident that these models will be transferable to other cultures? This is a particularly compelling question at the end of the Twentieth Century when we are witnessing, on a worldwide basis, increased levels of intense nationalism that many times rejects the contributions of foreign cultures.

Then there are issues that bridge the gap between culture and ethics. For example, should MMC software companies cater to the racial or sexist biases of non-Western cultures? Will software companies rationalize these issues and simply localize their MMC applications for such cultures by precluding the use of women, Caucasians, Orientals, Hispanics, African-Americans, tall people, short people,......?

Finally, there are issues that are clearly of an ethical nature. For example, some software suppliers are already having to respond to allegations that they are providing tools to foreign governments whose policies may be in conflict with acceptable international norms. As multimedia technology and interfaces improve, it is a certainty that such applications will provide those governments with even better tools to pursue their internal and even external policies.

The Challenge for Education

From an information technology standpoint, the 1980's were characterized by significant changes in corporate management policies and organization structures that, to a great extent, were brought about by an appreciation for the competitive value of information. That these changes took place in the decade of the personal computer is not circumstantial. The 1990's will see even more significant changes resulting from improved computer-based modes of information processing and data communications, much of it based upon the evolution of multimedia computing. In the context of globalization, MMC will provide the natural user interface that can dramatically affect information system-based worldwide communications. For these systems to be effective, it will be necessary for the information technologists who develop them to account for the broad cultural differences characteristic of a global community of end users. At the present time however, few post secondary educational institutions are equipped to train systems developers with the knowledge necessary to produce those future systems. There are a number of matters that these institutions must address to meet the challenges of the future:

a) Because of its complexity, it is essential for MMC to become part of the mainstream curriculum, teaching practices, and development activities of universities and industry. For example, computer science and information technology students and industrial trainees should be exposed to MMC technology through the use of existing MMC instructional and training technologies and media. For the most part, this means incorporating IVD and MMC materials into existing curricula. Companies such as Comsell Corporation, National Education Corporation, and the Minnesota Educational Computing Corporation have extensive catalogs from which MMC materials may be chosen.

b) Formal practices must be defined and documented to include the extra dimensions of media production/ integration into the development MMC applications. Currently, most multimedia computing consists of audio and video enhancements to existing, personal computer-based, single user applications. As our experience in developing multimedia applications grows however, both from a developer and from an end user standpoint, expectations of MMC will also grow. There will be a need to incorporate MMC into existing, complex, corporate information systems. The need to develop new corporate information systems that contain dimensions of MMC will also grow. When this happens, it will be essential to use formal design, development, and testing practices to produce these complex applications. Schools and departments of software engineering need to encourage graduate students, faculty, and information system development management to attend to the special problems of multimedia, and perhaps to consider how or whether existing CASE and/or rapid prototyping methodologies lend themselves to developing these systems of the future (Reisman, 1992).

c) Computer science and information science programs must begin to offer programs of study that specifically include principles of MMC application development. Such programs should be interdisciplinary, requiring the involvement of other (non technical) departments in the institution. Just as the role of the end user is now widely recognized in the development of information systems, so must the role of other subject matter experts be recognized in the development of MMC applications. Institution- and curriculum-accrediting bodies such as the ACM/IEEE, DPMA, and AACSB must recognize the importance of MMC, and alter their accrediting guidelines to reflect the role of an interdisciplinary body of knowledge called multimedia computing.

d) Finally, those responsible for preparing systems developers of tomorrow must recognize that future information systems will be used by an international community of end users. Because of this, information technology students must not only be trained in the technical aspects of MMC-based system development, they must also be educated about cultures and behaviors of others. This internationalization of the curriculum will not be easy. Few technical educators have the knowledge or skills to even begin this task. Colleagues in such disciplines as foreign languages, sociology, psychology, history, and geography must be called upon to assist in creating programs of study tailored for information technology students. As educators, the example of our own interdisciplinary cooperation will serve as the best model for the global technologists of the future.

REFERENCES

Anastasio, E. J. (1973). Evaluation of the educational effectiveness of PLATO and TICCIT. In J. M. Biedenban & L. P. Graywon (Eds.), *Frontiers in Education* (pp. 382-387). New York: IEEE Press.

Boeing Computer Services Company. (1981). *CBI classroom break-even analysis.* Seattle, WA: Education and Training Division.

Brandt, R. H. (1987). *Videodisc training: a cost analysis.* Falls Church, Virginia: Future Systems Inc.

Comcowich, W. J. (1989, March). The ages of videodisc. *Instruction Delivery Systems*, pp. 10-15.

DeBloois, M., Clauson Maki, K., & Ferrin Hall, A (1984). *Effectiveness of interactive videodisc training: a comprehensive review.* The Monitor Report Series. Falls Church, Virginia: Future Systems Inc.

De Marco, T., & Lister T. (1987). *Peopleware: productive projects and teams.* New York: Dorset House Publishing.

Gallupe, R.B., Bastiannutti, L.M, & Cooper, W.H. (1991). Unblocking brainstorms. *Journal of Applied Psychology, 76* (1), pp. 137-142.

Graham, M.B.W. (1986). *RCA and the videodisc - the business of research.* Cambridge, Massachusetts: Cambridge University Press.

Little, T.D.C., & Ghafoor, A. Spatio-temporal composition of distributed multimedia objects for value-added networks. *Computer, 24*(10), pp. 42 - 50.

Maher, T. G. (1988). *Hands-on verification of mechanics training; a cost-effectiveness study of videodisc simulation* (Research Rep.). Sacramento, CA: California Department of Consumer Affairs, Bureau of Automotive Repair.

McLeod, R. (1989). *Information systems, a problem-solving approach.* Chicago, IL: SRA.

Meghini, C., Rabitti, F., & Thanos, C. (1991). Conceptual modeling of multimedia documents. *Computer, 24*(10), pp. 23 -29.

Parkhurst, P. E. & Grauer, P. (1989, January). *An interactive learning resource center for medical education.* Instruction Delivery Systems, pp. 10-22.

Pollak, R. A. (1989, May). *Videodiscs: applications in education and training.* Instruction Delivery Systems, p. 27.

Reisman, S. (1978, March). Research in multimedia computer assisted instruction. Paper presented at the annual meeting of the American Education Research Association, Toronto, Ontario, Canada.

Reisman, S. (1987, September). Interactive videodisc technology. *IEEE Computer*, pp. 103-106.

Reisman, S. (1991). Launching a learning center:a case study. *Information Resources Management Journal, 4* (3), pp. 13-22.

Reisman, S. (in press). Development strategies for interactive videodisc applications. *Interactive Learning International Journal.*

Reisman, S. (1992). Power to the people: end users as developers. *IEEE Software, 9*(2), 111-112 .
Reisman, S., & Carr, W.A. (1991). Perspectives on multimedia systems in education. *IBM Systems Journal, 50* (3), pp. 280-295.

Reisman, S., Johnson, T.W., & Mayes, B.T. (in press.) Group Decision Program: A Videodisc-based Group Decision Support System. *Decision Support Systems Journal.*

Reisman, S. & Martin, D. B. (1977, September). Television technology in computer based training. *IEEE Conference Digest,* (pp. 38 - 40). Toronto, Ontario, Canada.

SALT *Proceedings of the Sixth Conference on Interactive Instruction Delivery* (1988). Orlando, FL: Society for Applied Learning Technology.

SALT *Proceedings of the Seventh Conference on Interactive Instruction Delivery* (1989). Orlando, FL: Society for Applied Learning Technology.

14 Intelligent Tutoring Systems for Global Information Technology Education

Anthony Verstraete and William Valonis
Pennsylvania State University

To accommodate the growing need for information technology education and the accompanying worldwide shortage of capable instructors, a variety of computer-assisted approaches to education are available. However, information technology education in a global setting requires systems which are flexible in responding to widely different cultural approaches to learning and great variations in the technological sophistication of users. Intelligent tutoring systems (ITS), with their ability to adapt to different student learning styles and environments, have outstanding potential in assisting with technology transfer and education. In this chapter ITS are contrasted with other computer-based technologies within a global context. The components of ITS are examined, and an illustration of a simple ITS is provided. A functionality test is provided to help potential adapters of ITS in distinguishing ITS from other computer-based instructional technologies. Finally, methodological guidelines are provided to assist developers of ITS where the intended application involves education in a culturally pluralistic environment.

There has long been a worldwide shortage of experienced instructors in the diverse domains of expertise associated with information systems technology. The recently developing nations in Asia and Africa are in critical need of instructors. Eastern European nations and the newly independent nations of the former Soviet Union are also eager to embrace modern information technologies but lack skilled instructors.

Various approaches for resolving this worldwide shortage have been proposed. The one traditionally used in technology development efforts involves the temporary assignment of non-local instructors to regions where the shortage is most acute. When this approach is not feasible, training native instructors within these regions may be attempted. Recently there have been attempts to use computer and communication technology to augment human instructors. This chapter will examine these attempts. It will especially focus upon intelligent tutoring systems, which provide a potential for combining many of the best features of these various approaches.

The use of non-native information technology instructors entails socio-cultural adjustment as well as logistical costs. Relocation requires a willingness of people to work away from home for extended periods, and also an ability to work within foreign settings. Before expatriating an instructor, an assessment should be made concerning the comprehensiveness and adaptability of the individual's expertise. Many expert information technology instructors may be unconsciously dependent upon the technological infrastructure of the home country, and would be unable to instruct effectively in an environment where this infrastructure was not in place. Living conditions in lesser developed nations may be incompatible with the living style of the majority of technology experts. With this difficulty comes the direct expense and logistical complications involved with maintaining educational facilities, such as offices and classrooms, that are acceptable to non-native workers.

It is unlikely that there will be, in the near future, enough capable instructors willing to teach abroad to meet instructional demands. Cost is prohibitive for many applications. Even assuming that we can find an adequate number of instructors willing to work in foreign settings, to be effective these instructors must acquire a working knowledge of the local culture and often must overcome language barriers. Such preparation adds substantially to the time and costs of instructor training. Without such training there is less likelihood of fully attaining the instructional goals of the program. This preparation is most essential when the social and technological disparities between the instructor's culture and the host culture are pronounced, which is often the situation when educational efforts are directed towards developing nations.

Similar problems are encountered when attempts are made to train local people to serve as instructors. The trainees must either be transported to centralized training facilities or local facilities must be established. Neither logistical approach fully eliminates problems associated with existing social and technological disparities. Once the initial training period is over, constant re-education is required to keep the native instructors abreast of rapidly evolving information technologies. Preparing instructors of the same nationality as their students does not necessarily guarantee the resolution of problems stemming from cultural or other social differences between the teacher and the student. The techniques in which they are prepared may not be ideally matched to the diversity of instructional environments. Many developing nations are a patchwork of widely differing social and ethnic groups and islands of technical capabilities. The "native" instructor may have to accommodate his instructional methods to differing groups and individuals as much as would a foreign instructor.

EDUCATIONAL TECHNOLOGIES

Even if the above problems can be resolved, the global shortage of information technology instructors cannot realistically be met solely by training more native instructors or relying on expatriate instructors. Demand will continue to outpace our ability to prepare instructors. Computer-based educational technologies can help to address these problems. They will work tirelessly in any environment capable of supporting their components for as long as required. An adequate workstation and a well-designed system is all that is required. They can be designed to be responsive to specific cultural and operational settings. Most importantly, they can be replicated and placed in a variety of locations at fairly low cost, with none of the direct risks associated with using human instructors.

Four technological approaches to replacing human instructors will be considered: **distance education using videoconferencing techniques, computer assisted instruction (CAI), expert systems (ES) advisors, and intelligent tutoring systems (ITS)**. In this chapter, we will review the first three of these approaches briefly, then discuss how intelligent tutoring systems can combine their advantages to provide flexible support for global information technology education.

Tele-teaching environments, in which students and instructors communicate via long-range voice and video links similar to tele-conferencing, have been discussed for many years. The use of distance education has been well established and proven to be effective in many international application areas (Abrioux, 1991). While many large businesses today use video-conferencing, they rely heavily on an advanced communications infrastructure. Without such an infrastructure, video-conferencing is effectively impossible. As many less developed countries lack reliable telephone networks and other telecommunication facilities, video-conferencing cannot be a practical method for providing information technology education within these regions.

Video-conferencing may not necessarily facilitate intercultural communication. Careful attention must be paid to issues concerning differences such as the meaning attributed to visual cues within a culture-specific context. Video-conferencing is applicable to limited application domains because it is better suited to explaining general concepts than imparting specific skill sets. Instructional platforms employing video-conferencing techniques may yield no better educational results than using videotapes unless effective instructor-student dialogue can be achieved. In attempting to leverage the supply of instructors by increasing the student-teacher ratio, such approaches often lead to reduced instructional effectiveness.

Another approach, computer assisted instruction, is a more portable technology. If personal computers are locally available, they can be used to run CAI programs. CAI is a stable technology that can be counted on to perform dependably within its limitations. One limitation of CAI is its relative lack of flexibility to individualize its pedagogical approach to conform to the student's personal attributes (Anderson, Boyle, & Reiser, 1985; Elsom-Cook, 1990; Yazdani, 1986). This rigidity makes CAI less attractive for many applications of global information technology education.

A common form of CAI program familiar to many computer users is the "on-line tutorial" which accompanies a wide variety of software packages. Persons familiar with computer technology frequently encounter these tutorials and seldom have difficulty in using them. Novices often require preliminary training prior to using them, while more advanced users find the plodding way of presenting the material annoying. CAI programs lack the capability to accommodate their instructional approach in response to individual differences. To provide such capability, the tutoring program would have to possess a diagnostic and reasoning facility.

Applications of Artificial Intelligence

Artificial intelligence (AI) is the study of mental faculties through the use of computational models. Intelligent tutoring systems are the product of AI research in the field of education. This chapter will focus on ITS and the role such systems can play in global information technology education (GITE). Many readers will be familiar with expert systems, which are closely related to ITS. Both types of systems are concerned with knowledge transfer, but their goals are different, and therefore their design must also differ. ES are focussed on giving advice towards solving a particular problem, while ITS are geared towards providing the student with enough knowledge about the domain to solve problems without assistance. Much of what has been learned through extensive ES research and development efforts within the last decade can be directly applied to ITS. The nucleus of an intelligent tutoring system is, in fact, an expert system equipped to provide instruction at the individual level.

Expert systems in teaching. Expert systems are computer programs designed to provide advice to resolve particular problems in a manner similar to human experts. Expert systems can only be applied to narrowly defined areas of procedural knowledge, called *domains*. They do not work well with large, complex areas of knowledge which do not possess clearly delineated rules, called *heuristics*. To create an ES, a knowledge engineer must "capture" knowledge from a human expert and engineer that knowledge so that it can be represented in a computer's *knowledge base* (Hayes-Roth, 1984). A user of the system can then ask the ES questions, which will be processed by the expert system's *inference engine* using the knowledge base.

Expert systems could be useful in providing instruction, although this is not their primary purpose. By repeatedly consulting an ES and observing its reasoning, users can slowly acquire their own expertise within the domain. However, ES are designed to help users solve one particular problem at a time, rather than teaching a general approach toward an entire class of problems. This is a primary difference between expert systems, which are designed to give advice, and intelligent tutoring systems, which are designed to endow the student with an understanding of the domain.

ES are not able to assess a student's performance in any detail, and they are generally limited in the variety of ways in which they can present explanatory information. There are many domains which are difficult to reduce to a set of production rules, which are the usual form for representing heuristic logic stored in knowledge bases. For these reasons, ES are not an ideal technology for providing automated instruction, although they can be effective in certain limited, well-structured domains. ES intended for instructional purposes could be difficult to introduce in areas that are technologically and culturally dissimilar to the system's country of origin for the same reasons mentioned in the above discussion of CAI.

Intelligent Tutoring Systems. Intelligent tutoring systems are computer programs designed to transfer knowledge about a particular narrowly defined domain through the use of individualized learning sessions. They may be viewed as the offspring of the marriage of CAI and ES technologies. ITS are meant to simulate human tutors in a one-on-one environment rather than human teachers in a classroom environment. Intelligent tutoring systems are among the most promising of emerging technological solutions for coping with instructor shortages. The ability to offer personalized, flexible instruction to individual students can enable ITS to successfully increase the effective supply of information technology instructors. While ITS cannot totally replace human instructors, they can greatly reduce the amount of time instructors must spend with individual students.

The focus on individualized learning is the primary difference between ITS and CAI. To truly be an *intelligent* tutoring system, the program must provide lessons that are individualized to accommodate each student's level of prior experience and preference for interacting with a tutor (Sokolnicki, 1991). The ITS must be able to generate exercises to correct the student's weaknesses, which requires more than the simple library of exercises typical of older CAI approaches. It requires the intelligence not only to locate a mistake, but also to ascertain the probable cause of the student error and to devise a strategy to keep the mistake from reoccurring. It is this intelligence facility which allows ITS to provide a flexible response to the cultural and technological diversity encountered in worldwide educational programs.

Another difference between ITS and many CAI programs is the objective of the system. CAI programs often concentrate on teaching facts to the student. If the student can repeat all the facts supplied by the system, the system is considered successful (Angelides & Doukidis, 1990). The problem with this approach is that the student may be memorizing the facts, but not truly understanding the underlying concepts. When the student tries to apply his knowledge to the domain, he may find himself unprepared in a manner similar to that of a well-trained parrot entering into a philosophical debate.

ITS can be designed to help the student develop an understanding beyond mere factual memorization. By allowing the student to make mistakes, and then assisting in the recovery from such mistakes, ITS help the student to see the "Why?" behind the facts. ITS can then offer the student problem-solving exercises to allow him to gain "experience" in the domain without incurring risk. When the student experiences difficulty in handling these real-world simulations, supplemental instruction can be automatically triggered.

COMPONENTS OF INTELLIGENT TUTORING SYSTEMS

Although ITS researchers are not always consistent among themselves concerning the partitioning and labeling of the architectural components of ITS, the components identified in Anderson's Advanced Computer Tutoring project are representative (Anderson, Boyle, & Reiser, 1985; Yazdani, 1986). Five major parts may be identified [FIGURE 1]: (1) An *interface module* which handles dialogue with the student, (2) a *tutor module* which administers lessons, (3) a *student model* which tracks student progress, (4) an *expert module* which contains the lesson's subject content, and (5) a *bug catalog* used to identify students' common learning problems. Various authors may use similar terms for components that may differ markedly in both construction and use (Brecht & Jones, 1988).

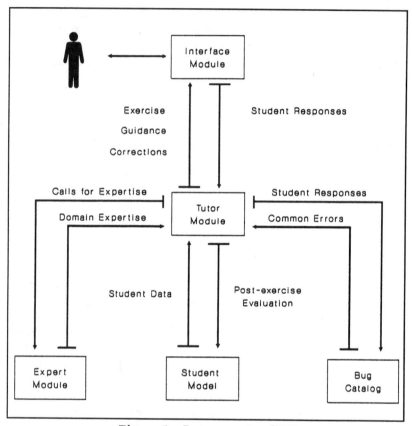

Figure 1: Components of ITS

To allow the reader to more easily grasp the principles behind the five components of ITS, this section includes examples of each of the components. These examples are separated from the main body of the text by use of asterisks and italics, as is shown below.

* * *

An example of an ITS intended to teach basic word processing skills will be used to illustrate the function of each of these components. The example is a simplification of a real working ITS, and is intended only for demonstrating the functions of each component. It was chosen as a subject domain concerned with providing instruction on performing rudimentary procedural tasks such as how to perform basic word processing functions: saving and printing documents, manipulating text strings, and checking spelling. Real world ITS would normally be much more substantial in their goals and content.

* * *

Interface Module

The interface module is the component which manages the communication between the student and the ITS. The design of this component requires special attention so that excessive time is not required to learn how to interact with the system. The goal is to have the student begin learning the subject matter as soon as possible. Any delay required to learn the interface incurs both costs to the organization and the annoyance of the student. As in many applications designed for non-expert users, the transparency of mechanical elements is an important factor in facilitating use. In designing the user interface, the focus should not be simple interaction, implying merely an exchange of actions, but instead meaningful human-machine communication, focussing on the exchange of ideas and concepts (Miller, 1988).

Interface design may use graphic or text oriented approaches. **Graphical User Interfaces (GUI)** make use of pictorial representations of files, devices, and so on. Well known examples of GUI are the MacIntosh personal computer's interface, IBM's OS/2 and Microsoft's Windows. ITS can utilize GUI to simulate control panels, schematics, and other visual models. Few GUI are purely graphical; most use text-based interaction in addition to graphics. Textual interfaces communicate via words rather than pictures.

Textual interfaces normally require the user to learn a command language before communication can take place. Menu-driven software is an improved form of textual interface that reduces the need for the user to memorize command language syntax. Neither of these forms of textual interface are recommended for ITS use. Command language interfaces are far from transparent, while menu-driven interfaces are often fairly cumbersome. Another difficulty with menu-driven interfaces for ITS is that the user may learn to approach a problem from a "multiple-choice" perspective that would be inappropriate when dealing with similar problems in real-world settings (Miller, 1988).

The most advanced form of textual interface is the **Natural Language Interface (NLI)**. The ideal NLI allows the user to communicate with the system as if talking with another person. Practical application of this interface style is beyond the current state-of-the-art systems, although pioneering efforts have been made using this technique in medical tutoring systems (Hagamen & Gardy, 1986). NLI are becoming more powerful, using more complex parsing strategies. Although they remain somewhat awkward, users can usually learn to communicate with a minimum of trouble by limiting their dialogue to the NLI's limited comprehension abilities. Such NLI interfaces still rely on a technologically sophisticated user who knows how to limit dialogue style and content to what the computer can reasonably comprehend (Chin, 1984). Developing NLI interfaces for several languages would be an overwhelming task, further complicated by dialectical and regional usage variations in the local language. Therefore, developing ITS using NLI would probably not be suitable for many global applications.

A diagnostic facility could be used to alter the textual interface strategy. A novice would receive complete explanations, while a more experienced user might only receive terse reminders. Approaches could shift from GUI or menu-driven to command-driven or even limited NLI. More than one interface could be concurrently available to the user. The diagnostic facility could be especially useful in GITE settings where there is a wide variation of user experience in using ITS-based instructional facilities or widely differing exposure to various interface styles.

* * *

The word-processing ITS will maintain both a GUI and a limited NLI. One section, or window, of the screen will contain graphical representations of the word processing function being taught. These representations will take the form of sample screens, allowing the student to associate what is encountered in the ITS with what will be encountered when using the actual word processor. Another window in the interface will permit natural language dialogue between the student and the ITS. The primary reason for use of this "split" interface is to allow the ITS to communicate with the student via the NLI window while the student explores the functions of the word processor via the GUI window. The student can move to the NLI window to ask the ITS for help or to respond to questions posed by the ITS. Individuals in some cultures may exhibit an overall preference for text-based instruction, and may rely more heavily on the NLI window, while others may better understand a pictorial approach, and thus rely on the GUI window.

* * *

Tutor Module

The tutor module is the ITS component responsible for preparing an exercise, guiding and helping the student during the exercise, and evaluating the student's success at completion of the exercise. The tutor module is essential to ITS, and differentiates it from other approaches to computer-based instruction. To function effectively, this component must be able to access and maintain the other components of the system, as will be demonstrated below (Angelides & Doukidis, 1990).

The first task which the tutor must perform is the preparation of an exercise. Two broad strategies may be used for the selection and presentation of course material (Halff, 1988). The first strategy is used for expository teaching. It uses the *web teaching* technique, which specifies that the first concepts to be covered should be ones that relate to the student's current understanding, and that generalities should be discussed before specifics (Norman, 1973).

The second strategy applies best to the teaching of procedures. Three objectives of this strategy are:

1. Manageability - The exercise should be solvable by the student at his current level of understanding.

2. Appropriateness - The exercise should require use of the procedure being taught.

3. Individualization - The exercise should be chosen to overcome the student's current weakness(es).

Proper implementation of any of these strategies requires information acquired from the student model.

Once an exercise is chosen, the tutor's next task is to guide the student through the exercise. While doing this, the tutor module may need to access any of the other ITS components. The *interface module* will be required to facilitate communication between the student and the tutor. The *student model* may be updated according to the student's responses. The *bug catalog* will be accessed to determine if the student is committing any predefined errors. Finally, the *expert module* may be accessed when it appears that the student requires additional domain information.

The tutor may offer guidance in two ways. It can respond to questions posed by the student, or it can intervene without the student's request. The second form of guidance can occur when the student makes a mistake that has been included in the bug catalog or when the student spends too much time involved in material that he already understands or is irrelevant to his educational objectives. By whatever means tutorial guidance is initiated, it must be executed as guidance and not as automatic error-correction. Simply correcting mistakes without helping the student to find the reason for the errors circumvents an important part of the learning process. (Halff, 1988)

The tutor module's third task is evaluation of student success at the completion of the exercise. This phase may be merged with the exercise-preparation phase to produce a continuing cycle of student learning [FIGURE 2]. This evaluation may involve maintenance of the student model to represent the student's increased skills. Alternatively, the evaluation may involve a comparison of the student's solution and the ideal solution as put forth by the domain expert. This type of comparison would pinpoint and attempt to analyze the differences between the two solutions. The tutor module's ability to analyze differing approaches and to maintain records of these differences is of special interest in GITE. It is presumed that there will be regional and cultural differences in student approaches to problem solving during the educational process. The tutor module can serve the designer by providing information about approach characteristics employed by certain populations. Knowledge of these differences can then be used to improve the design of educational methodologies targeted for that population.

* * *

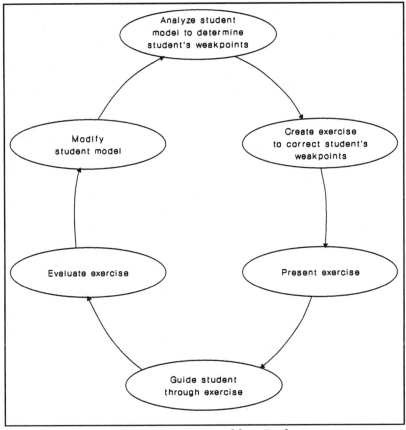

Figure 2: ITS Teaching Cycle

Following the web teaching strategy, our example ITS will begin by associating word processing with something that the student is already familiar with, whether it be writing, typing, or using another word processing application. Dependent upon the student's beginning expertise, the tutor may or may not require the student to complete some basic text entry exercises. Following this, the tutor might discuss the need for saving a document, and teach related concepts concerning volatility of main memory. However, for the student who has previously used applications requiring that a file be saved before exiting the program, the tutor may go directly to the procedure for saving files with this particular word processor. Other word processing skills will be similarly taught.

* * *

A key factor in designing ITS tutor modules for GITE is flexibility. While a flexible tutor is desirable in any ITS application, cultural plurality among users places much greater demands on the system. Not only might the tutor have to deal with language differences, but also with differences in educational background and pedagogical preference.

The tutor should not always choose lessons in the same order, but should instead be able to individualize selections to each student's needs. For example, a student who makes many spelling mistakes and saves and prints without using the spell checker may be given a reminder that the spell checker should be consistently used. The tutor module would know to analyze the student's spelling even though the spell checker was never activated. A student who doesn't use the spell checker because he rarely misspells words might not receive such a reminder.

The frequency of reminders and the general "intrusiveness" of the tutor module during a lesson should be designed to vary according to cultural and individual preferences. Certain individuals or cultural groups which stress individual control and initiative might find a proactive style of tutor more annoying than a tutor designed to be passive. Other individuals, perhaps members of a culture where it is not considered proper to explicitly request help, would be better served by a more intrusive style of intervention.

Student Model

The student model is the component of ITS which keeps track of information relevant to student characteristics, which is useful in determining pedagogical strategies. Among ITS' advantages over earlier forms of CAI, one especially relevant to GITE is the ability of ITS to tailor presentations to the individual user's characteristics. The student model constructs a database of information about each student. It also provides a diagnostic facility that dynamically refines the student model during the course of student interaction with the system (VanLehn, 1988).

Various types of student modeling techniques exist, and a three-dimensional method has been devised for their evaluation (Rich, 1983). The first dimension is the ability of the system to customize its approach to individual students. Some early techniques generated a canonical model to represent a typical user. This type of model is concerned with the "average" user, and is not adept at dealing with a heterogeneous group of users. Newer, more flexible techniques develop and maintain a collection of individual student models. The use of individual student models allows the system to personalize its approach to each user.

The second dimension to be measured is the ability of the ITS to determine for itself the student's relevant attributes. Techniques which rely on the student to configure the model allow the most freedom and power to experienced users, but beginners will be best served by a system that builds the student model on its own, based on the way in which the student interacts with the system. This is because most beginning students would be intimidated by system configuration-type questions.

The third measurable dimension is the tutor's ability to match short-term objectives to the student's ultimate learning goals. Short-term models are devoted to solving only the current problem. Long-term models keep current student exercises in line with their educational purposes. Short-term techniques do not record and save detailed information about student progress. Therefore, they may guide the user to a dead-end, relative to student learning goals, because of their inability to consider such goals and their relevance to current activities. Long-term techniques are better able to identify subtle trends to ascertain if the student is approaching his goals.

Individual student models can be constructed by employing one of two basic strategies. The stereotyping strategy analyzes actions to match the student with one of a set of generic profiles. As the student continues to interact with the system, the student's stereotype match can be further refined. This strategy is particularly suited to large, complex student models. The second strategy infers individual facts about the student based on his patterns of interaction with the system. While this strategy is more time consuming, it has greater potential for constructing an accurate student model tailored to the specific individual.

One method which applies this second strategy is the genetic graph approach. Skills within a subject domain are represented as a network of nodes and subnodes (Brecht, 1988). Each skill that the system is designed to teach will be represented by a cluster of nodes. Each node can represent either a concept to be learned or a failure in understanding. The system's goal is to move the student through the "positive" nodes while helping him avoid the "negative" ones. As the student progresses, the positive nodes will be marked to indicate that the student comprehends the concept. In the case of the negative nodes, marks will be made when the system observes a student error and erased as the student corrects his misconceptions. The links between the nodes symbolize either logical relationships between concepts or the specific deviation from a packet of expertise that leads to a failure to understand. By backtracking along the link between the negative node and the related positive node, the model can be used to determine which concept is misunderstood and suggest the proper corrective action.

Nodes can be partitioned into sub-nodes. In this manner, the model can break broad concepts down into a finer granularity. This technique can be used to avoid overwhelming users with large chunks of new knowledge. The capability to modify the granularity of the knowledge or skill components can be very useful, as it provides a mechanism for adjusting the learning curve to fit the student's prior experiences and ability to assimilate new forms of knowledge.

As a student uses ITS, the student model will be changed to reflect the student's learning achievement. As the student grows more familiar with the material, the student model would record the student's progress towards more advanced nodes. The model would also note the student's level within each node, indicating to the tutor module the necessary degree of granularity best used in presenting material to the student. The deeper levels of a student model would store more-finely grained concepts than the upper levels to allow students who are experiencing difficulty to learn in smaller increments.

* * *

Because the example is limited to a very narrow domain - a single word processing application - we could construct a genetic graph student model without being overwhelmed with detail. Our tutor will teach a small number of basic skills, such as entering a new document, saving and loading documents as files, some basic editing techniques, and use of tools such as a spell checker. These basic skills may be decomposed into subskills. Subskills of the document saving skill may include formatting a disk, saving the file before ending the application, and making backups. The subskills might even be further decomposed, which would be helpful for students beginning at a particularly low level of computer experience.

* * *

Expert Module

An oversimplified, but convenient, description of the expert module is to describe it as an expert system within ITS. The expert module contains the domain-specific information which ITS will attempt to transfer to the student. The most labor intensive task in building the expert module is encoding this domain information. The choice of the method used to accomplish this will determine both the required effort and the quality of the finished product.   There are three primary encoding strategies (Anderson, 1988).

One strategy is the "black box" approach, which does not require encoding heuristic knowledge. The use of mathematical models is one example of this approach.   Consider a simple system that generates electricity with a steam-driven turbine. A black box model of this system would treat electrical output as a mathematical function of steam pressure. The steam pressure would be affected by such factors as opening and closing valves or changing the boiler temperature. The black box method is relatively easy to execute, but the finished product is not well-suited for instructional purposes, as the student gains little insight into why the various mathematical formulae were used.

Another strategy is the traditional "glass box" expert system approach, in which knowledge is acquired from a human expert and represented within the system, typically as heuristic rules which can be manipulated by the system. This approach is best used to assist users without teaching them. While this approach can be used in an instructional mode by allowing the students to see the rules which were processed to arrive at a particular decision, it is not well-suited for ITS, which attempt to guide students to an understanding of the reasoning behind the rules.   An approach better suited to ITS is the "cognitive" approach, which requires abstract simulation of the expert's use of acquired knowledge. The most labor intensive of the three, this strategy has the best potential for helping the student to assimilate the domain knowledge, and not just to recite learned facts. The cognitive model should be able to deal with:

> *Procedural* knowledge, concerned with the steps executed in performing a task, such as playing a particular piece of music on a piano.

> *Declarative* knowledge, which provides facts in a framework which promotes reasoning. Explaining the various symbols of sheet music, and how they can be positioned, is a declarative process.

> *Causal* knowledge, used to explore the interrelationships of various parts of a system. Causal knowledge would allow a student to realize that an out-of-tune piano may need to have its wires tightened.

* * *

Our ITS will use the cognitive approach to constructing an expert module. The module will contain procedural knowledge in the form of how to operate the various functions of the word processor. Declarative knowledge will appear in the form of introductions to each of the functions, including explanations as to why each function is used. Causal knowledge will be transferred as the student views the effects of using each function.

* * *

Bug Catalog

The bug catalog is a collection of student mistakes commonly encountered within the domain. Originally developed as a method for teaching programmers by identifying common logical and syntactical errors, the bug catalog is now being used in diverse application domains. When the student makes errors, the tutor module will refer to this catalog to see if the mistakes resemble previously recognized patterns. If a catalogued pattern is recognized, the tutor module would then be able to respond with a repertoire of corrective actions designed to rectify the problem.

The bug catalog is not used in all ITS. In some ITS, other modules can perform functions similar to the bug catalog. In the expert module, the errors may be represented by mal-rules (Angelides & Doukidis, 1990), which are distortions of the correct rules. The student model may replace the bug catalog by using the techniques described previously. Conceptually simple, the bug catalog is still an important part of ITS, and should be approached with the same care given to the other components. When applied to GITE, the catalog could be modified to contain errors that are common to students with the same cultural background.

* * *

Since the word processing tutor is comparatively simple, we can implement the entire bug catalog within the student model. This is accomplished by creating nodes or subnodes for various typical errors, and then establishing links between these nodes and the nodes which represent the proper actions from which the errors are deviations. For example, within the editing skill group, we would have nodes dealing with cutting and pasting text. A negative node might represent the error of deleting a long string of text, then retyping it somewhere else. This node would be linked to the cutting node, which indicates that instruction in cutting (followed by instruction in pasting) will help the student to avoid repeating the error.

* * *

Functionality Tests

It is important for developers to be able to distinguish between simple CAI and true ITS. Since ITS are more complex than CAI, they require more time and effort to implement in international settings. However, the rewards of developing ITS that are sensitive to the cultural milieu in which they will operate are greater than those of adapting CAI to a particular culture. By asking a short list of simple questions, the two approaches can be easily distinguished. Although ITS is a technology which still lacks strict definition, these questions will be helpful in providing a better perspective.

Does the system alter presentation for each individual student?

A system must offer more than canned responses for each possible student reply to a particular question. The ability to personalize instruction is the hallmark of true ITS. To answer this question, one must observe multiple users of the system (Rushby, 1989). The system should know enough about the user to be able to respond in a manner which is comprehensible without being patronizing. The system should use different teaching methods to address an individual's particular learning style. As would a skilled human tutor, it should use various media to provide the best learning experience to a heterogeneous population. True ITS will also continue to modify their approach to challenge the student as new understanding is acquired (Bently, 1991). Simple CAI will go from one exercise to the next in an unchanging order, insensitive to the student's progress. ITS will examine the student model to determine if a given exercise is too simple to provide a challenge to the student.

Does the system make use of user feedback?

The system's evaluation of a student's responses should go beyond simply determining their correctness. The responses should be analyzed and used to develop and alter the student model. Feedback can be used to determine the appropriateness of the current teaching technique. Such feedback can also form a pattern which can help determine the student's level of understanding. (Angelides & Doukidis, 1990).

Does the system have a syllabus of training?

Simple CAI may merely present the student with a preprogrammed sequence of exercises. Once all the exercises are completed, the student is assumed to understand the material. ITS should have a set of skill goals for the student to meet. Exercises will be designed and presented to correct the individual student's weaknesses.

Does the system correct misunderstandings?

The system should be able to do more than grade a student for errors at the completion of the exercise. ITS are able to interrupt a student to point out errors. Once an error has been located, the system will explain why the response was erroneous. The system will also look for error patterns which may indicate some fundamental misunderstanding. The system will then offer suggestions designed to help the user overcome the misunderstanding (Kirrane, 1989).

DEVELOPMENT OF ITS FOR GLOBAL APPLICATIONS

Overcoming Cultural Barriers

ITS which have been successfully designed and implemented for use within one culture are not guaranteed similar success when transferred to other cultural settings. When the technology transfer is from a technologically advanced country to one which is less technologically advanced, the difficulties are particularly pronounced. (Kedia & Bhaghat, 1988). An understanding of the cultural obstacles to cross-cultural technology transfer is a prerequisite to successful implementation of ITS on a global scale.

Problems stemming from intercultural communication barriers may occur in a variety of ways. The most fundamental and intractable problems occur at the level of *core beliefs*, which involve the basic cognitive processes of individual members of a culture. Perception of time and its value, basic values of right and wrong, and individuals' overall view of the world fall into this category. At the level of *interpersonal relationships*, the designer is concerned with cultural conventions governing one-on-one interactions, including proper role behavior and personal communication style. Above the level of dyadic relationships is *social organization*, the approach that a culture uses to regulate the interactions of large groups of people within social institutions such as educational or business organizations.

Another aspect of cultural analysis which is particularly relevant to ITS design is *material culture*, the physical artifacts of human technology and how they are viewed and utilized by members of a particular culture. One culture may readily adopt technology from another, and thereby alter its own material culture. However, the culture will not readily change at the level of core beliefs; instead any new technology adopted by the culture will be used in a manner that is compatible with these deeper values (Adler, 1983).

By studying the relationships between the levels of culture and the components of ITS, application developers may better determine a strategy for transferring a tutoring system to a particular culture. A framework has been developed to help depict these relationships [FIGURE 3]. Before it can be applied in facilitating intercultural transfer or use within a culturally pluralistic setting, the developer must be familiar with the host culture. We will therefore discuss some basic guidelines on how to achieve cultural understanding.

Methodology for Cultural Understanding

The first step to understanding a foreign culture is learning its language. The most obvious reason for doing so is to overcome the exclusive need for an interpreter; trying to develop ITS through an interpreter is extremely cumbersome, if not impossible. Another reason to learn the language of the host country is to better understand the culture. For example, in many cultures core values place a heavier emphasis on "we" than on "I", reflecting a tendency to think of people as members of groups more than as individuals. To gain a deeper understanding of a foreign culture and avoid social blunders, some familiarity with the language is indispensable (Hofstede, 1980).

Once the developer has an understanding of the host language at the literal level, *cue-reduction* may begin (Herskovits, 1951). During this process, the developer will learn to respond to increasingly subtle cues that a culture uses to achieve communication among its members. Knowledge of idioms, euphemisms, and other non-literal devices helps developers to design interfaces which would be more acceptable to native users.

There are other methods for studying a culture's core values besides direct communication with its members. When observing popular activities, one can look "behind the scenes" to understand how the values of the culture are represented by the actions of its members (Grimaldi, 1986). A study of a culture's heroes will also lead to an increased understanding of the culture's values (Broms and Gahmberg, 1983). The popular image of the American frontiersman exemplifies the American values of individual freedom and self-reliance. Designs which allow users a high degree of choice in controlling their educational program and ITS interaction would be readily accepted in such a culture.

Culture and ITS Design Features

Once the developer has a working understanding of the local culture, it becomes necessary to apply this understanding to the development of the tutoring system. Suggestions and examples regarding the application of cultural understanding to the five components of ITS are offered below.

Interface Design. Hardware features and interface requirements interact to create a complex network of mutual constraints. In considering the hardware implications of interface design, the material culture has an obvious effect. The hardware that implements the user interface must be able to function in the environment of the host culture; environmental aspects include not only natural factors such as humidity and temperature conditions, but also technological elements such as the dependability of electrical and data communication links. Operational factors, including the availability of support infrastructures to provide repair service and expendable supplies, are also important.

The interface should attempt to capture the "flavor" of the culture. For example, Arabic cultures and the French find colorful, detailed displays appealing, while Germans tend to dislike "gaudy" displays (Hall, 1969, 1989). Observation of the material culture may yield important clues to underlying values useful for good interface design. Mass media is a useful guide; billboards, magazines and newspapers, and television programming may all be sources of insight into culturally based preferences.

The societal level of culture can affect the user interface. The legal system of the host culture may limit the hardware platform to products available from local vendors (Contractor & Sagafi-Nejad, 1981). Conversely, in some areas the use of imported technologies might have positive status connotations for the user. In some instances, traditional educational methods used in the society could be incorporated in the design of the interface. Issues such as who will use the system and the design of the instructional setting relate to societal norms of group behavior. Interfaces designed without an understanding of these norms may fail.

At the interpersonal level, the interface should adopt the communication style preferred by the culture. The context in which the culture presents information must be considered (Hall, 1989). *High-context* cultures, such as the French, assume that the listener already possesses significant background - contextual - information and therefore prefer to use terse statements. *Low-context* cultures, like that of Germany, assume that the listener does not have all the necessary background information and will provide extensive background information along with the new information. Interpersonal communication is an important issue in interface design. Multimedia techniques may be particularly useful in situations where the trainee has limited reading comprehension, interest or motivation is low, or where visual identification with a human instructor will help in the acceptance of the interface. The actors used in developing these segments should obey both the verbal and non-verbal communication norms of the society. Placement of gaze, loudness of voice, and the manner of demonstration are examples.

The core values of a culture affect the temporal perceptions of its members. Temporal perception regulates the way people view and use time. Members of a *monochronic* culture are generally aware of the clock, and tend to schedule their activities to prevent overlap. In these cultures, the student will usually schedule a block of time for using a tutoring system, and the probability of interruption is fairly low. The facilities available for providing student access to the system can be more easily centralized and scheduled.

In *polychronic* cultures, on the other hand, individuals tend to be concurrently engaged in many activities. An interface in this kind of environment should include features to allow it to accomodate various interruptions. A "save session" or "minimize" feature would be desirable, allowing the student to temporarily suspend the learning session while attending to other things. User facilities designed for polychronic societies should permit greater flexibility in scheduling and location to encourage their use.

Tutor module design. Social conventions for providing tutoring should be examined when developing features of this

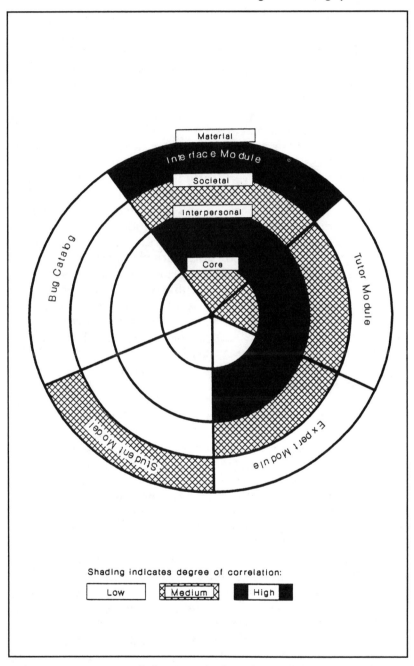

Figure 3: Framework for Transcultural Implementation of ITS

module, which should attempt to imitate accepted tutorship practices of the host culture. In cultures where apprenticeship approaches predominate over institutionalized education, the tutor may be modeled after the master-apprentice relationship.

The tutor module should be modified to fit interpersonal aspects of the relationship between teacher and trainee. This can involve adjustments to the frequency and style of correcting errors and verifying correct answers. A tutor module which is too active for the culture will seem intrusive, while a tutor module which is too passive may leave the student feeling lost. Similarly, the style of correction or verification should be adjusted to the culture.   Context preferences, as discussed in the interface section, are important here.   A high-context tutor in a low-context culture will seem cryptic to the student. Conversely, a low-context tutor in a high-context culture will seem patronizing.

It may be useful to consider temporal perceptions when modifying the tutor module's lesson-design facility. Monochronic cultures may find ITS more acceptable when they offer lessons that are relatively brief and easy to fit into a precise schedule. This type of culture will probably prefer lessons that are relatively intense and goal-specific, with minimal tangential issues. In polychronic cultures, lessons may be long, but they should be easy to interrupt when other business intrudes.

Expert module design. The societal level of a culture can have some impact on the design of the expert module. Legal restrictions on transborder data flow may directly impact the level of expertise provided by the module. Such restrictions may also affect the frequency and manner in which the expert module is updated to reflect changes in information technology. Any perceived threat to national security, economic competitiveness, or personal privacy could lead to local legislation which might hinder the development or modification of the knowledge base component of the expert module (Buss, 1984; Chandran, Phatak, & Sambharya, 1987).

A good knowledge of social norms concerning interpersonal relationships will be important to the design of the expert module if it is necessary to acquire expertise from local domain experts. The design process depends on a cooperative relationship between the one designing the system and the system's clients. The better the designer understands the local culture, the greater the opportunity to develop a successful working relationship. Managing relationships can become particularly complicated. Different tools and strategies should be used depending upon the background, personality, and status of the expert.

Student model design. The student model starts with a representation of an average student. As the student begins to work with the system, the student model is altered to become an individualized record of each student's characteristics. In order to speed the process of generating the individualized student model, the initial representation can be modified to resemble the average student of that culture. In a culturally pluralistic society, an initial representation could be provided for each group.

One of the functions of the student model, as discussed earlier, is to keep the student activities in line with their long term educational goals. However, students in polychronic cultures may prefer to explore side issues during the session. For such cultures, the student model could allow flexibility in permitting such digressions from the stated goals.

The material culture is a useful indicator of the average student's level of technological sophistication. Students from a technologically advanced culture will have a greater background knowledge concerning information technology than students from cultures that are less technologically advanced.

The societal level of culture, particularly the legal system, may affect the construction of the student model. Privacy laws could be interpreted to apply to student models, as they represent information regarding citizens of the culture. The information maintained by the student model may be perceived as an invasion of individual privacy in certain societies.

The status systems of the interpersonal level of culture could affect the student modelling process. In a class-conscious culture, the student model may have to include a factor for the student's social status. This may be needed by the system to modify the teaching style to one that would be appropriate for a member of the student's class.

Bug catalog design. The effect of culture on the bug catalog is difficult to predict. While different cultures may give rise to different common errors, preliminary observation of the culture may not be very helpful in determining what form these errors will take. The systems approach suggested by the four-level cultural framework will be less effective than experience gained through actual use for compiling the bug catalog. To permit the bug catalog to expand over time as members of the culture work with the system, a record of tutoring sessions should be kept and periodically reviewed to identify common errors.

CONCLUSION

ITS technology is not a universal panacea; there are areas in which ITS cannot yet provide an effective answer to instructor shortages. ITS require relatively high initial start-up costs, time and effort. At present, a tutoring system must have a potential for extensive use to recoup the costs of development. A modular approach to ITS may reduce the start-up costs for subsequent ITS projects. Developers may be able to reuse the tutor module and some parts of the student model.

Because of the relative youth of ITS technology, there is a lack of standardization in the field, as well as a shortage of basic tools and experienced developers. However, within the last five years significant advances have been made in the fields of knowledge representation and multimedia communications. These technical advances open up great potential for developers of ITS tools. As research continues and ITS technology matures, a wider range of tools will be available to help in ITS design. For example, it may eventually be possible to detect a student's attributes through frame representations, and customize a multimedia training session tailored to the student's language, learning preference, and technical background.

Areas in which ITS can be effective share some basic characteristics which have been identified by Johnson (1988):

1) A high student to instructor ratio.
2) Real training equipment is expensive, unavailable, or unsafe.
3) Training must be conducted at remote sites.
4) Need for recurrent re-training exists.

These are characteristics which are shared by many applications within the area of global information technology education.

ITS, like all computer-based systems, require constant monitoring to determine if they are successful or if they require further development and refinement. A wide range of established evaluation methodologies exists for assessing the impact of educational programs, and such techniques could be applied to ITS. But once in place, a well-designed tutoring system may require less intervention than other types of computer-based educational platforms because of its flexibility.

The diverse needs of more students can be better met through the use of ITS than through other forms of CAI. One of the greatest strengths of ITS is their ability to offer individualized instruction to each student.   ITS owe their strength to the capacity to dynamically alter an approach to suit the learning style of cultural groups and individuals. Although providing this capability makes ITS more difficult to design, it also increases the overall effectiveness of the final product by providing flexibility. The intelligent tutoring system is particularly adept at handling situations involving socio-cultural plurality within the educational environment. Another advantage of ITS is their transportability. This advantage extends beyond the initial move from the home culture to the host culture. ITS are also better able, in comparison to human instructors, to change physical location within a geographic area, such as from the large cities to provincial towns, serving to promote regional growth and technology transfer across wide areas.

The future of ITS is fundamentally tied to ongoing developments in related fields of AI. As progress is made in natural language recognition and generation, the current limitations on using NLI will be removed. Advances in ES techniques, especially those concerning the representation of knowledge, will be especially useful in advancing ITS. Newer techniques such as frame-based reasoning and object-oriented approaches to knowledge may be applied to ITS to provide a more holistic approach towards representing the domain of knowledge which the student is attempting to master. This would permit the student to more freely explore the domain area, gaining a broader perspective and greater understanding.

Increasing use of artificial intelligence technologies in education is natural and inevitable. While philosophical and ethical debates may continue to surround the field of AI, practical applications of knowledge-based systems are already well advanced. Many of these applications involve the operation and maintenance of information systems. Such systems are especially suited for support provided through expert system technology. The same attributes of information technologies which make them amenable to expert system diagnosis also make them excellent candidates for ITS.

Corporations and educational institutions should join together in coordinated research and development efforts in this area. Currently, the development and application of ITS technology is limited. Individuals and organizations with special interests in technology education within less developed nations are unaware of the potential of ITS and related technologies and lack the equipment and trained personnel required to initiate ITS applications. There is already a substantial body of literature in cross-cultural learning theory (Brislin, Bochner, & Lonner, 1975), but this knowledge has yet to be applied to the design of computer aided instruction systems in polycultural settings. Methodologies for ITS application development and maintenance have lagged behind the development of ITS tools. Such challenges must be addressed before the great benefits promised by ITS in meeting the growing need for worldwide information technology education can be realized.

REFERENCES

Abrioux, D. (1991). Computer-assisted language learning at a distance: An international survey. *American Journal of Distance Education, 5*(1), 3-14.

Adler, N.J. (1983). Cross cultural management: Issues to be faced. International Studies of Management and Organization, 13(1-2), 7-45.

Anderson, J. R. (1988). The expert module. In M. C. Polson & J. J. Richardson (Eds.), *Foundations of intelligent tutoring systems.* (pp. 21-53). Hillsdale: Lawrence Erlbaum Associates Publishers.

Anderson, J. R., Boyle, C. F., & Reiser, B. J. (1985, April). Intelligent tutoring systems. *Science, 228,* 456-462.

Angelides, M. C. & Doukidis, G. I. (1990). Is there a place in OR for intelligent tutoring systems? *Journal of the Operational Research Society, 41*(6), 491-503.

Bently, T. (1991, April). Computer talk: Intelligent tutoring. *Management Accounting (UK), 69*(4), 14.

Brecht, B., & Jones, M. (1988). Student models: The genetic graph approach. *International Journal of Man-Machine Studies, 28,* 483-504.

Brislin, R. W., Bochner, S., & Lonner, W. J. (Eds.). (1975). *Cross-cultural perspectives on learning.* New York: John Wiley & Sons.

Broms, H., & Gahmberg, H. (1983). Communication to self in organizations and cultures. *Administrative Science Quarterly, 28,* 482-495.

Buss, M. D. J. (1984, May-June). Legislative threat to trans-border data flow. *Harvard Business Review,* 111-118.

Chandran, R., Phatak, A., & Sambharya, R. (1987, November-December). Transborder data flows: Implications for multinational corporations. *Business Horizons*, 74-82.

Chin, D. (1984). An Analysis of Scripts Generated in Writing Between Users and Computer Consultants. *Proceedings of the National Computer Conference, 53*, 637-642.

Contractor, F. J., Sagafi-Nejad, T. (1981, Fall). International technology transfer: Major issues and policy responses. *Journal of International Business Studies*, 113-135.

Elsom-Cook, M. (1990). Guided discovery tutoring. In M. Elsom-Cook (Ed.), *Guided discovery tutoring: A framework for ICAI research.* (pp. 3-23). London: Paul Chapman Publishing Ltd.

Grimaldi, A. (1986, Winter). Interpreting popular culture: The missing link between local labor and international management. *Colombia Journal of World Business*, 67-72.

Hagamen, W. D., & Gardy, M. (1986). The numeric representation of knowledge and logic - two artificial intelligence applications in medical education. *IBM Systems Journal, 25*(2), 207-235.

Halff, H. M. (1988). Curriculum and instruction in automated tutors. In M. C. Polson & J. J. Richardson (Eds.), *Foundations of intelligent tutoring systems* (pp. 79-108). Hillsdale: Lawrence Erlbaum Associates Publishers.

Hall, E. T. (1969). *The hidden dimension.* New York: Anchor-Doubleday and Company.

Hall, E. T. & Reed, M. (1989). *Understanding cultural differences.* Yarmouth: Intercultural Press.

Hayes-Roth, F. (1984, September). The knowledge-based expert system: A tutorial. *Computer*, pp. 11-28.

Herskovits, M. J. (1951). On cultural and psychological reality. In J. H. Rohrer & M. Sherif (Eds.), *Social psychology at the crossroads* (pp. 145-163). University of Oklahoma: Harper & Boflers.

Hofstede, G. (1980). *Culture's consequences: International differences in work-related values.* Beverly Hills: Sage Publications.

Johnson, W. B. (1988). Pragmatic considerations in research, development, and implementation of intelligent tutoring systems. In M. C. Polson & J. J. Richardson (Eds.), *Foundations of intelligent tutoring systems.* (pp. 191-207). Hillsdale: Lawrence Erlbaum Associates Publishers.

Kedia, B. L., & Bhaghat, R. S. (1988). Cultural constraints on transfer of technology across nations: Implications for research in international and comparative management. *Academy of Management Review, 13*(4), 559-571.

Kirrane, P. R., & D. E. (1989, July). What artificial intelligence is doing for training. *Training: The Magazine of Human Resources Development, 26*, 37-43.

Miller, J. R. (1988). The role of human-computer interaction in intelligent tutoring systems. In M. C. Polson & J. J. Richardson (Eds.), *Foundations of Intelligent Tutoring Systems*. (pp. 143-189). Hillsdale: Lawrence Erlbaum Associates Publishers.

Norman, D. A. (1973). Memory, knowledge, and the answering of questions. In R. L. Solso (Ed.), *Contemporary Issues in Cognitive Psychology: The Loyola Symposium* (pp. 135-165). Washington, D.C.: V. H. Winston & Sons.

Rich, E. (1983). Users are individuals: Individualizing user models. *International Journal of Man-Machine Studies, 18*, 199-214.

Rushby, N. (1989, October). Training and education: ITS - a long way to go. *Personnel Management*, 125.

Sokolnicki, T. (1991). Towards knowledge-based tutors: A survey and appraisal of intelligent tutoring systems. *The Knowledge Engineering Review, 6*(2), 59-95.

VanLehn, K. (1988). Student modelling. In M. C. Polson & J. J. Richardson (Eds.), *Foundations of Intelligent Tutoring Systems* (pp. 55-78). Hillsdale: Lawrence Erlbaum Associates Publishers.

Yazdani, M. (1986). Intelligent tutoring systems survey. *Artificial Intelligence Review, 1*, 43-52.

Economics and Global Information Technology Education

15

J. Christopher Westland
University of Southern California

Information systems curricula have been criticized for failing to provide students with economic and control models consistent with those used for cost-benefit analysis in areas such as marketing, finance and accounting. In rebuttal it has been noted that the shortcoming is not in the curricula, rather that economic models to assign value to information and information technology do not exist in the discipline. Organizations thus face an ongoing challenge in assigning value to their information technology portfolio. This shortcoming is particularly disturbing in a global management setting. Multinational operations require more stringent accountability and control to overcome limitations imposed by distances, cultural disparity and language. The lack of an objective economic and control structure for information technology creates credibility problems in the classroom presentation of information technology management issues. Yet the complexity of information technology investments confounds attempts to directly apply traditional models from financial analysis in an information systems setting. What is needed is an economic language tailored for information technology assets, but consistent with traditional accounting frameworks. The current chapter explores the elements of such a language, and considers how these might be presented in a classroom setting. It describes the differences between tangible assets, around which traditional economic and control frameworks have been established, and information, and information processing assets which comprise information systems. It then shows how economic frameworks can be described and explored in the classroom via spreadsheet software. The last section discusses implications of this approach for the information systems curriculum, and extensions which are likely to be needed in the future.

THE GLOBALIZATION OF INFORMATION TECHNOLOGY AND ITS IMPACT ON THE FIRM: PROBLEMS IN CURRICULA AND PEDAGOGICAL SOLUTIONS FOR THE 1990'S

In a recent report on Andersen Consulting's CEO-CFO study for *Computerworld,* Maglitta [1991] observed that "the question that everyone is asking themselves is: 'Are we getting the value for our IS investment?' Nobody can really tell us." The study underscores concern over information systems' failure to deliver on promises of competitive advantages, efficiency and reduction of personnel costs. Nor is this an insignificant failure. The U.S. may spend as much as $200 billion annually on software, up to $100 billion annually on hardware and perhaps $200 billion annually on the update and maintenance of data (Computer Science and Technology Board,1990; Westland [1990d]). Peter Keene [1991] estimates that over 50% of corporate capital expenditures are directed toward information technology, even during periods in which drastic expenditure cuts have occurred throughout other industries[1]. Management may have difficulty formally cost justifying investments in information technology because of the unique character of platforms and inadequacies in accounting for these resources. Yet the need for cost justification of these investments has never been more urgent. Business schools are challenged to provide a new "language" for expressing issues, problems and subject matter in information technology. The current chapter argues for a "language" derived from models from economics, accounting, control and financial analysis.

The need for a standard language, and the accompanying tools for analysis and decision making is exacerbated by the increased size and scope — i.e. the "globalization" — of information technology investments that are impelled by new developments in information technology.   For example, the radical improvements in telecommunications hardware and software, along with the dramatic reductions in price of that capability, are forcing business to shift rapidly away from decentralized "islands of technology" toward distributed computing on a global scale. Because competition in intermediate and end-product markets is increasingly global, due to the ever increasing opportunities for consolidation and economies of scale offered by technology, these networks must be considered on a global scale.   But differences in culture, business, language, and facilities around the globe obviate many of the ad hoc analysis tools which supported information technology investment decisions in an era when systems were centralized and conducted under strict standards. One of the most important moves afoot is outsourcing, where some of the computing facilities, and perhaps software and data as well, are placed under the management of an external firm.   Outsourcing decisions are not amenable to decision making using traditional tools of analysis (Caldwell [1990], Ward [1991]).

These trends in information technology determine the education required of future business graduates to remain competitive in the coming decades.   Thus information technology education needs to incorporate into curricula a "language" which is able to express the problems, issues and components of global information systems in a fashion which can be effectively communicated to management and end-users.

Preparing future business graduates to deal with the ongoing trends in information technology is one of the more daunting challenges facing business education. Dijkstra [1989] has criticized computing curricula for neglecting mathematics; and Parnas [1990] has criticized information technology for neglecting engineering.   Three other areas of neglect have been criticized in the business information systems curriculum: the neglect of economics, finance and accounting for information technology. To this date, most business courses in information technology have concentrated on describing the technology, and associated methodologies.   Although managerial strategy has been discussed, particularly with the objective of predicting the impact of technology, business IS curricula have not been particularly successful in developing useful strategy models for investments in information technology (Maglitta [1991]).

Other areas in business education face the same problems and requirements, although nowhere is the business environment changing as rapidly as it is in information systems. The solutions adopted by finance, operations management and marketing have centered on an "economic language" provided by accounting, and objectives often (but not always) stated in terms of profits. An economic language can communicate global operations and investments across cultures. Language constructs, methods of reporting, and methods of maintaining data are well defined, and have weathered many courtroom tests around the world. But such a language has yet to be developed for information technology for a variety of reasons which are discussed in this chapter. It is important to educate future managers who must make decisions involving information technology in a manner consistent with the education they receive in finance, marketing and other areas.

Development of a business language for information technology is also important in integrating business coursework — an issue which has become increasingly important in MBA programs in recent years. The failure of IS education to address and characterize the financial investment aspects of information technology has sometimes created credibility problems for IS faculty within the business curriculum as well as within the school. The underlying paradigm of business education is the cost accounting and control paradigm of accounting. In practice, this paradigm provides the budgetary and actual cost and performance numbers for any facet of a business. Programs and investments are required to justify themselves in the terminology of this paradigm. The failure of information systems instructors to state their case in the standard terminology of business schools makes it difficult to convince students of the worth of information technology course material (despite a strong job market in information systems), and creates problems in communicating and integrating IS curricula with other facets of undergraduate business or MBA curricula.

The current chapter explores the potential for developing a language for the problems, issues and components of information technology which can provide this consistency across disciplines. The exposition develops as follows. Current issues, controversies and problems in the economics and control language presented by educators today are discussed, and in the following section, solutions to existing problems are recommended. Subsequently, the chapter provides an example of the manner in which this solution could be presented in class using spreadsheet software, and after that discusses future trends, and summarizes the approach suggested in the chapter.

ISSUES, CONTROVERSIES AND PROBLEMS IN CONVEYING INFORMATION TECHNOLOGY CONCEPTS IN THE CLASSROOM

The History and Current Exposition of Topics in Information Technology

Prior to prescribing new models for describing the problems, issues and components of information technology, it is worthwhile to review their current exposition in business curricula. A review of introductory textbooks in information systems, systems development, databases, telecommunications and other areas typically presented in the business curriculum reveals course content largely focused on describing available information technology, and the manner in which that technology is used in the business world. Normative models do not seem to exist, and this makes it difficult to answer student questions concerning decision making. Typical questions which are difficult to address given the content of current IS curricula are "How much is an information system worth?" "Should the current payroll system be replaced?" "Should our firm buy the more expensive packaged software?" Questions such as these arise whenever corporate management must make a strategic investment in information technology.

Contrast this situation with accounting, finance and marketing, where normative models abound. Accounting education is for the most part normative, prescribing how generally accepted accounting principles should be applied. In comparison, information technology classes may seem ad hoc and anecdotal.

A general economic and control model for information technology resources could be used for financial analyses associated with capital and discretionary budgeting. Development of such a model has become increasingly important as the scope of information technology investments has grown from domestic islands of automation, whose planning and acquisition are largely ad hoc, to global information networks which require sophisticated central planning, customization and procurement. Existing models seem to be inadequate in addressing the special problems of information technology platforms[2].

The lack of such models in information systems curricula arises from our uncertainty about the exact nature of information technology products. Contrast this with the products typically addressed in marketing and operations research courses — tangible products with comparatively large quantities of direct material and labor, and small amounts of R&D, selling and other indirect costs. Even finance, which deals with securities which exhibit both value and risk, seems to have a more easily definable product than does information technology. Software, one of the main information technology products, exhibits both value and risk, but its costs are almost entirely R&D and other indirect costs. Thus the first copy of a software product may cost millions of dollars; the second, third and so forth copies may have close to zero marginal cost. The problem of providing a language for information technology products is not only more difficult, but these problems are more difficult to communicate in the classroom. What is required is an extension of traditional accounting based business languages to allow a more flexible definition of the characteristics of information technology products such as software and data. Statistics indicate that expenditures on software and data are perhaps four to five times that on hardware, and thus it is these problematic areas that require our attention.

Accounting and the Description of Information Technology Assets

One of the best ways to broach the shortcomings of traditional accounting and financial analysis models in addressing information technology assets is by tracing the origins of accounting based business languages. Traditional accounting systems were designed to track property rights and rents that were radically different from those associated with today's information property.   These systems are rooted in the theory of accounting put forth by Fra Luca Pacioli (Fra=*fratello* or brother) a 15th-century Franciscan friar.   Pacioli was a mathematics professor at various Italian universities, and was a friend of popes, princes and artists, including Leonardo da Vinci, who drew the 'proportions of man' as an illustration for one of Pacioli's books.   Pacioli in turn computed the proportions for many of Michelangelo's sculptures.   Pacioli did not invent the double entry system (by about 200 years) but popularized it.   His treatise on "Double Entry" was a chapter in *Summa de Arithmetica Geometria, Proportioni et Proportionalita.* The system was attractive because of its mathematical foundations.   Double-entry bookkeeping was designed to meet the needs of the fourteenth century Venetian merchant marine, where portable, high value units of inventory needed to be transferred from one place to another.   Double-entry found near universal adoption in later accounting systems because it offered reliable error control when transaction volumes were moderate, and where transaction records were retained indefinitely, e.g. in a General Journal or Special-purpose Journal.   Unfortunately, it was not designed to meet the needs of accounting for information technology products - such products were not economically important until quite recently.

It is interesting to note the impetus driving the adoption of Pacioli's new method of accounting — the development of a vast transportation network for commerce by the Venetian merchant marine.   The products involved were tangible, and in the possession of the merchants for only a short time before they were sold or delivered on consignment. The next great advance in business language was the extension to accounting promulgated by British and American accountants at the end of the 19th century to track the growth and operation of U.S. railroads. The railroads in the U.S. provided a vast transportation network consisting of "depreciable" assets e.g., rails, ties, cars, and so forth.   Because railroads had access to long, uninterrupted rights of way on land, they naturally expanded into distribution networks of oil pipelines, and communications networks of telegraphs, and later telephone networks.

Problems with Accounting as a Business Language for Global Information Technology Education

The business language that provides the backbone for today's college business curricula originated with the U.S. railroads. But the U.S. economy is outgrowing this business language — the number of generally accepted accounting principles have multiplied almost 20-fold over the past 20 years in attempting to adapt the "railroad" system to the needs of the latter half of the 20th century. The problem lies in the types of products that are important in the economy — 50% of new investment consists of information technology products. The end of the 20th century marks the advent of a new network for communication and transportation, and requires once again an extension of the business language to describe the products delivered through these new networks. The logical place to present these extensions to business language is in the classroom.

There are other problems in "railroad" accounting of which students need to be aware. In particular, "railroad" accounting focuses only on the supply side of investments, because of an accounting principle called the Historical Cost Principle. The Historical Cost principle requires that assets be recorded at the historical cost charged in the arms-length transaction(s) that purchased it. The demand for the asset is ignored until a sale is made via another arms-length transaction. This was fine for the sorts of goods handled by the Venetian merchant marine - portable, excludable, rival and having (demand) value commensurate with the number of units owned (e.g. two barrels of wine are twice as good as one). But the pressing questions in business today concern the demand for information technology assets — e.g., "how much is this software worth?", "which programming language is better?" and so forth. These are also typically questions asked by students in the classroom, consistent with questions asked in finance, accounting, marketing and operations research classes.

Information technology, ideas and other complex products are different from the tangible assets of Pacioli's accounting, or "railroad" accounting in several ways. Defining how information technology assets differ from tangible assets is the first step in presenting students with a new business language suitable for a corporate world in which 50% of new investments represent information technology assets. Information technology assets tend to be distinguished by very large initial investments of time, effort and capital, and virtually free and unlimited use after initial acquisition. They are partially rival, i.e. consumption of a unit by an end-user affects the utility to other end-users through the network or congestion externality. They are also nonexcludable—one end user cannot exclude another end user from receiving the benefits of using a particular resource. This is considerably different from use of a tangible private good such as a unit of inventory. Inventory is both rival - consumption of a unit by the end-users denies any other end user of utility from that unit; and it is excludable - one end user can exclude another end user from receiving the benefits from a particular unit of the resource (see Olson [1965] for an extensive discussion). Traditional accounting systems misrepresent economic issues such as the demand (value) for rival and nonexcludable assets such as information technology platforms.

Conceptual Problem Encountered by Students Studying the Globalization of Information Technology

The Economics of Sharing and Information Technology Platforms

Information technology is typically acquired through investment in platforms, and annual expenditures are often locked in far in advance by these platform investments. An information technology platform is an information technology asset or resource that is shared by other information technology assets. The term platform has entered our vernacular as a result of standardization across vendors, industries, firms and individuals. The discussion of platforms has also become standard in introductory business IS curricula, and is an important part of systems development course work. Accounting for information technology resources or platforms is much more complex than traditional accounting because of the complex and developing state of property rights associated with these platforms.

Externalities

Information technology assets (platforms) are distinguished from those traditionally studied in the business curriculum by the importance of externalities. The value experienced from individual usage of an information technology resource will be affected by externalities arising from shared usage by the other end-users. An externality is a consequence of activity not fully accounted for in the price and market system. For example, cigar smokers polluting the air in a public building contribute a diseconomy as an externality (byproduct) of their consumption (purchase) of cigarettes. In the case of computer technology, individuals make personal decisions about how much of a computer resource to use; but the usage of other individuals, and the sharing of platforms affects these individual decisions through, for example, longer waiting times. Externalities reflect activities not fully accounted for in the individual decision making.

These externalities affect the perceived performance of the information technology resource, and thus alter its value on the demand side. For example, a sales accounting system receives value from the CPU platform as well as the operating system platform. Traditionally, the cost of this sharing, if information technology is accounted for at all, is accounted for through (full absorption) cost allocations - i.e. supply-side valuations. Cost allocations ignore congestion and network externalities, and thus may misrepresent the actual value that the user will receive from sharing a platform.

Congestion externalities reflect the nuisance caused by contention for shared resources - data channels and storage in business systems, or CPU cycles in real-time and scientific systems. The quality of computing services degrades as usage increases, e.g. through slower response times, higher failure rates and so forth, and this degradation is economically characterized as a congestion externality. These often result from queuing (i.e., lining up while waiting to be served by a platform).

Network externalities increase the value of hardware, software or databases as more users share them. Hardware and software become more valuable with greater use because there is more sharing of information about how to use, or how not to abuse, them. Databases become more valuable with greater use because there is more sharing of information about what is contained on the database, levels of data accuracy, and so forth. This sharing may be casual and verbal, may be facilitated by formal or informal user groups or may be formally documented in user manuals and reference guides. Databases, networks and other communications services increase in value through greater use, because they provide vehicles for larger groups of users to exchange and collectively retain information. There also may be better *de facto* support for heavily used software and databases by management, because of the unfavorable political consequences of disappointing large groups of end users.

Information Technology Property Rights

IS curricula are incomplete in their presentation of the characteristics of information technology; they seem to be silent on the legal aspects of information technology assets.   This reflects shortcomings in the law regarding information technology assets. Yet discussion of property rights and law regarding intellectual property, software, R&D and privacy are important if future business leaders are to be able to effectively assess their investments in information technology assets.   Traditional accounting for assets is predicated on the legal property rights associated with tangible commodities. The oldest and most developed laws are real estate laws.   In the U.S., product inventory generally comes under the jurisdiction of the Uniform Commercial Code. But important input factors for information systems - specifically those associated with data and software - receive little protection from the law. These must therefore be protected through secrecy, complexity, fast response, and fast obsolescence of data or software.   Business students must be aware of the changes in business structure associated with information intensive products which result from the inability of current law, both in the U.S. and abroad, to protect the property rights associated with information technology assets.

The characteristics of information property rights are difficult to convey in the classroom.   This is a reflection of the confusion surrounding information property rights in the legal and business communities. The globalization of the information technology industry has created its own complications because different nations interpret property rights differently — what is grey market in one country may be perfectly acceptable in another.   Yet the legal status of the information assets and activities are fundamental to any study of IS, and this must predicate the presentation of other topics in the classroom. Software and data property rights are still in the process of development. Software can be copyrighted, and the extent of protection is currently being tested by major information technology vendors such as Microsoft, Apple and Intel.   Data property rights are the subject of much current controversy due to recently enacted privacy laws in Europe and the U.S. — e.g., Prodigy (Sears / IBM) has come under criticism concerning the ownership and "rights" to privacy over user files on their system.

Telecommunications has emerged as an important topic in the classroom with the proliferation of options such as local area networks. The availability of cost-effective telecommunications alternatives has contributed greatly to globalization of information systems. Yet confusion surrounds property rights here as well. Laws concerning communications networks have changed dramatically since the deregulation of telecommunications carriers. New technology is integrating telecommunications and computing more closely than ever before, blurring the demarcation between them. Further complicating issues is the problem of the human interface. People cannot be owned, rather employment contracts provide schedules of rights. The acquisition and retention of "expertise" is a critical factor in software factories and other attempts to apply modern production techniques to the development, design and implementation of software. Property rights can evolve solely from prior investment in people (or expertise as this is called in software factories), and from investment in a network of interrelated technologies.

The ownership of "ideas," the stock and trade of the information technology industry, has become particularly contentious. Apple's recent lawsuit over the "look and feel" of their operating systems interface is perhaps the most visible example of the software industry's desire to protect property rights associated with ideas. Yet critics complain that creativity (and competitiveness) will be squelched if ideas can be effectively protected. Further muddying this issue is the lucrative "black" or "gray market" for software "clones" supplied by firms in many less developed (and controlled) economies. It is sometimes argued that this piracy oils the wheels of an over-regulated or tightly controlled market, which would otherwise be inefficient and protectionist. These markets undermine the legitimacy of established property rights, and generate serious long term inefficiencies. Issues such as these raise important insights in the classroom; they are issues which students should begin thinking about prior to accepting employment.

The complexity of property rights for information technology resource, and the possibilities for use of information in new and unforeseen ways has raised provocative questions concerning economic questions of value and cost. The majority of people in the developed world now earn their livings by dealing in ideas. But as management faces the problems of ordering the flow of ideas, they find that ideas are so different from the physical objects governed by most management approaches that the phrase " intellectual property" seems almost a contradiction in terms.   Stealing a car means that the thief has something which the owner does not: namely, the car. "Stealing" an idea means that the "thief" and the "owner" both have exactly the same thought. There already exist legal precedents which judge that ideas cannot in fact be stolen.   Examples can provide interesting discussions in the classroom. For example, one of the unusual consequences of confusion associated with information property rights is reflected in the manner in which the U.S. and other nations levy customs duties on software entering the U.S. The amount of the duty is proportional to the area of the medium on which the software resides.   Thus the same duty would be levied on one line of program code as on 100,000 lines of program code if both resided on, say, a 5.25 inch floppy disk, containing about 20 square inches of recording medium.

A Classroom Framework for Global Information Technology Education

An economic framework for global education in information technology starts with the definition of market structures which have arisen to acquire or produce information technology and its critical components - hardware, software, communications networks, data, ideas and people. The classroom framework should then define the activities associated with each of these components. Activities provide the opportunity for economic agents (1) to acquire or produce goods and services using systems of these components; (2) to acquire and protect property, quasi-property, or contractual "rights" ("property rights" for brevity) associated with information systems comprised of these components; and, (3) to extract "rents" from customers, creditors and third parties for receiving value (because of use, etc.) from information systems.   These activities provide the focus for decision models based on value and cost (Porter and Millar [1985]).

Once activities are defined, concepts of value and cost may then be presented to students. Since value and cost are necessary components of most of the models presented in the business curriculum, these provide links to global education in finance, accounting, marketing and so forth. In business, property, contractual rights, rents and so forth are typically projected onto a pricing, or valuation system via accounting systems or through financial analysis. Decision making requires a level of structure not currently offered by generally accepted accounting principles, which must reconcile the differing economic lives, and acquisition points, for hardware, telecommunications networks, software, data and people. Property rights and rents are typically addressed by depicting information technology as sets of shared platforms. A scientific workstation might serve as a platform for a Unix operating system. The Unix operating system, in turn, may serve as a platform for a database management system. The database management system may in turn serve as a platform for an accounting system that maintains data on customers. The accounting system may in turn be a platform for ad hoc reporting or query systems needed by the end-user. The distinctive feature of this framework is that each platform is acquired as a package at a point in time, information technology has a certain useful life (economic, technological, etc.), and when retired will be replaced by some other information technology platform.

Where the same computing requirements are experienced by many firms, there exists the opportunity to develop a platform that is industry-wide, or indeed global. Many platforms, e.g. Unix and C at AT&T, began with internal corporate projects to satisfy corporate needs. The research and development costs of complex technologies can then be shared by many firms if they can be sold as global platforms. The rise to dominance of systems integration as an IS support and consulting function largely reflects the proliferation of platforms. Firms find that they may be able to realize 80-90% of the functionality that they desire from a widely-used package with a low unit cost. They can garner the remaining 10-20% of the functions that they need from value added resellers (VARs) and systems integrators.

Platforms and Rents

Rents in the computer industry are often not obtained directly, rather they are predicated on a platform which is made cheaply and easily available (essentially a loss-leader), and then are extracted from add-ons which are highly profitable to the vendors. For example, many RISC workstation makers have virtually given away their base configuration of hardware; rents are collected through the subsequent sale of hardware peripherals (disk subsystems are a staple of storage hungry Unix), and software (which tend to be much more expensive on workstations than their microcomputer counterparts). Similarly, Microsoft and Apple virtually give away their operating systems and graphic interfaces; they are able to extract rents through greater market share for applications (e.g. Excel, Word) which use a preemptive knowledge of the operating system under which everyone in the market operates. The rent-seeking process has become both complex and interesting.

Economies of scale are highly pronounced in the extraction of rents from investments in information technology. They are also difficult to characterize. Both producers and users of information technology are forced to consider economies of scale in order to cost justify applications of information technology. There is strong motivation for participation in global markets.

The subsequent section presents a language for addressing these issues in connection with information technology. Such a framework is a natural extension of current economic paradigms which allow managers to review far-flung investments in traditional assets. The framework provides a language and a basis for both strategic and control problems faced by the manager. It allows the educator to effectively describe the behavior of idea- or design-intensive assets which dominate global markets in the 1990's.

Conveying Concepts in the Classroom: Recommendations for an Economic Language for Information Technology

This section presents an educational language for economics and control of information technology investments. Such a framework should be very useful to educators attempting to present information systems ideas to individuals whose prior background has primarily been in other areas of business. It provides a vehicle in which to express the components of decision models for information technology investment and operation.

Management faces two problems—a strategic problem of how much to invest in information technology, given a projected or targeted level of operations; and a control problem of how to encourage the individual users of information technology to use the amount of information technology services that is best for the firm. Decision models for both must be presented in the business educational curriculum. In the strategic, or long-run problem, management must *a priori* target or estimate specific usage levels for the information technology, and then determine an adequate investment in information technology to meet users' needs. In the control, or short-run problem, management must a priori purchase the information technology, and then determine how to motivate individual end-users to use this in a fashion which best achieves corporate goals. Representations of operations in both problems must be generic, and translate effectively into the various modes of business existing in the global marketplace.

Classroom presentation of decision models may begin by characterizing an information technology platform, asset or resource. Three things characterize an information technology resource or platform: (1) its economic life, from acquisition to disposal, (2) its price-performance, and (3) the other information technology assets which share its services. These three things, in our current context, may be measured in terms of (1) time horizon for information technology investment decision making, (2) marginal cost vs. marginal value, and (3) externalities, respectively.

One of the most interesting aspects of information technology arises from the central role, and rapid pace, of research and development. Information technology resources tend not to wear out; rather they becomes technologically obsolete. For example, computer hardware becomes technologically obsolete when replacement computers have such improved price-performance that the cost of operating the old machine exceeds the cost of buying a new machine. This is one of the main reasons for downsizing—the life-cycle costs of operation of LANs and standalone microcomputers for many applications (usually with smaller databases) is much lower than for the same application system operating on a mainframe (Scheier [1990], Caldwell [1990]).

Economic Life of Information Technology Assets

The economic life of several information technology resources used simultaneously in a firm's IS installation might be graphically represented on a time line as shown in Figure 1.

Hardware typically has an economic life of around three to seven years; software from around five to twenty years. Of all information technology assets, databases and files have the longest economic lives, sometimes approaching twenty to thirty years. Note that in accounting for economic life of databases, the databases themselves should be distinguished from the information residing on the databases, which can have either a shorter or longer useful life. For example, a publisher's database of classical literature could hold economically useful information which is centuries or millennia old; at the other extreme, stock market bids and asks may be economically useful for less than a second. The organization of data adopted by a firm (i.e. the database) tends to persist, and have a long useful life; the data itself may not. Typically, the time between archives of a database[3] is related to the useful life of data.

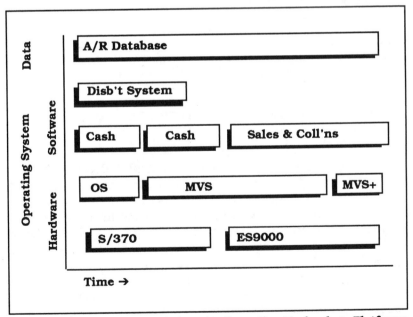

Figure 1: Economic Lives of Shared Information Technology Platforms

Performance Metric	Type and Characteristics	Related Usage Metric
Hardware MIPS,MFLOPS, etc.	Technical Metric	Number of Machine Instructions Processed
TPS A & B, SPEC Marks, etc.	Synthetic Workload	Number of Transaction Processed
Firm Specific Benchmarks	Natural Workloads	Amount of Work Completed
Software GOTO Count	Structuredness of Code	
Databases Precision & Recall	Amount of Useless Data Retrieved	
Type I & Type II Error (Neyman-Pearson)	Amount of Useless Data Retrieved	
Westland [1989] Net Benefit Measure	End User Value	

Table 1: Performance Metrics for Information Technology Assets with Related Usage Measures

Performance and Value of Information Technology Assets

Performance measurement is central to determining the value and demand for information technology assets. Because information technology usually reaches the end of its economic life prior to wearing out, the various accounting measures currently used to determine value—historical cost, net book value, fair market value or replacement costs value—provide misleading indicators of the revenue generating capability of information systems assets. Metrics generate a great deal of controversy in practice, since information technology products succeed or fail depending on the performance metrics used to

evaluate them. Students can be made aware of these measurement problems by surveying the available metrics, and discussing merits and problems of each. New metrics[4] are required for
information technology assets; over time these are being devised,
albeit in an ad hoc fashion. Table 1 provides a brief summary
of performance metrics for hardware, software, and databases.

Hardware performance metrics have evolved substantially with the proliferation of desktop computers. Hardware
performance has evolved from simplistic MIPS and MFLOPS
measures, to value oriented synthetic workload measures such
as TPS A and B, SPECMarks and so forth (Westland [1992a]).
Software performance metrics have similarly evolved over the
past 30 years, from simple nesting and GOTO counts, through
structuredness and complexity metrics, function and feature
points, defect and reliability measures, finally to business directed value measures. (Westland [1991c] ; Rubin [1991]). Data
storage performance metrics are less well developed, but in
general measure the quality of data indexing, and efficiency of
storage and retrieval. Information science measures of precision
and recall have traditionally been invoked to measure the value
of a given data organization, although these have been widely
criticized. Westland [1989] provided alternative metrics which
addressed the net value of a given storage organization.

Markets for Information Technology Assets: Information Technology's Counterparts to Markets Studied in Finance and Marketing Curricula

Decision models used in the business curriculum typically treat production decisions separately from marketing decisions. The theoretical foundations for this separation are found
in the work of Irving Fisher [1930]. Value based performance
measures provide a basis for the demand side of the analysis;
price charged by the vendor of the information technology
reflects the supply side of the analysis as shown in figure 2.

For practical application, it is possible to interpret demand and supply metrics in Figure 2 as follows: Demand=marginal
revenues=marginal cash inflows + marginal externalities; and
Supply=marginal costs=marginal cash outflows.

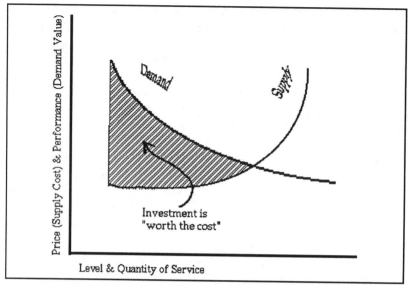

Figure 2: Price-Performance for Information Technology

A Framework for Presenting Decision Models in Business Education

Decision models used in the classroom assume some objective. The economic models described to this point provide management (who have purchasing authority) with a measure of the net benefits to their firm or operations provided by a particular investment. This investment may involve the purchase of hardware, software or data from an outside vendor, or development and implementation costs of software, and so forth incurred internally, since information technology resources may be "made," "leased" or "purchased" (Scheier [1990] and Caldwell [1990] provide examples of these Options).

Monetary objectives, such as profit, are the easiest for students to understand and assimilate into their overall business education. Business curricula emphasize profitability extensively, and profit is central to most financial analysis. A monetary basis for evaluation and control of global information technology investments has several desirable characteristics. First, the primary and most easily quantifiable goal of management is profit maximization, thus a monetary based accounting system justifies information technology investments to management in a way consistent with widely understood goals and

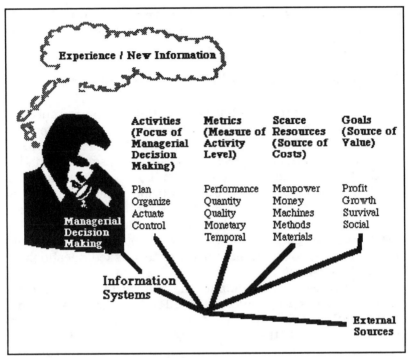

Figure 3: A Classroom Model for Describing Strategic and Control Decisions Concerning Information Technology Investments

agendas.   Second, profit maximization is important to other stakeholders in the firm, such as bond and stockholders, who may evaluate the firm only from a monetary perspective. Third, among all decentralized control mechanisms, price mechanisms are the most informationally efficient—they minimize the amount of information which must be exchanged between users (Hurwicz [1977], Walker [1977] and Osana [1978]), and they allow reliable decision making in the face of uncertain and incomplete information and uncertain task processing (Malone [1988]; Malone and Smith [1988]).

Figure 3 provides a useful classroom aid for visualizing the objectives and components of a decision model; this provides a framework around which the student may organize issues in information technology.

The information technology is used in systems which provide a feedback loop to keep the manager informed of events and the manner in which they influence outcomes and attainment of corporate goals. Thus figure 3 provides students with a schematic for the value-producing aspects of information technology.

Traditional Decision Models for Investment

Business programs have traditionally measured success of investments by one of three approaches— (1) Payback period (PB), (2) Internal Rate of Return (IRR), and (3) Net Present value (NPV). The formulas for each of these are discussed in the standard accounting and finance textbooks. Their specific application is important, since they provide explicit rankings of investments in terms of what is "better" or "worse." And questions concerning how one chooses the right technology investment, whether one technology is better or worse than another, and so forth are perhaps the most asked questions in college classrooms.

All three metrics simplify the real world, and this may contribute errors. In practice, NPV, IRR and PB approaches are used to rank investments in IS resources from most desirable to least desirable, until the capital budget is exhausted. Rankings, unfortunately, discard significant portions of the information collected for decision making. Their application is also complicated by factors such as costs, returns to scale, and intertemporal preferences. The NPV, IRR and PB approaches do not recognize the discretionary budget constraint (i.e. avoidable costs); instead they include acquisition and ongoing operating costs in decision making in an ad hoc manner.

Both PB and IRR ignore the magnitude of investment, which makes it difficult to determine the organizational impact of projects chosen with either approach. NPV provides a more complete metric for evaluation of projects, but requires a prediction of future discount (interest or cost of capital) rates, which is difficult if not impossible to do accurately. PB is often used because information technology requires the least amount of information input (i.e. future discount rates, and cash flows after the PB period can all be ignored).

PB period is the time that information technology takes for cash flows from customer demand to recover the initial investment in information technology resources. It ignores the time value of money (discount rate) and cash flows after payback, and strongly favors the short-run. The PB approach is the most popular ranking approach in practice, both because it is easy to compute, and because it emphasizes the speed with which the investment can be recuperated.

Shortcomings of Traditional Models for Evaluating Investments in Information Technology Assets: The Two-Part Tariff in Global Information Technology Education

All three traditional approaches are based on estimates of future cash flows. Outflows (from the firm, department, etc.) will be future out-of-pocket and sunk costs. Accrual accounting constructs such as depreciation should be ignored, since these provide alternatives to prediction of future cash flows specific to financial statements. In effective decision making with financial models, virtually all choice decisions are construed in terms of marginal costs and revenues - or in this analysis, marginal cash flows resulting from a given information technology investment. Accountants implicitly recommend the same approach, but couch this in terms of relevant costs and opportunity costs. Marginal cash flows usually are not explicitly available, but must be inferred or predicted.

Because congestion and network externalities affect the perceived value of information technology, the price at which an information technology resource is offered will influence its success in the market. Network externalities are especially important when information technologies are implemented on a global scale. Management typically tries to take advantage of network externalities through two-part tariffs.

A useful classroom example of a two-part tariff is found in the marketing strategy of King C. Gillette, inventor of the safety razor. In order to maximize the usage of his safety razor, he almost gave away the razor itself. His profits were made selling the disposable blades. Two-part tariff pricing strategies first lock the consumer into a given technology; then make a profit for the manufacturer with added usage. Two-part tariffs exert themselves naturally in information technology platforms because of the tight coupling between computer hardware, software and databases. With products in which the marginal cost of the first unit of output may be hundreds of millions of dollars, and subsequent units cost virtually nothing, two-part tariffs are needed for financial viability in the marketplace. Consider the production of computer software, where the hardware purchase represents the membership fee, and incremental software and database purchases provide the ongoing benefits of ownership of the information technology. An information technology strategy which has received recent attention has been the games of Nintendo, where an expensive hardware is almost given away, while inexpensive software is sold at almost the cost of the hardware. Classroom discussion of popular technology such as Nintendo games will tend to provoke interest in abstract concepts such as two-part tariffs and network externalities.

A CLASSROOM EXAMPLE DEMONSTRATING THE ECONOMICS OF SHARED INFORMATION TECHNOLOGY PLATFORMS

To this point, the chapter has presented components of decision models which are relevant to the global investment in information technology. These must find their way into the business curriculum, both in IS and in the functional areas such as finance and marketing, if students are to be adequately prepared to be effective managers. To be convincing, though, classroom presentation cannot simply terminate with a presentation of issues and components of an economic model of information technology investments. It must integrate these in a classroom example. The current section provides such an integrative example.

The ultimate value of management's portfolio of information technology platforms is realized through the firm's ability to support end user tasks through its application systems, which are in turn predicated on the performance of platforms required to keep them running. This section shows how various information technology resources may be accounted for in a spreadsheet format for a simple investment analysis of application software running on a hardware platform. Both formal and *ad hoc* analyses examine how the chapter's framework may be used to tackle various standard financial analyses required of business graduates.

Consider an example where the hardware congestion cost arises because tasks for the information system to perform have to queue up behind each other in a single line, and wait for the machine to complete them[5.]   A typical graph of the level of congestion $f(y)$ with respect to usage y of the information system appears in figure 4.

Similarly, the software network benefit g(z) at activity level z appears in figure 5. This is a benefit (versus a cost) of using software—the more information technology is used, the more benefit information technology provides.

The current example makes the assumption that y and z are commensurate, and either can provide a basis for performance or usage level of the system.   Assume that the total operating cost of this system includes not only the congestion

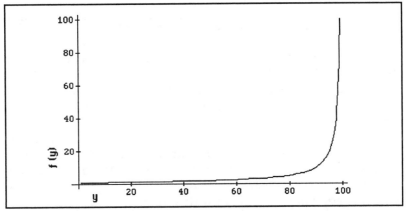

Figure 4: Hardware Congestion Externality $f(y \mid 100)$

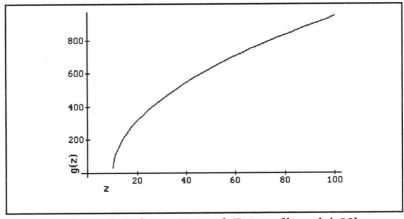

Figure 5: Software Network Externality $g(z \mid 10)$

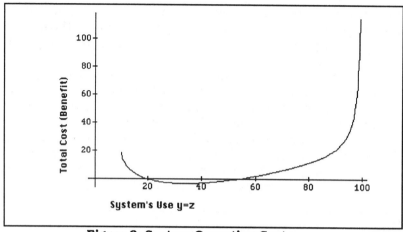

Figure 6: System Operating Costs

and network externalities, but also the fixed cost of running the system, e.g. air conditioning, rent on space, and so forth, set here to 10; and the variable cost, e.g. power consumption, maintenance and down time, set here to the level of usage y=z. The total cost of operations appears in figure 6.

Figures 4, 5 and 6 can provide students with insight into the mechanisms behind a cost analysis of an information system. In practice, the analysis would need to consider the timing of cash flows - this is best carried out via a spreadsheet. Because students are typically familiar with spreadsheet processing, this will provide a less threatening framework in which to organize the complexities of information technology financial analysis. An example of the same information presented in spreadsheet format (Microsoft Excel in this example) appears in figure 7, with and without formulas.

This gives only the simplest example of a financial analysis of information technology investments. Practical applications would require that each metric; e.g. MIPS for a CPU platform, database accesses for a DBMS platform, and so forth; on which a platform in the firm's portfolio of information technology investments was evaluated would appear on a line such as the usage line above. Then the demand (value plus externalities) and supply (factor fixed and marginal costs) cash flows would appear as functions of these usage levels.

Other extensions are also possible. The educator may address issues of global competitiveness through network ben-

	A	B	C	D	E	F	G	H	I	J	K	L
					Financial Analysis of IT Invest							
1	*Projections*	Jan-92	Feb-92	Mar-92	Apr-92	May-92	Jun-92	Jul-92	Aug-92	Sep-92	Oct-92	Nov-
2												
3	*Yield:*	10%										
4	Usage	0	0	17	86	43	79	40	67	55	3	
5												
6	*Demand:*											
7	Hardware (Congestion)	1	1	19	93	45	83	42	70	57	4	
8	Software (Network)	0	0	-74	-758	-331	-686	-299	-568	-452	0	-1
9												
10	*Supply:*											
11	Hardware (Cost)	10	10	10	10	10	10	10	10	10	10	
12	Software (Cost)	5	7	10	10	10	10	10	10	10	10	
13												
14	*Analysis:*											
15	Net Value	-16	-18	35	645	266	583	238	478	375	-24	1
16	Net Present Value	1920	2130	2308	1893	1816	1416	1319	973	695	789	7
17	(future value flows)											

Figure 7a: Spreadsheet Based Financial Analysis of Information Technology (values)

	A	B	C	D
			Financial Analysis of IT Invest	
1	*Projections*	32142	=B1+31	=C1+31
2				
3	*Yield:*	0.1		
4	Usage	0	0	=RAND()*100
5				
6	*Demand:*			
7	Hardware (Congestion)	=B4+1/(1-B4/100)	=C4+1/(1-C4/100)	=D4+1/(1-D4
8	Software (Network)	=-IF(10*(B4-10)<0,0,10*(B4-10))	=-IF(10*(C4-10)<0,0,10*(C4-10))	=-IF(10*(D4
9				
10	*Supply:*			
11	Hardware (Cost)	10	10	10
12	Software (Cost)	5	7	10
13				
14	*Analysis:*			
15	Net Value	=-SUM(B7:B12)	=-SUM(C7:C12)	=-SUM(D7:D1
16	Net Present Value	=NPV(0.1,C15:Q15)	=NPV(0.1,D15:Q15)	=NPV(0.1,E15
17	(future value flows)			

Figure 7b: Spreadsheet Based Financial Analysis of Information Technology (formulas)

efits. As information technology becomes more complex to use and build, larger and larger networks of users are required to justify its costs. This will tend to cause component parts of a system to be produced in widely dispersed locations. Computers and databases might be located in Europe, software developed in India, users located in the U.S. and telecommunications leased from an international carrier. The financial analysis of information technology investments in this situation must take into account currency fluctuations over perhaps several years, as well as interest rates and preference for present returns. Although accounting procedures exist for directing currency translations, the direct derivation of supply and demand cash flows from usage metrics offers an opportunity to sidestep currency valuation problems. For complex scenarios, it is probably best to use currency translations for computing out-of-pocket expenses and investments in foreign countries, and direct estimation from usage metrics for value and externality calculations.

Future Trends in Business Curricula: Establishing a Central Role for Economic Models of Information Technology

The prior sections have outlined a number of components which must be incorporated into classroom decision models for accounting for information technology. Prediction and discussion of future trends is one of the best ways to motivate students to study and master an understanding of these components. This section explores several topics which should be a part of the classroom offering.

As commodities in the future become more intelligent, continuing the trend witnessed in automobiles and consumer electronics over the past 20 years, their markets will behave more as information technology markets than as the markets for traditional tangible commodities. Business graduates need to be prepared for these radical changes in markets, and thus the changed jobs they will be competing for in the 1990's. The employment market for business graduates is expected to change even more, due to a trend described by Peter Drucker. Drucker proposes that the typical corporate organization will evolve during the 1990's into a much flatter organization, with very efficient communication channels supported by information technology — the prototype he used is a symphony orchestra. This evolution will require that future managers have a better understanding of how these information channels work. That, in turn, is going to require that a much larger portion of the curriculum be devoted to issues of telecommunications and associated information technology. Many of the positions lost in this "flattening" of the organization will be those traditionally thought of as entry level positions for business graduates.

Existing curricula are lacking in their coverage of the relevant areas of telecommunications and information technology. A recent interview of leading educators in Laplante [1991] found that MBAs are graduating with a basic understanding of desktop applications, but lack knowledge of how to manage information technology, either as a functional manager, or as a manger in information systems. Some of this may be explained by the fact that MBA programs in IS lack the unifying economic framework for management and control which are central to other business disciplines.

There is also reason to believe that traditional lecture and exam approaches to college teaching are not the most appropriate ones for information technology. The "active" and "interactive" character of information technology makes its education less amenable to teaching through classroom lectures and reading textbooks. While these vehicles may provide general guidance, and a chance for the student to discuss philosophy, they cannot relay the character, implementation and implications of information technology. That requires something more akin to the "open classroom" (Kohl [1969]) which was so highly touted in the 1960s. This approach to teaching also seems more consistent with Drucker's vision of the flattened firm of the future.[6] Two problems arise in the open classroom approach - motivation and grading (monitoring). Students, when left to their own devices will tend to shirk, and systems must be designed to keep them from shirking without seeming too autocratic. Grading will require more individual attention and monitoring, perhaps aided by educational computer systems. A third problem arises concerning how the University can obtain tuition revenues without the traditional classroom-lecture setup. Some insight on this latter problem may be gained from current discussions concerning whether or not circulating libraries are obsolete in the information age.

The change in character of the predominate resources, away from tangible commodities toward information technology, presents business schools with daunting challenges. Addressing these challenges will require creativity, as well as a willingness to abandon or modify existing programs of instruction. The rewards to those schools which can effectively meet these challenges will be great. Thus few can afford to ignore the major restructuring that information technology is bringing about in the corpus of business.

ENDNOTES

[1] How significant are IT expenditures in the U.S. economy is open to debate, since no single agency tracks information technology investments, and accounting does not require the segregation of information technology expenditures on financial statements. A rough idea of the size and extent of information technology expenditures in the economy as a whole may be gleaned from U.S. government statistics. Annual expenditures (circa 1991) on information technology are around $150 million for hardware, $150 million for software and $200 million for data acquisition and maintenance. (1990, Computer Science and Technology Board, National Research Council, Keeping the US Computer Industry Competitive, Washington D.C.: National Academy Press). The U.S. gross national expenditure is around $5 trillion, composed of $1.2 trillion for nondurable goods $1.8 trillion for services and $1 trillion spent by Federal, State and Local governments.

[2] For example, prior research by Kaplan and Atkinson [1989], Vancil [1978], Benke and Edwards [1980], Cushing (1976), Cotton (1975), Jensen and Meckling [1976], Miller and Buckman [1987] and Zimmerman [1979] suggests that cost allocations and transfer prices are poorly specified in practice, a problem which becomes more pronounced when demand based externalities influence the usage of assets with large initial costs and low marginal costs.

[3] Data is archived when it is either purged or recorded to a low cost medium and stored off-site.

[4] A "unit of measure" like a "mile" is a metric for length or distance

[5] The M/M/1 queuing model provides a simple straightforward example of a commonly encountered congestion effect in computer hardware. It is used here for simplicity, but the insights provided are true for general queuing models. The appropriate queuing model and parameters would typically be determined through hardware benchmarking performed by a firm's technical staff.

[6] Drucker's analogy of the symphony orchestra suggests IT education might adopt some of the methods and trappings of music performance education - e.g. the "Suzuki" method might provide a useful prototype.

REFERENCES

Benke,R. and J. Edwards (1980) *Transfer pricing: techniques and uses.* New York, NY: National Association of Accountants.

Boehm, B.W. (1984) Software Engineering Economics, *IEEE Transactions on Software Engineering*, Volume SE-10, Number 1, January 1984.

Caldwell, B. (1990) The Outsourcing Circus, *Information Week*, March 12, 1990, pp. 40-46.

Computer Science and Technology Board (1990) National Research Council, *Keeping the US Computer Industry Competitive*, National Academy Press, Washington, D.C.

Cushing, B.E. (1976) Pricing internal computer services: The basic issues, *Management Accounting, v.57*(4), April, pp. 47-50.

Dijkstra, E.W. (1989) On the Cruelty of Really Teaching Computing Science, *Communications of the ACM*, December, 1398-1404.

Feller, W. (1966) *An Introduction to Probability Theory and Its Applications*, New York:Wiley

Fisher, I. (1930) *The Theory of Interest*, New York:Macmillan.

Hurwicz, L. (1977) On the dimensional requirements of informationally decentralized Pareto-satisfactory processes, in K.J.Arrow and L.Hurwicz, eds., *Studies in resource allocation processes.* Cambridge, UK : Cambridge University.

Institute for the Future (1986) *Electronic Information Services*, Report R-71, Park

Jensen, M.C. and W.H. Meckling (1976) Theory of the Firm, Managerial Behavior, Agency Costs and Ownership Structure, *Journal of Financial Economics*, October, pp. 305-60.

Kaplan, R.S. and A.A. Atkinson (1989) *Advanced management accounting.* 2nd ed. Englewood Cliffs, NJ: Prentice-Hall.

Karlin, S. and H.M. Taylor (1975) A First Course in Stochastic Processes (2nd ed.), New York:Academic Press.

Keene, P. G.W. (1991) *Shaping the Future: Business Design Through Information technology;* Boston:Harvard Business School Press.

Kohl, H.R. (1969) *The open classroom; a practical guide to a new way of teaching* New York:Random House.

Laplante, A. (1991) Making the Grade, *Infoworld*, February 11, 1991, 50-52.

Maglitta, J. (1991) It's Reality Time, *Computerworld*, April 29, 1991, 81-4.

Malone, T.W. (1988) Modeling Coordination in Organizations and Markets, *Management Science*, v. 33(10), 1317-32.

Malone, T.W. and Smith, S.A. (1988) Modeling the Performance of Organizational Structures, *Operations Research*, April-May, 1317-32.

Miller, B. and A.G. Buckman (1987) Cost Allocation and Opportunity Costs, *Management Science, v.33*(5), 626-639.

Olson, M. (1965) *The Logic of Collective Action*, Cambridge:Harvard University Press.

Osana, H. (1978) On the informational size of message spaces for resource allocation processes, *Journal of Economic Theory, v.17*: 66-78.

Parnas, E.L. (1990) Education for Computeing Professionals, *Computer*, January, 17-22.

Porter, M.E. and V. E. Millar (1985) How Information Gives You Competitive Advantage, *Harvard Business Review, v. 57* (March-April), 149-160.

Rubin, H. (1991) "Measure for Measure" *Computerworld*, April 15, 1991, 77-79.

Scheier, R.L. (1990) Kodak Unit Overhauls IS and the Business Process, *PC Week*, April 1990, p. 127.

Swanson, E.B. (1988) *Information System Implementation*, Homewood, IL:Irwin, 58-73.

Vancil, R.F. (1978) *Decentralization: Managerial Ambiguity by Design*, Homewood, IL:Dow Jones-Irwin

Varian, H. (1984) *Microeconomics* (2nd ed.), New York:Norton

Walker, M. (1977) On the information size of message spaces, *Journal of Economic Theory, v.15*: 366-375.

Ward, B. (1991) Hiring Out, *Delta Sky, v. 20*(8), 36-45

Westland, J.C. (1989) A Net Benefits Approach to Measuring Retrieval Performance, *Information Processing and Management*, October 1989, v.25(5), 579-581

Westland, J.C. (1990a) Topic Specific Monopolies in the Information Services Industry: Evidence from the DIALOG Group of Databases, *The Information Society, v. 6*, 127-138

Westland, J.C. (1990b) Scaling Up Output Capacity and Performance Results from Information Systems Prototypes, *ACM Transactions on Database Systems*, September, 341-358

Westland, J.C. (1990c) Assessing the Economic Benefits of Information Systems Auditing, *Information Systems Research, v.1*(3), 309-324

Westland, J.C. (1990d) Competing in the World's Computer Market, *Scientific American*, November, 152

Westland, J.C. (1991a) Economic Constraints in Hypertext, *Journal of the American Society of Information Science*, February, 178-184

Westland, J.C. (1992a) Problem Vectorizability and the Market for Vector Supercomputing, *Information Processing and Management, v. 27*(5), 499-515

Westland, J.C. (1992b) Network and Congestion Externalities in the Short Run Pricing of Shared Computing Services, *Management Science*, in press

Zimmerman, J. (1979) The costs and benefits of cost allocations, *The Accounting Review.* (July): 504-521.

Section VI

Research Issues in International IT Education

Designing Research Education in Information Systems:

16

Toward a Global View

A. Trevor Wood-Harper, Raymond K. Miles and
Paul A. Booth
University of Salford

*This chapter deals with the development and philosophy
of the Doctoral Program in the Department of Mathematics and
Computer Science at the University of Salford. One of the two major
streams of this school is Information Systems (IS), and the need for
education in this area is addressed. Criticisms of the current UK
approach to doctoral education and study are offered, and it is
suggested that the drawbacks of this approach are largely responsible for the particularly low completion rate in the UK. The
alternative offered at Salford attempts to retain the best aspects
of the UK approach, while drawing on experience and practice
from other academic cultures. The Salford initiative is then described in some detail, and its implications for research education
and training are examined in global terms.*

In this chapter the aims, structure and content of the
Doctoral Program in Information Systems, recently established
at the University of Salford, are described and discussed. The
program is one of the first of its kind in the UK, and marks an
important departure from the conventional approach to Ph.D.s
adopted within the United Kingdom (UK). The overall aim is to
achieve a doctoral education structure which retains the strengths

of the UK approach, but which offsets the drawbacks of that approach by the inclusion of established practices from the US doctoral school model. It is argued that this *marriage* of two distinctly different approaches taken from two countries is a significant step towards the globalization of IS/IT education. First, the supervisor-student model which is prominent in the UK and the US doctoral school vehicle are outlined as two contrasting approaches to doctoral education. The position of the Salford initiative within this framework is then explained. The formative forces of the Salford initiative are further elaborated through a consideration of the special research demands of IS and the potential contribution of doctoral research in IS towards globalization of IS/IT education.

Second, the need for and the general direction of a new approach to doctoral IS education in the UK is discussed. This is done through an explication of the strengths and weaknesses of UK conventional practices, an examination of alternative approaches, and a consideration of the internationalization opportunities in IS. Third, the Salford doctoral program is described, giving particular attention to its design criteria and the means by which it addresses the shortcomings of established UK doctoral education practices. The program's contribution to the globalization of IS/IT education is then discussed by focusing on the nature and composition of the research community which underpins the Salford initiative. The chapter concludes with a discussion of possible implications of the Salford program for the globalization of IS/IT education.

DOCTORAL EDUCATION IN INFORMATION SYSTEMS

Doctoral Education: the 'Emergent' Approach

Higher education within the United Kingdom's Universities, Polytechnics and Colleges has changed considerably over the last decade. While the concentration on academic rigor at all levels has been maintained, the isolationist perspective of academic life being divorced from industry and commerce has been almost totally displaced. Now there is an emphasis on education that is relevant to the general needs of society—or at least this is the picture at bachelor and master levels. Those who have obtained Ph.D.s in the UK in recent years will most likely have found that the old customs and attitudes endure, and education at doctoral level has remained almost untouched. Although the topics of some Ph.D. theses may be more industry-oriented, the attitudes and practices encountered by those obtaining these degrees will be much the same as they were twenty, or even forty years ago.

Circumstances, however, are changing. The research councils, who fund much of the research in the UK, have become increasingly concerned at the inordinately low completion rates for doctoral degrees. Those who receive funding for doctoral degrees are expected to complete their full-time research and submit a thesis within three to four years. Unfortunately, under 50% of postgraduate doctoral students achieve this, with the completion rate being as low as 30% in some areas. Many students fail to complete at all, and it is against this background that some academics are beginning to question the British approach to the Ph.D., the D.Phil., and the like. There are many qualities of the 'UK approach' that almost all UK academics wish to retain, yet there is general agreement that much has to change, although little has so far been done.

While doctoral school education might be characterized as a *managed* approach to higher research degrees (which we will discuss later in this chapter), the predominant attitude towards advanced research education in the UK is one where research is allowed to *emerge*. The culture of individualism within UK academia is such that postgraduate students are expected to make their own way in the research world, albeit under the wing of a supervisor who will help to point them in an appropriate direction. Though there are many differences of opinion as to the exact position of the supervisor, to be effective, he or she might have to play the role of academic expert, teacher, 'hands-off' research manager, confidant or counselor.

For their part, doctoral students are expected to analyse research areas for themselves, and to produce proposals and plans for research. Thus, the UK *emergent* approach emphasizes individualism and self-reliance, thereby seeking to develop a student's confidence in his/her own abilities. One consequence of this individual 'hands-off' approach is that some research is misconceived, and that students sometimes only recognize this after considerable effort has been expended. It can be argued, however, that such realizations, together with the resulting reappraisal of the research plan, encourage some considerable depth of thought. They facilitate an appreciation of the importance of having clear research objectives, and help to develop the student's understanding of the subject matter.

Accordingly, the emergent ethos is one in which the student is placed in an apprentice role, albeit one in which they are "given enough rope to hang themselves." The objective is to allow students to prove themselves—fostering the creativity and flair that is vital for good science. Judging by the position of UK science in the world academic community, we might argue that the emergent approach has been successful in this respect. On the other hand, it is the UK emergent approach that appears to be responsible for such a low completion rate.

Doctoral Education: The 'Doctoral School' Approach

An established alternative to the UK emergent ethos is that of the managed approach to doctoral education. The philosophy differs in that research is viewed as something that can be taught, particularly the acquisition of research skills. Doctoral students take part in a managed program of activities that culminate in the presentation of a thesis. The activities included in this sort of program include planning, topic selection, research topic formulation, and the like. Bodies such as the Science and Engineering Research Council (SERC 1991) and Economic and Social Research Council (ESRC) in the U.K. have recognized the importance of such activities and recently issued guidelines to this end (ESRC 1991). This orientation, as applied to information systems doctoral research, is prominent in the United States, with notable examples of doctoral schools at Minnesota, Indiana, and Georgia State University (Vaishnavi et al., 1991).

The Salford Approach

The Department of Mathematics and Computer Science at Salford University has responded to the issue of low completion rates by establishing a Doctoral Program in Computer Science which aims to build on the respective strengths of both the emergent and managed approaches. Although the Department has experienced and research-productive staff, together with very good contacts within the academic and industrial research communities, there's no tradition of doctoral education in computer science. Consequently, the aim has been to focus research within the department upon the program, and to build upon the general strengths of the University. In particular, the University of Salford has the most extensive contacts with industry and commerce of any educational institution in the UK, as well as the highest proportion of students from overseas. The prime objective then, has been to develop a program, set within an international framework, in which the research is of both theoretical and practical importance, as well as being of social and economic relevance.

Special Demands of IS Research

The doctoral program in computer science at Salford contains two streams, IS and software engineering linked by a central theme of human-centred systems. Though equal importance is attached to each stream, it is IS rather than software engineering that forms the focus of attention in this chapter. This is partly due to the fact that the doctoral schools that have so far been established are largely in the IS area, and so concentrating on this aspect aids comparison. However, it is the special demands of IS research that are of more direct interest to internationalization.

In the field of IS, the range of applicable and proven research methods is extensive. These methods extend well beyond the sometimes restrictive hypothesis and test approach. The need for a wide range of methods arises from the nature of the information systems area. In our ideal world we might wish to implement slight variations of a system in several identical organizations and observe the effects upon them. Clearly, this is not possible, and the complexity of organizations and the human issues that are involved in this area necessitate approaches which build overall pictures rather than prove or disprove. Galliers (1991) lists fourteen research approaches, including laboratory experiments, field experiments, surveys, case studies, action research, etc. (see Booth, 1989, for a list of the wide variety of methods that can be used to evaluate a system). Moreover, as some of these methods involve significant interaction with outside organizations, and individuals within these organizations, certain consultancy skills are also required. Consequently, the need for some research training for doctoral students before they embark upon research in the information systems area is quite apparent.

Globalization of IS/IT Education: The Contribution of Doctoral Research

The need for information systems, computer-based or otherwise, is universal. They are an essential ingredient of human activity at both individual and group levels. This would seem to be a prime causal factor in the explosive growth of the IT industry as a world-wide phenomenon. Thus, in some respects, one starts from the base that practice has been extensively internationalized. There could, therefore, be major all-round gains in the effectiveness of information systems if IS/IT 'theory' were also to be internationalized. IS research is well placed to move in this direction, especially if increased attention is applied to action research or action learning, a cornerstone of IS research methods. Action research is a framework in which theory and practice are complementarity; action (or practice) generates new/revised theory which in turn generates more practice. A pooling of action research experiences at an international level would greatly enhance our understanding of ,and competence in, the method itself. Indeed, once an organized move toward internationalization is initiated, the very nature of the method lends itself to the formation of a virtuous circle, the process possessing a self-generated momentum. The key question is how to initiate the process.

The view taken at Salford is that such a step needs to be pitched at doctoral research level and beyond. An important feature of action research is that it demands sophisticated skills, often on a par with those exercised by seasoned consultants. At this stage, it is not realistic to expect to find such prowess at undergraduate or masters levels. Indeed, the research initiative will make significant development demands on academic staff. Nevertheless, it is expected that a highly visible doctoral research program, spanning the discipline as a whole, will exert a strong pull effect on undergraduate curricula and practices, especially in terms of promoting an international outlook.

Accordingly, an internationalization initiative on the action research front (not to the exclusion of other IS research methods) needs to be directed and managed. A doctoral school combining managed and emergent educational approaches is a much better vehicle for this than either model taken separately. The objective is to create a two-dimensional research matrix where, along one axis, particular IS/IT issues are pursued and, along the other axis, research methods are developed, the two dimensions feeding on one another and the whole set in an international context.

DOCTORAL EDUCATION IN THE UK: THE NEED FOR CHANGE

Key Problems with the UK Emergent Approach

Criticisms of UK doctoral education have been voiced for some time (e.g. Baddeley, 1979), and although much of the debate has occurred within the social sciences area, the problem appears to pervade almost all areas of academia. In particular, the aforementioned low completion rates of doctoral students has attracted considerable attention. So, what are the causes of this problem? Alternatively, some might ask whether there is a problem—maybe the low completion rate is a reflection of a system with a high degree of selectivity, in which only the best succeed. It is doubtful, however, that many UK academics would agree with this view. All too many are aware of talented individuals who have abandoned their Ph.D.s. Given that this is the case, and that there is a significant problem, we need to identify the central causes. It is not argued that any of the suggested causal factors discussed below constitute the major reason, rather that they are all aspects of an unsupportive, and sometimes even hostile, academic culture.[1]

Changes in research direction. It is commonplace for doctoral students to embark upon a program of research and then, when they have learned more about their subject area, to abandon this program. In essence, they recognize that their proposed research is not as potentially fruitful as they had once thought. This has already been mentioned, and while the reappraisal that results from the realization that research is misconceived may be of use in prompting thought and analysis, it also has the effect of discouraging and even depressing the student. If such a realization comes late in the program of study, the student may feel that his research cannot be rescued. While those who emerge from such problems may do so with an increased confidence in their own abilities, many do not overcome such difficulties—they either have the courage to recognize their problems and give up, or more often allow their research to drift on without direction into fourth or fifth years, or even longer. Others still submit theses that reflect a significant change in direction, and risk being judged by their supervisors, or examiners if it reaches this stage, to have failed to construct and pursue a coherent and productive program of research.

A key problem, then, is that doctoral students are frequently expected to develop a program of study, often with little support, at a time when they are novices, resulting in programs that are sometimes fundamentally misconceived. Good supervisors should recognize this, of course, but even the most talented academics may miss such problems, particularly when they have high workloads and may not have the time to think through the program in the necessary depth. When students recognize the problems with their research (and they usually do at some point), they may have already invested considerable effort and feel unable to continue.

Isolation. Research is rarely an easy activity, yet many students lack the social support they need for the difficult periods of their research. Many are socially isolated, and sometimes also physically isolated in unwanted rooms in their department. Their contact with the rest of the research community can be limited to as little as a once-a-week meeting with their supervisor. Even for those who have the good fortune to have a strong community of friends, research can be a lonely activity if none of these friends has interests in the student's own particular research areas. Unfortunately, the social aspects of any form of work are often overlooked. For example, those companies that employ home workers frequently have to introduce extra mechanisms to integrate such employees into their organization. Otherwise, employees tend to feel little contact with and no loyalty towards either the company or the individuals within it.

Yet, the emphasis within the emergent approach upon individual research tends to reinforce isolation. It negates the need for a lively environment in which research is the topic of everyday conversation. Even when such lively departments exist, the apprentice role that accompanies the emergent ethos and is sometimes forced upon doctoral students often results in their exclusion from such discussions, and even the physical

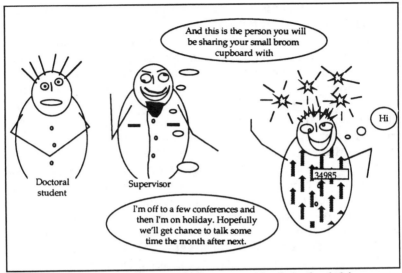

Figure 1: Many students are isolated within their own departments.

arena of the staff common room where discussions usually take place. In short, doctoral students often fail to receive the social support that they need, particularly at such crucial times as when formulating their research, or writing their thesis, when they may have doubts about both their research and themselves.

Dependence on the supervisor. It is possible to point to examples of poor environments compensated for by good supervisors. Unfortunately, most supervisors do not have the necessary time and exceptionally wide range of skills to provide every aspect of support a doctoral student requires at different times. Indeed, Phillips and Pugh (1987) found that difficulties with supervisory skills was a central problem, and one which constituted a considerable obstacle for many students.

Supervisors will sometimes complain that students expect too much of them, yet the student often has few sources of support, and supervisors tend to forget the problems they experienced when studying for their doctoral degree. Moreover, it is unreasonable to expect one person to play the roles of academic expert, teacher, 'hands-off' research manager, confidant and counselor to a variety of personalities, some of whom they might not always agree with or feel sympathetic towards.

For these reasons, the relationship between the student

and the supervisor is crucial to success within the emergent approach. A poor relationship—a mismatch of personalities—and failure in one form or another is quite possible (see Wray, 1991). Moreover, this failure can take several forms, including abandonment of the research or a failure at the final examination. A supervisor does not only have to support the student in the ways suggested above, but also has to select the most appropriate external examiner and informally defend the thesis (pointing out an examiner's misunderstanding can be a delicate process). Indeed, this may, in part, be seen as a problem in a system in which one person, the external examiner, can ultimately pass or fail several years work. There are undoubtedly cases in which the choice of the wrong external examiner—someone unsympathetic to the approach that had been taken, and possibly a little rigid in his or her beliefs—has led to good work being failed. The importance of the supervisor in this context is probably best illustrated by an old joke, commonly told in UK academic circles:

> A fox, walking through a wood, sees a rabbit. He is about to pounce, when he notices that the rabbit appears to be writing. The fox presents himself and asks the rabbit what he is doing. "I'm writing my thesis," the rabbit replies. Astounded, the fox asks the subject. "It's about rabbits eating foxes." The fox begins to laugh, and so the rabbit invites him into a nearby cave for a demonstration. Meanwhile, a wolf has been watching this, and is surprised to see the rabbit emerge from the cave, with no sign of the fox. The wolf then presents himself, and asks the rabbit if he thinks he can eat a wolf. "I'm sure I can manage that," answers the rabbit. As the wolf approaches the cave he sees a shadow in the corner. "What's that?" he asks, and the rabbit replies, "Oh, that's the lion, he's my supervisor."

The moral of the story is that, no matter how ridiculous the thesis, it is the size of the supervisor that counts. This is, of course, an overstatement, although many will be aware of odd individuals who fit this characterization of a supervisor. It was never intended that a supervisor should play such an important role in this respect, but such a role exists nevertheless. To recapitulate: an ideal supervisor, then, has to be a manager, a diplomat, an expert in his/her subject area, and a clinical psychologist. In addition, the supervisor needs to be a very well-known figure in his or her field, with plenty of time to spare. Consequently, fulfilling the role of supervisor is a difficult one, especially when UK academics are also expected to be researchers, administrators, teachers, and fund-raisers.

An additional and obvious problem for doctoral students in this respect is that not all academics have the necessary skills to supervise a Ph.D. Almost all have the academic knowledge and expertise, but not always a personality that easily fits into a supportive role. Some supervisors are unwilling to give up the time to discuss research issues with students, while others view doctoral students as assistants whose role is to aid them with their research. Such supervisors show little concern for the student's development and work towards a thesis. It is also noticeable that such forceful characters often use the apprentice role as an argument to justify their unreasonable behaviour. Indeed, some supervisors have developed a succession of such poor relationships with their students that they have had only one or two students complete their theses, despite nearing retirement age, being well-known in their fields—holding chairs or similar positions—and having accepted an average of one doctoral student a year for the past twenty years.

Fortunately, such extremes are rare, although they do emphasize the 'pot luck' that doctoral students take when being assigned a supervisor. The single supervisor norm does, however, tend to exacerbate such problems. It is often the case that students in trouble are not expected to consult other staff, as this might be viewed as interference on the part of these staff. Students with two supervisors can, sometimes, fare better. Alternatively, some students are placed in a position in which they can never satisfy the conflicting demands of their different supervisors.

Other Problems with the UK Emergent Approach

We have considered some of the problems that appear to lead to the exceptionally low completion rate for UK doctoral students. Nevertheless, there are other problems with the UK approach, even though these drawbacks may not significantly contribute towards to the poor completion rate.

Inapplicability of research findings. Many doctoral

students produce theses that have little applicability, or even general relevance, to science, society, or sometimes even their own subject area. The emergent approach, with its emphasis upon individuality and creativity, may produce some brilliant doctoral theses, but the majority are destined to remain untouched on dusty shelves in the more obscure corners of university libraries. For those who recognize that a doctoral degree (for better or worse) generally only requires a demonstration of an ability to construct and pursue an appropriate program of research, then this does not necessarily prevent them from submitting their work. Other students, however, who may have pursued well-conceived programs of research, sometimes implicitly appear to decide that their research is not worthy of a doctoral degree, and incorrectly believe that they will not pass. Such students fail to recognize that a significant contribution to knowledge need not, necessarily, be a large step. Alternatively, they struggle to present their work as being applicable in some domain or other when it is clearly not of relevance. Such a realization is common during the writing of a thesis, and again may arise from an approach that requires students to identify research questions before they have fully come to terms with an area, as well as lack of support during a crucial phase.

Lack of knowledge of research methods. Most students begin their research with only the knowledge of research methods that they acquired at undergraduate and masters level. In some cases this knowledge might be reasonably broad. Subjects such as psychology tend to entail large components on research methods and analysis. By contrast, engineering subjects, including computing, put more emphasis on what is known, rather than how we came to know it. Unfortunately, doctoral students in the UK tend to pick up research skills as they go along, and less often start with a clear idea of the research methods that are available to them, and their uses.

While it might be argued that a doctoral program approach similar to the one adopted at the University of Salford would be of relevance elsewhere in UK education, there is a particular need for such a program in the computer science area. Although there is an emphasis upon research methods in undergraduate subjects such as psychology, there is more of a concentration on knowledge acquisition in subjects such as computer science, sometimes at the expense of research methods and approaches. Consequently, students from a computer science background are often in particular need of an introduction to research methods.

Alternative Approaches

Some alternatives to the traditional UK approach have been briefly described by Davies (1990). Baddeley (1979) suggested a route to a Ph.D. in which students would have to submit a literature review and two published papers. The problem, of course, is that many journals take a long time to publish papers, and this could actually extend rather than reduce the time it takes to obtain a doctoral degree.

An apprenticeship route has been suggested as an alternative to the 'lone gentleman scholar' approach (see Phillips and Pugh, 1987). Here the student would be attached to established researchers. The problem with this is that it appears little different from present practice. Moreover, the notion of the apprentice is sometimes used by less caring supervisors as an excuse for pressing their students into acting simply as research assistants. This sort of abuse is dealt with later in the paper.

The Economic and Social Research Council (ESRC) has proposed a research program route (ESRC, 1989). Here, students would attend a one-year introduction to research methods, etc., at particular schools. The students would then proceed to the university or college of their choice. This, however, while similar to the doctoral approach we will describe below, entails students moving between departments during their study. Given that one of the major arguments in favour of the Salford approach is that it promotes a sense of community within the department, it is argued that the ESRC model overlooks the social aspects of the support that doctoral students require.

Compared to the approaches outlined above, it is the US doctoral school approach which offers the most to counter the problems of the UK situation. However, the notion of a cohort of doctoral students following a shared and closely monitored framework of research development runs contrary to the individualistic ethos of the UK emergent approach. Indeed, the difference is such that it might be doubted whether such an approach would be generally accepted, or even considered acceptable, within the UK. The clash between the doctoral school culture and the UK emergent ethos does not focus principally on the teaching of research methods and the like, but rather on the

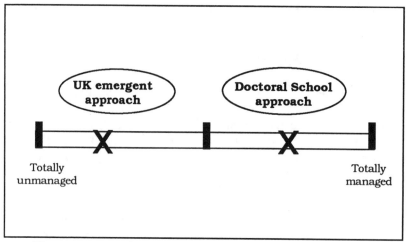

Figure 2: A continuum showing the doctoral school and emergent approaches.

principle of *managing the research student.*

While many UK academics would accept that there are serious problems with doctoral education in the UK, few if any would want to lose the most attractive aspects of the UK doctoral degree, most notably the element of students 'proving' themselves in the research arena. Indeed, those students within the UK system who have been too closely guided can fail if their viva demonstrates that their work has not been sufficiently independent.

To balance the equation, so to speak, the philosophy that has been adopted at Salford is one of promoting *self-management* among research students. One way in which the Salford doctoral program might be characterized would be as being in the middle of the continuum shown in figure 2. This, however, would be a simplistic and inaccurate perspective. The aim of the program is to teach students to manage their own research, and remains very much within the spirit of the UK tradition. One manifestation of this is that possessing a masters degree is not a prerequisite for entry into the program, as is often the case within US doctoral schools.

The doctoral program, however, has not only been developed by analysing alternatives to the UK approach, such as the Doctoral School philosophy, but also through the analyses developed by both the postgraduate students involved in the school and some undergraduate students as well. A number of such analyses have been performed, most of which have been via the medium of the Multiview methodology (Avison & Wood-Harper, 1990; Wood-Harper et al, 1985).

The structure and content of the Salford program, together with an explanation of how it seeks to address the problems described above, is presented in the next section. But first it is useful to return to the international focus.

The Internationalization Dimension

In the thinking which underpins the Salford program, internationalization of IS/IT doctoral research education is a prominent factor. It is seen as a highly desirable, even essential, enabling mechanism to bring about the required changes. Three important factors come into play.

First, the introduction of research cultures other than that of the UK should, at the very least, serve to "broaden the minds" of staff and students alike. More positively, for those steeped in the UK tradition, the very presence of alternative approaches, in the forms of visiting experts from other countries and international groups of students, should engender a reappraisal of the British way of doing things.

Second, IS research and development issues are already the subject of widespread international attention and cooperation. Nowhere is this more evident than in the field of IS methodologies, apparent as long ago (relative to the history of IS as a discipline) as the 1981/2 internationally-based comparative survey of design methodologies (see Olle, Sol & Verrijn-Stuart, 1982). Indeed, there hardly seems to be a significant IS research topic that is not being scrutinized by academics from numerous countries. It is no longer a case of a few prominent participating countries. It is a truly worldwide phenomenon. Thus, IS researchers, in order to do justice to their research, must take an international outlook. Their research environment should facilitate and not obstruct that purpose. Of course, the same observation applies to many disciplines, but then that only serves to emphasize the potential of the Salford program to serve as an exemplar within IS and other fields.

Third, the internationalization of research, almost regardless of the field of study, has been greatly facilitated by the deployment of IT. Witness the numerous international research communities in which electronic networks greatly enhance communication. It is therefore incumbent on the very discipline concerned with the development and application of IT to lead the way.

THE SALFORD INITIATIVE

An Overview of the Salford Doctoral Program

The Salford doctoral school is designed as a three-year program, the first four terms being largely devoted to research preparation. At this juncture it is useful to examine the principal ingredients of the Salford doctoral program (a detailed exposition of the full program is to be found in Appendix A).

The first year is largely taught, students participating in workshops and seminars covering the following areas:

- foundation studies in Information Systems and/or Software Engineering;
- an exploration of research methods;
- the development of critical and analytical skills;
- planning a viable research program;
- the development of presentational and writing skills; and
- an exploration of research topic areas.

Research topics are developed from the two major foundation streams: Information Systems and Software Engineering. The research topics reflect these streams, but an integrative perspective is adopted by placing an emphasis on a central theme of human-centred systems. Topics are selected from the following areas:

- artificial neural networks;
- theory and practice in information systems;
- automated tools for systems development;
- human-computer interaction;
- management of information systems;
- computer-supported cooperative work;
- systems development methodologies and environments; and
- re-usability of software.

The students spend the fourth term of this research

preparation year developing their research proposals, identifying a research question and detailing a program of research.

Although it has yet to be developed, it is proposed that students can, after this first year, take a M.Sc. in either Software Engineering or Information Systems. This provides a 'stopping-off' point for those who, for one reason or another, cannot proceed to a Ph.D. Another intermediate exit point is being considered for the award of an M.Phil. degree on completion of two years. These 'stopping-off' points reflect the progressive structure of the doctoral program. It is intended as a means by which students might be given reasonable support, and encouraged to complete their doctoral degree within three to four years. On the other other hand, there is an explicit recognition that circumstances and sometimes motivations change, and that students need to be aware of junctures at which they can bring their studies to an end and still finish with a valued and meaningful qualification. Almost all UK institutions of higher education offering research to doctoral standard provide such — stopping-off— points, but they are infrequently used, and there have been suggestions that students have sometimes not been aware of these points. Moreover, an M.Phil. is sometimes viewed as a failed Ph.D.—this is a quite inappropriate perspective that encourages the dispirited to leave without qualification, rather than officially acknowledge what they know to be a reasoned and sensible decision. Within the Salford scheme, these are to be promoted as reasonable points at which progress can be brought to a satisfactory conclusion, and certainly not as second-class degrees that imply some form of failure.

Thus, the program at Salford aims to support the various and sometimes changing needs of individual students. In the first year students are introduced to a variety of methods and areas, while support in the second and third years takes the form of involvement in the active and stimulating research community at Salford. This critical and constructive environment allows those involved to share ideas and research experiences with fellow students, as well as with more accomplished researchers. The aim of such a supportive atmosphere is to make research more productive, effective, and enjoyable. The benefits for the student are that there is support available from a wide variety of sources, including a world-wide network of consultants and advisers. The benefits for the department are that the school focuses research effort, and that the students who form the program contribute towards the academic community.

As the students pursue their own research on an individual basis, seeking support where they feel appropriate. With a supervisor playing the role of guardian rather than sole academic reference, the program still allows the development of the creativity and flair that's vital for good science, but within a disciplined framework. Students have the freedom to prove themselves, but within a supportive environment, in which they are encouraged to be independent only when they have a firm grounding in research methods and a good understanding of various topic areas.

The central ethos of the doctoral program is that it is not replacing the key aspects of the British approach; rather, it is supplementing them with a firm grounding in research methods and topics, and then providing the academic and social support to enable the individualism and creativity which is central to the UK approach.

Important Features of the Salford Program

Having discussed the fundamentals of the Salford ap-

| UK needs | Design features of doctoral program | | | | |
	taught parts	regular support	scheduled events	community support	supervisory team
changes to research	X	X		X	
isolation				X	
dependence on supervisor				X	X
inapplicable research	X	X	X	X	
research methods	X	X		X	

Chart 1: Connections between doctoral program features and the needs of UK research education

proach, it is now useful to consider those features of the doctoral program that have been included to address the needs of the UK emergent situation. These design features and their respective links to the drawbacks of the UK emergent approach are outlined in Chart 1.

This chart illustrates the doctoral program's main aspects:

- taught components;
- planned advisory and supervisory support;
- scheduled key events;
- an advisory/supervisory team for the program as a whole; and
- an identifiable research community.

To elaborate on the chart, there follows an explanation of how these components of the doctoral program relate to the deficiencies of the traditional UK approach to research education.

Changes in research direction. The doctoral program is intended to tackle deficiencies in three ways. The first is by introducing topics areas so that doctoral students have a thorough understanding of an area before constructing their research proposals. The second way is by providing support to identify when change is necessary and advising on such change. The third is the provision of the necessary social support for students who have to revise their workplans.

Students are expected not only to develop a proposal, but also to present and to justify it to both staff and fellow students in workshop settings. It is intended that this, together with the introduction to their own and related topic areas, will lessen the chances of students embarking upon misconceived research programs.

Nevertheless, even if a program is well conceived, it is still possible that the results from earlier parts of the research will necessarily entail some adjustment in the research program. The commitment by students to explain regularly and to justify their research to others in the program, as well as to staff, should help students identify points where adjustments are required, as well as allow staff and fellow students to advise.

Lastly, revising a program of research can be difficult and sometimes dispiriting. The research environment at Salford is intended as a community that supports such difficult periods, offering the reassurance, as well as the empathy that arises out of shared experiences.

Isolation. Salford's approach to the problems of isolation entails students interaction with one another, as part of a community—one that has a program of social as well as academic activities. The division between the academic staff and the students is intended to be minimal, with the former in the role of more experienced, though fallible researchers. For this reason academic staff also present their work and research plans for students to criticize at various workshops so that students feel they are an integrated part of this community.

A further point to consider in this respect is that many doctoral degrees are not taken by those who we might normally place in an apprentice role. For a proportion of students a Ph.D. is a mid-career development (or non-career interest pursued). For such individuals a doctoral degree provides a goal and helps them to focus and tp distill their experience within a structured framework.

Dependence on the supervisor. Again, it is the social environment of the program that should, in part, overcome this problem. The supervisor is not the sole source of academic reference, but a guardian-like figure who has responsibility for ensuring that a student is progressing although the course of that progress is determined by the student. The consequence of such a relationship between the student and the supervisor is that the student is expected to consult other members of staff, the consultants and advisors to the program and fellow students. Such consultation is not an infringement on the supervisor's role. This places supervisors outside the almost impossible role the emergent approach expects and allows students to choose those who most advise them, and consequently influence their work.

Inapplicability of research. The process of introducing students to topic areas, and of students then presenting argued perspectives on these topics is intended to provide a firm grounding in the relevant research areas. The later activity of constructing and justifying a research proposal and program should also help to develop the student's knowledge. Consequently, the research that arises from this process is less likely to be of little or no interest to either industry, commerce or society at large.

A further mechanism for encouraging the relevance of research to real problems is the company associate scheme.

Commercial organizations may become associates of the doctoral program and have the opportunity of presenting their own ongoing research; of presenting problem areas that are of interest to them; of participating in workshops; of making their own organization available for study; and of offering placement visits for doctoral students. This aspect of the program is intended to be complementary to research and development activities within commercial organizations, affording a longer-term research function, in addition to providing an avenue for staff development. The program enables companies to use the expertise within the Department of Mathematics and Computer Science at the University of Salford and to become acquainted with postgraduate students who they may view as potential employees. Accordingly, the process of involving outside organizations ensures the relevance of the research pursued within the program. It is also, however, a two-way process by which associate companies learn new ideas, perspectives, methods, and techniques.

Research methods. The doctoral students are introduced to a range of relevant research methods and analysis techniques during the first year of the course. Moreover, in identifying their research and detailing programs of investigation, they have to clearly state the methods they intend to use. It is at this stage that more experienced researchers are able to suggest methods students might have overlooked. Importantly, however, research proposals are not formulated until students have some overall perspective on the methods that are available, and which might be most appropriate in any given circumstance.

Finally, a word about the *single examiner* issue. The problems and inconsistencies of having individual external examiners, as opposed to boards that reach consensus, is not something the doctoral program can address. This is a national issue that has to be resolved between the awarding bodies. However, it is hoped that by using the collective knowledge within the department, its consultants, and its advisers, the most appropriate examiner for any particular thesis and student might be selected.

An International Research Community

Chart 1 clearly shows that the community serves as the *integrating* contribution. It has also been argued that the very nature of IS/IT, especially in a research sense, demands an international perspective which must therefore be reflected in the research community. This is where the internationalization dimension of the program comes to the fore. How then is it to be achieved?

The Salford response has been to construct a model of a research community in which equal weight is attached to its two principal participating groups—staff and students. They in turn are bound together by the research curriculum. Each of these three components must be internationalized in an internally consistent manner. In other words, one must pay due regard to each and all of the three components and how they relate to one another.

Starting with the research curriculum, the bonding agent of the community, the view has been taken that its content—research topics and study areas—should encompass research themes in IS which are of current or potential global interest. Typically, these include the application of IT within small businesses, the adoption of IT in developing countries, IS methodologies, and new computer architectures. This is internationalization of the intellectual framework.

One can then move to *interactive* internationalization by consideration of staff and of student groupings. In the Salford doctoral program, the research community functions within two domains: an inner domain, comprising resident students and staff, and an outer domain embracing contacts *beyond* Salford, both in the UK and in other countries. Mechanisms for this include staff and student exchanges, a team of consulting experts from both academia and industry, and electronic networking to enable the two domains to interact. This arrangement engenders an international perspective in operational terms.

An International Faculty

It is worth elaborating on the staff component, as it constitutes an international faculty. The international faculty, while normally playing no part in the admission of students into the program, initially reviews a student's research proposal. The interaction between the international member and the student is usually via electronic mail. From this first contact, a relationship should be established. While it is possible for students to telephone the international faculty members, the emphasis is upon the use of electronic mail to maintain contact, and to discuss research issues. This has the added advantage of allowing students to keep a record of their interactions and to look back on it when necessary. There are funds available for students to visit international faculty members, and the international faculty members make regular visits to the Salford campus. In this way, the international faculty can interact at a distance, and supplement this with regular face-to-face contact. This enables advice to be given at key stages, such as topic selection, and provides students with a broadly based research leadership that can respond to their needs. In addition, faculty members participate in assessment and appraisal or research progress and findings.

IMPLICATIONS OF THE SALFORD INITIATIVE

The Doctoral Program in Computer Science at the University of Salford is directed at providing the academic and social support students require when studying for a Ph.D. Its ethos has been influenced by various approaches, although it might best be characterized as combining a doctoral school approach with the highly individualistic approach of UK academia. It is intended that the program should evolve in response to both the demands of the discipline and the needs of staff and students. Those within the computer science and information systems areas are well-used to rapid change. Consequently, a development such as this might be best pioneered in such an environment.

The political context in which the program operates, and might operate in the future, is becoming increasingly international, especially as a result of the fundamental political changes in what was once the Eastern bloc of communist countries. Although 'distances' between research communities, cultural as well as physical, remain significant, competition in the educational world is becoming international. The Salford program is intended to bridge such gaps. It is envisaged as one part of an international network of schools, interacting with one another. It is expected that the program will exchange students and staff with other schools to debate philosophies, share information, and promote debate in the subject areas.

This two-way process of exchange has already been established with industry. The University of Salford is centrally involved in the two-way process of having its research informed by the developments in industry while itself informing industry. However, it appears likely that even this might become increasingly international in the next few years.

In the UK, changes to the educational system, particularly the removal of the binary divide between universities and polytechnics, provide an opportunity to reassess the role and nature of doctoral education. The program at Salford has attempted to retain the best of the traditional UK approach, while making the doctoral education more compatible with international norms. Nevertheless, we cannot be sure that there are not better ways of arranging such research training. Further research is needed into the approaches and academic cultures that inform the approaches within different countries, and even between different universities and colleges within the same country.

One of the wider implications arising from the work at Salford is what may be described as a 'pull' factor exerted on educational levels below that of doctoral research. In the UK the design of an undergraduate program, especially its content, usually reflects the research interests and projects of the department responsible for the course. Therefore, one can reasonably expect steps toward internationalization at doctoral level to filter through to taught courses at Masters and first degree levels.

Finally, it needs to be stressed that the creation of the Salford doctoral program carries with it international ramifications which extend beyond the field of computer science. The very act of constructing a doctoral program which draws on two distinctly different educational approaches taken from two different countries is itself a step towards globalization of the discipline concerned. The resultant program is likely to possess an emergent property of potential international practice not previously manifest at a national level. This is perhaps most evident at Salford in the form of the doctoral school community, one in which the status of staff and students is secondary to their respective and complementary roles. The benefits of this kind of community are not restricted to research activities in IS/IT. Indeed, it should be possible to generalize the Salford model of an international faculty to other universities, disciplines and cultures. Even when funds are limited, a faculty based on electronic mail contact alone could nevertheless, be of considerable value.

However, IS/IT academics and practitioners are in a privileged position to lead the way. The Salford initiative would be consolidated and enhanced if IS/IT researchers from other countries were to actively participate in similar developments. At Salford it has been a case of the UK looking toward US practices. It follows, at least in principle, that US researchers might also benefit from the Salford experience. It is hoped that the Salford doctoral program will serve, at best, as an exemplar for others to follow or, at worst, as a catalyst for productive change in the globalization of IS/IT education.

APPENDIX A
The Doctoral Program Rationale in Computer Science, The University of Salford

Introduction

The Doctoral Program in Computer Science is the first of its kind in the United Kingdom, and provides postgraduate training in research to Ph.D. standard. The research pursued within the program is of both theoretical and practical importance as well as social and economic relevance. Having said this, students entering the program are not assumed to have any previous research education, apart from a general introduction at undergraduate or masters level.

The program places students within an active and stimulating research community. This critical and constructive environment allows those involved to share ideas and to research experiences with fellow students as well as with more accomplished researchers. The program affords a supportive atmosphere to make research more productive, effective, and enjoyable. The specialized research training provided, together with the environment, aims to produce what might best be characterized as 'knowledge creators' whose work is of relevance and interest to academic, industrial, and commercial communities across the globe.

Overview of the Program

During the first year of the Doctoral Program students

take part in workshops on research methods, critical and analytical skills, presentational and writing skills, and are introduced to the various research topic areas. The two major streams within the Doctoral Program are Information Systems and Software Engineering. The research topics reflect these streams, although an integrative perspective is adopted with an emphasis on a central theme of human-centered systems. These topic areas include: artificial neural networks; theory and practice in information systems; automated tools for systems development; systems development methodologies; human-computer interaction; management of information systems; computer-supported cooperative work; software development environments; and re-usability of software, amongst others.

In addition to attending and contributing towards workshops, students are expected to produce a detailed review of their area of interest. This forms the background to research proposals the students produce in the fourth term in consultation with their supervisors. The proposal provides a plan of research for the following two years. The research that is undertaken in years two and three must constitute a significant contribution to existing knowledge that is presented in a written thesis and defended during an oral (viva voce) examination. All full-time students are expected to complete their research by the end of the third year although some may take an extra fourth year in exceptional circumstances.

The initial year—Aims . The initial year of the program contains taught courses and an integrated year of study. The year covers the following areas.

- assisting the student in preparing an appropriate research topic;
- preparing the student for a scholarly selection and application of appropriate research methods;
- introducing the student to critical research issues in appropriate fields;
- developing the student's ability to critically evaluate other related published research work; and
- assisting the student in preparing a research plan so that the process of managing a research project to the constraints of an appropriate time framework can be monitored and controlled.

The courses are provided to allow for these aims to be met. Each of the courses is evaluated to provide feedback, to encourage a disciplined approach to study, and to allow students to develop a realistic approach to self-assessment regarding the research they intend to carry out.

The initial year - course content. The overall program consists of a one-year taught program containing the following elements:

- Information Systems Research Foundations
- Software Engineering Research Foundations
- Foundations of Inquiry
- Topics in Information Systems
- Selected Topics
- Research Methods
- Literature Survey of Chosen Area
- Research Proposal—to be assessed by a selected committee;

These are arranged into four termly/quarterly modules as follows:

Term 1 Concentration seminars - Information Systems and Software Engineering
Term 2 Research Topics
Term 3 Research Methods
Term 4 Research Proposal Preparation

The taught program. The initial year prepares the student conducting empirical work and for developing a thesis for examination. The courses given in the initial year prepare the student for these tasks and for the overall management of the research project.

Each component is taught through a seminar format. In the seminars students prepare a critique of a given paper and develop the main threads of ideas regarding the form of inquiry and the view of knowledge argued by the author to be most appropriate to that paper.

Objectives

1. The primary objective of the course is to develop the students'

480 Wood-Harper/Miles/Booth

skills in critical analysis. The research argument in each paper is concentrated on so that the view of acceptable research can be highlighted and discussed.

2. Each paper deals with a particular problem area of relevance to information systems research. The seminar approach allows for these areas to be exposed and understood so that those which are felt most relevant to individual research topics can be discussed.

3. The process allows the student to develop an appropriate topic by revealing the strengths and weaknesses in the research frameworks adopted by existing researchers in that area.

Course Requirements

1. All students must adopt the role of seminar leader and primary presenter in each course. In this role they prepare and present a 1 to 1.5 hour seminar using the assigned material and then lead and coordinate the discussions of that area.

2. During each seminar each student must be an active participant in the discussions. Additionally, each student is expected to prepare a diary document assessing each presentation which will be assessed at the end of the seminar course. The diary should attempt to criticize the ideas presented in a disciplined and rigorous professional manner.

3. Several assignments are required for each component of the course. Students must submit the required number of assignments in a standard that demonstrates understanding of the different areas.

4. Students must attend all of the taught program which consists of the following elements.
   Concentration seminars - Information Systems and Software Engineering. These courses are aimed at 'rounding and filling' the student's background knowledge in the concentration areas.
   Foundations of Inquiry. This course is aimed at developing the students' rudimentary understanding of re-

search. This is necessary so that a research thesis can be developed which is defensible as a contribution to knowledge. The student is exposed to critical issues in information systems research and software engineering as well as   the debates regarding appropriate forms of investigation. The topics covered include the following:

- **Foundation 1:** Systems and Inquiry
- **Foundation 2:** Paradigms of Inquiry
- **Foundation 3:** Information Systems Research and Practice

Foundation 1: Systems and Inquiry. The objective of this component of the course is to introduce student s to new forms inquiry, so broadening their perspective on science. The reasoning for adopting this view as opposed to a traditional hypothesis and test approach will be debated so that the nature of information systems research can be understood as a social scientific form of inquiry which deals with a holistic, and hence systemic framework for inquiry.

Foundation 2: Paradigms of Inquiry. The objective of this component is to introduce the student to a meta-level analysis of inquiry frameworks. The concept of paradigms will be used to convey this. The different paradigms of thought currently dominant in information systems research will be discussed. This allows the student to develop the capability for critically categorizing different research approaches and arguments.

Foundation 3: Information Systems Research and Practice. The objective of this component is to develop the students' ability to put the frameworks for inquiry into research contexts. This means that analysis of information systems research can be conducted in a disciplined and rigorous manner. The practical aspects of doing information systems research are considered alongside the theoretical issues. During this seminar program students are likely to be required to select a further paper from the literature to present and to justify why the chosen paper is relevant.

Topics in Information Systems. The aim of this part of the course is to develop a contextual understanding of information systems research. A series of topics are covered in a seminar format similar to the foundations components, and these change as the program evolves. Topics currently covered include the following:

- systems development/evolution methodologies;
- organizational and managerial aspects of information systems;
- human-computer interaction;
- strategic information systems and competitive advantage;
- information systems assessment; and
- computer-supported cooperative work.

Each of these topics has been selected because of its topical relevance to current issues in information systems research. Reading lists are given for each topic and seminar presentations of the readings are required.

Selected Topics. The student will be part of a program involving other students. Each student will have particular topics which he wishes to cover beyond the set components of the course. This component allows for those topics to be developed. It consists of seminars run by students who are interested in particular topics. These individuals provide a short reading list of key papers for their chosen area and these are presented and discussed by that group of students to the first year program group as a whole. This allows for a more refined understanding of a chosen topic to be covered. It also allows for a preliminary consideration of whether or not the chosen topic is an appropriate one for doctoral research in information systems.

Research Methods.This prepares the student for carrying out the empirical work. Various research methods will be covered by both criticism and practice with qualitative and action-based research methods being concentrated on.

Literature Survey of Chosen Area Each student will develop a literature survey of a chosen area that must be written up in the form of a critical analysis of that area. The learning from the previous components is expected to provide input to this survey. The student should rely heavily upon interaction with the supervisor, both in choosing the topic and in starting the literature survey. The survey will be a document of not more than 10,000 words which will be formally assessed.

Research Proposal.The research proposal represents the culmination of the learning regarding the initial year of the program. It also provides the basis for the research to be conducted in the remainder of the program. The proposal to be developed should be no longer that 10,000 words, and should be in the form of a structured proposal, i.e., report style rather than essay style. The proposal should contain the following elements:

1. a rigorously defensible statement of the identified research issue and related research topic. (Answers the question "What is to be done?");

2. a statement defending the importance of the research (Answers the question "Why should it be done?");

3. a review of significant prior research which includes

- selected material from the literature survey
- critical analysis of focal issues and/or papers
- an argument substantiating why the chosen literature is relevant to the proposed research (Answers the question "What else has been done?") ;

4. a critical review of the strengths and limitations of the chosen research methods, approaches, and/or methodologies. (Answers the question "How is it to be done?");

5. plans of how the research is to be carried out over the set timescale. This is to include landmarks and to prioritize which activities are essential and which can be reconsidered if time becomes a problem during the research. The student is reminded to include holiday periods in the planned time framework. (Answers the question "How is the research project to be monitored and controlled?");

6. a critical review of the potential outcomes of the research. These can only be surmised but it is a good discipline in managing research to consider these prior to doing the research. This consideration should deal with the likely theoretical and practical implications of the research. (Answers the question "What is the research likely to lead to?"); and

7. a statement justifying how the research will be defensible as a complete piece of research independent in its own right. (Answers the question "How will you know when the research is finished?").

The proposal is highly significant in the taught part of the program. The student is expected to form an assessment committee of academics who are willing to examine the final proposal. This should include the supervisor and a chair (who should be someone other than the supervisor) and two other individuals. The importance of the proposal is paramount to managing the research project successfully through to thesis and oral examination. It provides an important framework for the proposed research. It fulfills purposes that include communication, planning, and contract negotiation and commitment. Each of these provides a sound basis for both the doctoral work and for future research projects. These are expanded upon below.

Communication. Research must be communicated to become a contribution to knowledge. Writing the proposal educates the research student in selectively analysing and communicating ideas and proposed actions. This is fundamental to the attainment of a Ph.D., in which written and oral communication become the primary modes of assessment. The discipline gained from this serves the individual throughout a research career, both in writing research papers and in writing research proposals. Defense of the proposal at committee helps prepare the student for the viva voce and for future research interviews with research grant providing bodies.

Planning. Research, by definition is not wholly predictable, but this should not form the basis of an excuse for taking an undisciplined approach to the management of research. Planning the research means that critical time periods can be appreciated, prioritization of key research events can be negotiated, conflicts can be uncovered and managed, and the monitoring and controlling processes needed for useful self-evaluation can be developed and applied. Doing a Ph.D. is demanding both conceptually and personally. Self-discipline is required and a plan helps in achieving this.

Contract Negotiation and Commitment. When doing a Ph.D., students enter into a series of contracts with the university, the supervisor, and even implicitly with themselves and their partners. These contracts have to be negotiated and explicated, and commitments to joint actions must be made. The proposal makes the requirements of the various contracts more visible, thus making them easier to negotiate. Writing the proposal and presenting it for examination signifies that the necessary commitments to those negotiated contracts are being made by all members for the duration of the whole Ph.D.

program. The proposal has to be delivered to a chosen committee as outlined above, and this delivery includes a viva voce style negotiation. This allows for the members of staff to become committed to the proposed research.

When the proposal has been completed and examined and all other coursework and seminar work has been completed and passed, the student must start the proposed empirical research. It is crucial that the proposal is applied to this process and used as a guide for the research. This prevents the research from becoming unnecessarily long and keeps the student within a reasonable timescale—something that is particularly important when action-based research is being undertaken. Without relying upon the proposal, the student may lose track of his research objectives. It is these objectives which have to be defended in the thesis, and so they are of paramount importance.

The students are encouraged to conduct their research in their work settings, which means that they need to have some point of clarification on where they are going. The proposal achieves this. However, it is open to renegotiation with the supervisor, who must be satisfied that any changes are both relevant and achievable. At the end of the period of conducting empirical research, the writing up of the thesis is required which leads to examination with the intention of completion of the Ph.D. and attainment of the doctorate. The program cannot guarantee this achievement but can help avoid many of the pitfalls which may prevent it.

APPENDIX B
Doctoral School Faculty

A. T. Wood-Harper (Coordinator), Professor and Head of Computer Science. Information system applications in education, health care, and developing countries; information systems methods, evaluation and tools.

A. M. Addyman, Senior Lecturer. Networks and communications; object-oriented programming.

J. Ashworth, Lecturer. Telecommunications and satellite communications; parallel computing.

P. A. Booth, Lecturer. Human-computer interaction and user errors; artificial neural networks.

R. J. Eldridge, Lecturer. Systems Analysis and software tools.

H. McIntyre, Lecturer. Software environments; microprocessor applications.

R. W. Paulson, Senior Lecturer. Software quality and software tools.

S. Vadera, Lecturer. Expert systems, applications in health and safety; formal methods and natural language.

J. R. G. Wood, Senior Lecturer. Information system methodologies, parallel computing tools.

F. Walkden, Professor and Chairman of Department. Evaluation of software tools; educational applications.

Consultants to the program in the Information Systems area:

D. Avison, Professor, Southampton University, UK.

N. Bjørn-Andersen, Professor, Copenhagen Business School, Denmark.

W. Cotterman, Professor, Georgia State University, USA.

L. Davies, Senior Lecturer, Griffith University, Brisbane, Australia.

P. A. Dearnley, Senior Lecturer, University of East Anglia, UK.

G. Fitzgerald, Research Fellow, Oxford University, UK.

D. Flynn, Lecturer, UMIST, UK.

R. Galliers, Professor, University of Warwick, UK.

N. Janaratne, Lecturer, Heriot-Watt University, UK.

K. Kumar, Associate Professor, Georgia State University, USA.

P. Ledington, Senior Lecturer, University of Queensland, Australia.

L. Mathiassen, Professor, Aalborg University, Denmark.

R. Miles, Head of Computing, Lancashire Polytechnic, UK.

T. Reponen, Professor, Turku School of Economics and Business Administration, Finland.

L von Hellens, Asst. Professor, Turku School of Economics and Business Administration, Finland.

Acknowledgements:: The authors are grateful for the help of Dr. Lynda Davies, Griffith University in jointly preparing the doctoral course outline.

REFERENCES

Avison, D. E. & Wood-Harper, A. T. (1990) *Multiview: an exploration in information systems development.* Oxford, UK: Blackwell.

Baddeley, A. (1979) Is the British Ph.D. system obsolete? *Bulletin of the British Psychological Society, 32,* 129-131.

Booth, P. A. (1989) *An introduction to human-computer interaction.* Hove, UK: Lawrence Erlbaum Associates.

Davies, G. (1990) New routes to the Ph.D. *The Psychologist: Bulletin of the British Psychological Society, 6,* 253-255.

Economic and Social Research Council (1989) *Discussion paper on research training in the 1990s.* Swindon, UK: ESRC.

Economic and Social Research Council (1991) *Guidelines on the provision of research training for postgraduate research students in the social sciences.* Swindon, UK: ESRC.

Galliers, R. D. (1991) Choosing appropriate information systems research approaches: a revised taxonomy. In: H-E Nissen, R. A. Hirschheim, & H. K. Klein (Eds.) *The information systems research arena of the 90s.* IFIP 8.2 Workshop, Copenhagen, Denmark, 14-16 December, 1990. Amsterdam, The Netherlands: North Holland.

Olle, T. W., Sol H. G., Verrijn-Stuart, A. A. (1982) *Information systems design methodologies: a comparative review.* Amsterdam, The Netherlands: North Holland.

Phillips, E. M. & Pugh, D. S. (1987) *How to get a Ph.D.* Milton Keynes, UK: Open University Press.

Science and Engineering Research Council. (1991) *Research chief condemns government indifference* by William Bown reporting on a statement from Mark Richmond, New Scientist, 21 September.

Vaishnavi, V. K., Yoon, S.J. & Buchanan, G. C. (1991) Research in computer information systems at Georgia State University: a balanced approach. *IEEE Transactions on Computers, 40,* 500-509.

Wood-Harper, A. T., Antill, L. & Avison, D. E. (1985) *Information systems definition: the Multiview approach.* Oxford, UK: Blackwell.

Wray, S. (1991) How to choose your Ph.D. supervisor. *New Scientist.*

Section VII

Related Materials

Glossary

Application. A set of programs that automates some business function

Application specialist. A person with particular competence in the use of computer programs, usually within an area, such as marketing, production or finance.

Application technologies. Techniques or devices that support the development of business applications.

Artificial Intelligence (AI). The study of human thought processes through computational models.

Audio Visual Connection. IBM IVD multimedia application development product

Bedouin. Derived from an Arabic word "Bedou" which is the name given to the tribal desert dwellers. Not so many years ago, almost all of the Arabian Peninsula inhabitants were Bedouins. As Saudi Arabia modernizes, true Bedouins are becoming increasingly hard to find. Many have abandoned their tents and camels to work and live in cities.

Capital expenditures. Expenditures on goods which yield benefits over more than one year, and whose costs are recognized over several years.

CD-ROM. Compact disc read only memory; optical, high volume digital storage medium for data and multimedia

CD-ROM drive. DASD for CD-ROMs CMI - computer managed instruction

Central Academy of Information Technology (CAIT). The education and training division of JIPDEC. CAIT was established in June 1987 when the old Institute of Information technology (IIT) was reorganized and renamed.

Client object. An object that is requesting a service of another object.

Communication technologies. Media for communicating and integrated networks linking people for communications.

Computer Aided Revolution On Learning (CAROL). Computer aided instructions course ware which is developed by Information technology Promotion Agency (IPA) according to MITI's project. The first version was completed in 1988. the curricula of CAROL are based on educational guideline which is developed by CAIT.

Computer Aided Instructions (CAI). Using computers as an instrument for education. A student responds to questions presented on display by typing keyboard or pointing by mouse etc.. Special software is required.

Computer Assisted Instruction (CAI). Any pedagogical technique which uses computer technology to assist the learning process.

Computer infrastructure. An organization's choice of computer hardware and software and telecommunication equipment to allow internal and external integration.

Congestion externalities. Congestion externalities in information technology reflect the nuisance caused by contention for shared resources - data channels and storage in business systems, or CPU cycles in real-time and scientific systems. These often result from queuing (i.e., lining up while waiting to be served by a platform).

Cost accounting and control. A formal system of bookkeeping and reporting, which tracks production of goods and services; also called managerial accounting

Cost-industrial society. A society in which knowledge or information (rather than land, family, capital or raw materials) is the route to power. This is the evolutionary stage following agrarian and industrial societies.

Data Base Repository. Software providing a means of defining the characteristics and storage for objects in applications environments.

Department of Education. A government body, has a large number of activities under its administration. Primary, secondary, university, social and adult education are its primary responsibility. It also administers educational research, youth welfare and other related activities.

Department of Electronics. A government agency, entrusted with policy formulation and implementation in the field of electronics and computers. It is also entrusted with the implementation of various regulatory and promotional aspects of electronics industry.

Depreciable assets. Goods which yields benefits over more than one year, and whose costs are recognized over several years.

Diploma Program in Computer Applications. A one-year Information Systems program offered by many Indian universities and computer centres.

Double-entry bookkeeping. Method of acquiring, organizing and reporting economic information; see Pacioli

Dyadic relationship.   A pairwise relationship between two individuals, such as an instructor and a student.

Economic language. A verbal method of communicating a particular body of knowledge in economic terms — value, cost, demand, supply and so forth.

Economic life. Length of time over which an asset still yields positive value.

Economies of scale. Pertaining to supply of goods and services, implies that greater total quantities of production yield lower per.

Electronic Data/Document Interchange. The substitution of electronic messages for standardized commercial documentation so as to eliminate the need for actual physical copies of the documents.

End-products. Goods produced to be sold to parties external to the firm

Equifinality. Many paths lead to the same goal.

Excludable. Pertaining to information technology assets, one end user can exclude another end user from receiving the benefits from a particular unit of the resource

Expert Systems (ES). Computer programs designed to provide specific advice like a human expert.

Externality. A consequence of activity not fully accounted for in the price and market system.

Formal communication. The interchange of voice, picture, and data among people through an (electronic) channel which may allow input, storage, manipulation, enhancement, and distribution.

 Full motion video. Full-screen, color video playing at 30 frames/second

GIO (Global Information Officer). A Chief Information Officer of a multinational corporation who is responsible for IT issues on a global level.

Globalization. The tendency of components of a single information system to be procured from many different countries, or to be installed and used in many different countries.

Graphical User Interface (GUI). A technology allowing a computer user to communicate with a program through the use of visual images rather than words.

Heuristics. Specific knowledge within an application area that is expressed as rules of good judgment.

Hierarchic lattice. A logical grouping of objects that describes their inter-relationships.

High tech. Incorporating sophisticated technology into the product or service being produced. The informationtechnology industry is an example of a high tech industry.

Historical Cost Principle. The accounting principle underlying most valuation on accounting reports. The Historical Cost Principle states that asses should be valued at the cost incurred in an arm's-length transaction.

HyperCard. Apple Computer's application development product

Incubator. An institution which assists entrepreneurs in establishing start-up companies. Often associated with a university or government agency, it provides office space, business consulting, and sometimes financial assistance to young companies.

Informal communication. Face to face communication among two, or a group of, people which includes, among other things, spoken language, body language, and smell.

Informatization. Becoming information intensive or information oriented. This is translation of "Jouhouka" in Japanese.

Information economy. That portion of a nation's economy which derives from "information work." That is, the manufacture of information technology, the development of software and systems, and the provision of information services.

Information industry. Tthe industry comprised of information technology firms.

Information service.   Services associated with data entry, processing, storage, retrieval, and communication.

Information Processing Engineers Examination (IPEE). A system of national examinations whose aim is to provide the technologies level to be acquired and educational target for information processing engineers and an objective criteria for evaluating their skill and qualifications

Information Processing Society of Japan (IPSJ). Academic organization of computer scientists in Japan.

Information technology. The combination of computer and telecommunication technology to create (business) applications.

Information technology engineers (IT engineers). All kinds of technical people who engage in information technology utilization in organizations. They include systems analyst, systems engineer, programmer or coders, system development project team managers, telecommunication engineers, system operators, and system auditors.

Information technology firm - a company whose primary product or service is information, information technology, or information services.

Information technology sector - those members of a nation's labor force who are engaged in information technology work.

Information technology work . Hardware manufacture, software and system development, and information services provision.

Infra-structure. Usually defines countries' installed base of equipment and services for communications, transportation, and services. Infra-structure relating to information technologies describes a country's installed base of computers, telecommunications, and supporting software, including, for instance, data base and networking software.

Intellectual property. Property that is produced by mental effort.

Intelligent Tutoring Systems (ITS). Computer programs which mimic human tutors by adjusting their pedagogical approach to individual users.

Intermediate products. Goods produced to be used by parties within the firm

International Standards Organization (ISO). An international group that develops interconnection standards about telecommunications networks.

Japan Information Processing DEvelopment Center (JIPDEC). A non-profit organization whose objectives are to promote information processing by computers throughout not only industry but also the entire society and thus to contribute to the overall economic and social development of Japan.

Language. A set of tools and methodology for communicating a particular body of knowledge. Languages are especially important in the classroom where students have neither prior exposure to the concepts, nor are they conversant in the terminology of the topic area.

Leap frogging . The phenomenon of a nation moving directly from an agrarian to a post-industrial society. That is, leap frogging over the industrial society.

Line managers. In manufacturing organizations, the hierarchy of managers between the (Divisional) Executive Officer and the foremen on the jobfloor.

MAIT (Manufacturers Association of Information Technology): an autonomous apex industry association of hardware manufacturers, software developers, training organisations and hardware and software service organisations. It has considerable say in the formulation of policies for export, import, manufacture and training in the information technology sector.

Management Information Systems (MIS). An integrated, user-machine system for providing information to support operations, management, and decision-making functions in an organization. The system utilizes computer hardware and software; manual procedures; models for analysis, planning, control and decision making; and a database (Davis and Olson, 1985.)

Managerial applications. Knowledge based, decision oriented applications used for problem recognition and analysis

Masters in Computer Applications. A three-year graduate program in Information Systems offered in many Indian universities and colleges.

Messages. Requests from some client object to some supplier object for some service.

Ministry of Education, Science and Culture (MESC). A ministry of Japanese government which takes responsibility for national education, science and culture.

Ministry of International Trade and Industry (MITI). A ministry of Japanese government which takes responsibility for national industrial and trade policy and control.

Multi-media. The integration of object orientation, data base and storage technologies in an application environment.

N1 network. A national academic telecommunication network for major national universities.

Natural Language Interface (NLI). A technology designed to allow a human to converse with a computer program through the use of normal conversational language.

Network externalities. Network externalities increase the value of hardware, software or databases as more users share them.

Nonexcludable. Pertaining to information technology assets, one end user cannot exclude another end user from receiving the benefits of using a particular resource. information technology assets are considerably different from tangible goods such as units of inventory. Inventory is both rival - consumption of a unit by the end-users denies any other end user of utility from that unit; and it is excludable - one end user can exclude another end user from receiving the benefits from a particular unit of the resource   Traditional accounting systems misrepresent economic issues such as the demand (value) for rival and nonexcludable assets such as information technology platforms.

Objects. Entities from the real world about which an application maintains information.

Object classes . Groupings of objects which have *identical* properties, attributes, and processes.

Object orientation. A method of developing applications which packages data and the allowable processes on that data together.

Off-shore data processing. Assigning some or all aspects of a company's information processing function to a location in a country different from its headquarters to take advantage of cheaper labor rates real estate, and time differences.

Open System Interconnect model (OSI) . A seven layer standard defining how telecommunication networks logically and physically interconnect.

Operational applications . Transaction processing applications used by first line managers support day-to-day business functions.

Outsourcing. Business restructuring where some of the computing facilities and perhaps software and data as well are placed under the management of an external firm.

Pacioli. Fra Luca Pacioli(Fra=fratello or brother) was a 15th century Franciscan friar and mathematics professor at various

Italian universities. He was a friend of popes, princes and artists, including Leonardo da Vinci who drew the 'proportions of man' as an illustration for one of Pacioli's books.   Pacioli in turn computed the proportions for many of Michelangelo's sculptures. Pacioli is best known for his treatise on Double-Entry; but he did not invent the double entry system (by about 200 years), only popularized it.

Platforms. An information technology asset which is shared by many users for many activities.

Portable. information technology assets which are capable of operating on several platforms.   Portability is important in software design and development.

Price-performance. One way of finding points on the demand curve for an information technology asset.   Price is the price charged for an information technology asset, say a computer. Performance is a measure of its value to the end use. If the price is less than the end users willingness to pay for that level of performance, there will be a sale.

Processes. Operations on data that transform it in some way. Also called services.

Proprietary information technology. Computer hardware and software and telecommunication equipment that in principle can be used within the architecture of one producer only.

PTT: Postal, Telephone and Telegraph. The state-owned telecommunications monopoly present in most countries and responsible for provision of (almost) all telecommunications services.

"Railroad" accounting. The modern system of accrual accounting whose constructs were developed largely as a result of investments in the railroads in the U.S. at the turn of the century.

Rival. Pertaining to assets, consumption of a unit by an end-user affects the utility to other end-users through the network or congestion externality. information technology assets are considerably different from tangible goods such as units of inventory. Inventory is both rival - consumption of a unit by the end-users denies any other end user of utility from that unit; and it is excludable - one end user can exclude another end user from receiving the benefits from a particular unit of the resource Traditional accounting systems misrepresent economic issues such as the demand (value) for rival and nonexcludable assets such as information technology platforms.

Satellite network. Telecommunication network systems which employ satellites as communication node.

Service. A process performed by a supplier object.

Shared data bases. One or more inter-related files accessible, in a read-only manner, by multiple departments or organizations.

Sharia. Islamic law and teachings that govern the Moslem's relationship to Allah (God), people, and other entities in the society.

Societal infrastructure. The institutions, services, and utilities which comprise the underlying structure of a society. Examples are education, health care, transportation, and telecommunications.

Software crisis. Increasing shortage of IT engineers in Japan. Totally 966,000 IT engineers are estimated to short to demand in 2000. Software crisis may become a bottleneck for the future informatization of industry and may lessen the competitive power of Japanese firms.

Storage Technologies. Devices that provide different types of storage facilities in a computer environment.

Strategic applications. Applications used by senior management to do environmental surveillance and analyze decision consequences.

Supplier object. An object which performs a process requested by another object.

System development specialist. A person with particular competence in building computer and/or telecommunication applications. The person may be a specialist in one or more areas, for example; business analysis, requirements determination, information analysis, programming, and implementation.

Technology transfer. Large scale introduction of a new technology to some previously non-technical environment.

Transborder Data Flow (TDF or TBDF). Transfer of computer generated data across international borders over telecommunications media.

Transmission control protocol/internet protocol (TCP/IP) . A set of rules developed by the U.S. Department of Defense defining how to connect networks from different vendors.

Two part tariffs. Pricing schemes where the interrelationship of two assets allows the seller to give away one asset, and overprice the other. Common in hardware and software sales.

University Grants Commission. An autonomous body under the Department of Education. Its main role is the promotion of university education and maintenance of standards of teaching, examination and research in universities.

Value of an information technology asset. Potential for end-users to improve their economic position through ownership of an information technology asset.

Value added resellers (VARs). Firms which modify and sell an information technology asset for a substantial mark-up.

Video conferencing technology . Devices and software that integrate television, computer, and communication technologies to transmit audio and video signals that simulate face to face meetings.

Biographies

Abdulla H. Abdul-Gader is Assistant Professor of Management Information Systems at King Fahd University of Petroleum and Minerals (KFUPM), Dhahran, Saudi Arabia. His degrees include a B.S. and MBA from KFUPM and a Ph.D from the University of Colorado. Dr. Abdul-Gader has contributed to such journals as the Journal of Management Information Systems, Information Resources Management Journal, Information and Management, and the Middle East Economic and Business Review. His primary research interests are in the areas of Knowledge-based systems development, end-user computing, and social impacts of information technology.

Paul Booth's background is in human-computer interaction. He obtained his first degree in Behavioural Sciences and later his Ph.D. (concerned with error analysis in HCI) from Huddersfield Polytechnic.

Sue A. Conger is an Assistant Professor of Computer Information Systems at Baruch College, the business school of The City University of New York. She has a B.S. in psychology from Ohio State University, an M.B.A. in finance and cost accounting from Rutgers University, and her Ph.D. in computer information systems from the Stern School of Management at New York University. Her research interests are innovation of information technology, software development, information technology use for work, and management of the IS function. In addition to teaching and research, Dr. Conger has an extensive consulting practice which draws on her work experiences from 20 years in the information systems field.

Candace Deans is an Assistant Professor of Management Information Systems at Wake Forest University. She received her Ph.D. degree from the University of South Carolina with a major in Information Systems and minor in International Business. Her current research activities focus on global information systems issues. She has articles published on this topic in the Journal of Management Information Systems and the Journal of High Technology Management Research. She recently completed a book with Dr. Michael Kane, International Dimensions of Information Systems and Technology.

Martin D. Goslar is Associate Professor of Business Computer Systems at New Mexico State University. Dr. Goslar has several years of industry and academic experience in the area of international information systems. Most recently publishing in the international area, he is currently involved in the investigation of technology transfer in the Latin American Community. He is widely published in the information systems literature, including articles in such journals as Decision Sciences, Journal of Management Information Systems, Journal of Computer Information Systems, and Journal of the Academy of Marketing Science.

Jatinder N.D. Gupta, PhD, CFPIM, is currently Professor and Chairperson of Management Science, Professor of Information and Communications Sciences, and Professor of Industry and Technology at Ball State University, Muncie, Indiana. He received his B. E. (Mech) from University of Delhi, M. Tech in Industrial Engineering and Operations Research from Indian Institute of technology, Kharagpur, India, and a Ph.D in Industrial Engineering from Texas Tech University, Lubbock, Texas, USA. Co-author of a textbook in Operations Research, he has published numerous research and technical papers in Production Scheduling, Management Science Implementation, Information Systems, Small Business Management. His current research interests are in production scheduling, manufacturing systems analysis, and information systems applications.

Rekha Jain completed her Ph.D. from the Computer Science and Engineering Department, Indian Institute of Technology, Delhi, India in 1985. Before that she worked in an apex level bank for a year. Since 1985, she has been a faculty member with the Computers and Information Systems Group at the Indian Institute of Management, Ahmedabad, India. Her current research interests include computer systems in organisations, management of large IT projects, computer networks and database management systems. She has publications in international and national journals.

Tor J. Larsen is associate professor at the Norwegian School of Management, Department of Organization and Management. He got his Ph.D. in Business Administration (specialization, Management Information Systems) from the University of Minnesota in 1989. In 1990, the Norwegian School of Management appointed him chair of the committee for the revision of the four year, full time, business administration program. He was also charged with the responsibility of developing a new structure for the basic undergraduate courses in MIS. Doctor Larsen has published recently in the Journal of Information and Management and at Hawaii International Conference on System Sciences. His main research interests are in the fields of managers use of computers, innovation, and the globalization of information technology.

Karen D. Loch, Ph.D., is an Assistant Professor of Decision Sciences in the College of Business at Georgia State University in Atlanta, Georgia. She received her Ph.D. in Management Information Systems from the University of Nebraska. She has published in MIS Quarterly, Interface, case and text books, and in the areas of simulation and management of information resources in other MIS and management science publications. She has presented papers at national conferences of Decision Sciences Institute, The Institute of Management Science, and

Hawaii International conference on System Sciences. Her research interests include international management of information technology, telecommunications and management support systems.

Louis C.K. Ma is a senior lecturer in the Department of Computing at the Hong Kong Polytechnic, where his teaching and research interests are in information systems management. Mr. Ma graduated from the Hong Kong Polytechnic in Systems Analysis and received his MBA at the University of Technology, Sydney. His current doctoral research is on Information Systems Planning at the University of Warwick (UK). He has gained over 15 years experience in systems development/management, IT education and consultancy. Prior to joining the Hong Kong Polytechnic in 1987, he was manager of the MIS section at the State Bank of New South Wales, Australia. He is a member of the British Computer Society, Hong Kong Computer Society and the Hong Kong Management Association.

Raymond K. Miles has an extensive industrial and international background in IS/IT, having worked both as a project manager and as a contultant across a wide range of industries, including the electronics, construciton, automotive, metals, and petrochemical sectors. Since the early 1980s, he has worked in the UK polytechnic/university sector where his work current position is that of Dean of the Faculty of Management, Business and IT at the North East Wales Institute, Wrexham. His research interests include the application of soft systems methods to strategic management, especially in respect to organizational structures and the corporate impact of IT. He is a visiting research fellow in the Department of Mathematics and Computer Science, Salford University.

Prashant Palvia is Associate Professor of Management Information Systems in the Department of Management Information Systems and Decision Sciences at Memphis State University. He received his Ph.D, M.B.A. and M.S. from the University of Minnesota, and B.S. from the University of Delhi, India. In addition, he has nine years of experience in industry. Dr. Palvia is the Editor in Chief of the *Journal of Global Information Management*, and was the conference chair of the 1991 International Conference of the Information Resources Management

Association held in Memphis, Tennessee. He serves on several editorial boards, and is the Associate Editor of iInformation Resources Management Journal. His research interests include international information systems, strategic information systems, end user computing, database design, software engineering, SDLC methods, and MIS in small businesses. He has published extensively; his publications have appeared in Decision Sciences, ACM Transactions on Database Systems, Information & Management, Journal of Systems Management, Information Resources Management Journal, Information Systems, Interface, and Information Sciences.

Sorel Reisman is an Associate Professor of Information Systems in the Management Science Department of the School of Business at California State University, Fullerton. He joined the University in 1986 after more than 15 years in industry where he was involved in research, development, marketing, and sales of educational and multimedia computing hardware, software, and applications. Dr. Reisman founded and co-directs the university's Interactive Learning Center and has written numerous articles on multimedia computing. He is an editorial board member and regular columnist in the publications IEEE Software, and MPC World. Dr. Reisman is also on the editorial board of the Journal of Global Information Management.

B.C. Saxena is a Reader in the Department of Computing at the Hong Kong Polytechnic, where his teaching and research interests are in management support systems, end user computing and information systems management. He received his BSc and MSc from Lucknow University, India and his PhD in management from Gujarat University, India. Dr. Saxena has over 20 years of teaching, research and diversified industrial experience in IT management and information systems development. Prior to joining the Hong Kong Polytechnic in 1982 as a senior lecturer, he worked as a management consultant, and as computer services manager in a leading business school in India which was set up in collaboration with the Harvard Business School. Dr. Saxena is the author of over 40 articles and papers on information systems and is the originator of a decision support system development methodology called "decision support engineering". He is a member of the British Computer Society, Institute of Data Processing Management (UK), Association of Computing Machinery (USA), Society for Information Management (USA), Information Resources Management Association (USA), the Institute of Management Sciences (USA), International Society for Decision Support Systems, Hong Kong Computer Society, and Hong Kong Management Association.

Osam Sato is an Associate Professor of MIS in the Department of Management at the Tokyo Keizai University. He graduated from Hitotsubashi University. He had been working as a member of Research Committee of Information Processing Education at CAIT. He also had worked as editorial board member of some Japanese academic associations including Association of Management Information, Japan Society for the Study of Office Automation, and Japan Society for System Audit. He has published in Information and Management, some Japanese journals, and some books in Japan.

James A. Senn is Director of The Information Technology Management Group at Georgia State University in Atlanta and Vice-President for International Affairs of the Society for Information Management, an organization of corporate information executives. He is known internationally as a dynamic speaker on management and information technology and on developing winning strategies for personal and corporate success. Senn consults widely with business and is the author of several leading books on information technology along with numerous articles and papaers.

R. Ravichandran is an assistant professor of information systems at Ball State University, Muncie, Indiana, U.S.A. He received his Ph.D. in Management Information Systems from Indiana University, Bloomington. His articles have appeared in Decision Sciences and other journals. He is a member of the ACM, Decision Sciences Institute, TIMS and American Association for Artificial Intelligence. His current research interests include decision making, decision support system, database design, management of MIS, and systems design.

Eileen M. Trauth is an Associate Professor of Management Information Systems in the College of Business Administration at Northeastern University. Her research interests include organizational impacts of information technology, information management, global information technology issues, and telecommunications policy. She has also published several papers about information systems education. Her articles have appeared in such journals as ACM Transactions on Information Systems, Information and Management, Journal of Systems Management, MIS Quarterly, and Telecommunications Policy as well as in several scholarly books. She is co-author of *Information Literacy: An Introduction to Information Systems.* During 1989-90 she was a Fulbright Scholar in Ireland. During 1992 Dr. Trauth lectured at the University of Ottawa and was a Visiting Professor at the Free University of Amsterdam. She received her Ph.D. from the University of Pittsburgh.

William Valonis is a graduate of the Penn State University, where he received both his Bachelors and Masters degrees in Management Information Systems. His research is directed towards applications of Artificial Intelligence in business and education, and cross-cultural technology transfer. He has taught programming and been involved in the design and development of computer assisted instruction.

Anthony Verstraete is Senior Lecturer at the Pennsylvania State University, where he has taught a wide variety of courses, including management information systems, systems analysis, database management, decision support systems, expert systems, and business data communications. He has also taught internationally. Prior to joining the faculty at Penn State in 1980, he spent ten years developing information systems for government and education. His doctoral work focussed on the study of human problems in technological change. His current research is directed towards methodologies for the design and implementation of systems which cross cultural and national boundaries. He is currently engaged in several projects involving the use of expert systems in student advising and instructional development.

J. Christopher Westland is currently an Assistant Professor of Information Systems at the University of Southern California. Previously he worked in industry for eight years, first as a Certified Public Accountant for Touche Ross in Chicago and later as Database Administrator and Computer Security Analyst for

Rockwell International He has been awarded an Andersen Foundation Fellowship, a FLAS Fellowship by the U.S. Department of education, several Paton Fellowships, a Dykstra Fellowship for Teaching Excellence, and a FRIF Grant to study politics and conflict resolution in information systems resource sharing. His current research focuses on the economics of information systems management and information technologies, on new technologies for software engineering, and on organizational and strategic applications of information technology.

Trevor Wood-Harper's degree is in Computer Science and his Masters in Systems Engineering, and his PhD in Information Systems Methodologies. His major thrust is development methodologies and he is mostly widely known for Multiview Methodology. Prior to his academic career he was a senior systems analyst at Granada Television and British Airways. Dr. Wood-Harper is an active consultant using Multiview, and has also worked as a lecturer and senior lecturer, reader and professor at polytechnics and universities in the United Kingdom, Denmark and the United States. He is currently Professor of Computer Science at Salford University and heads the research group in information systems methodology and evaluation. He has published widely with more than 50 research articles and five books to his credit.

Index